BAR

ESSAYS ON HIS WORKS

WRITERS SERIES 24
SERIES EDITIORS:
ANTONIO D'ALFONSO AND JOSEPH PIVATO

Canada Council   Conseil des Arts
for the Arts   du Canada

ONTARIO ARTS COUNCIL
CONSEIL DES ARTS DE L'ONTARIO

Guernica Editions Inc. acknowledges the support of
The Canada Council for the Arts.
Guernica Editions Inc. acknowledges the support of the Ontario Arts Council.

BARRY CALLAGHAN

ESSAYS ON HIS WORKS

EDITED BY PRISCILA UPPAL

GUERNICA
TORONTO – BUFFALO – CHICAGO – LANCASTER (U.K.)
2007

Priscila Uppal, editor
Guernica Editions Inc.
P.O. Box 117, Station P, Toronto (ON), Canada M5S 2S6
2250 Military Road, Tonawanda, N.Y. 14150-6000 U.S.A.

Distributors:
University of Toronto Press Distribution,
5201 Dufferin Street, Toronto (ON), Canada M3H 5T8
Gazelle Book Services, White Cross Mills, High Town, Lancaster LA1 4XS U.K.
Independent Publishers Group,
814 N. Franklin Street, Chicago, Il. 60610 U.S.A.

First edition.
Printed in Canada.

Legal Deposit – Second Quarter
National Library of Canada
Library of Congress Catalog Card Number: 2006933707
Barry Callaghan : essays on his works / edited by Priscilla Uppal. – 1st
ed.
(Writers series ; 24)
ISBN-13: 978-1-55071-253-7
ISBN-10: 1-55071-253-5
1. Callaghan, Barry, 1937- – Criticism and interpretation.
I. Uppal, Priscila II. Title.
III. Series: Writers series (Toronto, Ont.) ; 24
PS8555.A49Z62 2006   C818'.5409   C2006-905168-2

CONTENTS

THE FICTION

The Black Queen Stories, The Way the Angel Spreads Her Wings,
When Things Get Worst, and A Kiss Is Still a Kiss

THE NON-FICTION

Barrelhouse Kings, Raise You Five, and Raise You Ten

CONTRIBUTION TO THE ARTS
The Man, The Publisher, The Mentor, The Translator, The Teacher, The Archive

CODA

INTRODUCTION

*Up, Up, and Away with Barry Callaghan:
An Introduction to* Essays on His Works

PRISCILA UPPAL

Barry Callaghan: Essays on His Works began over four years ago, when I sent a letter to a dozen or so writers, academics, and visual artists, inquiring as to whether or not they might be willing to submit to "a collection of artistic responses and critical appreciations of Barry Callaghan's work." My rationale was that as a poet, journalist, visual artist, editor, and publisher, Barry Callaghan has produced a significant and internationally acclaimed oeuvre; yet, critical articles have been scarce. A corrective to this omission was certainly required: a volume celebrating, assessing, and contextualizing his contributions to Canadian and international literature and the arts, to facilitate and encourage lively, intelligent, and impassioned discussion of one of Canada's most important and recognizable man of letters, and to pave the way for future contributions to research and discussion of both his work and life.

But, of course, these are busy times, and miserly times to be artists and intellectuals, and would I find enough people who would graciously commit themselves *pro bono* to such a task? Would they too agree that as members of literary, artistic, and intellectual communities, we are in many ways bound to give praise where praise is due, and to foster discussion, dialogue, and even (or perhaps especially) controversy where it is warranted? With relief, my initial list of contacts responded generously and enthusiastically, raising my confidence about the ability to create such a book. I approached Antonio D'Alfonso, publisher of Guernica Editions, and asked if he might be interested in adding this book to his popular "Essays and Their Works" series (which includes such writers as Margaret Atwood, Al Purdy, and Alistair MacLeod, among others). He quite literally jumped at the opportunity to be the publisher of essays on – much in the manner of Joyce Carol Oates who once claimed Callaghan as "probably the only real poet in Canada" – what he called, "one of the only true writers in this country."

After these preliminary successes, and upon reflection, other contributor names were added to my initial list. Other names were suggested to me. The list grew longer. I contacted more people. Then, of all surprises, people started contacting me, proposing pieces, offering their services and support to the project. The list grew longer. Then, I thought it would be helpful to readers of the book, and to future writers and researchers of Barry Callaghan's work, to reprint some of the reviews of his books that had come out at the time they were first published, as well as a dozen or so important introductions and existing articles that have been written over the years. And so, in short, a small corrective collection has blossomed quite naturally and miraculously into a nearly definitive book assessing and celebrating almost all aspects of Barry Callaghan's career thus far. I say "nearly," because my sincere hope is that this collection, with as large a scope as it does possess (examining his career from the 1960s to the present 2000s), will not stop here, but will act as a seedbed for vibrant and engaged literary analysis and artistic discussion in the future.

But for now, more about the pieces collected here, and the structure of the book. As stated, some pieces are reprints of national reviews (at least one review from a major newspaper has been included of each of Barry Callaghan's poetry, fiction, and non-fiction books), and some are reprints of academic articles or articles in literary reviews; yet, an overwhelming majority of what is included here are original pieces written specifically for this book in a variety of forms: essays, academic articles, reminiscences, letters, meditations, notes, homages, poems, songs. These original pieces are offerings by contemporary poets, novelists, journalists, professors, radio personalities, television producers, visual artists, public intellectuals, musicians, screenwriters, documentary film makers, archivists, and others; from Canada, the United States, France, Ireland, Italy, and elsewhere. In fact, even a quick perusal of the list of contributors in our Table of Contents attests to the excellent artistic and intellectual company from around the globe the reader is about to encounter. It is a prestigious, diverse, and heady list, with each contribution adding purposefully towards a fuller understanding of Barry Callaghan's artistic visions, his literary commitments, his national and international impact, and his potential lasting contribution to arts and letters.

Barry Callaghan's career could be fruitfully studied as a model of supremely executed multi-tasking, as much of his poetry, fiction, non-fiction, journalism, visual art, radio and TV work, professorial teaching, editing, translating, and publishing, have not been undertaken discreetly from one another; however, for the purposes of providing the reader and researcher with some direction in terms of what works of Barry Callaghan's might be discussed in a given individual piece, it has been necessary to impose a strict and easily discernable structure on the collection. I have divided the book into four sections: The Poetry (Hogg *The Poems and Drawings* and Hogg *The Seven Last Words*): The Fiction (*The Black Queen Stories*, *The Way the Angel Spreads Her Wings*,

When Things Get Worst, and *A Kiss Is Still a Kiss*); The Non-Fiction (*Barrelhouse Kings*, *Raise You Five: Vol I: Essays and Encounters 1964-2004*, and *Raise You Ten: Vol II: Essays and Encounters 1964-2004*); and, lastly, The Cultural Contribution (pieces relating to Barry Callaghan's work with other writers through *Exile: The Literary Quarterly* and Exile Editions publishing house, his work as a translator, his archives, and so forth; essays not specifically about his authored works, but about other aspects of his authorial life). While the categories accurately reflect the main textual foci for discussion, the pieces themselves frequently delve into discussions and appraisals of other books and/or aspects of his career. A few pieces could transfer easily into other sections. Nevertheless, overall, I think the integrity of the structure can be trusted.

Some further structural notes: the pieces in each section are discussed according to the publication chronology of the book under discussion, that is, *The Black Queen Stories* is discussed, then *The Way the Angel Spreads Her Wings*, then *When Things Get Worst*, then *A Kiss Is Still A Kiss*; not the historical chronology of when the pieces were written (to help readers contextualize in this way, individual pieces will be identified below as either reprints or original contributions). In Callaghan-esque spirit, an original poem or score, written specifically for this book, opens each section.

Following this introduction, it is useful to note that a Chronology of Barry Callaghan's life – of use to those who are not aware of his biography, but also a handy reference for others – and a Published Works list (up to the point of publication of this book) are included. A recent interview with the author conducted by William Kennedy ends the collection.

*

Here I will give a brief summary of each authored piece included in the collection in order to provide readers and researchers with a clearer sense of what piece one might want to read next, as sometimes the titles of the individual pieces do not make such assessments immediately self-evident. It also gives me the chance to offer the reader or researcher an overview of the entire book in all its variety of form and content, and to highlight some recurring themes and points of interest. Discussion of each piece will follow the Table of Contents exactly here:

THE POETRY: *Hogg The Poems and Drawings,* and *Hogg The Seven Last Words:* An original poem by the great French poet Michel Deguy, "Homage to Hogg," begins this section, an artistic offering to the character and poetic persona Hogg. With Hogg as his model, Deguy strips the landscape of nature and gods alike to confront the vast unknown of the self and its relation to others. Then Margaret Atwood's "Barry in the Underworld," a reprint of the Canadian icon's introduction to the Croatian translation of *Hogg,* introduces novice readers to the mythic underworld (archetypal, psychological) of the poem, unearthing the poet as risky explorer. Next is Adele Freedman's review of *The Hogg Poems and Drawings* from *The Globe and Mail* from 1978, which documents not only how positively the book was received at the time, but how surprising and original the poetic mission was in Canadian literature. Freedman speaks most enthusiastically about the "hallucinatory experience" of the poems, the vitality created out of a mishmash of visual and auditory experiences. Then Susan Beckman's "Hogg in the Holy Land," a reprint of an academic article that appeared in *Contemporary Verse 2,* contextualizes the work within the genre of the Canadian poem sequence (Michael Ondaatjee's *The Collected Works of Billy the Kid*, and Margaret Atwood's *The Journals of Susanna Moodie*, among others), and explores the archetypal and local quests undertaken by Hogg, as well as his sexual search for salvation. Branko Gorjup's "Twice Born Hogg," written later than Beckman's piece as an introduction to the Croatian translation of *Hogg*, gives an even fuller account of *Hogg* in terms of the Canadian tradition of the long poem (which has only grown since the late 1970s), documenting how it has "enriched the Canadian imaginative space with a powerful vision that brings together the topographies of two disparate urban landscapes, Toronto and Jerusalem."

For more philosophical discussions and notes on *Hogg*, we move along to Brunella Antomarini, a respected Italian philosophy professor, and her "Stone Yearning to be Water: Hogg's Philosophical Realism for the XXI Century," an original contribution, in which she argues that Barry Callaghan possesses a unique philosophy, one based on contradiction and paradox, and on the absolute necessity of such to create a singular being. In her reading, Hogg is a modern Dante, with a vision that is brought about not through meditation, but through uncertainty, chance, action, and the coexistence of love and death; in short, "the musical accord of opposites." Professor Ray Ellenwood's "some notes on callaghan's *hogg poems and drawings*" is a reprint of an article that appeared in *Brick* magazine in 1979, where he postulates Hogg as the antithesis of the man Barry Callaghan, and purports some thoughts on Hogg's spiritual journey of many transformations. In a similar vein, poet Joe Rosenblatt's original piece, "3 Meditations on Hogg," grows into a correspondence with the author (perhaps in the guise of Hogg), which nearly drives the poet to madness as he faces all the fictions, riddles, blasphemies, and sleights of hand found within the poems. Of particular note is his trip to the Toronto archives that calls into question the generally accepted "historical" version of Hogg as related by several authors and critics included in this book.

Three writers then provide us with a sustained discussion of a single poem from *Hogg The Poems and Drawings* (with brief mention of others). The American poet Jim Hart writes about "Sisyphus the Crack King" from the point of view of his personal experience as an ex-crack addict, detailing how the poem authentically captures and mimics the range of emotions and bodily experiences before, during, and after a crack high. (He also suggests that school children be taught the poem as a way to steer them away from drugs.) Professor David Lampe's "Hogg's Roman Nose: Callaghan's Sardonic Sonnet" focuses on the array of traditional (classical, medieval, renaissance) poetic forms that can be found in *Hogg*, particularly as they relate to religious and political verse, citing the sonnet "The Imperial Beak" as a prime example. Then writer and professor Bruce Meyer's "What the Darkness Tells the Light: Barry Callaghan's 'Judas Priest'" argues for the prescience and forward thought of "Judas Priest" in light of the recent controversy in Catholic circles over the unearthing of *The Judas Gospels*, a fourth-century Gnostic text that suggests Jesus shared the foreknowledge of his betrayal and death with his disciple Judas, a scenario also explored in the Callaghan poem.

As a bridge between the first Hogg book, *Hogg The Poems and Drawings*, and the second, *Hogg The Seven Last Words,* are two articles focused on the Hogg drawings. Visual artist Vera Frenkel examines the Hogg drawings from the point of view of "one autodidact to another," in an article created for an exhibition of the drawings at Carleton University Art Gallery in 1997 and reprinted here, entitled, "The Hidden Precinct of Desire." Her vast knowledge about the process of visual artistic expression informs her complex discussion regarding the genesis and execution of the drawings, particularly how autobiographical elements may have deeply influenced the work to reveal "a crisis of the body," which turns into an epic quest for a new life. Michael Bell's "The Whole Hogg," written for the same exhibition (he was the Director of the gallery), is a very comprehensive analysis of the drawings that contextualizes them within a "text-image" framework informed by psychological and literary theories, with special attention to their place within Surrealist and Anti-Rationalist movements. Lastly, before turning attention to the second installment of Hogg, a reprint of celebrated American poet Hayden Carruth's introduction to the revised edition of *Hogg The Poems and Drawings* is included, where he hails the work as a "momentous and lyrical triumph," that combines "a conspicuous intermixture of the sensibility of the North American underclass – Irish, Jewish, and especially African American," to create a heavily rhythmic language "full of street idiom."

We then begin our section on *Hogg The Seven Last Words* with a reprint of George Elliott Clarke's review from *The Halifax Herald*, where he characterizes the work as a powerful "poem-novel" that provides readers with "a discourse on the lousy twentieth century" through juxtapositions of wise tales, haunting images, and fatal ideologies. A longer assessment, David Sobelman's "Fishing for Hogg in the Midnight Sun," an original work for the collection (but part of a larger work, entitled *Belletters*), written as a letter to a friend, provides us with a provocative and complex reading of various poems, highlighting not only what he understands to be the poetic genius of the poet, but also the importance of the poetry in his own life. The dialogue between the writer and his recipient quickly extends into a conversation with Hogg, Barry Callaghan, Nietzsche, Heidegger, and others. Then lauded French poet Robert Marteau, in "Margaritas Ante Porcos," reminisces about his first encounter with Hogg and Barry Callaghan the man in Montreal in the late 1970s, and discusses his more recent epiphanies regarding the genesis and meaning of the Hogg poems since reading *Barrelhouse Kings*, especially as related to the significance of the "pig" resonances. Genesis is also prodded in poet David Wevill's original piece, "The Seven Last Words," which describes how the love affair in *As Close As We Came* turned into the key love story in the second installment of Hogg, and how these new poems bring together "satire, political comment, and intimate personal lyric." Novelist and actress Gale Zoë Garnett responds to the visual and aural elements of the poems in "A Slaviceltic Circus Poet," another original piece for the collection, revealing how Slavic film and music have influenced not only the subject matter and poetic sensibility of the oppressive KGB-riddled Russian landscape of these later poems, but also their aesthetic execution. Lastly, writer and professor Janice Kulyk Keefer in "Against Forgetting: Notes on Barry Callaghan's *Hogg The Seven Last Words*" offers readers a detailed summary of twentieth-century Russian history as the backdrop for reading the poems – an essential original piece – without knowledge of which, she argues, one runs the "risk of impoverishing the art and its impact on us." She then provides a reading of the poems that contextualizes them within a genre of literature that remembers and witnesses world events through recreating history in artistic, fictional form.

THE FICTION: *The Way the Angel Spreads Her Wings, The Black Queen Stories, When Things Get Worst,* and *A Kiss Is Still a Kiss:* The section starts with an original score by recently deceased jazz and blues saxophonist and life-long friend of Barry Callaghan, Doug Richardson, entitled "Barry's Lament." Over the last few years, Doug Richardson had played at nearly every Exile Editions launch party, as well as at several of Barry Callaghan's personal reading events, in Toronto and elsewhere. Think of this contribution as the soundtrack to this array of articles, reviews, and responses to Barry Callaghan's fiction, much of which has been inspired by jazz and blues rhythms and personalities, and much of which is discussed in terms of musical genres and styles. The more formal discussion of the fiction begins with a reprint of celebrated late-author Timothy Findley's review of *The Black Queen Stories* from *The Globe and Mail*, where he describes the collection of short stories as a dark, magical book, and the Black Queen as a figure that enters both the concrete and imaginative landscape of multicultural Toronto, representing all who are struggling to find themselves. She is "there in all our lives and we have to learn how to cope with her." Michael Trussler's reprinted academic article then dissects the three-page title story in detail, in "The Short Story as Miniature: Barry Callaghan's 'The Black Queen,'" after examining the difficulties and complexities of theorizing and discussing short stories as a genre, as well as how short stories achieve their effects on a reader. Close-reading two stories (one from *The Black Queen Stories* and one from *A Kiss Is Still a Kiss*; "The Cohen in Cowan" and "Our Thirteenth Summer," respectively) is screenwriter and journalist Norman Snider, who argues that in defiance of politically correct movements that seek to discredit any artistic appropriation of voice, particularly "the moral and psychological confusions caused by the flights from ethnic and religious identity," Callaghan has managed to write authentically about the Jewish experience as a non-Jew. Attention then shifts to *The Way the Angel Spreads Her Wings* with a reprint of a review by Paul Williams Roberts of Barry Callaghan's first published novel. Roberts claims that "few first novels have been as eagerly awaited as this one," and then goes on to champion the book not only as a blending of a poetic style to prose, but also as an Oedipal triumph whereby the son refuses to battle the father, but instead creates an arena and space of his own. Highlighting other aspects of the novel, Alef Graf van Steijn's "Complexity, Circularity, and Distanciation: Notes Toward a Reading of *The Way the Angel Spreads Her Wings*," an original contribution, argues that the musicality of the autobiographical novel's non-linear structure is polyphonic and cubist in nature, and that this framework is intended to represent the contradictions of the modern mind struggling with the truths of twentieth-century modernity and war.

Next is a reprint of a review by Ann Diamond from *Books in Canada* of Callaghan's second novel, *When Things Get Worst*. Intrigued and affected by the tale of this young nameless woman and her husband Evol, and the religious Lute, the writer searches out Callaghan to discuss faith and evil with him under the dark lights of a Bay Street bistro. Then poet Kathleen McCracken and writer Seán Virgo articulate their admiration of the storytelling skills evident in the execution of the novel in two original articles. McCracken examines how the author writes with keen understanding of the highlands and lowlands of western Ontario Grey County, creating a believable twenty-two-year-old female narrator and other characters "whose lives are beset by misfortune and despair, yet punctuated by moments of incisive joy and insight"; whereas Virgo, comparing the narrative technique to the musical *fugue*, outlines how the novel works as "a sustained hopscotch with time, back and forth and across three generations," with motifs appearing and reappearing in new combinations and contexts throughout the book.

A reprinted review from *The Globe and Mail,* continues this argument of sustained artistic vision, this time in terms of the short story collection, *A Kiss Is Still a Kiss.* Entitled "A Complex Beauty," Joan Thomas suggests that although the characters do not reappear in subsequent stories, the stories might nevertheless benefit from being read as a linked sequence, because of the ways in which they intersect with each other through common themes and images and, most notably, through characters that can be described as "the living dead." Conversely, concentrating on the "affirmation and celebration of life" in Callaghan's work is the writer Leon Rooke. In an expansion of an introduction that first appeared in the Italian translation of *Never's Just the Echo of Forever* (a novella originally published as part of *A Kiss Is Still a Kiss*), Rooke christens the tale of the school crossing guard as Callaghan's "best story, and certainly one of the most perfectly accomplished and haunting Canadian fictions that I know." Writer and biographer Rosemary Sullivan then explores the art of storytelling in an original piece that examines "Because Y is a Crooked Letter," which she argues is "a perfect model of what a story can be," tracing her reading of the narrative as she tries to unlock the mystery of how it works. Lastly, I offer my own original article, "Orpheus in Retirement: Love, Myth, and Questions of Audience in Barry Callaghan's 'Nobody Wants to Die,'" one of my favourite works, here read as a compelling modern mythical revision of the Orpheus and Eurydice myth into a love story of an older couple and a tale of a grieving widower that asks important questions regarding the artist-audience relationship.

THE NON-FICTION: *Barrelhouse Kings, Raise You Five: Essays and Encounters: 1964-2004, Raise You Ten:*

Essays and Encounters: 1964-2004: Irish poet and long-time contributing editor to *Exile: The Literary Quarterly*, John Montague produces an original poem, "Homage," recalling memorable incidents and people in his decades-long friendship with Barry Callaghan. Next, writer Anne Michaels, in an original piece, offers a few words on intimacy in *Barrelhouse Kings*; both the intimacy explored between father and son, and writer and reader. Paul William Roberts' review of *Barrelhouse Kings*, "A Son's Lament," reprinted here from *The Ottawa Citizen*, also expresses amazement at the genuine intimacy of the father-son relationship between Morley and Barry – a love through debate – both in life and in print, and calls the work a "staggeringly great book, and something quite unique in our own literature," a family story that is a love story. Dennis Lee then provides us with an original extended discussion of the memoir in "'The Truth Was Always in the Telling': Storytelling in *Barrelhouse Kings*," where he examines the layered storytelling technique used in the book and postulates on how earlier fictional works might have contributed to the methods employed in *Barrelhouse Kings*; an important discussion "more on the craft than content" of the memoir. CBC Radio personality Bill Casselman also veers away from the content of *Barrelhouse Kings* to discuss how the public, more specifically the Canadian public, has responded to Barry Callaghan, as well as to address the complexities of relations between father and son, particularly their public differences.

Assessment of *Raise You Five: Vol 1: Essays and Encounters 1964-2004* and *Raise You Ten: Vol II: Essays and Encounters 1964-2004* begins with a reprint of professor Michael Keefer's review of *Raise You Five* from *The Globe and Mail* entitled "Just What We Needed: A Critic with 'Duende.'" Keefer hails the work as "literary criticism and cultural history of a high order," pointing to the depth, breadth, and intelligence of thinking evident in the book, comparable to other great Canadian literary critics like Northrop Frye, but he separates Callaghan's critical practice from this group by acknowledging his additional intensity of feeling as defined by Federico Garcia Lorca's term *duende*. Since these books have only recently entered the public domain, I've decided to include another review of *Raise You Five*, a slightly expanded version of writer Ray Robertson's *Quill and Quire* review, and a review of both *Raise You Five* and *Raise You Ten* by Diana Kuprel for the University of Toronto publication *Idea&s* to offer a few more entry points into these works. Robertson argues that Callaghan is extraordinary in his ability to create art "out of whatever raw material he chooses or is chosen for him," and he cites several examples of this from his literary journalism; Kuprel extends this notion to Callaghan's ability to include himself within the act of relating, and applauds how he records "the author's own internal journey as a writer encountering other worlds." Then David Sobelman, in a Herculean feat of philosophical rationalism, provides us with a second original contribution (another selection from a longer *Belletters* piece), where he outlines a six-part taxonomy through which to understand Callaghan's literary journalism as presented in both *Raise You Five* and *Raise You Ten*. This is a rare look at a man's extensive reading (both professionally and personally) of another man's work and life, as expressed in a letter to another friend.

THE CULTURAL CONTRIBUTION: *Barry Callaghan The Man, The Publisher, The Mentor, The Translator, The Teacher, and The Archive*. In an original poem, "For Barry Callaghan," poet Patrick Lane starts us off by painting a literary portrait of the writer as a Black Irishman of verve and vitality. Then the celebrated French-Canadian writer, Marie-Claire Blais, in an original piece, reminisces in "Barry Callaghan" about meeting the man in New England in the 1960s, and expresses her deep admiration for the work he has done since as an author and as a publisher, holding true to his youthful convictions, especially that writing is "the visionary art that combats all mediocrity, an art that denounces and accuses." Alexandre Amprimoz's "The Thinking Heart: Barry Callaghan's *Exile*" is an essential piece for anyone interested in Canadian publishing history and the inner workings of and personalities associated with a long-standing international publishing house and literary magazine. Written as a companion for Exile Editions' Tenth Anniversary celebration, "a unique event in our literary history," Amprimoz argues for the cultural and artistic importance of Barry Callaghan's work as publisher and editor of *Exile: The Literary Quarterly* and Exile Editions, for his creation of a "seedbed" for creativity, experiment, debate, and dialogue, and how he has acted as a mentor and cultural hero for many Canadian and international artists. One such mentored writer, Lauren B. Davis, in "The Big Man," another piece written specifically for this collection, revisits the publication of her first story in *Exile: The Literary Quarterly*, and confesses how joining *Exile*'s literary circle and Barry Callaghan's circle of family and friends literally saved her life, suggesting in the process that he must have saved many others as well. Ray Ellenwood, respected translator and regular *Exile: The Literary Quarterly* and Exile Editions contributor and collaborator, then tackles Barry Callaghan's role as a translator, and as a publisher of works in translation, particularly French-Canadian and East-European works, in "Barry Callaghan, Translation, Exile." This original piece offers a rare behind-the-scenes view of translation history in Canada, as well as the translation process. It also includes an extremely valuable resource put together by

Ellenwood and the Exile Editorial Board: an appendix listing *all* the translations that have been published in *Exile: The Literary Quarterly* and through Exile Editions.

Turning to Barry Callaghan's contributions to the teaching profession are Michael Keefer and Jon Brooks, the former a Teaching Assistant of Barry's in the early 1970s and now a professor and journalist, the latter a talented musician and one of Barry's last students. Michael Keefer claims that Barry Callaghan's interdisciplinary and historically, culturally, and politically informed teaching style, predates official academic Cultural Studies courses and programs. (Keefer also tells some funny anecdotes in this original memory-piece that are not to be missed.) John Brooks then explains how his own original contribution to this collection transformed from an essay on "Never's Just the Echo of Forever" and the character Albie Starbach, "the most disturbing and thus true Canadian literary archetype," into a piece and a tribute song expressing gratitude to the writer who has shown him his city in fiction and the beauty of powerful narrative. Lastly, Christopher Doda, poet, archivist, and *Exile: The Literary Quarterly*'s new submissions editor, provides researchers with an extremely important resource in "As Thoroughly as Possible: Barry Callaghan's Papers," detailing the extent of the author's records, as well as those of Exile Editions, including both literary and non-literary items; a necessity for current and future research and future biographers.

As a coda to the book, another long-time friend of Barry Callaghan's, the novelist and journalist William Kennedy interviews him at the horse races in Saratoga. Kennedy prods Callaghan to expand on his views of the relationship between reporting and storytelling, non-fiction and fiction, and truth and lies, including the mysteries of storytelling, its relationship to religious experience, how writers have hidden their intentions from censors, to issues concerning authenticity of voice. Not surprisingly, the bets at the end of the day pay out.

*

This has been a project undertaken by one editor for the last four years, but supported by many. Thank you again to all the contributors – obviously, none of this would have been possible without your generosity, your intelligence, your let-me-know-if-there's-anything else-I-can-do's, and your great taste. Special thanks to Ray Ellenwood for translations of Marie-Claire Blais and Robert Marteau, and to Christopher Elson for the translation of Michel Deguy. Thanks to Bruce Meyer for various supports. Thanks to all those who extended permissions. Thanks to Michael Callaghan and Gabriela Campos for index help, Marilyn DiFlorio for all the typing and correcting, and my graduate assistants, Matthew Carrington and Christina Sacchetti, for various help throughout the production of this book. Thanks to Antonio D'Alfonso for his enthusiasm for this project and for publishing it. Thanks as well to the many well-wishers for your support. Thank you, Claire, for putting up with all this, and for feeding me. Thank you, Chris, for the same, as well as for textual assistance.

I'd like to reiterate that it is my intention with this book to generate discussion of Barry Callaghan's work and life, a subject which has hereto garnered too-little attention considering its enormous significance to and impact on many aspects of public life. Herein, people disagree, contradict each other, interpret differently; this is to be expected and encouraged. Our contributors stem from all different backgrounds nationally, linguistically, ethnically, religiously, culturally, aesthetically, and politically. There is much to enjoy here, much to agree with, much to disagree with, much to ponder; and much more that could be written. I hope others will see fit to write about, as Ray Ellenwood has suggested, the over thirty years of visual art that has appeared in *Exile: The Literary Quarterly*, or the role violence has played in Callaghan's work, or how sensual some of his prose writing can be; or more about those complex female characters whose minds he keeps entering, or about the upcoming book *All In: Essays and Encounters 1964-2004* and the critically acclaimed new book of short stories, launched only a month before this book returned from the printers, *Between Trains*.

Alexander Amprimoz writes, "The mystery for a man who is so much on the road, is how he has managed to be there so often to those who've knocked?" It's a great question and impossible to answer. I am, admittedly, a fan of Barry Callaghan, a friend, regular guest, privileged Exile Editions poet and *Exile: The Literary Quarterly* Editorial Board member, and also, through the years, with my co-vivant Christopher Doda, an honorary child (we spend Christmas evening with Barry and Claire every year). As I sometimes put it, "I met Barry Callaghan because Branko Gorjup took my poems to him and he said he would publish them. Six months later, I was managing his house and his dogs." What generosity he has shown to so many; many more than appear in these pages. More people wanted to contribute, several being older contemporaries, but they were unable to due to personal circumstances and/or illness. Some whose words should likely be included here (Yehuda Amichai, Irving Layton, William Ronald, Zachary Solov, Harry Somers, Robert Zend) have, unfortunately, like Barry's beloved father, passed on.

In order to calm myself down during the last torturous weeks of my comprehensive PhD exams, I asked Christopher to read to me one story each night from *The Black Queen Stories* and *A Kiss Is Still a Kiss* as I fell asleep. Those stories remain with me, while many of the lines I so deliberately and painstakingly memorized for the exams are already lost.

One day he won't be here when we come knocking (although I sincerely hope that day is decades away). However, he will still be welcoming us with the words that he's left behind, and hopefully, in these appraisals too.

In short: read this book. Then re-read Barry Callaghan again. And again.

CHRONOLOGY

1937: Barry Callaghan was born in Toronto, in the Annex area July 5, 1937, the second and youngest son of famous modernist Canadian writer Morley Callaghan (b. 1903) and his wife Loretto (Dee) Callaghan (b. 1902). He was raised in a quiet tree-shaded street, the upper floor of a fourplex. Several of his stories – "Our Thirteenth Summer," "Intrusions," "A Drawn Blind" – are set on this street, as is the opening of his novel, *The Way the Angel Spreads Her Wings.*

1942-1949: During the Second World War years, Callaghan attended St. Peter's Grade School, on the southeast side of Bathurst south of Bloor. He skipped grade seven. He sang in the choir of St. Peter's Church, on Bathurst Street, northwest of Bloor. The choir director, Harry O'Grady, figures in many of Callaghan's fictions. He also played for the St. Peter's baseball team, and for several years they were City CYO Pee-Wee and Bantam Champions. They played in Christie Pits, site of the Thirties anti-Semitic race riot.

1950-1956: Attends St. Michael's College School. Taught by Basilian priests. He plays football, basketball, track, wins the Public Speaking trophy four years in succession. Becomes a basketball star, and fails grade eleven. In 1951 the Callaghans move to 20 Dale Avenue in Toronto in Rosedale. In 1954-55, he discovers – though he is under-age – the low life of Yonge Street and the "Porters' Hall" on College Street, the only "Black" dance hall in Toronto. Several of his stories are set in this world – "Poodles John," "Crow Jane's Blues," as well as the poems "John the Conqueroo" and "Judas Priest." He meets Doug Richardson, who will become a fine tenor saxophonist and his lifelong friend. He fails to graduate from high school.

1956-1958: Enters Assumption College Windsor (later, the University of Windsor) to play basketball, but is influenced by a remarkable gathering of young priest-teachers. In the summer of 1958, he joins Canadian Press (Broadcast News) as a summer replacement and becomes a young reporter about town, especially the world of Yonge Street and the Barclay Hotel, the city's only nightclub. Back at college, he discovers the futility of his dream of playing in the NBA, and quits basketball. He leads a college delegation to a Model United Nations at McGill University. In 1956-57, he writes his first poem, "The Outhouse," published in the College Magazine, *Kaleidoscope*. This long sequence – unwittingly in the manner of the Beats – causes a good deal of consternation.

1959: In the spring of 1959, he sells his first short story, "The Muscle," to CBC radio Windsor. Summer, works as a reporter for CBC Television News, Channel Six, the local news. One of his first interviews is with a talking horse. In the fall, he moves back home to 20 Dale Avenue and enters the undergraduate program at St. Michael's College, the University of Toronto.

1960: Reporter, for the summer, at CBC Television News, Channel Six. Meets Edmund Wilson, takes him to the Barclay nightclub, which he later writes about for *Toronto Life*.

1961-1962: In his final year, he is director of The All-Varsity Review, a musical. The lead dancer is Denise Cronenberg (sister to David Cronenberg, cousin to Claire Weissman Wilks, with whom Callaghan will eventually come to live for thirty-five – and counting – years). Out of a dispute over his grade for a paper he wrote on Milton and Eliot, comes an invitation from the President of the Pontifical Institute of Medieval Studies, Rev. Lawrence K. Shook, to become a teaching fellow in the graduate program. He graduates with a BA. Declines offer to become a Rhodes Scholar.

1963: Graduates with an MA from the University of Toronto and enters the doctoral program in English and studies there under the direction of Donald F. Theall until 1965. Declines an offer to become a fellow of Massey Hall. Begins appearing on CBC radio where he talks about books once a week. He marries Nina Rabchuck and not long after they buy a house on Eastbourne Avuenue, in the Oriole Parkway neighbourhood of Toronto. On their honeymoon in London, he meets poets Patrick Kavanagh and George Barker, and in Paris, the engraver S.W. Hayter, and poet John Montague. He and Montague become lifelong friends (in 1972 will begin his tenure as contributing editor to *Exile: The Literary Quarterly*, and in 1982 Callaghan will edit Montague's first *Selected Poems* published simultaneously for Dolman Press, Wake Forest University Press, Oxford University Press, and Exile Editions).

1964: Son, Michael Paul Morley is born. Hired to work in television on the cultural program, *Show on Shows,* which becomes *The Umbrella,* hosted by Group of Eleven abstract expressionist painter, William Ronald, who becomes his lifelong friend.

1965: Hired as lecturer at Atkinson College, York University, by Donald F. Theall, continues to work on *The Umbrella;* meets and interviews, through 1965 and 1966, Le Roi Jones, Marie-Claire Blais, Margaret Laurence, John Updike, Patrick Kavanagh, Allan Sillitoe, Saul Bellow, Philip Roth, Arnold Wesker. First published critical article: "The Writings of Margaret Laurence," Tamarack Review, No. 36.

1966-1967: Working with producer/director, R.J. (Paddy Sampson), he writes and performs in *The Blues,* a film of live performances featuring Muddy Waters, Brownie McGhee, Sonny Terry, Otis Spann, Willie Dixon, 'Lonecat' Jesse Fuller, Mabel Hillary, Booker T. Washington White, Sunnyland Slim, and James Cotton. Callaghan is hired to edit the Literary pages of the *Toronto Telegram*, where he works until he resigns under pressure in 1971.

1968: Hosts a television conversation among theologians, "The Pope and the Pill," on the occasion of Pius XII's papal cyclical on birth control. Becomes one of four hosts for the news and public affairs program, *The Public Eye* (the other hosts are Peter Jennings, Norman Depoe, Jean Sauvé). Travels across Canada with Pierre Trudeau; is given unheard-of space in the Telegram, three folio pages to write about Trudeau. Writes about New York ("Desolation Row") over four folio pages. Writes and directs a one-hour documentary for CBC, "Callaghan's New York."

1969: Before beginning to work for the television program, *Weekend,* he writes and hosts a one-hour documentary, "Israel." Program causes nervous rumblings in Jewish community. In Jerusalem, he meets poet Yehuda Amichai, who becomes his lifelong friend and contributing editor to *Exile: The Literary Quarterly* in 1972. He meets the Israeli actress, Saya Lyran. Their affair, which leads to the breakdown of his marriage, will give rise to *The Hogg Poems and Drawings,* 1978. Callaghan, as film maker, covers not only the Middle East, but the social upheaval and violence in Quebec, the student revolution in the United States, the Chicago Seven trial, and is thought of, by right-wing network brass, as a left-wing radical. His affair with Saya Lyran comes to an end.

1970: He moves into the Fontainebleu Apartments on Rosedale Valley Road across the hall from public affairs researcher and artist, Claire Weissman Wilks. Begins relationship with Claire. Goes to Cairo, Beirut, and Amman. Is arrested by Saica guerillas (Syrian branch of PLO), is released and travels to Jordan where he is caught in The Black September War. Returns to Toronto where he makes films about the War and the Palestinians, both broadcast during the October crisis. He conducts a conversation with Prime Minister Golda Meir during which he challenges several assumptions about Israeli policy. Meir is furious. Uproar in Jewish communities in Winnipeg, Toronto, and Montreal. General audience approval index, however, is ninety-one.

1971: Callaghan is made Assistant Professor and acting Chairman of English Department. Interviews Angela Davis, charged with conspiracy and murder in support of the Black Panther Party, in her California prison cell. The CBC had ordered him not to meet with Davis; he does; when she is freed, the CBC broadcasts the interview and fires Callaghan. He resigns from *The Toronto Telegram.* Following the Meir controversy, he is initially denied tenure, but his academic career is saved through the direct intervention of Dean Harry Crowe (a well-known Zionist) with the President, who overrules the Senate. At the urging of Crowe, he founds *Exile: The Literary Quarterly*; Callaghan says it will be "one of the two best literary journals in the world."

1972: June: first issue of *Exile*.

1973-1975: Continues to teach. Is offered no work as writer or as film maker or in television. He will never again appear on CBC television as a cultural or political commentator. Begins writing *The Hogg Poems*. He is admitted to hospital in state of shock caused by severe arthritic pain. Moves to Church Street, across from St. Michael's Cathedral.

1976: Begins Exile Editions with a book of drawings by Claire Weissman Wilks. Moves in with Claire at Fontainebleu Apartments in Rosedale Valley. Forms Villon Films with friend/cameraman/producer, Peter Davis, of the United States. He makes film about Rhodesia at war. Goes to South Africa. Is arrested and put in prison by secret police while making film with Davis about the Afrikaaners. Is expelled from South Africa. John MacFarlane of *Weekend Magazine* publishes "The Muscle." Alan Coren of *Punch* publishes "The Muscle," the first of *The Black Queen Stories*. Regular on CTV's Canada AM as a weekly contributor on films and eventually becomes a weekly "columnist" until 1979.

1977: Tom Hedley (formerly of the *Toronto Telegram* and *Esquire*) becomes editor of the new, revamped *Toronto Life*. Callaghan travels to Puerto Rico, gambling in the casinos, and subsequently receives National Magazine Award for "Luck in Men's Eyes," published in *Toronto Life*. Travels through Bavaria to Dachau and Munich.

1978: Publishes *The Hogg Poems and Drawings*. Book is launched with an exhibition of the Hogg drawings at the Isaac's Gallery, Toronto. Downchild blues band perfoms. Invited by Tom Hedley to write a regular fiction and/or reportage column, "Callaghan," about people in the city. Many of these columns become stories published in *Punch* ("The Black Queen," "Crow Jane's Blues," "Springwater,"

"Dark Laughter," "A Drawn Blind"). Works on *Atlante*, translations from the French of poet Robert Marteau. Meets Jerry Tutunjian for whom some of his best travel writing will be written for *Leisure Ways*. Is hired by John McFarlane and Gary Ross to travel to Gabon and Cameroon to write about Cardinal Léger, Albert Schweitzer, and leper camps.

1979: Lives in Munich, then in Paris at 22 rue de la chaise. Works on engraving in S.W. Hayter's atelier. Meets Samuel Beckett. Feted at legendary Punch Lunch. Returns to Toronto, becomes host of the show that succeeds the Morton Schulman Show on CITY TV, *Firing Line*. Wins National Magazine Award and President's Medal for Excellence for "Albert Schweitzer's Dark Continent." Publishes *Treatise on White and Tincture*, translations from the French of Robert Marteau. Travels to Moscow and Leningrad. Meets Marina Golovchenko, giving rise to *As Close as We Came*.

1980: Publishes *Interlude*, translations of prose by the French poet Robert Marteau.

1981: Buys a house with Claire Weissman Wilks on Sullivan Street, in Toronto's Chinatown. Claire opens one-woman show of 100 erotic drawings at Charles Pachter's IGA Gallery. Callaghan meets Yugoslavian poet, Miodrag Pavlovic. Travels to Macau, Hong Kong and Tokyo with publisher George Yemec, who becomes lifelong friend. Ostensibly, Callaghan is to meet Stanley Ho, one of the richest men in the Far East, and owner of casinos and race tracks. In fact, Callaghan and Yemec are on an extended tour of race tracks in Hong Kong and Tokyo. This is the beginning of Callaghan's devotion to the "nags." Travels to England's Lake District with Claire to visit territory of Coleridge and Wordsworth. Travels through Germany with his son, Michael, and to Ireland where they stay with John Montague.

1982: Publishes *As Close as We Came* with Stoddart and Exile Editions, sequence of poems based on his time in Moscow and Leningrad. Louise Denys publishes *The Black Queen Stories* at Lester and Orpen Denys as part of their International Fiction List. Publishes Miodrag Pavlovic's

Singing at the Whirlpool, a translation. Travels to Berlin. In August, travels to the town of Saratoga Springs for the legendary August horse races. He and Claire attend every August since.

1983: Wins National Magazine Award for "Year of the Horse" and the National Canadian Travel Writing Award for "Berlin." Travels with Claire Weissman Wilks, making pilgrimage from Paris to Santiago de Compostela, following medieval route.

1984: Wins ACTRA Award for Best Television Host for the CITY TV show, *Enterprise*. Wins the National Magazine Award and the University of Western Ontario's President's Medal for Excellence in Magazine Articles for "The Night the Balloons Wouldn't Come Down and Join the Party," published in *Toronto Life*. Travels to Calgary. Travels to Beograd to appear with John Montague, Miodrag Pavlovic and Robert Marteau at International Poetry Festival. Travels to Venice and Rome. At Saratoga, he and Claire meet Zachary Solov, former principal dancer with Balanchine. Thereafter, until 1995, they stay in Saratoga at Solov's house every August. Loretto Callaghan dies. Her death affects Barry deeply as they shared a closeness he describes in his memoir, *Barrelhouse Kings*.

1985: Travels by ship with Latvians, Estonians, Lithuanians, to protest – under leadership of Soviet dissident Vladimir Bukovsky – the ratification of the Helsinki Accords. Wins the CBC Award for Fiction for "A Childish Mistake." Receives Gold Award for Fiction from the Foundation for the Advancement of Canadian Letters and Periodical Distributors of Canada for "Looking for the End," published in *Toronto Life*. Publishes *Fragile Moments,* translations of Quebec poet Jacques Brault. Publishes *A Voice Locked in Stone*, translations from the Serbian of Miodrag Pavlovic. Travels to Rome for a one-woman exhibition of Claire's work.

1986: Wins International Authors Festival Literary Award (shared with Margaret Atwood). Travels to Alaskan glaciers with Claire Weissman Wilks.

1987: Celebration of Fifteen Years of Exile and Exile Editions held at Bistro 990, Toronto. Downchild blues band performs. Travels to Beograd and Rome, where he is Writer in Residence. Publishes *Flowers of Ice: Selected Poems: Imants Ziedonis*, a book of translations from the Latvian, and *The Selected Poems of Frank Prewett,* co-edited with Bruce Meyer. Travels to Rome, Beograd, Venice and Bologna. Travels to Stockholm and Jerusalem for one-woman shows by Claire Weissman Wilks. October: suffers terrible vandalism on his Sullivan Street home. Wins Lowell Thomas Award (US) for his writing about travels to Alaskan glaciers.

1988: Publishes *Stone Blind Love*, dedicated to his mother as muse, his third book of poems; decides immediately that the poems really belong to The Hogg sequence, that the publication – despite fine reviews – was a mistake. Wins National Magazine Award for "Act of Vandalism," an account of the actual vandalism on his home, published in *Toronto Life*.

1989: Publishes *The Way the Angel Spreads Her Wings*. Refuses to be put forward for full professor status at York University. Receives Pushcart Prize for Non-Fiction in the United States for "Motiveless Malignancy" (a version of "Act of Vandalism"). Writer in Residence, University of Rome. He publishes (along with Ray Ellenwood) *Wells of Light: Selected Poems of Fernand Ouellette* and edits, introduces and publishes *Canadian Travellers in Italy*, an anthology of writing by Canadian writers.

1990: Allows name to be put forward and is made full professor at York University without debate. August 25th, Morley Callaghan dies. The funeral mass, held in St. Michael's Cathedral and attended by several hundred guests, as well as the procession to Mount Hope Cemetery and the wake at the family's favourite restaurant, Le Bistingo on Queen St. West, are described in great detail in Barry Callaghan's memoir, *Barrelhouse Kings*.

1991: Moves with Claire into 20 Dale Avenue, Barry's childhood home, where they remain until today.

1992: Travels to deliver lectures in Rome and Prague.

1993: Publishes *When Things Get Worst*, his second novel. Receives Toronto Arts Award for Writing.

1994: Travels to address conferences on Canadian literature at the University of Bologna.

1995: Publishes *A Kiss Is Still a Kiss*, his second collection of short fiction. Edits and publishes an anthology of short fiction, *This Ain't No Healing Town: Toronto Stories*. Lectures in Milan, Bologna, Trieste and Venice. In August, he and Claire start to stay in Albany rather than Saratoga, beginning their relationship with retired journalist Joe Gagen and novelist William Kennedy. Because John Montague is Writer in Residence at William Kennedy's The Writers Institute in Albany, Callaghan agrees to march in 1996 for the first time in the his life in a St. Patrick's Day parade.

1996: Travels to Venice and Bologna to consult on the translation of *The Black Queen Stories* into Italian.

1997: Publishes *Hogg The Poems and Drawings*. "Drawings by Barry Callaghan – The Whole Hogg," a retrospective exhibition is presented at the Carleton University Art Gallery. Named in Salute to the City: Toronto's 100 Outstanding Citizens. Travels to Havana, Cuba, to address a conference on Canadian Fiction and to launch an anthology of Canadian short fiction that includes his "The Black Queen." Travels to Bologna where he addresses a conference on Canadian Women's Studies.

1998: Publishes *Barrelhouse Kings: A Memoir*. He is given the inaugural W.O. Mitchell Prize for Mentoring By A Writer Who Has a Body of Work. *Selected Stories* and *Hogg The Poems and Drawings* are published to acclaim, in Croatian, in Zagreb.

1999: Honoured with a Doctor of Letters at State University of New York at Buffalo. Travels to Venice, and then to Mexico City to give a series of readings.

2000: Made member of the Founders Society at York University. Gives series of lectures and readings in Udine, Venice, Bologna and Rome.

2001: Gives a keynote talk at the Monterey Festival of Writing from the Americas. Claire has a one-woman exhibition to open the Monterey State Cultural Centre. Travels with John Reeves and Claire to Denmark to meet and photograph various Danish writers for *Exile: The Literary Quarterly*. Travels to Paris to give a reading introduced by Michel Deguy.

2002: Travels to Mexico to launch an anthology of Canadian short fiction with Margaret Atwood, Alistair MacLeod, and others. Claire has an exhibition in Mexico City's Museo del Choppo and at the Gallery of the National Assembly.

2003: Retires from teaching at Atkinson College. Is appointed Professor Emeritus and Distinguished Scholar at York University. Travels to Bratislava for publication of *Temny smiech [Selected Stories]*.

2004: Son Michael Callaghan marries Mexican artist Gabriela Campos on Feb 14th, in official ceremony at Toronto City Hall, but then later in a cathedral wedding in Oaxaca, Mexico. Barry Callaghan and Claire and many friends and family travel to Mexico for the wedding. Travels to Turin, Italy, to launch at Turin Book Fair *Di male in peggio [When Things Get Worst]*. Travels to St. Petersburg and to Riga to meet Imants Ziedonis for the first time, the national Latvian poet whom he translated into English in 1997.

2005: Publishes first volume of his non-fiction, *Raise You Five: Essays and Encounters, 1964-2004*. Travels to Rome to launch at Rome Book Fair, *Niente è solo l'eco de sempre [Never's Just the Echo of Forever]*. *Exile: The Literary Quarterly* is officially handed over to son Michael Callaghan as publisher. Barry Callaghan remains Editor-in-chief, but a new Editorial Board is established.

2006: Publishes second volume of his non-fiction, *Raise You Ten*. Travels to Rome to read at Romapoesia, and while in Rome begins writing short stories for *Between Trains*. To Paris, to launch *J'amais est l'echo de toujours [Never's Just the Echo of Forever]*. Exile Editions is officially handed over to son Michael Callaghan as publisher. Barry Callaghan remains Editor-in-chief, but a new Editorial Board is established.

2007: Publishes *Between Trains*.

PUBLISHED WORKS

Between Trains. Stories. McArthur & Co. Ltd.: Toronto, 2007.

Raise You Ten: Essays and Encounters, 1964-2004. McArthur & Co. Ltd.: Toronto, 2006.

Raise You Five: Essays and Encounters, 1964-2004. McArthur & Co. Ltd.: Toronto, 2005.

Hogg The Seven Last Words. Poems. McArthur & Co. Ltd.: Toronto, 2001.

Barrelhouse Kings: A Memoir. McArthur & Co. Ltd.: Toronto, 1998.

Hogg The Poems and Drawings. McArthur & Co. Ltd: Toronto, 1997.

A Kiss Is Still a Kiss. Stories. McArthur & Co.: Ltd Toronto, 1995.

When Things Get Worst. A Novel. Little Brown: Toronto, 1993.

The Way the Angel Spreads Her Wings. A Novel. Lester & Orpen Dennys, Toronto, 1989.

Stone Blind Love. Poems. Stoddart: Toronto, 1988.

As Close As We Came. Poems. Exile Editions Limited: Toronto, 1982.

The Black Queen Stories. Lester & Orpen Dennys: Toronto, 1982.

The Hogg Poems and Drawings. General: Toronto, 1978.

Books by Barry Callaghan
Which Have Been Translated

Jamais est l'écho de toujours (Translated by Claire and Louise Chabalier). Les Allusifs: Paris, France, 2006.

Niente è solo l'eco di sempre (Translated by Carla Pezzini Plevano). Cosmo Iannore Editore: Isernia, Italy, 2005.

Di male in peggio (Translated by Carla Pezzini Plevano). Cosmo Iannone Editore: Isernia, Italy, 2004.

Temny smiech (Translated by Marián Gazdik). Juga: Bratislava, Slovakia, 2003.

A Kiss Is Still a Kiss: Racconti (Translated by several hands) Supernova: Venice, Italy, 1999.

Hogg (Translated by Giga Gracan and Borivoj Radakovic). Konzor: Zagreb, Croatia, 1999.

Crni Smijeh (Translated by Zdenka Drucalovic). Konzor: Zagreb, Croatia, 1999.

Slepog a Kamena Vliskost. (Translated by I. Malenkova & M. Pavlovic). KOB: Beograd, Yugoslavia, 1991.

Crna Kraljica I Druge Price (Translated by Jelena Stakich). Izdavacko Preduzece Rad, Beograd, Yugoslavia, 1991.

Lo mas cerca qua estubemos (Translated by S. Wald & L. Zeller). Hyperion: Barcelona, Spain, 1989.

Tako de desilo (Translated by Miodrag Pavlovic). Beograd, Yugoslavia, 1989.

Les Livres de Hogg (Translated by Robert Marteau). Quinze: Montreal, Canada, 1978.

Book Translations by Barry Callaghan

Eidolon. Robert Marteau, Exile Editions Limited: Toronto, 1990.

Wells of Light: Selected Poems of Fernand Ouellette (Co-translated with Ray Ellenwood). Exile Editions Limited: Toronto, 1989.

Flowers of Ice: Selected Poems. Imants Ziedonis. Exile Editions Limited: Toronto, Canada, 1987.

Fragile Moments. Jacques Brault. Exile Editions Limited: Toronto, Canada, 1985.

A Voice Locked in Stone. Miodrag Pavlovic. Exile Editions Limited: Toronto, Canada, 1985.

Singing At The Whirlpool. Miodrag Pavlovic. Exile Editions Limited: Toronto, Canada, 1982.

Interlude. Robert Marteau. Exile Editions Limited: Toronto, Canada, 1980.

Treatise On White And Tincture. Robert Marteau. Exile Editions Limited: Toronto, Canada, 1979.

Atlante. Robert Marteau, Exile Editions Limited: Toronto, Canada, 1978.

THE POETRY

Hogg The Poems and Drawings
and *Hogg The Seven Last Words*

HOMAGE TO HOGG

Michel Deguy

No longer are there Gods
No longer the Dead, the Shades
No longer the Beasts, the great parietal magi figures of
    the anthropomorphosis
There is no more Nature
There is not even the hereditary Enemy

. . . At last alone?
Whence comes then the terror?
Could there only be the among-*us*
To be brought about and cared for
– first of all by inventing the *us*?

The third party, the other other than otherness, the
    Other,
Could it be Space, the astrophysical elsewhere
For which deterrestration agitates?
Nihil
Obstat

 Let us begin again:

Who is the host, who the guest? Every guest is wholly
"other"; every host is wholly other. Inasmuch as the
guest is no longer a god (Demeter unrecognizable at
Celeo's hearth, or the untouchable god at the inn in

Emmaus...) how can hospitality reinvent that uncondi-
tionality with which the philosopher – it is Jacques Der-
rida – charges it again? There are no monsters other
than the absolutely other ("every other is wholly other,"
he liked to say). It is a question of changing monstrosity
into . . . ? Into the *wholly other,* the thinker tells us.

*

Yesterday the African (man or woman) in a red *boubou*
That man-woman right here whose identity decapitates
(his or her badge hanging it in effigy from his or her
     buttonhole)
I attributed to those cheeks
"*la forme entière de l'humaine condition*"

Let us call *Uprightness* in her, in him
That which is aimed at in each and every one of us by
     the capital letter of
Rights
As long ago the second *ousia* of the Stagyrite

If becoming-a-guest requires a metamorphosis
Into what is now the question.
By what conversion, we would have said in the time of
     religions.
Into Jew, into Christian, into Muslim?
Into what human of the future?
For *others* will no longer do, nor *neighbour,*
I have proposed: into an orphan
So that we might adopt one another.

Translated by Christopher Elson

44

BARRY IN THE UNDERWORLD

Margaret Atwood

There's a poem by Gwendolyn MacEwen that ends, "There is something down there and you want it told." She could have been speaking directly to Barry Callaghan: what's *down there*, and *telling it*, have been the two poles around which his work in all its multiplicity has long revolved.

Down there is the underground, the underworld – of gambling, of petty criminals and drunks, of "social undesirables," of outcasts and immigrants, and, as in the title of his fine literary magazine, of exiles: those who either fall to the bottom or are thrown there or who dive *down there* deliberately. *Down there* is also the world of repressed wishes, of surrealism – the flip side of reason and logic, the dream-world, the cave you enter in search of treasure or lost Eurydice, or else the nightmare Minotaur. Then, too, it is the subterranean realm of passion and rage, of volcanic emotions. It's the sadness beneath the clothes, the skeleton beneath the flesh: *down there* is *beneath*. *Down there* is also where the angels went when they were kicked out of heaven, and Barry's work goes hurtling off in search of them – them, and whatever else may be down there. Eccentric pen and outrageous pencil, and hook, line and sinker are his tools, and big fish are what he's after: the big fish *down there*. Some of them are angels *manqués,* but some of them are sharks.

So Barry Callaghan is – among many other things – one of those wild-eyed, depth-defying explorers of the Underground. It's always a risky vocation, and he's taken his risks; and the work – *his telling it* – is the result. Telling it is also, of course, one of the risks. Each

45

of his pieces is the end of a rope, a rope you can haul in or climb down, which may or may not be a lifeline. What's at the other end? Something you can't see yet, something with teeth. Some sort of monster. Whatever he's hooked.

You.

THE HOGG POEMS AND DRAWINGS

Into the bloodstream like an amphetamine

ADELE FREEDMAN

Reading *The Hogg Poems* is like falling through a rabbit hole (a seal hole, if you wish) into a world as crazy and hallucinatory as Alice's Wonderland. With only a couple of quotations serving as incongruous signposts – one from Henry Scadding's *Toronto of Old* and the other by Henry Miller – we are plunged into the visionary mind of Callaghan's Everyman, the pig-headed Hogg. First Hogg is fed the question. "How," asks a voice in the Prologue, "does a man live through an endless winter of endless nights, and how does he stay sane while sitting squat hour after hour by a seal hole in the ice?" How, indeed? Hogg's response, like that of Ecclesiastes who addressed the same question centuries before, is to undertake a search for the meaning of life – the spring of water trapped beneath unyielding sheets of stone.

Hogg escapes to Jerusalem to commence his multidimensional voyage of self-discovery. He is a pilgrim of old, but he is also a tourist. Callaghan wrings a wry sort of humour from Hogg's ability to straddle time periods: a supplicant addresses him:

> See the blind stair, that's where
> Christ leapt upon his cross;
> and close by, Mr. Hogg, the best
> coffee in Jerusalem.

Hogg's peregrinations unfold as a series of discrete scenes which are as compelling and perfectly formed as dreams. On the Abu Gosh Road he meets a man with an eye like a mole. Suddenly he is at the Hotel Tarshish with a woman feasting on roast dove and olives. He makes love in a cemetery. He accepts arcane wisdom from a sphinx-like café proprietor after being shown a tin box of cigarettes, each neatly scissored in half.

At the centre of Hogg's stay in Jerusalem, like a pit embedded in a peach, is his love affair. The individual poems comprising it are compilations of surface details that suggest an impenetrable sensuality. Hogg luxuriates in the proliferation of surfaces as though they were velvet cushions. He is totally vulnerable to sensory captivation. He savours every detail of his beloved's room on the Avenue of Suleman the Almsmenor:

> an oil lamp from Thessalonika hangs between the rooms.
> in the drawer of her dresser her father's
>
> violin, the bridge and strings broken. he loved
> Wagner. two novels on the bedside table: Light
> in August, Death in Venice.

Alas, *Death in Venice* wins out over *Light in August*. Hogg's woman leaves him for another, leaving him no choice but to return to Hogtown – but not before he tosses off sixteen paintings meant to recapture that precious state of pre-consciousness that precedes the use of words. These consist mainly of mix and match noses, fingers, toes and penises (there is also a red angora nipple) – all of them withered and most of them done in shades of yellow and purple that recall bruises. As a species they are unforgettably hideous.

It is obvious from his art that Hogg still has a way to go. But before he is allowed to come up for air, it seems that he must continue his travels in the heart of darkness – in this case the Toronto subway network. It is here that he does his stations. He penetrates as far north as Sheppard Station. At every stop, subterranean characters afflicted with inner-city madness proffer advice: dwarves, hermaphrodites, sadomasochists – even a crap shooter called Doctor Ded. It's like Fellini in blank verse (mostly); every poem hits the bloodstream like an amphetamine.

At long last Hogg climbs up out of the seal hole. He is rather fazed by his experience in the underground – who wouldn't be? – but has arrived at some kind of acceptance of the human condition. He is "nonetheless alive to hope as more than survival, to prayer as more than madness, to death as more than a sigh."

What Callaghan has accomplished in *The Hogg Poems* is something rare. He has used the archetypal structure of descent and rebirth as a scaffolding on which to set scenes from contemporary reality memorable for their acute sensitivity to street language and visual minutiae. These aren't cerebral poems, although they are thoughtful. They aren't decorative, although they're visually lovely. Callaghan has given us something more existential. We are the wedding guests held captive by the glittering eye of the Ancient Mariner – in this case Hogg. We stand in the same relation to Hogg as he does to the woman and prophets of his psychic landscape. In other words, we are essentially receptive – not because we want to be passive but because the compelling direct-ness of *The Hogg Poems* demands that we be. Our open-ness turns out to be a reflection of the poet's own receptivity, which has allowed him free passage among the interpenetrating levels of consciousness that make up our inner lives.

HOGG IN THE HOLY LAND

Susan Beckman

Barry Callaghan's *The Hogg Poems and Drawings* provides further evidence of the ongoing interest among
Canadian poets in the possibilities of the poem
sequence, an interest that has recently given us works as
diverse as Ondaatje's *The Collected Works of Billy the
Kid,* Atwood's *The Journals of Susanna Moodie,* Gut-
teridge's *Tecumseh,* and Davey's *Arcana.* The individual
poems of Callaghan's books are chapters in the narrative
of the resurrected life of James Hogg, a nineteenth-century religious zealot responsible for erecting "the shell of
a place of worship" in the Don River Valley that came to
bear his name.

Though the quest structure of *The Hogg Poems* is
archetypal, the impetus behind them is purely local. The
ancestral spirit of Hogg's Hollow, having lain in its
wooden suit for some one hundred and thirty years, is
disturbed when the Yonge Street subway extension is
pushed through his resting place. Dragged unwillingly
into the surrealist world of the twentieth century, the
resurrected Hogg is, ironically, immediately crucified at
the hands of the subway workers:

> . . . they thunder-
> clapped him with a two-by-four, roped him up
> by the arms between two trees and nailed
> this inscription to his jaw-bone latch:
> HERE HANGS THE KING OF THE HATCHING
> DEAD.

("The Hatching of Hogg")

Over a century of reading nothing else but his own mind has convinced Hogg that there must be

> one place where the last words
> on the dice were
> Holy Holy Holy,
> he went to Jerusalem.
>
> ("Inside His Wooden Suit")

But the vision of the Holy Land turns out to be a false one, for the monks Hogg meets there direct him not to spiritual salvation but rather to

> . . . a medieval guidebook that provided
> pilgrims with the Hebrew words for: "woman, let me
>   sleep with you,
> I will give you gold."
>
> ("On Abu Gosh Road")

Thus, the landscape Hogg explores in Israel is primarily a sexual one, his guide being the reincarnated prostitute, Mary Magdalene. She fails to give him the sought-after Word, but gives instead the "gift of tongue":

> . . . he and his
> woman were naked and
> ignored the language
>
> of moss along the bone,
> and all grief, calumny,
>
> rage, fell from his eyes
> when she knelt and gave him
>
> the gift of tongue, so too,
> the moon swallowed

the sun, his cry named
her and in reply

they heard the muezzin
in his minaret,

that stone shaft into
the mouth of god.

("The Gift of Tongue")

Jerusalem is seen not as a holy city, but as a giant Golgotha, one whose present peace is disturbed by the "air-
/ sucking-thwap of an army helicopter" and one that in
the past has witnessed the destruction of thousands in
the name of a religion that now has lost its meaning.

. . . and how they have
gone down, crowded, into the crypts and cairns
and muddle of the common boneyards:

gone down the Imperial Beak,
gone down Bishop Arculf and Saewulf,
gone down the Perfumers of the Rock and the Kadi of
    the Mount,
gone down Tancred and Baldwin and Blake's vision of
    Skull Hill,
gone down Montefiore and Rabbi Yosef Warsawe and
    Rabbi el Bagdadee,
gone down Halebim of Aleppo and al-Ghazzali,
gone down to the Vale of Gihone,
gone gone with stone anointing lamps to the caves
on the road
to the sea;
only watchmen remain on the walls,
and in the chapel of Veronica there are
loan-sharks with whips of hippopotamus hide,
and on one's sleeve, the supplicant from the Sepulchre:
"See the blind stair, that's where
Christ leapt upon his cross;

and close by, Mr. Hogg, the best
coffee in Jerusalem."

("Skull Hill")

Here, as in many other sections of the collection (most
notably the subterranean world of Book Three), the
themes and technique of ironic juxtaposition are reminiscent of *The Wasteland*. Yet the lovemaking of Hogg
and Mary has an eroticism, albeit an eroticism tinged
with guilt, that finds closer parallels in "The Song of
Solomon" than in the Eliot poem:

> Shower water tumbling, down
> her belly and into his mouth
> (whose proverb? – that a fish
>
> begins rotting from the head)
> they spend the whole afternoon in bed,
> four pillows of goose down, fresh
>
> fruits from the coast, cold white
> Ashkelon wine, she has painted
> her toe-nails red. He smears the
>
> pulp and seed of berries over
> her breasts . . .

("The Silver Hook")

The bestiality of their love and the sexual landscape in
which they exist are reflected in the colour drawings
that form the core of Book Two. The visions of the tortured and distorted or dismembered human bodies with
obsessively prominent genitalia are the product of
Hogg's disturbed consciousness. The recurrent motif of
the setting sun suggests a dying civilization and the sub-
human figures are often depicted in a recumbent state,
sometimes, indeed, already partially buried. The surreal-

istic imagination that shapes the poetry, that gives it graphic as well as intellectual form, is at work in the nightmarish arrangement of symbolic objects and body parts that are the focus of the grotesque drawings reminiscent of Salvador Dali and René Magritte.

The drawings are the physical manifestation of Hogg's being driven back to that "place beyond words" that is the cradle of human experience. Having been seared by his experiences in the Holy Land, he concludes he is "not of this place, where the sun / strafes everything in sight" and comes to appreciate, by the point in his quest marked by the beginning of Book Three, the wisdom of the Irish proverb which forms the epigraph to the Toronto section of the sequence,

> go to Rome,
> long journey, little profit.
> the God you seek
> lives at home.

The subterranean world to which Hogg returns is no less profane than the place he has left, but the description of the classic descent into hell is modified by a wryness of tone and a colloquial idiom that characterize the last book of the poem:

> But how in hell did his destination
> come to be at Sheppard Station?
> Where was that? And why?
> Am I dead? Where I am, am I?

The damned that Hogg encounters, from the dope-crazed musician Sweet-Meat Manzone, through the bridegroom of death and Hell's Belle (who voices her awareness of modern man's captivity, "we're here / doing digital time") to Doctor Ded, are black caricatures of the city's human scum, Hogg's movements among them from subway stop to subway stop are cast as a parody of the Stations of the Cross, culminating in the final sacrifice with which his wandering began:

"Hogg Dreams Veronica"

Who is up there keeping vigil
who will wipe the face of Hogg
gaunt, unshaven, stations done,
mounts the stairs, dreams of one
who is up there keeping vigil
who will wipe the face of Hogg
cleanse his wounds, staunch his bleeding,
in her veil his pain left sleeping.

But, among the hopelessly degraded, Hogg finds his salvation. Gambling with Doctor Ded, Hogg wins the right to hear the truths of this latter-day prophet who tells him, "you intend to suture / what you is to what you'd like to be"; and from Bad Blood Jeremiah Stuck, who has himself plumbed the very depths of a living hell, Hogg hears the Gospel of "Judas Priest." Jeremiah, like his Biblical counterpart, finds the powerful priests, prophets and institutionalized religion of his day corrupt:

the church is led by those who have
the bread, while
the priests ration out Christ's compassion,
and Jesus is
their bag man, collecting dues, but that's
all a lie,
that's bull, not one apostle in the gospel
of good news
had any kind of special pull . . .

He reminds Hogg of Christ's mission to redeem the most desperate sinners, speaking in jazzy rhythms and employing facile rhymes that authenticate him as a voice speaking to the people. His knowledge is born of his own suffering, but it has taught him to understand the agonies and motivations of others:

> Old Jeremiah Stuck
> can tell you, when you reach out, sleepless,
>   for the walls
> of your hole, and all you touch is the darkness
>   of your soul,
> you scrutinize how and why a man dies,
>   why, when Jesus had him
> dead-to-rights, he broke the bread and said,
>   Eat your fill, Judas,
> I know who you're going to kill.
>   The question's this,
> Why's the kiss the ancient invitation to the abyss?
>   Well, I've come to see
> what above all Jesus knew, that built
>   into love is
> betrayal . . .

Judas is seen in the light of the "fully aware / fall-guy" who was willing to "shoulder the sin of suckering Him"

> because he foresaw that double-dealing
>   dealt his life
> new meaning – that once he had his own hide hung
>   in perfect imitation
>   of God's begotten Son,
> then he and Jesus would be One, and that is
>   what he done
> for you and me, shared this complicity
>   in death, so we do
> draw today deliverance breath, that's why old Stuck
>   has come undone,
> free, and telling you the essence of all
>   be not mendacity
> but complicity, for if Judas and Jesus are One,
>   if by betrayal

the beautiful is begun, then not only Judas
  be in you,
but Jesus, too, you wear His face no matter
  your disgrace.

Girded with these new insights, Hogg emerges from the underworld "alive to hope as more than survival,/to prayer as more than madness, to death / as more than a sigh." From the battered spirit dragged from his resting place and the fragmented being of mid-quest, Callaghan renders his completed man, "the whole Hogg."

The reader may be left with a sense of dis-ease at the final product of this journey because the apparent seriousness of Callaghan's themes are so deliberately undercut by the closing pun. Is it a daring stroke of comic genius, or merely fatuousness? It is true that Hogg first appears as the incarnation of the collective Canadian unconscious, a nineteenth-century mind striving to find its place in the twentieth-century world, as a contemporary Everyman, but it is also true that from the outset he is presented in a comic light, as a blubbery seal body mistakenly hauled from the frigid waters of oblivion:

Hogg came up for air,
before he was half out of his hole they got him,
lugged him, along the killing floor, yellow lips,
jawing how he was the wrong one . . .
                              ("The Hatching of Hogg")

Hogg's quest, while not without its serious meaning, its real degradation, despair and pain, is primarily a mock-heroic quest.

The highly literary consciousness that records Hogg's progress characteristically maintains a distance, and yet has a fine eye for ironic juxtapositions. Thus, of the rooms of Hogg's lover in Book One, he observes:

> . . . In the glass-doored case along the wall,
> there are old play-scripts and one photograph of her,
> chalk-faced in The Ghost Sonata as The Daughter
>
> of the Caretaker's Wife and the Dean Man.
> An oil map from Thessalonika hangs between rooms
> in the drawer of her dresser her father's
>
> violin, the bridge and strings broken, he loved
> Wagner, two novels on the bedside table: Light
> in August, Death in Venice.
>
> ("The Silver Hook")

There are, however, enough moments of sympathy with the suffering observed – such as this from the "Prologue": "how does a / man live through an endless winter of endless nights," and this lyrical expression of Hogg's knowledge of his desertion by his erstwhile lover in the Holyland: "she will not come, a door, / slamming, a wooden clapper / gone mad in the mouth / of the wind, strikes twelve" – to suggest a shared pain. If this is true, then the distance, however it is expressed, in wryness of tone, parody, caricature or biting satire, is perhaps nothing more than a defensive screen to mask the involvement of the reporting consciousness.

The other point that needs to be made about the creator of *The Hogg Poems and Drawings*, is that, though he is keenly aware of the suffering in his world, he is also an artist with a highly developed sense of humour and a quick wit. This manifests itself in the exquisite modulations of contemporary slang that Callaghan turns to such effect. This he does in ways as different as creating a character called Hell's Belle and putting into the mouth of a subway labourer, working at his peril in the wintertime, the statement that "we were frozen stiffs." Callaghan's is a highly entertaining wit that does not hesitate to operate on the sacred preserves of our civilization and complacency whether by equating Christ's Holy Stations of the Cross with Hogg's profane Toronto subway ones, or by carrying the logic of the Judeo-Christian creation story to a disconcerting conclusion:

> . . . I am the image
> of my maker, ex nihilo nothing . . .
>
> ("Doctor Ded")

It is a wit that dares and has earned the right to make that culminating pun, so that in the end the attuned reader will accept "the whole Hogg."

TWICE BORN HOGG

Branko Gorjup

Originally published as *The Hogg Poems and Drawings* in 1978, the work was, in the words of Hayden Carruth, "an event of singular importance, registered as such in the consciousness of certain readers throughout North America." However, Hogg was destined for a second birth, almost twenty years later. In the intervening period, Callaghan had written two other collections of poetry: *As Close as We Came*, 1982; and *Stone Blind Love*, 1988. It was the latter collection that dovetailed with *The Hogg Poems and Drawings*, expanding its already significant scope – the individual's quest for singularity in a divided world – reinforcing its central theme of hope lost and regained. In 1997, Callaghan collapsed the two books, revised the texts, and the new Hogg was reborn in *Hogg The Poems and Drawings*.

Both Hoggs have enriched the Canadian imaginative space with a powerful vision that brings together the topographies of two disparate urban landscapes, Toronto and Jerusalem, superimposing one upon the other, collapsing the time that separates their historical beginnings. The representation of the two cities is unique in Canadian poetry, not only by juxtaposing them along the lines of "new" and "old," "profane" and "holy," but also by making them, through inversion, into a demonic parody of each other. Hogg's Jerusalem is a palimpsest of ancient religious fervor, unquenched zealotry and transcendence, a mythical and mystical "New Jerusalem," with its gates forever closed, forever assailed, a place of deferral. But it is also a place of physical reality, of sensuous and sensual encounters, of war, darkness and decay, a trap, an illusion, and an impossibility. Hogg's Jerusalem is where the inexplicable, that has eluded pilgrims for centuries, is transformed into the phenomenal, where myths appear as flesh. Similarly, Toronto – the young metropolis in the New World, a utopian mirage in the cranium of its politicians and urban planners, a glowing city of glass and steel where new pilgrims come from around the world to chase their illusions, is revealed through its actual voice. The voice Hogg hears and recounts is, in fact, a polyphony of a hybrid city, an amazing array of unofficial cadences and rhythms. All this is contained within a poetic form, the long poem, that is most appropriate for the task at hand. The journey of Hogg the pilgrim, the questing contemporary urban consciousness, requires the fluidity and the duration of the form, which Callaghan, with Hogg as his doppelganger, achieves.

The "long poem" phenomenon is particularly interesting and somewhat mystifying to those reading Canadian literature. It is one of Canada's more conspicuous literary genres, attracting to itself some of the most significant poets the country has produced. The reason for its sustained popularity, according to some critics, has to do with its protean, indefinable form, with its ability to continually transform itself. Its flourishing in Canada has been sometimes associated with the vastness of the country itself, with its incompleteness, its varied and diverse culture. In his 1946 essay, "The Narrative Tradition in English-Canadian Poetry," Northrop Frye observed the frequency with which the long poem was attempted in Canada with "remarkable success." Frye, obviously, had surveyed the period leading up to his own time, referring to the early Canadian "classics," including Oliver Goldsmith's *The Rising Village* (1834), Joseph Howe's *Acadia* (1874), Isabella Valency Crawford's *Malcolm's Katie* (1884) and E.J. Pratt's *Brébeuf and His*

Brethren (1940). All of these poems were informed by the ideal of the European humanistic tradition. Their narrative form was a convenient vehicle for telling a story about Canada, the Canada that was still engaged in the primary task of writing itself into literary existence. Looking at these long narratives, the reader would encounter two impulses. One was directed toward the immigrant's imaginative appropriation of the physical world, focusing on the bridging of the gap between the old culture, inherent in language, literary forms and conventions, and his or her experience of the "new" land. The other impulse strove to give form and coherence to the country's short past, celebrating the power of civilization over nature and natural man. Today, nineteenth- and early twentieth-century long poems are read as discursive narratives, as representations of the myth of creation, with the national anxieties that such a myth inevitably embodies.

In contrast, the contemporary long poem, frequently identified as postmodern, is less concerned with the nineteenth-century epic ethos, the assuming of the voice of the nation, or a people, or a civilization. Likewise, it is less interested in staying put within the discursive mode, within impersonal, public speech. Instead, it shares the emotive tonalities and symbolic textures of the lyric, though resisting brevity – with the monumentality of the archetypal situation inherent in the epic, let us say, the hero's obligatory descent into the underworld. The contemporary long poem is a hybrid form, constantly under the siege of deconstruction.

It allows for cross-generic interplay, embedding into itself other forms of representation, from documents – true and apocryphal photographs, musical scores – to drawings, interviews, memoirs, etc. It can undercut the highbrow purpose of a traditional narrative with the irreverence of parody, self-parody; it can slow itself down with deferrals, with the sudden sidestepping into the unanticipated, and speed up with leaps that can join eons, collapsing time, becoming omni-directional.

The proliferation of the contemporary long poem in Canada in the past quarter of a century has had a great deal to do with the attractiveness of the form itself, with its cross-generic nature. But also, it has to do with its closeness to the epic, one of the genres that has always been at the heart of the Western literary canon. That extraordinary inheritance – from Homer, Virgil, Dante, Ariosto, and from Milton, Wordsworth, Browning to Whitman, offers the writer familiar with the works of these poets the challenge of a new beginning, a deliberate departure from the mighty forms that "stare" down at them from the heights of history. The contemporary long poem poet – according to Robert Kroetsch, a distinguished Canadian writer and literary critic – is faced with one problem, the need to honour "our disbelief in belief;" to "recognize and explore," in other words, "our distrust of system, of grid, of monism, of cosmologies perhaps, certainly of inherited stories and at the same time to write a long work that has some kind of (under erasure) unity."

Since the 1960s, the Canadian literary chronology has been regularly punctuated by the appearance of an astonishing number of long poems, all of them unhinging "inherited stories" – from Phyllis Webb's *Naked Poems*, with its linguistic sparseness and a Jungian claustrophobic enclosure, to b.p. Nichol's ten-volume poem, the *Martyrology*, which, dealing with the sanctity of words, could end only with the death of the author. Nichol's ongoing work was, as Eli Mandel described it, "a life-sentence," both life-imprisonment and a life-long poetic line. Margaret Atwood, in *The Journals of Susanna Moodie*, and Michael Ondaatje, in the *Collected Works of Billy the Kid*, revisited historical/legendary personalities and re-cast them as our contemporaries. In the process, they interrogated historical assumptions about two different cultures, the Canadian colonial steeped in the garrison mind-set, and the American "frontier" mentality of conquest, whether physical or neurological. Behind both poems lurk the mighty shadows of other peoples' stories. Likewise, though with a difference, behind Daphne Marlatt's *Steveston* and Christopher Dewdney's *A Paleozoic Geology of London, Ontario*, we discern a shadow imposed by a genius loci, by its historical text, its archeological/geological script. While Marlatt inhabits the propreceptic vision, played with by William Carlos Williams in his long poem, *Paterson*, Dewdney applies the geological methodology of a scientist, turning nature, from fossil to moth, into a personae dramatis. And, of course, one could go on naming other poets and describing other poems, particularly those that deal with the non-European immigrant experience, such as Dionne Brand's *No Language Is Neutral* or Andrew Suknaski's *East of Myloona*. The list is long and varied.

What *Hogg: The Poems and Drawings* has in common with other long poems is the notion of locality and history. Callaghan's Hogg is not a displaced person looking for a place and an identity. Rather, he is locked within a specific locale even when he travels elsewhere, because the locale where he situates himself is his perception of an actual place. His Toronto/Jerusalem is *logos poeticos,* in the Herodotean notion of history.

Like Atwood's Susanna Moodie, Callaghan's Hogg is our Gothic ancestor, someone who forcefully inscribes himself onto the Canadian landscape (he allegedly constructed a place of worship in what is today Hogg's Hollow, a suburban part of Toronto). And like Moodie, Hogg embodies what can be described as the primal Canadian immigrant experience, the white man's fear of an alien and inhospitable environment, an environment Callaghan describes as a "land of eelgrass and ice and snow." However, this is the point where the similarity between the two characters ends.

While Atwood and her Susanna Moodie are distanced because of the existence of another text – Moodie's own *Roughing It in the Bush*, a well-known first-hand dramatization of the immigrant experience – Callaghan and Hogg are hardly distinguishable from each other, the lines of their identities are blurred. Callaghan did not accommodate Hogg's "historical" voice, Hogg as a document. He created a voice for him and turned him into fiction. He metaphorically ate him; he ate the pig.

What we know of the historical James Hogg is a trace, which makes him an archetypal Canadian. He is known to have built a place of worship on his land and to have betrayed the 1837 Mackenzie Rebellion, a liberal uprising against the Tory (conservative) oligarchy. The fact that he found, as Hayden Carruth has observed, "his destiny in betrayal," influenced the poem's thematic, structural and moral make up.

Callaghan could not have chosen a more unlikely double. Hogg is the "antithesis of everything I am," he has written: "Scot, ambitious farmer, Tory, and an informer . . ." As his doppelganger, Hogg represents Callaghan's own demons, which are our demons: the dark, tormented and vulnerable side of one's embattled psyche. The idea of betrayal, of being a traitor, is, for Callaghan, a reality lurking behind every human impulse, directed not only outward, but also inward. In betraying a cause, a revolution – Hogg also betrays himself. As William Kennedy has suggested, Hogg is what the Irish would call "the traitor betrayed." And yet, because of his name (hog is a pig and Toronto is still called in popular terminology "Hogtown"), Hogg becomes a porcine metaphor who stands for appetite and abundance, but also for cleverness and toughness. Hog images are sustained throughout the work, keeping it anchored in earthly experience.

Another important feature of the contemporary Canadian long poem is that of the journey. The questor – a familiar Canadian fictional type – is released into a larger world from the one he has known and outgrown so that he can map out the "geography" of his presence in time and space. The completion of the quest is signaled by the birth of a text, which in Canada, because of the country's late and colonial beginning as a nation, is of particular significance. The Canadian quest – and here Callaghan's poem is an excellent example – is a double journey: a journey away from and towards a home. Metaphorically, the double journey that Hogg undertakes is a return from death and darkness to life and light, and from a divided world of betrayal and self-betrayal to that of wholeness and redemption. In actuality, Hogg returns to a place where he can claim his singularity and, in turn, recognize the singularity of his place of origin, his Toronto.

The beginning of Hogg's quest – Callaghan calls it a pilgrimage – is situated in a displaced reality, in a world of nightmares where metamorphosis and the collapse of time regulate the poet's vision. The historical Hogg enters the poem – comes up for air – through the frame of rebirth. But the rebirth is, in fact, an orgiastic, sinister and humiliating sacrifice. He is crowned with a "dead pig's tit," dragged and feathered and broken with "a two-by-four." Hogg, like Christ or Osiris, is turned into a public spectacle. Because he is "a man in search of his singularity," as Callaghan describes him, he is always "thunderclapped by life" and by his "fellow men." Hauled back from the dead into the violent world of the living, the contemporized Hogg prepares to commence his quest with his own ritualistic diving into the murky waters of Lake Ontario, in what can be described as a sacramental act of cleansing. He leaves behind on the shore of desolation, decay and death "a mound of bristle and maggot."

Even though the water is cold and slimy, it feels like "ointment." As Hogg re-emerges, "crashing into the air," he "gulps down" the darkness that has surrounded him. In the act of "swallowing," he erases, at least momentarily, his past and present and relocates himself in Jerusalem.

The first of the three books that constitute *Hogg: The Poems and Drawings*, describes Hogg in Jerusalem, on a new ground he must traverse.

Pages are now the site where his relationship with a local woman matures into a consummate love affair. Presented in a sequence of intensely lyrical love poems unlike anything that can be found in the usually timid Canadian repertoire, the privacy of the relationship begins to suggest entrapment. The more Hogg wants to protect the interiority of the relationship from any outside interference, that is, the lovers' overwhelming world, the closer he comes to arresting his quest, which is far from over.

He must be moving on along that obligatory trajectory imposed by the long poem that passes through the "underworld," where the protagonist's true self is tested. Love, which propels this part of Hogg's journey, is rich, dark, and dangerous and, above all, ambiguous, not the one found in a romance quest. It is, to quote William Kennedy, "achingly real, indissoluble – that will go nowhere but forever." The woman, with whom Hogg falls in love, though she will betray him, is not a stereotypical temptress, a mere object of male desire. She is an active presence who gives and takes, capable of transgression but also of fierce loyalty. She completely occupies her environment, assimilates to herself all its contradictions. She is the place – a place that has entered our imagination as both heavenly and terrestrial and she gives Hogg the key to enter its true dimension. In one of the central poems in this section, "And So to Bed," the lover, as Eve, sees that light is simply an absence of darkness, and the other way around, too. She points out the fraudulent nature of a binary world that keeps the white and the black sheep separated in a sort of apocalyptic anticipation. Adam is God's dark side. The second Adam, who enters the poem to hang himself in the first Adam's stead, reinforces Callaghan's idea that the two are inseparable, that the sinners and the sinned against are part of the same circle, that the divine/mythical cannot be disentangled from the human.

The love lyrics in this section are interspersed with poems that annotate Hogg's acute observation of Jerusalem from his singular point of view. Hogg's voice shifts as he wanders through the labyrinthine pathways of the ancient city, it modulates itself from being irreverently loud to contemplatively hushed. The place comes alive with strange characters, powerful smells, exotic foods, mysterious sounds, unexpected colour schemes. The entire city, though real in its particulars, is like a mirage. Hogg's forward peregrination expands referentially. City streets are accounted for and places of worship named – we walk along The Street of Chains or witness a scene at the hillside cairn for Saint Eulalia of the Severed Breast. The lyrical moves into the documentary; the self-referential becomes historical; the margins that separate the present from the past are erased. Hogg's attention, focused on the present, keeps dissolving as he introduces his reading of the past texts. In the poem "The Emperor's Imperial Beak," he leads us through Suetonius's fragment into the nightmarish vision of Flavius Titus' defeat of Jerusalem: "Centurions sealed the gates with molten lead / and of the dangling, paltry dead / they made a hanging garden." The only way to bring the past closer is by erasing the distance that separates us from it. In Callaghan's Jerusalem, everything occurs simultaneously. The city itself is a text, a palimpsest in which we can trace ourselves through time.

Leaving Jerusalem, Hogg begins his homeward journey, commencing the second leg of the quest. The moment he exits the dream of Jerusalem he finds himself in the dream of silence, which constitutes the second book in the collection. Here, Hogg externalizes what must have been a disorienting recognition of a collapsed relationship with a woman he loved and of a bungled quest in a sequence of extraordinary visual images, introducing into the structure of the Canadian long poem a new feature, the pictorial fragment. Through this sequence, the inexplicable and the unspeakable are laid out before the reader, a world that obviously reflects Hogg's psychic landscape. As we enter this world and begin to meditate on its symbology and its spatial representation of images, we are struck once again with the extent to which Hogg's sense of the world is both fragmented and whole at the same time. In this reassembled body-landscape, the boundary between illusion and reality is broken down.

As in Hogg's life, as we have come to know it, everything is and is not what the eye sees and what the rational mind translates into conventional codes. Hogg's drawings, unlike his language, de-codify his world, turning it literally into flesh – the word is incarnate, the landscape anthropomorphized. Art critic Nancy Beale, reviewing an exhibition of Hogg's drawings at the Carleton University Art Gallery, encapsulated Hogg's pictorial energy as unbound: "There is a sense of freedom in letting the body go in all kinds of fleshy directions. As though a mental corset's been loosed." Indeed, the reader is allowed to glimpse a private psychic space, is carried on by the current of a pictorial stream of consciousness. To Vera Frenkel, Callaghan's drawings are so "given over to pain that they contradict the forward trajectory of the poems."

Pain? Whose pain? By reading Frenkel, we discover that the drawings were produced by Callaghan at a time when he was hospitalized with severe arthritic pain. For Frenkel, this biographical fact is important because it explains the presence of pain in the drawings. The drawings, as she sees them, are the representation of the body in a state of crisis. This disclosed "self-reflexivity" in the construction of the meaning in Callaghan's long poem draws our attention to both continuity and discontinuity within the work. The pictorial fragment is both a hermetic metaphor, enhancing our understanding of Hogg's silence, and an autobiographical map of pain and suffering, featuring the author's all-too-human need to find an outlet in art. Yet, regardless of pain, or because of it, the forward-moving trajectory of the quest remains in place.

Hogg has not yet completed his journey. What his pictorial nightmare has given back to him is an understanding of the precarious and transitory nature of order and stability. What he sees in his experience, and what prepares him for his next destination, the entry into the underground world of Toronto, is the notion of how singular every aspect, every detail of life, is. His experience leads him to a vision of life as an extraordinary kaleidoscopic rose, a life that constantly reconstitutes itself and flows, to quote Frenkel again, "from one form into another: a toe is pure erectile tissue, a breast becomes an eye, a vulva straddles space like a vast mouth, and every torn limb in this angry romp through woods and wounds is in a process of self-healing through unexpected capacities for pleasure."

In Book Three, Hogg is back home, a home he must still reclaim and repossess. The obligatory underworld trajectory in this section is transposed into an actual descent into the bowels of Toronto, which one of its mayors called "a whale of a city." The subterranean world of the recently built subway line provides Callaghan with a rich metaphor and ready-made structural principle. The subway not only connects the northern outskirts of Toronto – Hogg's place of origins, known today as Hogg's Hollow – with Lake Ontario, the city's southernmost boundary where Hogg began his descent, but it also serves as a contemporary *via dolorosa*. The subway stations are the Stations of the Cross, which Hogg must now traverse in order to strengthen his faith in himself, his place and his time. The journey is a form of prayer, echoing, at this point, more laudably the Christian mythopeic ethos. At the same time, the poem becomes broader in scope – it embraces a larger social vision of the city, reflecting Hogg's expanding consciousness. Hogg's personal quest assumes epic proportions by foregrounding the multiplicity of voices that make up the story of the city, by figuratively becoming himself the city. Toronto is no longer just a geographical site, but also a linguistic one, a place of multiple meanings encoded in the ways its citizens speak. In the sequence of poems, including "Sisyphus the Crack King" and "Judas Priest," Callaghan shows an extraordinary ability to recreate authentic voices that belong to their speakers, who themselves belong to the world seldom visited by most of us and even more seldomly acknowledged as real. Hogg's ear hears for us, and by letting us hear what he hears he transforms absence into presence.

Toronto is not a fixed ground. As we pass with Hogg, our trusted guide, through Toronto's underworld stations, a whole New World takes its place next to the one we have known, revealing what Adele Freedman has described in her review of the first Hogg, a Felliniesque carnival of "characters afflicted with inner-city madness."

Although the characters of the underworld are on some level distortions and deformations of the daylight reality, they are mostly parodic emanations of a sanitized vision of life embodied by Western man's obsession with scales and hierarchies, with high and low forms, with sacred and profane. Characters like Canned Heat the Hermaphrodite, Hell's Belle, John the Conqueroo Decatur, Bad Blood Jeremiah Stuck, and so on, are really only "freaks" in the Rabelaisian sense, whose main function is to invert and remake public norms. Although marginalized by the dominant forms of culture, Hogg reconstitutes them into a kind of wholeness he has been searching for because he realizes that heaven and hell occupy the same space, that one is merely a parody of the other.

In one of the central poems in the book, "Judas Priest," all the various aspects of Callaghan's design structure, theme, and world view come together. They coalesce in a vision of an undivided world, a world in which we have come to see, together with Jeremiah Stuck and Hogg, what Jesus knew: that betrayal is built into love. Because the essence of all life, according to the gospel of Jeremiah Stuck, is not mendacity but complicity, we are all Judas and Christ in one. With this revelation, Hogg's dark wanderings come to a halt. He is born again, this time cleansed of self-pity, into a healed world. With his rebirth, Hogg has assimilated to his consciousness what is common to both individual and collective humanity. Callaghan has created an extraordinary long poem, mythopeic in magnitude yet located within the passions and anxieties of contemporary reality.

STONE YEARNING TO BE WATER

Hogg's Philosophical Realism
for the XXI Century

Brunella Antomarini

1. Chance

Philosophers are haunted by what they learn from the way the poet or storyteller thinks. Individual events, as described by a poet, as facts that have occurred, bear their own meaning, to the exclusion of prior events. What has occurred is singular and what is singular – as such – resists being known, resists comprehension within the terms of broader concepts. From a philosophical point of view, then, the question is: How is it possible for something to be both true and non-universal?

The act of thinking while one is on the road (or as Callaghan's Hogg would have it, on the run) – thinking as a reporter does or as a documentary film director does, is very different from thinking for the sake of thinking. On the road, you think of "something" and that something leads you down a particular alley or causes deviations in your thoughts. You correct yourself at every step, sometimes you feel compelled to suddenly stop, to think again in the middle of a dangerous action, or in a state of shock: you are in a condition of constant self-transformation.

Philosophy, to the contrary, implies meditation, that is, it situates itself in an abstract domain so that it may embrace the oneness of a concept, or of the universe. But in doing so, it loses touch with the things of this world. So, naturally, philosophy turns to those rare miracles of writing in which universality is contiguous with the concreteness of things.

I can say that Barry Callaghan has a philosophy. And a much needed one today. It is a philosophy arrived at through the living of an active life, through the observing of events, and by giving those events a general sense of being that does not deprive them of their uniqueness.

To describe the poetic, linguistic, and metaphysical strategies required to achieve such a result, I will comment on two books: *Hogg (I)* and *Hogg (II)*, as well as two or three prose works in the background.

*

Hogg, as it turns out, is a modern Dante who lands in a modern Purgatorio (Jerusalem) and Inferno (Leningrad). Like Dostoevsky's archetypal protagonist in *Notes from the Underground*, Hogg has gone in search of what sets him apart in the world *aboveground* – he is in search of singularity as a space, and then – as we learn –

when his search for singularity
was done

pig-headed Hogg was able to cry: *"Behold the whole Hogg"* (this bold assertion that contains a self-deprecating joke indicates Callaghan's habit of mind, the risks he is prepared to take).

*

Singularity: what is singularity? Singularity is what haunts every philosopher when he is done with generalities. Singularity is elusive, it is slippery; yet, it is there, waiting for identification. Either we have a name for it,

74

and in that case it is not totally singular, falling under a wider notion, or we do not have any name, and in that case, it is what might *not* be there, might *not* have occurred. But it has.

In this context, Callaghan's language is experimental; he tries to find singular identification within an image, within assonance, within the description of contingent details. In the two Hogg books, Callaghan has decided "to re-enact a lost drama" (as the citation from Henry Miller states at the beginning of the poem), a drama that will start in Jerusalem. Why Jerusalem? Because it is

> one place where the last words
> on the dice were
>
> Holy Holy Holy.

In the throw of the dice lies the direction of holiness! Chance brings contingencies, what might not be there, but it can also bring – "by accident" – what we hold as the highest possible goal: holiness. What is saintliness then? It seems to lie in the search for a truth, a disruptive search if the truth is to be revealed, not just by the creatures of chance, but by chance itself.

Most human beings, however, want to leave nothing to chance – they want to feel safe, and they believe safety comes from living behind a wall, where they can live a life of half-truths.

In Callaghan's prose piece, "Berlin," the actual wall, when it was standing, guaranteed half-truths, whereas the collapse of the wall, the bringing down of the wall, indicated a desperate need to look for and secure whole truths, a space wherein the left hand *will* know what the right hand *is* doing. A short dialogue between a man and a writer sitting at a café in East Berlin presents the complex consequences of this conception of the truth:

Question: How long have you been working on your novel?

Answer: Four years. I'll finish it this year. It takes up sixteen empty notebooks.

Question: What is the theme of the novel?

Answer: The spoken word. Something is said; but a word, once spoken, vanishes.

Question: How does it end?

Answer: I don't remember.

The long, slow work of the writer leads not just to a vanishing word, but to an end which is not even remembered. The more authentic, the more slippery our vision of the real, the more attracted we become to the truth as opposed to half-truths, the more unsafe we are: "The Bible was wrong. They didn't want to be safe and to know only half-truths" ("Berlin").

We know something, therefore, about Callaghan's idea of the truth. The truth is, *in and of itself.* It sounds like the medieval idea of essence: what has substance *is* – in and of *itself.* But is Callaghan looking for essences?

*

A recurrent image in Callaghan's writing is the act of hatching: being born as an act of resurrecting, but also the animal act of being born full of uncertainty and fear: after all, "What if we are not being hatched?" ("Berlin").

Like Dante, having been hatched, Hogg (I) is thrown out of the city; he is hung between two trees and an inscription is nailed to his body: "Here hangs the king of the hatching dead." This is how he starts his Dantesque journey ("The Hatching of Hogg") emerging from underground to immediately pass through humiliation and betrayal. The fact is, Hogg (I) is born to begin to re-redeem himself.

So, as birth is a descending, the Purgatorio is an ascending, and these two counter-movements coincide in Jerusalem, the place where the Scriptures encounter a new religious thought: celestial Jerusalem and the Kingdom of God are one and the same with the horror of the world. How to translate Judeo-Christian thought into these terms? By forcing the reader in our time to accept the assonance between good and evil, chance and necessity, destination and the path to destiny, the messiah and the traitor, the upward and the downward. The truth is what must be left as it is, intact, with its contradictions and paradoxes. The truth is an earthly revelation deprived of superimposed order. When we learn this, we are ready to cope with a certain *natural* essence of reality.

If the Scriptures served to overcome the absurdity of chance in existence, now, in our time, we are required to take the next step: to make absurdity thinkable, and therefore, to find the sense *within* it. If it is not possible to overcome paradox, we must enter it.

Paradoxes are at the core of Hogg, and frequently, paradox is connected to stone: stones are seeds, hatching, tears, swallowed, burning, teeth – water locked within – God locked within – walls – eggs – medusa's work – restless; light inside: "Stone needs water as bone needs the beating of blood."

When Hogg descended, he reached

a cove of slate grey water
He undressed and slid
down a stone shelf
into the shallows.

Water is reduced instantly to a pool and it will soon dry up, leaving that space to stone: the "water locked within stone." The slough has the function of ointment, and while descending, Hogg's senses contract, allowing a song to pierce his ears.

This contraction, this reduction of the senses, corresponds to a reduction of the landscape: Hogg enters Jerusalem, which is "a sea of stone," dry water opening the way to the *natural* essence of things: contingency presented as the essence of the holy city, contingency, the secret core of eternal law. And the more the paradox deepens, obsessionally, the more we are unable to deny the achieved awareness that Jerusalem is

> suspended somewhere
> between prayer
> and the hanging rope

where "the worst lie is a loving look in the eye." This is how we enter into and engage the paradoxical feel for the Jerusalem wall shared by men who press their ears to that wall in order to

> hear the dry wave
> at the earth's
> centre.
>
> Stone
> needs water.
>
> Bone
> needs the beating
> of blood

But are not paradoxes arbitrary? *Ex absurdum quodlibet?* We are *in* the real empirical world, engaged in an interplay of organic with inorganic elements. A stone owes its form to the moulding of water; a bone owes its life to the blood that feeds it. What appears to be a rhetorical device, is in fact an aesthetic, a perceptual description that opens up the real world to us. A paradoxical realism?

Some paradoxes lead to hermeneutical freedom, disassembling any possible commitment to ontology. Hogg's paradoxes lead to realism, to a faithful description of reality. In a poem introducing Hogg's drawings, the silence of meditation metaphorically matches the silence of privation, the last verbal image providing a real landscape

Where
no voice
is
heard
no bones will be interred.

*

Metaphor and realistic description intertwine: that the rituals of death need prayers, need voices, is something that can be materially perceived and symbolically contemplated at one and the same time.

The second book of *Hogg (I)* has drawings which consist of limbs, short circuits of bodies and skin which we feel like touching, much more than looking at; they seem to make clear that a descent into the netherworld is a descent into tangible reality.

A poem in *Hogg (II)* tells of a "lonely mother" who flees

on snowshoes
over snow thirty feet deep,
tangled her feet in the tops of the trees
where she died
and was found in the spring
reaching for the earth.

This is the description of a bare fact, and the bare fact carries its own candour, its own poetry, its own sense, even its own music within itself. Hogg has only to perceive it, we have only to listen and to see.

Callaghan's philosophy becomes apparent in the beauty of such a *real* image. There is no place left for interpretative indulgence or symbolism; what seems to be implied is that reality has no meaning, but *images* are real.

The detached description of facts implies that meaning is engaged in a struggle with chaos; such a descriptive accomplishment is rootes in re-enacting the heterogeneity of the world. Order and chaos are not mutually exclusive. "He took the universe personally": so it is said of Rasputin in *Hogg (II)*. Such a titanic effort to embrace the whole world includes the violent gyring of what is flat (flattened by an order that is meaningful) into the multiple dimensions of chaotic occurrences. A Michelangolesque effort.

Chance is characterized all through the poems and prose works as purity, directness, as a guess: guessing how to get in tune with the flow of occurrences; as a mixture of good and evil: something is good by chance; actually how could something good not be touched by evil?

In the third book of *Hogg (I)*, we do not witness a final revelation at the end of his journey. Instead, Hogg starts again: resurrection is but a temporary and continuous repetition of a rising from the dead. The syncopation, the musicality of the verse is symptomatic:

> Hogg came up into a squat.
> He read the writing on the wall.
> This much was clear; what was was not.

Again a paradox, the rhyme of *squat* with *was not*: he's being hatched again, into nothingness again.

2. Intensity of Disinterest

If chance determines events and occurrences, disinterest determines the appropriate way to depict it. The poet-reporter's writing is an act of non-intervention. He lets things accomplish themselves through words.

An example is the narrative in *Hogg (II)*, "A Stolen Kiss," in which a girl lies with men whom her brother, a thief, beats to death. But one of them offers her water and when her brother beats him, she kills her brother and they steal his stolen gold; but the man, as he declares their freedom, falls into the flames. The quick sequence of events dislocates the reader as images gently lead him on: water, fire, music, kiss and kill. In a few lines, there is a concentrated deployment of a plot; up to the last line we expect more to happen.

The model for this verse narrative is music. We cannot say what the narrative deals with until we listen to the last movimento, a light in hindsight being cast on the whole. The poet, like Walter Benjamin's *flâneur*, touches on perceived events in total disinterestedness: that is the best way to grasp beauty, for, as Kant said, beauty has no interest in the object but only in its effects on the viewer. This is the way to the truth *in and of itself*.

The introductory poem to *Hogg (II)*, "Not a Thorn, Not a Tree," offers a series of negative images: someone is singing like the seed of an *unborn* bird, singing about being a knee, *no more* than a knee, *not* a thorn *nor a tree*. These images deploy over a short span of time, without shaping a complete form in the reader's mind, so quick is the touch. As a *flâneur* in Jerusalem, in Leningrad, in Berlin, Hogg observes things in their metamorphosis; he catches the change, the moment of the gesture, that prevents something from not being other than itself. The natural essence of things is change, the writer-*flâneur* is an Heraclitean logos at work.

3. God and Laughter

If sense can come from contemplating a drama devoid of sense, irony is another of the best devices to show it.

In "Himmler's Law" in *Hogg (II)*, Biblical angels are about to be wishboned from behind by Sodomites but they strike their persecutors blind. Out of a merciless morality, Sodom is burned. That's how Himmler described the holocaust camps. Is this Himmler's morality? Or the angels'? Do the angels take vengeance on Himmler? We are left with an ambiguous sense of ethical aims. Violence is an act of justice although justice aims at overcoming violence.

*

Both *Hogg (I)* and *Hogg (II)* are about creation and God: what is created needed violence, needed the partiality, the error of particularity, or better – what Hogg calls his search for singularity: the sin (the error) and the necessity of it (the actual world).

What is God then? He is a torn-apart God, a gambling God, an acrobat. He exists in these poems, not as a human projection or a figure of mythic omnipotence, but as something real, something to experience, something to be defied, teased, attacked. The key Gospel in Hogg's world is called the Gospel of Judas; it is Judas who plays the deeply human role, that is, if creation begins with the betrayal of the divine essence. It begins, in fact, when a natural essence is found in the wrong creatures. And Hogg himself sounds like a dangerous Gospeler disseminating a "news" which is not really "good," or which is good only in so far as it is disruptive. Disruption is what we can never escape; Hogg's paradoxes bring it under our eye at every step. It is music piercing our ears, hard to endure.

*

The harsh irony at work in *Hogg (I)* is also to be found in "True Stories," at whose core is a concern with lies, lies as they play out the role of enhancing the truth – "the more layered the lies the more biting the truth. Such is art." The fact that something is known to be and believed to be the truth is due to an acceptance of the *story* of the truth, a *form* of it, and therefore an acceptance of the lies inherent in the truth.

In "Sour Grapes," *Hogg (II),* two dead men laugh about what it is like in life when "it's never over"; their laughter turns into green grapes in the mouth of a woman, the grapes pass from her mouth to Hogg's mouth with a kiss. In another verse,

> laughter is glass
> and has bones
> that can be broken.

Laughter plays an active role: it carries a message from mouth to mouth and the message is the changeable character of the world.

Although we yearn for the overcoming of conflict, Hogg seems to be possessed by a craving for Hell itself, a desire to go deeper and deeper into the misery of Leningrad. Again we are confronted by a reversal – as direction – away from God, who is where we were headed. There is, instead, a new start, as if something of the previous journey were still left to be understood, a plausible Hell. An actual Hell, to be described as a journalist would: for there will be no light without darkness:

> All light seeds the dark
> total darkness is irretrievable and so too
> despair. All men need is
> air, air, air.

83

And in "Sleepwalker":

> Nothing is what it seems.
> When dark is closing in,
> it will be light
> opening up
> at the seams.

Seems/Seams: appearances are deceptive – in accordance with the great Platonic tradition – words 'betray' a deeper meaning, bespeaking the opening up of seams in darkness. Light does not erupt into darkness and dissolve the dark, as in theological metaphysics. It appears in flashes or little rays, unable to take darkness away, but able to prevent darkness from being total. Despair is to be endured by breathing, by retreating to the primary human need, air.

For those who understand, who engage these paradoxes, that *air* either explodes in laughter, or takes the form of the seam itself, that silent laughter between notes, that seam of laughter between darknesses. In this respect, God and His agents laugh at His atrocities, as when the poet Mandelstam is tortured in Stalin's gulag with electrical impulses and his "seraphim" look at him; they sit and listen to his heart beat:

> not the beating
> but the silence in between.
> eternity atrophied into an ellipse.

Infinity is not the opposite of finitude; it is not Dante's celestial destination; it is inside finitude, in the void of an interval between beats. No verticality accompanies the path to God, only the beating. Rhythm and suffering and God are caught simultaneously.

4. Uncertainty

> They ask Hogg:
> "you are the one? more and more
> they come along this road so ill-prepared to die."

Nobody was really sure that *he* was the Messiah. This was the *true* story, as told in the Synoptic Gospels, a true story which, through centuries of dogmatic theology, was interpreted, codified, and distorted, until a new *true* story became the story of pre-destination, the claim that Jesus knew his destiny in advance, as the elected victim, elected by his Father. From then on, nobody has been allowed to doubt whether *he* was the one. There would be, however, no Christianity without that initial uncertainty.

In "The Heart of the World: Yehuda Amichai," Callaghan – trying to describe the certain "strength" that is inherent in "uncertainty" – hears Amichai say that in order not to be broken, the Jews have learned through the centuries how to endure collapse by putting themselves into little pieces, because "it's much harder to break little pieces than to break one big piece." Amichai:

> I am composed of many things
> I have been collected many times
> I am constructed of spare parts
> Of decomposing materials
> Of disintegrating words.

5. *The Poetic Form of Chance: The Oxymoron*

Dolci asprezze e soavi, aspri e noiosi
Vezzi, frali ragioni al mio ben tarde,
Menzogne vere, verità bugiarde.

> Isabella Andreini
> (Italian poet and actress
> of the sixteenth century)

Now we are ready to clarify what is essential to
Callaghan's poetry: the frequent use of oxymora does
not have a rhetorical but a philosophical function: anything can be linked to anything else; all things are connected, like the bonds between lovers who

must
pass
in the dreaming
skulls
of the unloved
planted
as milestones
toward
home.

Love is accomplished by passing through the pain of the
unloved. There is no paradise if it lacks the transmutation from good to evil and from evil to good. In *Barrelhouse Kings*, there is a dialogue between a Mexican girl
and Callaghan.

"There are tiny fish in your fingertips," she said. "You
will have to feed them."
"How?"
"There is no cruelty in your tenderness. Fish have
teeth."

In this brief moment we have myriad images: caressing fingers, grabbing fingers, tenderness and cruelty, eagerness close to voracity, reproach and appreciation. The result, in its form, is a limited totality in which tenderness and cruelty, if they are real feelings, are one. For this, we need a poetry, or verse, or a game of paradoxes, that makes difficult truths bearable. By alternating assonance and dissonance, we are liable to lose our co-ordinates, become disoriented, like Hogg (I) in his egg, before the hatching, doubting he will ever be hatched. We find tragedy inevitable and normal, we retrieve our strength in syncopated music, in a quasi-rap musicality that leaves our "ears singing," our lungs filled with song, our spirits surrendering to "the searing light" in a perfect accord between sound and sense as

> Stone
> needs water.
> Bone
> needs the beating
> of blood.

We accept the "assonance in atrocities," that most challenging of attitudes for ethics, for existence. This can be an anti-ethical ethics of art, or an aesthetic ethics. And this is the divine paradox of creation: creatures bearing the trace of their creator, remaining forever an error in divine hands.

6. *Musical Accord of Opposites*

In his essay on poetics, "Conversation with Dante," Osip Mandelstam says that poetry uses longer words than those of normal usage. Ordinary language, he says, has an economic function, expressing a maximum of meaning with a minimum of effort. Poetry, however, reaches back to the slow naturalness of words, tries to catch the *singular* sense of something rather than aiming at commonplace meaning. This is why such words are slow, because they have to re-enact what they say. It takes a long time before we are able to make what is said actually appear. Music plays the role of making the word appear again and again as we read and re-read; music makes us surrender to the writing, and so, Mandelstam argues, it is rhythm that provides us with a revelation of the form before our eyes, in our ears.

Music, always present in Callaghan's work and life, is often expressed in Hogg as something material; it is metonomically identified with the ear (a receiving force) or with a voice that fills the lungs, in a reversal of direction: a voice turned and headed inside the body. Music seems to be an internalized form. The body must bear witness "in the bones" and be music's guardian. In music, the sense of coincidence of opposite tendencies is rendered through the common space of the body, which receives, conceives, keeps and expresses. This explains why a sun may be in the brain ("Sisyphus the Crack King") or the moon in the throat ("Southbound Hogg").

The clear philosophical implication is that forms (musical forms, visual forms, perceptions in general) are not created as objects of beauty but are received – as closely as can be – as they *are*, in and of themselves. Music is, in fact, what is most difficult to judge in concepts, or to put in words.

Maybe because of his work as a journalist, traveller and translator, Callaghan has often been concerned with incidental encounters between people or between different languages. Translation is an occasion for the cultural expansion of verbal and perceptual associations. If a translator is perfectly aware of the dramatic impossibilities of matching sense and sound, and knows that he must often choose between one or the other, he develops a certain capacity for loss; in translation, the writer surrenders his personal need for affirmation, in order to regain it through the remedy of loss, and in order to become conscious of how much of reality is left outside of our efforts to grasp it in details, in pieces, in partial revelations.

We are confronted with a kind of musical logic in which sense is continually lost and retrieved: one sound makes sense by being accorded to the next. Harmonization takes up a formal task, in which reality is completely absorbed. We do not need to find any additional meaning than that pleasure for the ears. Ready to lose it, we know that we cannot retrieve it until the next listening.

In fact, Callaghan's poems and prose must be read with regard to a certain musical tonality; it may be jazz or blues. His is essentially an oral poetry.

7. *A New Realism for a New Philosophy*

Philosophical tradition has always coped with contradiction and found ways to solve it or give it a deeper meaning. Paradoxes are only what appear *to be*, but *are not*: that is the claim, followed by another claim – that reality must have an order; God does not play dice, as Einstein would say.

But Callaghan challenges traditional rational thinking. Reality is chaotic, and though there is chaos that chaos must have a partial order, it must have a relative rule. Aesthetic devices are functions of this partial and temporary order of chaos. This is the challenge of Callaghan's oxymora, in which even what seems to be distant contains some small similarity to its opposite, though it may be just a musical accord.

In this philosophical context, meaning becomes the potentiality of empirical reality, always surrendering to the next possibility, to the next rhyme, to the next visual association, generously welcoming and yielding.

What might, therefore, be taken for weakness or a neutral attitude, is indeed respect for appearances. What we call reality is but the flow of appearances and it must be endured as it is. And this is not neutral at all, because it demands strength, the strength to not ignore the violence of singularity, that mixing of Judas and Jesus, who together constitute a well-formed lie, a musical lie, a possible truth. The courage required to leave wounds open is no weakness at all.

This is the humanity of Hogg's poems: a wildly disparate community of people, slippery subjects in metamorphosis (like "Heartbeat" in *Hogg (II)*, in which subjects change from line to line and we have to shift with the image from line to line; someone starts as a man, becomes *they*, and then a *she* appears, addressing someone with a *you*). The effect is often that of an amorphous crowd suddenly accruing around an inner landscape and turning it into a shared theatre. Nobody takes sides with the event occurring, some make comments, others act violently, but there is no distinction made between good and evil. Hard on the heels of twentieth-century theories and ideologies, Hogg has envisaged our twenty-first century; he has begun with absurd conflicts and tragedies, from which no ideology can provide an escape, and brought us into a world of things, of real bare contingencies, unredeemed or redeemed only by poetry. And as readers, we are present, witnessing and acting with Hogg, forever lost in the perception of his reality – as it is, as it is not.

SOME NOTES ON CALLAGHAN'S HOGG POEMS AND DRAWINGS

RAY ELLENWOOD

I looked up with outrage at that appetite for the treacherous which rides the Irish like a leper . . .
Norman Mailer, *An American Dream*

The three sections of the book (two poem cycles separated and united by drawings) are prefaced with the "Prologue" which in turn is preceded by two quotations: one from Henry Scadding's *Toronto of Old,* on James Hogg and his Hollow, the other from Henry Miller, establishing the central myth of the book, describing the poet's "heroic descent to the very bowels of the earth, the dark and fearsome sojourn in the belly of the whale, the bloody struggle to liberate himself, to emerge clean of the past." Using this time-honoured myth allows for all sorts of echoes and allusions. The poet dangles in the same wind with Oedipus, Jonah, Lazarus, Dante, Baudelaire and others, all chiming together with major or minor tonal variations.

*

Hogg's town is no *paradise terrestre*. The "Hatching Hogg" comes up for air like a seal, is dragged to the killing floor, thunder-clapped with a two-by-four, strung up. Down he goes then, for 130 years of meditation inside his wooden suit, emerges, goes to Jerusalem, is thunder-clapped in a different way, sinks once more and begins again in Toronto's underground from which he finally arises to learn, perhaps, what it all means. In the

Prologue "Cleft of Light" poem, a hunter waits to drag a seal through a hole in the ice while, all around him, the closing of the cleft of light is imminent. Hoggahan is seal and hunter.

[A note by Callaghan on this note: "I, too, have hauled old James Hogg out of his grave: antithesis of everything I am – Scot, ambitious farmer, Tory, and informer (he alerted York to the advance of Mackenzie's rebellious troop in 1837); unlike those who've become figures of old – Graves in *I Claudius* – I've brought his shell (of worship and skin) alive, have stood in it, forced him to live my life, hauled him around the world (Judas and Jesus are one). Also, however, Hogg is the singular man in search of his singularity: such a man is always thunder-clapped, by life: winter, night, death; and his fellow man – Prologue is the metaphysical condition for pig-headed, hatched Hogg."]

*

If Hogg was in his wooden suit 130 years and "believed died in 1839," that makes his re-emergence and trip to Jerusalem date around 1969, which is pre-history for me but which, according to rumour and other reliable sources, would rate the poems directly to some very critical events in the poet's life when he was a newsman in the Middle East and after.

*

Hogg's spiritual journey begins in a kind of stunned innocence. He goes to Jerusalem seeking something holy, not knowing where to find it at home. Everywhere are images of dust, heat, sterility, death, decay, fear and hopelessness, except in the lush oases he shares with a nameless woman in their "Days of/undress and incantation/when love swung through the air/like a great bell." Contrast the violence of Hogg's hatching with the tense, sensuous calm of these Jerusalem poems – porcelain, stone and nibbled fig. Hogg cried, "I am not of this place, where the sun strafes everything in sight," but it is not clear what happens to provoke the drawings and the need to begin again at home. There are biographical causes for this movement, perhaps, but Callaghan as poet is interested in showing effects. The drawings (obviously the products of a diseased mind, as I overheard someone observe) are presented in the movement of the book as an intermediate stage between the Jerusalem and Toronto experiences.

*

The drawings – metamorphic scrambling of parts, exchanges between landscape and anatomy, garish colours, obsessive manipulations of faces, feet, hands, breasts, genitals. Forbidding and funny at the same time. A man wrapping his arms around the nipple of a mountainous breast; flaccid, pig-eyed physogs staring from behind pricks of rock or tree-stump; all are grotesquely humorous and begin the transition from Hogg's Jerusalem innocence and vulnerability toward the sardonic but hopeful vision he will have at the end. [Note: An appendix of four of these drawings appears at the end of this collection of essays under Appendix A.]

*

In Book Three, especially, we hear voices and see apparitions: creatures like Canned Heat the Hermaphrodite, Hell's Belle, John the Conqueroo Decatur, the Northbound Woman and the Bachelor who weds the subway tracks. There is an astonishing variety of tone, mood and rhythm.

*

The *Hogg Poems* are a sequence of dramatic scenes which carry the personal, lyrical, spiritual movement of Hogg's transformation. For me this dramatic quality, which is not at all common in Canadian poetry, is the main strength of the book. In the last section we jump between jive talk and melancholy musings. Under the surface while loons and spiders dance above there is a strange mixture of hip street folk and echoes of the Laurentian Shield (Mrs. Moody never shows).

*

André Breton says in *Nadja* that he strove "in relation to other men, to discover the nature, if not the necessity, of [his] difference from them." The same urge, which gives Hogg his singular vitality, is recognized and mocked by one of the hellish figures of the subway:

> the man who asks why, figures he's got a future
> beyond what he's been,
>
> so I tell you true, you intend to suture
> what you is to what you'd like to be,
> you're on the road on the run,
>
> whereas me, I am the image
> of my maker, ex nihilo nothing, Doctor Ded . . .

Of course Hogg escapes into the light of a topside world which offers few joys, but at least gives him exposure to the gospel according to Jeremiah Stuck in a marvellous sermon which should be sung to a tune by Brownie McGhee. Its essence is:

> Well, I've come to see
> what above all Jesus knew, that built
> into love is
> betrayal.

"Judas Priest" is the climactic moment of an ambitious book, a fine poem, very close to the bone of Callaghan's mind as far as I know it. Nice people won't like it at all, at all. What will they make of all this lust and brutality threaded with a sacred iconography of gesture, ritual, bells?

THREE MEDITATIONS ON HOGG

Joe Rosenblatt

1

Every animal that has a split hoof not completely divided or that does not chew the cud is unclean for you; whoever touches the carcass of any of them will be unclean.

Leviticus 11:26

Out of the Ice Hole: Behold the Whole Hogg

Hogg, in his "Prologue," invokes the image of an Arctic hunter, harpoon poised to dispatch a seal once its snout breaks the surface of an ice hole. In "The Hatching of Hogg," Hogg, who has decided to ascend out of that ice hole, finds himself hauled and *lugged* like a seal across a frozen surface. Led by a *headman bearing icons,* a gang of phantom berserkers tar and feather him, even as he begs for mercy *with yellow lips, jawing how he was the wrong one.* His pleas, far from placating them, spur them on to further violence. An imperious shape-shifting bastard, their *headman* could have easily filled Pontius Pilate's golden sandals. He directs his underlings to break Hogg's legs *in accordance with the law.* Compared to him, our Zansibarian wonder demon, the *popobowa,* is a playful pussycat high on catnip.

Hogg seems aware of who his oppressors are. During *the casting of lots for his limbs,* he charges someone or several – the actual naming doesn't seem to be important – with being a *Christ-quisling. Quisling,* a word synonymous with betrayal? Are they former disciples who in some previous life shared a Passover meal with him, breaking matzo at the long table of the Last Supper?

Enraged at his accusation, they have him *thunderclapped*. He is roped to a scaled down *two-by-four*, in lieu of some serious Golgotha timber. In their *quisling* rage they rope his arms between *two trees* (suspiciously symbolic of the *two* thieves who shared Christ's fate on adjoining crosses on Skull Hill) and for a final entrée in this banquet of mind-numbing sadistic delights, they nail an inscription to Hogg's salient *jawbone latch*: HERE HANGS THE KING OF THE HATCHING DEAD. What an awful bloody way to break out of the shell!

However, I have the feeling that Hogg, the primordial victim, at rest on *slime* and *eel grass* – given who he is to become once he gets on the road – has only got his due. Those spooky thugs were tipped off. God ordered the hit. The omniscient Creator, who sees and hears all with every passing nanosecond of the universe, might have put up with Hogg sniping and sneering at all the *panhandlers for the* Lord he meets, money-grubbers at ease in their *crooked ecclesiastical sheets*, but he wasn't going to let Hogg's ode to the joys of heterosexual and metaphysical oral sex on Olivet Hill ("The Mount of Olives") pass Him by unpunished – a poem bizarrely implying that God is gay. Nobody can question God's procreative heterosexual ways and go *unthunderclapped*, not even so stout a pig-headed poet as Hogg.

Our imperious porker, as he waves, *en passant,* a psychic dorsal at fresh and salt water Biblic personalities – all operating under the arcane but informing number 3 – wants to be the whole triadic Hogg + 1: the Son, the Father and Holy Ghost, and the *taboo* or outlaw Hogg as well (see the black gunslinging kid, John the Conqueroo, who declares – "I am the man who am, in short, I is"). Hogg wants the whole theological ham-hock on the supernal hoof. That's what I call Chutzpah! He has not only got an attitude problem, but theologically, he has one ferocious bipolar disorder – wanting to be an outlaw winner and a sainted loser at the same time, so no wonder he's been pulled asunder, and left bloodied. If only Hogg had possessed a smidgen of Scandinavian bacon – like that supernatural hoofer, *Hildisvini,* the warrior boar of Norse mythology – then the blood on the ice wouldn't have been his alone.

In the follow-up poem, "Hogg Descending," Hogg survives his blood-letting and makes it down to the shore, but as he does he pulls his conflictive mindset along – like a placenta. His survival, as he moves on his belly, has few if any pleasant associations: images of corporeal decomposition are evident. On the land there is a decaying *mound* of raccoon lying on a pathway ripening with *bristle and maggot.* Hogg sees and smells death along a dogwood trail. It is present in the damaged and dying dogwood trees that have given up their leafy ghosts to *the hanging cocoons of tent caterpillars.* There's a sublime application of *memento mori* in the poem when Hogg scrambles down a *stone shelf* (intonating a memorial headstone) and eases in the buff into a slime-filled slough that suggests primordial (incarnating) birth. His *ears singing* he moves through braided roots of plant life at the bottom, *gulping down the dark.*

2

Why if it please you my Lord, your name is Bacon, and mine is Hog, and in all Ages Hog and Bacon have been so near kindred, that they are not to be separated." "I but," relayed Judge Bacon, "you and I cannot be kindred, except you be hanged; for Hog is not Bacon until it be well hanged.

Apothegm 36 in *Resuscitatio,*
Dr. William Rawley, 1671

"What an arrogant bastard . . . Who the fuck does he think he is, the Sun King?"

A poet from down under speaking
of Barry Callaghan to Joe Rosenblatt

Sharing the Hogg Dialectic: A Gift of the Sun King

If Tough Love in this century can still be viewed as a *Theatre of War*, then Barry Callaghan's name must be added to that casualty roster of such notable Canadian romantic poets as Margaret Atwood, Gwendolyn MacEwen, Milton Acorn, Michael Ondaatje, Leonard Cohen, Patrick Lane, and Lorna Crozier. Ever innovative in works of the imagination, Callaghan has elevated the term *love junkie* by buffing it with a certain spiritual fluorescence, while taming his demons, transmuting them into particles of creativity in his role as fiction writer, poet, journalist, broadcaster, professor of English, canine-fancier, autodidact draughtsman, discriminating gastronome, an aficionado of "quail breast and pigeon with truffles," an imbiber of the finest cognac and scotch, serious betting man on and off the track, and literary publisher.

"What an arrogant bastard...who the fuck does he think he is, the Sun King?" a poet from down under, more porcine than portly in his own transfiguration, groused while we quaffed pints of plain in a darkened seventies Toronto pub. He had only moments before got off the phone with Callaghan and was torrentially livid with the cool reception he had received on the phone. Piqued by his outburst, I calmly replied that Callaghan *indeed* was our Sun King, for didn't he keep publishing our poetry when he could have more profitably published fiction – or non-fiction! – and for a tell-tale sign of unadulterated lunacy, he was one of the few publishers in the country who still directly answered his phone, at home, obviously a dangerous practice considering that poetry attracts a wide spectrum of grousing nutters.

A more sympathetic, intrepid interviewer might ask if racial memory, particularly as it relates to the 1840s' catastrophic potato blight that ravaged Ireland, might have brought light to the eyes of his emerald muse. Depending on the lyric potation imbibed, and the time of day, that query might induce Callaghan to declaim that, "The People of the Book" were not only the scribes, scholars and bibliophiles of the Israelite Diaspora, but the same such progressive folk were palpitating amidst the Irish Diaspora, for rather than face extinction from starvation, his ancestors – literate all – had set out in "coffin boats" to cross the waters to where they had ended up being treated as Simians – treated as "the Yemenite Jews of the English empire," a sentiment he has eloquently elaborated upon in his bold essay, "The Simian Irish" (See *Raise You Ten*).

It is surprising, therefore, to find that in the early 1970s Callaghan adopted as his central protagonist one James Hogg, a Protestant settler said by the poet to have betrayed the 1837 uprising of small farmers in Upper Canada, republican citizens who were in burgeoning revolt against the Family Compact, an elite of corrupt Anglican clerics and wealthy landowners, the kind of stuffed shirts with stuffed pockets who found the very utterance of praise of an elected parliamentary assembly a seditious offence worthy of transport to Australia as convict labour.

It's bizarre, finding that a poet steeped in the traditions and lore of Irish republicanism, has adopted a reactionary like Hogg as his alter-ego; but more incredible is his admission that he was happy to find that Hogg was the "antithesis" of everything "I was, or am" – a "Scott, an ambitious farmer, a Tory and informer." So, why then did Callaghan choose a reverse Paul Revere to ride south on horseback to warn the authorities about a bourgeois democratic insurrection, when he could have chosen a true rebel, like the martyred Samuel Lount, who was hanged in Toronto after the collapse of the rebellion? In response to my query Callaghan wrote to me, and while his reply didn't directly address the underlying reason for my enquiry, it nonetheless was evasively entertaining. Scribed on *Exile Editions Dark Horse* letterhead, it arrived as a fax.

"Hogg," he declared in his inimical hand writing, a filigree of letters so lyrically delicate and tiny, that it was barely visible to the naked eye, "is a gambler . . . pigs are born to be sacrificed . . . Eaten. The taboo food, delicious, so sweet to the taste." And at the heart of the letter lay half the answer to my Hoggish question: "Hogg, the sacrificial pig, resists the police even as he resists God. He rides a horse to get away . . ."

Surely the man had become unhinged. Look at this ego-less writing, letters so diminished and fragile they seem intended to be cryptic, like wee hieroglyphs engraved onto the surface of a lapis lazuli canopic jar. Surely, I mused, a man whose handwriting is so minuscule must be hiding something? Let's see: I ask him a simple question and he sends me fleeting replies that germinate more questions than they answer. This poet was playing with a loaded pair of mythopoetic dice. I became darkly suspicious – enough to check the Toronto archives and do some historical research, for I suspected the swinish odour of historical revisionism in Callaghan's long poem, and worse – fiction! As it turned out I was right. The person who rode to Toronto under a barrage of hot rebel lead to warn the authorities of the armed insurrection wasn't a Hogg, but one Cornelia De Grassi, the teenage daughter of Phillipe De Grassi, an Italian-born officer dutifully serving the Empire.

Perhaps it was only at a subconscious level, but it seems to me that Callaghan the mischief man chose James Hogg as a mask – and in a wild charade – he did this to play off who he actually is against a man who stands for everything he is not – so that we could engage in the drama of watching who he is not become who he is. He played this Hogtown g-card, putting in an extra g, to conceal his real intention; to set out into the world as *a no one from nowhere* – like an unknown Scandinavian warrior king in the guise of a militant warthog, in the guise of a bristly and thunderous deity of unfathomable strength and brutal courage. From the beginning, this cautious yet devil-may-care Hogg intended to end up free and fast at a mile and 1/16 on the turf, the seeming heavy-footed porker moving silkily to the finish line, not to have his gizzard slit by unionized butchers in some refrigerated abattoir but to stand in the winner's circle, warmed by a blanket of roses. This swine was, in fact, not only fast, he had a pair of steely balls filled with singing testosterone.

I stubbornly queried Callaghan again, face to face, about James Hogg and the matter of betrayal.

He advised me to reread the poem, "Judas Priest." All, he promised, would be revealed. Sure! Hadn't I just figured out that his pig's ear actually was a silk purse. It occurred to me that I had actually popped the wrong question: I should have asked about his more feral choices, his voice appropriations lifted off Toronto's meaner streets. I found myself increasingly pissed off with his ennobling of society's drug addicts and deranged transvestites and other miserable lumpen types, other scum who would sell their mothers' organs to buy crack. What could possibly motivate this poet to ennoble the utterances of those who have defecated and urinated in lanes, dropped needles in public parks, all of their cockroaches infesting the breadbox of civilized society.

Where a poet like Milton Acorn identified with the world's proletariat, Hogg/Callaghan has reached beyond the proletariat to an even more damaged segment of society, what Marxists have often referred to as the *lumpen proletariat*. And Hogg is not only a complete and seemingly forgiving democrat at ease among "the scum of society," but he is gender blind. He is a *crypto feminist*, true not only to the principle of equality of the sexes but he is a man in touch with *real* women, corporeal, shapely and passionate women who fuck. My antennae, however, have also picked up powerful and polar pulsations in the veins of this carnal pig, and that is the *idea* of the Divine Presence of Mary: she is alive, she is there in the pulsations of ideational purity that always occur in this man's brain-pan, at the most surprising time, in mid-fuck.

3

I loved the Hogg poems, strange, disturbing, beautiful and awful . . . all those things that make the flesh creep and send shivers up and down the spine...more of the same please . . .

Gwendolyn MacEwen in a letter
to Barry Callaghan, May 1, 1978

Pain, a Shape-Shifting Son of a Bitch

The first Hogg to surface arrived *editio princeps* in 1974. Titled *The Cleft of Light,* and later retitled, *The Hogg Poems and Drawings,* this stunning 1978 edition came embellished with coloured drawings – experimental palimpsests scribed directly onto drawings depicting penis legs, floating vulvas, contorted mouths in agony, raging eyeballs, and other individuated mutant biology. They appeared to thrive on their own feral energy, but also seemed willing enough to peacefully co-exist with white semi-circular wafer moons, eerie alabaster fingers, opalescent breasts – and severed pale white feet that looked suspiciously like sculpted one-footed demons, a gargoyle humour sculpted for the purpose of terrifying potential sinners flocking through medieval cathedrals.

The more I studied these Hogg-driven grotesqueries done with coloured pencils, magic markers, and drawing pens, the more salient they became. In their frenzy, those severed anatomies appeared to be in revolt against the central Judaeo-Christian precept that God created Man in His own likeness.

There was something about those drawn fingers that wasn't quite right. They appeared elongated, stiff and swollen. Callaghan, I knew, had experienced recurring bouts of arthritis. It could and would flare up without warning, and the inflammation and pain had been so severe on occasion as to land him in hospital in a state of shock. But I suspected that more than arthritic pain was involved as a catalyst in the creation of the hallucinatory mutants in his Hogg drawings. There was, of course, another kind of crippling disease involved in the creative process: romance, the pain lovers feel when a romantic relationship goes bad. But almost certainly involved, too, was love's opposite – repressed hatred – for there have been men in his life who have earned his hatred, who deserve his hatred.

After all, his life by the late 1960s, and on, had become a pincushion for anxiety's needles: as a journalist covering Quebec in 1968 and 1969 he had been attacked in the *Anglophone* press; covering the 1970 Black September civil war in Jordan, he had been trapped in a battle zone, and must have been trapped to some degree by post-traumatic nightmares, images of war, mutilated bodies and wanton destruction – all this must have found their way into his drawings. And other blows had to have shaped Callaghan's metaphorical visions: the television conversation he had with then Israeli Prime Minister Golda Meir, earning her wrath by insisting that, in fact, the Palestinians did exist and, in fact, weren't going to disappear. He lost his job as a result of that interview. He lost friends. He was vilified. Doors to his talent were closed forever on the CBC air-waves (few know this because he has never publicly complained). And there were those of the Zionist per-suasion who conspired to drive him out of the universi-ty (they failed, but only after the President of the university – forcefully urged by Callaghan's Dean, Harry Crowe (see *Barrelhouse Kings*) – reversed a Senate deci-sion to deny him tenure). Other loveless events fol-lowed, such as a beating he took at the hands of the Afrikaner secret police, and adding to his trauma, his story of going into leper colonies in Gabon and Cameroon, where he received what he daintily called, "the leper's blessing, a kiss." Taking into account the accumulative effect of the shocks he endured, so many betrayals, it is not at all surprising that he had to save his sanity by dealing with the demons haunting his head. However, from my perspective, what I found even more disturbing than Callaghan's images of mayhem, was my core reaction to some of the more truncated forms of humanity prancing around in the buff, particularly those of the penis heads which stared up from a glossy page, penis heads that look like space aliens. Severed feet, legs, or private parts, something in my psyche told me that they should be clothed, like shingles on a serpent, or trees that have the decency to be properly attired in bark, as the Almighty intended.

What got me going when I first leafed through the Hogg book was the predominance of what Michael Bell (then the director of Carleton University's Art Gallery) would refer to as "cock and cunt" in his prologue to a luxurious catalogue titled *The Whole Hogg: Drawings by*

Barry Callaghan (published for an exhibition of the Hogg drawings held at that gallery between April 29-August 3, 1997). In that prologue, Bell elaborates on Callaghan's "egalitarian view" – his giving fair visual representations to both sides of the gender divide, especially in his depiction of male and female genitalia.

Bell further noted that Callaghan, by his skillful juxtaposition of conflicted anatomies, had created his own unique vocabulary, which could be conceived of as another form of writing. This "draughtsman-poet" was cognizant of not only the "organic nature of the body," but also its "extremities. They included toes, fingers, eyes and nipples etc." – those extremities distorted and writhing in an agony reflecting Callaghan's bouts with acute arthritis. The issue hasn't gone unnoticed.

The installation artist Vera Frenkel sees Callaghan's "forced immobility in the Wellesley Hospital in 1972" as impelling him to deal with his pain by drawing, by getting to the experience that lies beyond words.

If that is true, one has to say that Hogg has borne his pain in silence, and with dignity. Drawing aside, he displays no stigmata. On the contrary, and to the consternation of his enemies, he exudes the *joie de vivre* of the sybarite. But this air of the exultant sybarite who is engaged in a dance of death is surely another deceptive ploy. After all, he once admitted to me, "I have not slept without waking in the night in pain since I was twenty-two." It is small wonder that Hogg identifies with the pain of Good Friday on the cross, as Callaghan carries a cross (of 22. karat gold, of course) over his heart under his shirt as he jets off to sites of prayer like Jerusalem, or to sites of poetry and pain like Leningrad, or to the most sybaritic race tracks on this terrestrial orb.

Sadly, unlike God – who can fix a race at any of the earth's tracks – Hogg is not to be saved by wearing front bandages and running on lasik. He is slated – if cops and ecclesiastics are ever going to have their way – to be hog-tied, butchered and packaged as sausages on a plate at a prayer breakfast celebrating received opinion. Still, Hogg has an ace up his sleeve. He will, missing a few bristles to be sure, eventually end up a winner and he will remain a winner because he has been wise enough to "know the facts" and paranoid enough to make himself a moving target, moving through diverse incarnations and transformations, his willingness to be lucky, his readiness to be reborn – his willingness to get on the hoof (whereas cattle will stand still even as they are engulfed by flames, pigs are always – long before the conflagration – looking for a way out, escape). In a sense, Hogg's incarnations have provided him with an anodyne to block out the pain from those psychic nails driven into his soul by the phantasms of adversity. Pain, like the devil – who wants to nail our souls to eternity – loves to burrow into fingers and toes and other ligaments (to travel to the farthest reaches of the psyche) to make its terrible nests. Pain is a shape-shifting son of a bitch, but cuckoos (and Hogg certainly is *cuckoo*) know how to take over nests and sing and then fly away from them. Hogg has sung in the nests of pain, and then has hit the air currents.

BARRY CALLAGHAN'S
"SISYPHUS THE CRACK KING"

JIM HART

Git down, git down,
you got to get down
on your hands and knees
and keep your ear close to the ground.
There are druggies
who honey-dip around parking lots
playing the clown,
looking for
peddlers of high renown
as in H,
or dealers doing sap of the moon plant,
crack and smack.
. I used to dial a vial
myself,
a little digital digitalis,
the speed I dropped
absorbing the absence
in the air
with a light so rare
it baked
the shadow of despair
on a wall that wasn't there.
God almighty, it was a time
in fields of asphodel.

Ah the hit of crack, the rock. The rock which when it
properly sears the brain cuts off all pain and sunders so
blissfully all consciousness and of course all tragedy. All
drugs have the same purpose, I suppose, but having tried
a few, nothing does it with the speed and power of rock.
It is not the slow pushing of the boulder uphill, but like

a cartoon version of the myth, it is sped up in some fast frame that always shocks the user, and like the face of Sisyphus, the user's face quickly becomes as the rock.

Callaghan's poem begins with the demand and desire of everyone who takes the first hit: "Git down, git down you got to git down on your hands and knees." It is the urgency that shakes the drama of the myth and makes the absurdity crackle with the speed of its wit. No longer is the struggle the same by the time the second hit occurs, motored in the poem by rhyme, fuel-injecting rhyme; you are released into a victory over the drama. The absurd power of its rush makes you a king over all you survey and with the next roll of the stone one is frantically searching "forever" for the "sap" of the "moon plant" and it solves and seeks the answer to all of the most personal and intimate dilemmas; "it bakes the shadow of despair." The sublime subtlety of that line mirrors the seductive sensuality of the clear, white stream of smoke as the user exhales out into the night from a New York fire escape.

As the poem moves on, picking up speed, it master-fully weaves the tragic and brilliant escape into ephemera with the great false hope of mystical, cabbal-istic knowledge. But Sisyphus doesn't leave us there – he gives us our final necessary triumphalism: "Warned me never to leave no traces of the knowledge I knew. Called me the King of Crack."

Now I got to keep my head clear,
my nose clean,
and all my seed inside a dark clock.
This is quarry country,
the Bunsen burner
is a holy fire and funeral pyre,
the only begotten son
is dumb, deaf, crippled
and blind,

                    his syllable gone to seed
                      in the mind of
                     all those old carp,
                      the godfathers
                     who got the lock
                  on the chemical combinations,
                     XYZ down to a T,
         the formulations of obloquy and obscurity.
                   I was in their graces,
            and they put me through the paces,
             warned me to never leave no traces
                of the knowledge I knew.
               Called me the King of Crack.

All esoteric, philosophical, chat aside, this is a poem we
should be learning with our school children to let them
know that coming down "is worse than being bung-
holed." And that the problem is so much worse and better than that, for the Crack King goes on to tell us, "I got
this shameless stone, a dead sun inside my brain." It is
eternal biology, an even longer metaphor.

                  But I put on my eye-patch
                    and pranced uptown
                    and came unlatched
                 playing pin-ball with the sun.
            Being all butt, backbone and no brain,
                      I broke the trust
                 and left a trail of angel dust
                    so wide you'd swear
                    a snail had crossed
                        my nerves.
                 Too late, I clapped a coin
                     under my tongue,
              played dead among the misbegotten,
            but they beat the living Jesus out of me
               and hung me from this fire escape
                    where coming down
                 is worse than being bung-holed,

not just gored but gutted
by the privation
of salvation.
It's all up hill from here on in.
I got this shameless stone,
a dead sun,
inside my brain,
a curse I roll toward
a relief only the condemned thief
could understand
a long way east of Eden.

The ultimate urgency is that "The stone don't constitute no pain"; it's only the lack of stone that is the problem, just like the pause of Camus, the intrusion of the certain limitations, of that thing we each call consciousness, and to make matters even worse, as even the simplest of school children learn, "What's terrifying is the gods will come again."

Over the brow of the hill
the gods are at play.
Your father, mine.
It's never night,
always day as they lie,
cheat, vilify,
and replete with codes and codicils
pop a pill and change their shills to toads.
Your father, mine.
The gods got no shame,
so who's to blame for the stone
inside my brain?
They complain I broke a trust. Haw!
Roll on, baby, roll.
The stone don't constitute no pain.
What's terrifying is the gods will come again,
and the narcs, too,
taking a leg, a hand,
they is all sharks.

As someone who has watched the rock crackle and melt against the screen at the end of a pipe, it is the evocation through perfect random images that gives the poem so much of its power that is so much like the compilation of the crack high. The juxtaposition of clowns, gods, asphodel, dark clocks, cripples, ends of the alphabet, Kings, Jesus, Eden, the thief and the sharks. These images fit the crime, a crime almost impossible to survive, so "roll on, baby, roll."

HOGG'S ROMAN NOSE

Callaghan's Sardonic Sonnet

David Lampe

> *One can smile and still prove a villain.*
> Hamlet

1

Hogg's pilgrimage to Jerusalem and his return to Hog-town via the Toronto stations of the subway cross, is a quest as wild as any such in Mandeville. On both sides of Hogg's crossing of the water, the ordinary is made extraordinary, whether it is a monk on the road to Abu Gosh who has the enamelled eye of a mole or a ball-breaking Medusa down among the Toronto moochers – figures who have been much admired for their incanta-tory paranoia or their signifying street talk (the demon-ic reincoded with revelry) – their perspective, their meaning "bent" like notes in the blues.

What should also not be missed in the sensual, some-times blasphemous, sweep of Hogg's book, is that other poetic modes frame these Jeremiahs and junkies: – "Hogg Dreams Veronica," "Skull Hill," "Out of the Tomb Sheets," and "At the Lazarus Stone" are poems that provide contrast and counter-point. Meditative in tone and practice, both prayers and lamentations, these poems to my surprise, after careful reading, employ the forms – and play with the images – of medieval and six-teenth- and seventeenth-century English religious and political verse. My examples – and they will highlight, among other things, how well-read and how deeply rooted in history Callaghan's work is – will be excerpts from two poems, "Hogg Dreams Veronica" and "Skull Hill," plus Hogg's sonnet, "The Imperial Beak." I will consider this last poem in the context of renaissance sonnets, and how – in such sonnets – the past was used to inform present politics.

2

But first: a litany was and is a medieval form of liturgical prayer. The tone taken in a litany was and is crucial; tone was and is a way of turning private supplication into public invocation. At its most rudimentary, a litany went and still goes like this:

Holy Mary *pray for us*
Holy Mother of God *pray for us*
St. Michael the archangel *pray for us*
Holy Virgin of virgins *pray for us*
St. Joseph *pray for us*
Protector of the Holy Church *pray for us*

Sir Philip Sidney, familiar with the litany form from the Book of Common Prayer in the sixteenth century, wrote:

Therefore from so vile fancy,
To call such wit a frenzy,
Who Love can temper thus,
Good Lord, deliver us!

Here is Hogg as he dreams Veronica:

Who is up there keeping vigil
who will wipe the face of Hogg
gaunt, unshaven, stations done,
mounts the stairs, dreams of one
who is up there keeping vigil
who will wipe the face of Hogg
cleanse his wounds, staunch the bleeding,
in her veil his pain left sleeping.

3

Sound, as we know, was particularly important to medieval verse – the simple repetition of words and phrases that were a familiar rhetorical figure and appropriate to oral delivery as the poet established ethos and honed his homiletic power. Here are lines from the conclusion of Chaucer's "Troilus and Criseyde":

> Switch fyn hath, lo, this Troilus for love!
> Switch fyn hath al his grete worthynesse!
> Switch fyn hath his estat real above,
> Switch fyn his lust, switch fyn hath his noblesse!
> Switch fyn hath false worldes brotelness!

And Hogg, at Skull Hill:

> . . . and how they have
> gone down, crowded, into the crypts and cairns
> and muddle of the common boneyards:
> gone down the Imperial Beak,
> gone down Bishop Arculf and Saewulf,
> gone down the Perfumers of the Rock and the Kadi of
> the Mount,
> gone down Tancred and Baldwin and Blake's vision of
> Skull Hill,
> gone down Montefiore and Rabbi
> Yosef Warsawe and Rabbi el Bagdadee,
> gone down Halebim of Aleppo and al-Ghazzali,
> gone down to the Vale of Gihone,
> gone gone with stone anointing lamps to the caves
> on the road
> to the sea

4

And then along came the Italian, Francesco Petrarca, better known as Petrarch, who, for poets writing in English, became father to the sonnet. The Petrachan sonnets were poems of passion, poems of priapic lament, courtly concupiscence and court politics. It is the politics that concern us, specifically in the work of Thomas Wyatt and Henry Howard, Earl of Surrey.

In sonnet 105 (translation Wyatt)[1] ancient Babylon is Petrarch's contemporary Avignon: "Vengeance must fall on thee, thou filthie whore of Babylon" – and so it is that

> golde and pryde, by one accorde,
> In whichednesse so preadd thie lyf abrode,
> That it dothe stincke before the face of God.

English readers, confronting this sonnet in translation in their own context, would have understood that Avignon as Babylon in fact implied London.

And so, Sonnet 107 plays a variation on this theme, calling for a purging of Babylon (Avignon – cum London), that "den of cursed ire, scoole of errour, temple of heresye."

A dangerous game!

In Wyatt's own political sonnets, and in Henry Howard, Earl of Surrey's sonnets, an historical character like Sardanapalus, the Assyrian King, is almost certainly intended to be read as Henry VIII, as a monster of depravity who "Murdered him self, to shew some manfull dede." Within a coterie of English men and women like Wyatt and Surrey who knew their classics, as well as their Petrarch, these were not only poems that took a particular slant on the past, they were poems in which the present was informed by that slant on the past. Henry didn't like being told that, by anybody's implication, he was a monster. Incautious in a world where courtiers wore lace ruffles to protect their vulnerable necks, Surrey lost his head before he was thirty-one.

5

The Imperial Beak

*Titus, who was the darling of the human race,
thought the day wasted when he had
not made a friend.*

Suetonius

So, he came, absorbed by the tall
grass along the road and how green it was in the sun,
Flavius Titus, and in the month of Av, it was done.
Pick-ax, wallop, into the belly of rebellion.
The zealot's empty eye-pouch a medallion
of defeat. Centurions sealed the gates with molten lead
and of the dangling, paltry dead
they made a hanging garden. An infantry of owls
picked the bones clean. Oil, sacred towels,
incense in offertory dishes, these did no good.
Where once the prophet stood
an old crone consulted a dog's eye and found no
     meaning.
She spat at Caesar's soul in the fire and entered, keening,
into colloquy with God, face to the wall.

Protest poems – Denise Levertov's Viet Nam verse or recent anti-Iraq invasion rants – are seldom so subtle as Petrarch or Surrey or Wyatt. We've grown all too aware of overt polemic, poetry as propaganda. Perhaps that is why the generic inventiveness of Callaghan's sonnet – and its political allusions – have not been recognized.

Although "The Imperial Beak" conforms to the 14 line structure, it also departs from convention on several structural counts. Scansion might seem random, varying between 9 and 13 feet, with some lines of 13, 14, and even 16 feet, but that is using traditional syllabic measure. All becomes much less seemingly haphazard if one listens for accent. For example, the opening of line 3, "Flavius Titus," can be heard as an initial spondee (")

117

followed by a trochee ('u) – or, in the idiom of the *Hogg* sequence as a whole, as three stresses followed by a rimshot – *Kaboom*! Moreover, six lines are end-stopped, eight enjambed. Only someone who understands the strict sonnet form could play so freely within the grid while reinforcing that form.

Instead of the octave-sestet pattern of the Petrarchan sonnet, or the three quatrain final couplet form invented by Surrey and used by Shakespeare, Callaghan uses six rhymed couplets contained within an envelope rhyme (the first and last lines). This framing device – framing Titus *and* the fate of the zealots – points to the architectonics of the whole text, and also signals how this formal sonnet – set in the past – informs a more informal prose poem set in the political present:

> Now it is their own city and even the blind can feel free. So the two blind men who have never been outside the walls are walking toward Dung Gate. Beyond is the ridge that overlooks the ruins that lie in the long grass at the bottom of Dung Hill cliff, the ruins of David's house. The men hurry, holding each other by the arm, asking soldiers the way south. They go out through the Gate. They want to stand on the ridge and hear below them the voice of their forefather who had also held the city. They go a long way, talking excitedly, but then they grow silent, and soon stop. The road has petered out into rubble. They don't know where they are, but they hear voices, low, whining voices, children, coming closer, circling them.
> – Ask which way's the road.
> – They hate us, they'll lead us over the cliff.
> – What'll we do?
> – Don't move.

To understand how prescient this poem was and is – in association with "The Imperial Beak," consider that in 1970, the year of the experience behind the poem, Prime Minister Meir said that the people – the Palestinians – to whom the children in Callaghan's poem belong, "did not exist," and she forecast in a conversation with Callaghan (see *Barrelhouse Kings*) that in twenty years they would be forgotten: Callaghan forecast that those children – after decades of hatred and murderous "stand-still" – would initiate and sustain a children's war, an *intifada*.

6

"The Imperial Beak" is the only poem in the first *Hogg* sequence that bears an epigraph (the other such poem is "Himmler's Law" in *Seven Last Words*, which has marked thematic similarities to "The Imperial Beak"). The epigraph is from Suetonius, his *Twelve Caesars*, and it is really Callaghan's condensation of an anecdote in which Suetonius praises Flavius Titus, the eleventh Caesar, as an ideal administrator:

> Titus was naturally kind-hearted . . . He also had a rule never to dismiss any petitioner without leaving him some hope that his request would be favourably considered. Even when warned by his staff how impossible it would be to make good such promises Titus maintained that no one ought to go away disappointed from an audience with the Emperor. One evening at dinner, realizing that he had done nobody any favour since the previous night, he spoke these memorable words, "My friends, I have wasted a day."
>
> (Graves 290)

Callaghan's citation is obviously not exact. Why? Why does Callaghan not only compress this passage, but why does he "betray" the Suetonius text (the role that betrayal plays in love, in redemption, is a theme that runs throughout the Hogg poems)? Does he betray Suetonius' text so that he can reveal a different significant truth?

Consider how classicists in our time react to the Suetonius passage. For example, "Is there not something corny about [this] saying that Suetonius found so laudable?" Michael Grant asks. Callaghan is certainly not trying for the "corny" in his condensed epigraph and his sardonic sonnet. Rather, he has described the ways in which Titus, the seemingly bland and kind-hearted administrator, actually "walloped" the Jewish rebellion and destroyed the Jewish temple in 70AD. In so doing, Callaghan makes us aware of how the benevolent bland smiling face of an occupying authority betrays itself by becoming its other face – a brutal imperial or ideological or theocratic force.

7

Flavius Josephus, in his *War of the Jews,* left us a first-hand account of the fall of Jerusalem. We all – to one degree or another – rely on his report, written after Flavius Titus had laid siege to the city. Josephus, the Jewish general who so famously changed sides and betrayed his cause to serve as Titus' translator says a temperate Titus tried to stop the fires in the temple (VI. 4.5-6) and tried to stop the looting carried out by his troops, soldiers who had violated his command (VI. 4 7-5.1). Callaghan will have none of it. "The Imperial Beak" – with its vision of brutal force – has more in common with the story told by Sulpicius Severus (fifth century) who apparently followed Tacitus' lost account, and the poem supports the Talmudic tradition, which credits Titus' early death to divine punishment for his brutality.

8

Brutality is a certain fact in "The Imperial Beak." Though at first the "he" of line 1 is ambiguous, it is clear by line 3 that "he" is the jovial Titus, "the darling of the human race" "absorbed" in the vitality of the green grass and sun, and it is clear that "he" – the darling lover of nature – has ordered the all-out attack "in the month of Av," the fifth month on the nineth day – the date traditionally ascribed to the first (Babylonian) destruction of the temple.

Titus, according to Callaghan, issued no neat administrator's executive order. He directed a vicious "pickax" blow "into the belly of rebellion." Titus, having decided that the zealots were fools who, so blinded by fanaticism that they had refused his conciliatory offers, were now rewarded with literal blindness (an "empty eyepouch"), the appropriate "medallion of defeat." The locks to the gates are "sealed with molten lead," the "dangling paltry dead" are "made a hanging garden" to be eaten by raptors, by "an infantry of owls" – rather than given proper burial.

None of the temple ceremonies – "oil, sacred towels, incense in offertory dishes" – have availed. Instead of "a prophet," the voice of the temple has become "an old crone," who has "consulted a dog's eye" and "found no meaning." As the voice of a failed national zealotry she has "entered keening into colloquy with God," "face to the wall."

Like Wyatt, Surrey, and Shelley, Callaghan has used the past as a mirror through which to reflect on aspects of the present, to realize that there is always an "infantry of owls" on the fly, the destroyers, who devour and digest the occupied, offering – as darlings of the human race – the bland face of good intentions, good works and favours to the unsuspecting. Callaghan's sonnet not only re-inscribes history but his sonnet also subverts the form's tradition and gives it new resonance and new meaning.

Note

1. The translation of Petrarch attributed to Wyatt – and perhaps Wyatt was following in the steps of Chaucer whose translation of Petrarch's sonnet in the *Troilus* employs 21 lines (11. 400-421) – extends well beyond the compact 14 lines of the genre. Callaghan has adhered, in his own way of course, to the 14 line form.

WHAT THE DARKNESS
TELLS THE LIGHT

Barry Callaghan's "Judas Priest"

Bruce Meyer

The Judas Gospels, recently unearthed, offered readers the possibility that Jesus shared foreknowledge of his death with his disciple Judas. This particular Gnostic text has been preserved in a dry, Egyptian cave since the fourth century. Now that it is out, and translated, it has triggered a furor, but what should interest our readers, putting that furor aside, is Barry Callaghan's own Gospel of Judas, and, given what we now know, his pre-science.

Callaghan's man, his "Judas Priest" – *The Hogg Poems and Drawings* (1978) – is a former Yonge Street pimp who has done jail time and is now out and has become a sidewalk preacher. He is a certain Jeremiah Stuck, who declares:

> there must be more to human affairs than being
> belly-up in despair.
> Three years, friends, three in the hole.
> But I'm back,
> shifted my gears, and I don't pretend
> to save your soul,
> but old Jeremiah Stuck, he's going
> to lay some strange
> saving words down, so stick around.

Stuck, who preaches the Gospel of Judas to Hogg, has been paroled – not quite from the prison of Canto XXXI-II in Dante's *Inferno*, but from Corrections Canada. Hogg is akin to the Saint Brendan who is found in an eleventh-century Irish immram (the Celtic term for an epic voyage narrative involving fantastic settings and experiences). Brendan is a supplicant who sailed around in circles in search of redemption. In the *Navigatio Brendanum* or *Life of St. Brendan the Navigator*, Judas appears to Brendan as a lonely, windswept, shiveringly naked figure who is trapped on a rock off the coast of a purgatorial Iceland:

> St. Brendan espied a shape in the sea that looked like a man perched on a rock. A length of cloth, the size of a cloak, hung down in front of it from two spits. The whole thing was being battered by the waves like a skiff in a whirlpool.

As volcanoes spew and fume behind the haggard figure of the fallen disciple, Brendan questions Judas (as Hogg questions Stuck) and finds that he is free from Hell on a day-pass:

> "I am of all men the most wretched," came the answer, "for I am Judas Iscariot who foully bargained away the life of his Master . . . Sitting here is like being in the Garden of Delights, compared to the torments to which I can look forward this evening."

Callaghan's lonely, shiveringly naked persona, Stuck, has been to Hell, too:

> ... they
>   stuck me in the looney –
> bin, going to 'lectric shock me
>   back to Doctor Spock,
> and maybe Doctor Ded, which is
>   what they said, but
> never done. Just sat me on my buns
>   in solitary, for
> three years, and the walls in that room
>   sweated tears.

makes you think, alone with the deadfall
    of your own fear
there must be more to human affairs than being
    belly-up in despair.

The story of Judas that Stuck tells to Hogg is quite different from Brendan's. Stuck's Judas did not "bargain away the life of his Master." Quite the contrary. He entered into a bargain *with* his Master, a bargain in which the zealot disciple assists Jesus in the fulfillment of "the plan":

    Old Jeremiah Stuck
can tell you, when you reach out, sleepless,
    for the walls
of your hole, and all you touch is the darkness
    of your soul,
you scrutinize how and why a man dies,
    why, when Jesus had him
dead-to-rights, he broke bread and said,
    Eat your fill, Judas,
I know who you're going to kill.
    The question's this,
Why's the kiss the ancient invitation to the abyss?
    Well, I've come to see
what above all Jesus knew, that built
    into love is
betrayal . . .

Judas was not an accidental agent in the death of Jesus, but a co-conspirator. This is also the assertion made in the Gnostic text of *The Gospel of Judas*. In the final book of that gospel, Jesus turns to Judas and confronts him with the truth of their situation: Judas will not be the betrayer of Jesus, but rather, he will be necessary and complicit, the most trusted figure in the actions that will result in the crucifixion:

"But you will exceed all of them. For you will sacrifice the man who clothes me.

Already your born has been raised
your wrath has been kindled,
your star has shown brightly,
and your heart has [. . .]

Lift up your eyes and look at the cloud and the light within it and the stars surrounding it. The star that leads the way is your star."

Judas lifted up his eyes and saw the luminous cloud, and he entered it.

Through betrayal, Judas sacrifices the man-Jesus who clothes or cloaks the God-Jesus in order to reveal the Christ who leads mankind to everlasting life. The "luminous cloud" signifies that he is not only a willing but a knowing participant in the events of the Passion rather than a simple agent of evil or fear, and that the greatest motivation that binds people together is love to the point of "betrayal" so that a cause can be served.

In Judas' story, as Stuck tells it, the lover mirrors his beloved, and the highest act of devotion is to respond by imitating the death that he causes: "like his Lord, / not in hatred, but in love, / he hung himself dead." Stuck argues that "Christ's benevolent / intention was our subsequent redemption," and given that intention, various players had to play their roles in a larger drama, a tragedy that – because it is redemptive – ended as a comedy in which the lover and the beloved became bonded and were made One, "not by mendacity / but complicity:"

. . . double-dealing
     dealt his life
new meaning – that once he had his own hide hung
     in perfect imitation
     of God's begotten Son
then he and Jesus would be One, and that is
     what he done

for you and me, shared this complicity
    in death, so we do
draw today deliverance breath, that's why old Stuck
    has come undone,
free, and telling you the essence of all
    be not mendacity
but complicity, for if Judas and Jesus are One,
    if by betrayal
the beautiful is begun, then not only Judas
    be in you,
but Jesus, too. You wear His face no matter
    your disgrace.

"Judas Priest," as a poem, dares to see that at the heart of love is conspiracy. The word, *conspiracy*, in its Latin roots, literally means "to breathe together." The fact that Jesus and Judas are conspirators is blasphemous in Catholic doctrinal terms, but as Jesus and Judas "breath together," they share not only words but the life that lives in words and promises – inspiration. From "inspiration," the "act of breathing into something," comes the divinity that allows mere dust to live, and life to exceed itself. Stuck calls this a "complicity in death," suggesting that the sacrifice of Christ for everlasting life is something everyone shares in, from the most pious church-goers to the pimps at Yonge and Dundas; for we are not only Judas, but Jesus, too. This is the great secret that Callaghan shares with a fourth-century Gnostic writer.

THE HIDDEN PRECINCT OF DESIRE

Barry Callaghan's Hogg Works

VERA FRENKEL

I

Governing Narrative

"I was nineteen," says Barry Callaghan, "when W.W.E. Ross, the country's first modern poet, looked at me and said – in this very house – 'What's it to be, lad, poetry or painting?' Ross was a friend of my father's and he could see for himself what I'd been up to. 'Make up your mind!' he said. Truth is, I couldn't tell him which it was to be because I didn't know myself."

We are in the kitchen and Barry is preparing me for the images I am about to see set out on the dining room table or framed and hung throughout the Dale Avenue house in Toronto where he lives and works with his partner, artist Claire Weissman Wilks. Over the course of the evening, I see drawings and paintings from his young years and since, ranging from intimate journal sketches to many-paneled composite mixed media drawings behind glass, all continuing a private gloss, alongside his public writer/editor/publisher self.

"What's it to be . . .?" asked Ross. But for Callaghan, as with a number of painter-poet colleagues in Canada, from Barker Fairley to P.K. Page to Doug Fetherling, the real question hovering above pen and easel is: Must one decide?

Decision postponed indefinitely, we find at one charged intersection of Callaghan's paths, literary and visual, *The Hogg Poems and Drawings.*

II
The Pleasure of the Autodidact

Barry Callaghan is a naturally skilled draughtsman. His only formal art instruction, begun after the *Hogg Drawings* were completed, consisted of a two-month immersion course in engraving at Stanley William Hayter's Atelier 17 in Paris. It was clear long before then that "he could draw," which is a way of saying he was good at the romance of representation. He now wanted to use his skill to address the metal plate and the reversing image of the print.

The autodidact's special contribution is to trace and reflect the schooled illusions of contemporary practices, holding up for scrutiny the governing art rhetoric of the day and allowing us to imagine the path not taken.

I suspect that Barry might enjoy being seen in the company of a curmudgeonly William Blake who wrote in his *Epigrams on Art and Artists:*

You say their pictures well-painted be,
And yet they are blockheads, you all agree:
Thank God! I never was sent to school
To be flog'd into following the Style of a Fool.

and again:

Send battle, murder, sudden death, O pray!
Rather than be such a blind Human Fool,
I'd be an ass, a hog, a worm, a chair, a stool.[1]

Which is not to say that this view is justified, but that Blake's doggerel marks a familiar feature of the outsider's journey as it circumnavigates and scrutinizes from afar current assumptions within a discipline: exasperation with the presumed cant of those on the seeming inside.

Lest it be assumed from this that I am a fan of orthodoxy, I should mention that I myself did not attend art school, except, as it happens, for a single printmaking course, not with Hayter in Paris where Callaghan had *carte blanche* and a permanent bed under the stairs, but with Albert Dumouchel, Hayter's admirable antithesis, at the École des Beaux-Arts in Montréal. There I was told, "your portfolio is pretty strong for a woman . . . guess we'll take a chance" and was ruefully admitted. Despite an inauspicious beginning, the experience that ensued was one of the most rewarding and pleasurable I've had in any context, contributing to the notion I've had ever since that no matter what else I do in life my country of origin is the visual arts. So I'm game to carry out with pride the role of honorary blockhead that Blake would assign to me as a result, but it is primarily as an unschooled writer that I tangle with the Hogg works, one autodidact contemplating another.

The task requires that I look past and step around my usual habits of mind and, in doing so, I see a Callaghan world of image making that, like Velikovsky among the physicists, participates in another reality from mine, both foreign and interesting.

Setting aside notions of centre and periphery, and whatever chagrin each stance may induce, the pleasures of the autodidact are many: a presumed innocence and freshness of perspective; an absence of adherence to factions; the delights of savouring applause for pulling unexpected rabbits out of hats; a fetching and persistent trust that art is an unmediated, purely intuitive practice; in short, all the symptoms of a foregrounding of a vocation over profession.

While in this sense tiptoeing gently along with Callaghan through the undisciplined tulips, I find myself face-to-face suddenly with his complicated and painful images, no less painful for their whiff of self-mockery, and I begin to see there's a price to be paid for being unwitting.

III
Flesh, Image, Text

The *Hogg Poems*, justifiably lauded on their 1978 publication as a major contribution to Canadian writing, map the psyche and soma of place and time through the travels of the resurrected James Hogg, Torontonian, birth date unknown but dead by 1839, 130 years before Callaghan sends him to Jerusalem.

In the poems, Hogg, our Hogg, the Hogg of Toronto's Hogg's Hollow, like his namesake James Hogg, the respected Scottish poet, voices the spiritual through the vernacular. Contemplating a brace of Hoggs – writer and written – I see that they have something else in common: each savours sin and redemption in the same instant, through the flesh.

And it is through the flesh that we come to the originating impulses and working conditions for the *Hogg Drawings,* begun just prior to a period of severe arthritic pain and forced immobility in the Wellesley Hospital in 1972. The collapse of the love affair recounted in the *Hogg Poems*, and other events that had proved overwhelming, saw Callaghan hospitalized in what he describes as a total state of shock. His way of dealing with the dual outrages of illness and treatment was to draw. The subject was pain and the intensifying and telescoping of meanings that accompany a crisis of the body remain present in the drawings.

Pain is Satan's last, best weapon for turning Job against God, writes David Morris in *The Culture of Pain*:

His accusations against the silent, inscrutable, vengeful God who afflicts him find expression through exceptionally violent images in which the entire self is dismembered:

I was at ease, and he broke me asunder;
he seized me by the neck and dashed me to pieces;
he set me up as his target;
his archers surround me.
He slashes open my kidneys, and does not spare;
he pours out my gall on the ground.

(16:12-13)

. . . Body and spirit are afflicted together. [2]

The Hogg of the poems makes the pilgrimage to Jerusalem, and returns to echo its meaning through a chain of Toronto subway stations. Callaghan, who took him there and back, sketches an anguish that is at its worst at the Wellesley, but had already begun on his return from the Middle East, with its roots, as he pointed out to me, in long experience with bodily pain, "unseen most of the time by anyone, because of my propensity to frolic, footloose . . ."

A gift for ironic self-deprecation meant to achieve the opposite of what is said merges most often when Callaghan's claims to Irishness are on the menu. In that regard, hospital anthropologist Mark Zborowski, in his controversial study of attitudes towards pain among male veterans in hospital, found that among Irish patients, for example, "pain often became an occasion or source of pride . . . in effect interpreting their pain as something to be 'taken' . . . the ability to absorb punishment becoming a semi-heroic sign of courage and endurance,"[3] an attitude to pain as different from Job's as the poems are from the drawings.

Late twentieth-century readers are understandably suspicious of the suggestion that love, work, and, especially, statecraft, can have epic qualities. We've seen demagogues promising a new life and recognize the price paid for illusory escapes and, inured to the accompanying rhetoric, remain safe in our caves of irony. But anyone even remotely interested in the mythic properties of everyday life can savour, along with the history and mischief of his name, the epic journey of Hogg traced in the poems. The drawings, offering commentary through a sometimes ghoulish, sometimes tender play of forms, are of another order, so given over to pain that they contradict the forward redemptive trajectory of the poems. There is no rebirth in the drawings, but instead, Styx-like humour called out from the oarsman's position in the middle of the river, his arm tucked cozily around Cerberus.

Seamus Heaney, in a letter on the motives for writing his play, *The Cure at Troy*, suggests that what led him to adapt this play in the way he did was, "A sense that pride in the wound is stronger than the desire for a cure. A sympathy with that reluctance to shed the haughtiness of the hurt spirit for the humdrum and *caritas* of renewal."[4]

Haughty or not, Callaghan and Hogg managed to escape a brush with Jerusalem Fever, the syndrome observed with surprising frequency in travellers to the Holy City who pass out and wake up believing they are the Virgin Mary or Jesus. Actually, Hogg, preoccupied with the betrayal that sets him free, doesn't notice that he may be, among other things, Jesus, but Callaghan knows he's Hogg. Laughing, Barry tells me that in the sitting room off the kitchen, next to a likeness of Claire, hangs a portrait of a pig. Cheerfully, he calls it a self-portrait and cites the closing, accepting words of the cycle, "Behold the whole Hogg!"

Hogg's Jerusalem pilgrimage and the transformations it brings about have been detailed elsewhere. What matters here is the nexus between the poems and the drawings, the transfer point where metaphor informs both text and image. For example, in *On the Abu Gosh Road*, Hogg, taking shelter with the monks at the convent of the Holy Spasm, hears them pray:

> we do not forget
> that Seth
> brother to Abel and Kain
> planted the tree of mercy
> in the mouth
> of Dead
> Adam.

In one of the drawings we see a mouth at a tree's root, but a mouth disconcertingly alive, sensual, about to kiss or speak. This is no dead Adam. Something has happened between text and picture, a shifting to-and-fro of meaning, each providing commentary on the other. Where a root metaphor is at work, arising differently in the poems and in the drawings, the unsettling discontinuity creates tension, and bounded by the respective topographic limits of poem and drawing, alludes to a space-between.

Looking at the drawings separately, what do we see? Inked forms, heavily hatched and cross-hatched or hanging together on a light fluid line; water colours of various levels of density; generously applied pastels; and most intriguing of all, mixtures of all these in the image-annotated poems, drawings layered over typewritten and corrected *Hogg Poems*. Texts, embraced and subverted by intricate ornamentation, form palimpsests of words and visual gloss. Obsessive underminings of the uneven marks of typewriter keys reframe text as texture. This is drawing in process, rather than *a* drawing: a progressive permeation, ivy-like, of the brick of typescript.

Reading these poems-in-progress is a very different experience from reading the published Hogg cycle. Different versions of the same poem wrestle on each page with new and different efflorescences of imagery. Phrases emerge from a visual tangle of body protrusions and orifices, hang unconnected.

To call this a language of dreams is too simple. The drawings are almost documentary. They impose themselves on the vulnerability of the working manuscript, where we see penultimate or discarded versions of poems being groomed and smoothed, or roughed up, for public presentation. Visual and textual annotation meet and intertwine on the same page in a symbiosis of the unfinished. The order of the poem is disordered by the image, the image pierced by the poem.

In two quite different kinds of time, Hogg is born and Callaghan leaves the hospital.

IV

At Root

We are in a world of changed scale, boundary, and function. A moon pale as a communion wafer hovers between gigantesque thumb and forefinger; a tree root is a full-lipped mouth with toes; a huge phallus rises tall and tumescent out of the earth; limb extremities and genitalia exchange roles and in their altered states become one with the landscape. All is eroticized, strange, even frightening. The double life of body parts is here revealed. By day they have some relation to discernible function. They all walk by night.

We enter Hogg's incubator, moving together with him, as the Henry Miller epigraph to *The Hogg Poems and Drawings* reminds us, into a "heroic descent to the very bowels of the earth, the dark and fearsome sojourn in the belly of the whale, the bloody struggle to liberate himself . . ."

Here, transcending specific organs, sexuality permeates the body and the landscape. Flesh and earth dissolve into each other in one undifferentiated dance of amputees and their reconfigured parts. Yet there is a curious autonomy in the heart of this non-differentiation, each fragment of flesh serving as its own seat of consciousness. Life flows from one form into another: a toe is pure erectile tissue, a breast becomes an eye, a vulva straddles space like a vast mouth, and every torn limb in this angry romp through woods and wounds is in a process of self-healing through unexpected capacities for pleasure.

The cruelties of form that abound are all the more unsettling for being delicately expressed, imagery that affirms the far-reaching power of the polymorphous perversity underlying human life. Gazing at these truncated body parts, sexually charged and omnivorous, we are reminded that at root, in limb and orifice, hair and tooth, we are all everything.

Echoed in the titles of the two books beside his lover's bed, *(Light in August* and *Death in Venice)*, the poems and drawings hum with the transgressive but inevitable congress of sex and death. In "The Gift of Tongue," Hogg and his woman, naked among gravestones, make love, the moon swallows the sun, and as Hogg cries out in pleasure, they hear *"the muezzin / in his minaret / that stone shaft into the mouth of god."* Word, flesh, and image meet and change places.

There is a sense in these works of convergence at the source, of an early, primordial fusion, as in the presumed oneness of painting and poetry, suggesting the state of human expression before we emerge from the amniotic floating warmth and everything begins to divide into the chill cloisonné of specialization. Past their surface wars and seemingly surreal imagery, the *Hogg Drawings* allude to a place where these dividing walls have reverted to a natural permeable state, where word and image are one in a longing from which all art emerges.

With Callaghan's Hogg, that longing is for redemption. Though the drawings don't provide that option, Hogg, sinner and innocent, is redeemed in the poems. Between the playful and the malign, we discern him galumphing through his rebirth and arriving bleary-eyed at a renewed innocence. Along the way eyes or their substitutes are everywhere:

> the enameled eye of the mole who never sleeps;
> Jet glass eyes sewn on the hem;
> the zealot's empty eye pouch;
> an old crone consulted a dog's eye;
> baskets of beheaded fish, the eyes are best for soup;
> two boiled eggs . . . here are my man's eyes;
> he will not forget the holyman's eye, a wheel rolling, and
>   within the wheel another wheel rolling;
> the Eye in the sky;
> You dead-eye dick;
> and the amber-eyed cops;
> the eyes of horses and riders;
> his one good eye laced
> by blood, staring;
> The perturbed loving look in the eye; and,
> Even the blind can feel free . . .

V
Cultural Haunting (In Search of Hogg)

Limbs, like garments, may hang on poem-trees, or a wind of lust fill nipples and mouth and phallus, but the protagonist is no longer in the picture. His is the face in extreme close-up on a separate page, coming together out of strokes and squiggles, eyes bewildered; free of his sacred terrors. Hogg is here, in his secular daze, counting and recounting subway stations on his way home.

Hogg had become for me a compelling presence. I could see what was remarkable about him. To flesh out the ordinary was more difficult and my search took me to the curious window on the world that is the Internet. It would be a matter of minutes, I thought, using my favourite Internet search engine, to find the details of Hogg's background. We know from Henry Scadding when he died – 1839; no one seemed to know when he was born. Surely, among all the Hoggs, from Dollar, Clackmannanshire to New South Wales, I'd find the Hogg of Toronto, of the poems and drawings.

My confidence was misplaced. Seeking out Everyman and Pilgrim, I was quickly wooed away from my task, finding instead the Hogg Foundation for Mental Health in Texas, the Hogg maker of T-shirt transfers in Arkansas, and from Boston to Vancouver innumerable James Hogg dentists, doctors, and geneticists. Tucked among these and a good many others, almost contemporaneous with the Toronto Hogg, was a James Hogg – born in 1770, in the Parish of Ettrick in the Scottish Border Country, second son of Robert Hogg, a shepherd, and Margaret Laidlaw, a doctor's daughter. Known somewhat mischievously then and since as the Ettrick Shepherd, after the valley of his birth, and a cherished poet, he was also author of *The Private Memoirs and Confessions of a Justified Sinner.*[5] In a curious case of cultural haunting,[6] the title fits.

I now had two of them moving through each other's lives and work, and mine. One Hogg dissolved into another, authors into their texts. For a while, I confess, I abandoned the one Hogg for the other, dipping into other Hogg lives en route, but with a special affection for the Ettrick Shepherd. I began a journey into an unanticipated region of ghosts and shadows, where, as John Wain writes in his preface to the *Confessions*, quoting T. Earle Welby's introduction to the first edition, "Poe never invented anything more horrible or with so much spiritual significance." The atmosphere of his novel, writes Wain, "is in artistic resonance with the story he has to tell; it results from the author's sustained contemplation of things repugnant to his nature." Whether by elision, revision, or a kind of diagnosis by hypotenuse, his description suits the *Hogg Drawings*.[7]

For my sins, I find myself engaged in correspondence with Hogg scholars in Scotland and the U.S.A., exchanging biographical details with a James Hogg in Australia, and gauging the program of the Hogg Foundation as a research tool. I am reading the *Confessions*, a book in which the devil is made palpable, and am fascinated by three different introductions, including that of André Gide beside himself with admiration. Oh, Callaghan, where have ye led me?

I am far from Hogtown. In a tunnel of lenses, mirrors, and Möbius strips, seeing through the shape of James Hogg of Hogg's Hollow to the James Hogg of the Ettrick Valley and Edinburgh right into the heart of nineteenth-century fanaticism and Gothic romance. And the reverse journey is equally strange, the earlier Hogg serving as a lens through which I revisit Callaghan's poems and reconsider the drawings. "As usual," writes Norman Cohn in his book on cult practices, "the route to the Millennium leads through massacre and terror."[8] These congruencies are arrived at not entirely by chance. Still of this century, we like to imagine there is no chance, only synchronicity.

There is in Hogg the poet, Hogg the poem, and the *Hogg Drawings* something of the Gothic chill of the *Confessions*, a shared capacity for staring open-eyed at the disturbing and the forbidden and describing it in obsessive detail.

Rick Incorvati attributes the curious energy of the *Confessions* in part to its oscillation between two discourses, one closing about reason, one open to mystery,[9] and energy at work as well in the *Hogg Poems* (see, for example, "Hogg Begins Again"), where the vernacular meets the bureaucratic: folk-rhythm and rhyme (*"but how in hell did his destination / come to be at Sheppard Station"*) meets the institutional administration of desire (*"we poured reinforced concrete into forms requiring two million / board feet of lumber, put the stations under light, and / the only problem since then has been suicide . . ."*).

The protagonist of the *Confessions*, unable to shake the Devil, hangs himself and is buried by frightened neighbours. A century later, in an epilogue to the memoir, the Ettrick Shepherd, quoting a letter he has written about this matter to *Blackwood's Magazine*, reports the opening of the grave and the discovery there of the manuscript we have just read. The curious lads tugged on something and, "behold the body came up into a sitting posture, with a broad blue bonnet on its head, and its plaid all around it, all as fresh as the day it was laid in!"[10] Unaware of this, but at about the same time, Callaghan's Hogg emerges from his "wooden suit" ("Inside His Wooden Suit") 130 years after his own burial and begins his journey.

VI

Clearing the Ground

In supposing cultural memory to be alive and well at the university, a generous supposition, what better context for the Callaghan exhibition than the daunting array of explorations of word/image relationships at the Third International Congress of the International Association of Word and Image Studies which took place at Carleton

University in 1993. The first two hours of the program alone, even before the first coffee break, offered a startling range of topics: "Toward a Rhetoric of the News Photo," "The Amalgamation of Sign Systems: Ekphrasis, Pornography and Alchemical Search," "Fusing Word and Image in the Case of the Comic Strip," "Isomorphic Structures in the Work of Later Chinese Poet-Painter-Calligraphers," and so on.

In what seems like a whole revision of assumptions regarding visual art and poetry, metaphor and meaning, there is discussion of the work of, among others, Lawrence Wiener, ee cummings, Kyo-Den, Odilon Redon, Delacroix, Kurt Schwitters, Joyce, Cézanne, Hugh Hood, Donatello, Vermeer, Courbet, Ovid, Barthes, Bataille, Balzac, Nadar, Alice Munro, Poe, Klee, Apollinaire, Browning, Pound, Whistler, Baudelaire, Magritte, Duchamp, and even Van Gogh. A territory of languages is being charted.

Echoing Incorvati's notion of discourses of reason and mystery, Marxist psychoanalyst Joel Kovel writes in *The Age of Desire* of two histories intersecting, "the public one seizing the stage and driving the repudiated private fantasies deeper into the hidden precinct of desire."[11] In the *Hogg* Drawings it is the repudiated fantasies that seize the stage. We are in desire's hidden precinct, accompanied by fear and darkest wit, where Callaghan, drawing his poems and writing his drawings, opens a private gate and Otherness walks in.

Notes

1. Blake, William, "Epigrams on Art and Artists," *The Poems of William Blake,* ed., John Sampson, (London: Studio Editions. Reprint of), 272-3.
2. Morris, David, *The Culture of Pain* (Berkeley: University of California Press, 1993), 140.
3. Morris, *The Culture of Pain*, 54.

4. McDonald, Marianne, "Seamus Heaney's *Cure at Troy: Politics and Poetry,*" in *Classics Ireland,* (Vol. 3, 1996, University College, Dublin), unpaginated electronic version.

5. Hogg, James, *The Private Memoirs and Confessions of a Justified Sinner, Written by Himself, with a detail of curious traditionary facts, and other evidence, by the Editor,* ed. John Wain. (Longmans, 1824). Various modern editions have been published.

6. Rogoff, Irit, "Body Missing: Uncanny Histories and Cultural Hauntings." Paper presented at the Symposium *Kunst als Beute,* Gesellschaft fur Aktuelle Junst and University of Bremen, November 1-3, 1996.

7. Hogg, *Confessions,* ix.

8. Cohn, Norman, *In Pursuit of the Millennium* (London: Secker and Warburg, 1957), 116.

9. Incorvati, Rick. "Dialogue and Marginality in James Hogg's *Confessions of a Justified Sinner.*" Paper given at *Prometheus Unplugged* Conference, Emory University, Atlanta, April 12-14, 1996.

10. Hogg, *Confessions,* intro André Gide [1947], 220.

11. Kovel, Joel, *The Age of Desire: Reflections of a Radical Psychoanalyst.* (New York: Pantheon, 1982), 83.

THE WHOLE HOGG

Michael Bell

. . . the doodle could become the instrument and token of the freely creative imagination.[1]

Redolent of the mystical, the sensual, the base, and profound human passions, Barry Callaghan's *Hogg Poems and Drawings* (first called *The Cleft of Light*), when it was published in 1978, offered a rich banquet of images, characters, and incidents, sometimes horrific, sometimes beautiful, sometimes humorous, sometimes tragic, but always infused with a humanism that allows us to find ourselves perhaps all too human. Known primarily as a journalist in print, television, and radio – a purveyor of prose – and a university teacher, the *Hogg Poems* were Callaghan's first sustained verse works. The drawings, too, were a sharp surprise, for their exhibition, coincident with their publication, in the Isaacs Gallery in Toronto would have had no public precedent.

Born of a period of gloom, the *Hogg Poems and Drawings* record a rebirth. For there to be a rebirth, there necessarily has to be a loss, a metaphorical death. Loss of a high profile career in journalism when he had to resign from the *Toronto Telegram* in 1971, loss of a correspondent career with the CBC, loss of a lover, and his hold on the university position tenuous and threatened . . . the world of Irish-Catholic Callaghan, still in his thirties, for whom success came easily and early, was in a state of accelerating disintegration in 1971.

Like artists before him, and surely many after him, he turned to his preferred medium, writing, and turned from prose to poetry, picking up on something born of the love affair with an Israeli actress while on assignment in

Jerusalem for the CBC in 1969 and 1970. Turning inward, in search of singulairty[2] and leaving behind the denizens of Toronto night life, Callaghan retreated to Swimming Snake Island, a distant island in Georgian Bay. There he sought to relieve the burden of loss, initially in the first person, but eventually in the persona of James Hogg (a real person of some notoriety), of Hogg's Hollow (a real place and a source of the pejorative name for Toronto, Hogtown) – pilgrim and poet, hero and outcast, loved and betrayed. In the retreat, the quest revealed.

I

Defiance, error, anomaly – all drawings by writers are decidedly troublesome.[3]

The realization of the poems is traceable in the manuscripts and typescripts Callaghan kept after publication of *The Hogg Poems and Drawings* in 1978.[4] They are, however, not mere manuscripts and typescripts. Callaghan has made these supports of transient expression carry another form of imagery: drawings executed after and over the texts – periods of silence. At the most fundamental material level, the paper is a type of tinted drawing paper. The text is sometimes written in ink, sometimes typed, often revised. The drawings may be ink (often fugitive felt-tip pen), sometimes enhanced with colour, sometimes overwhelmed by colour. The text is not sacred and may be found effaced, a shadow of itself. Callaghan did not retain all the sheets (some were sold, some were given away, others lost track of). There are over one hundred and fifty sheets of drawings, experimental palimpsests corresponding to the contemporary notion of the work of art as an event, rather than a thing. Such events – here drafts and drawings – are inseparable from their conditions and possibilities. They:

Track the making – the eventuation or becoming – out of a work of art whose object hood could already be said to be under erasure, as the visible track in the cloud chamber marks the path of an electron whose position and momentum are not simultaneously knowable . . . the boundaries of [the work's] achieved from (however exquisitely executed that form may be in itself) are virtual, provisional, permeable by the evidences of its own history as by the known, unknown, and unknowable conditions of its making.[5]

The combination of text and image presents a myriad of challenges. Is drawing a kind of writing? Is writing a kind of drawing? Should text and image be addressed separately, or as a combined phenomenon? What *is* this combined phenomenon? Graphic can refer to writing or a picture. One commentator has proposed a spectrum of the image and text phenomenon: at one end is the text, pure and simple; at the other end is the pure representational image, *sans* text. In the middle can be found all the variants of text and image combinations, carefully graded by the ratio of text to image. Surely these Hogg hybrids would find a position on that spectrum.[6] Some sense of the distinction between words and images is helpful. It can be put as simply as "words have a performative power of evocation . . . make present in the spirit something otherwise absent . . . The illustration presents,"[7] rendering the magical evocative properties of the text impotent, even dead. But this does not seem to occur in the Hogg hybrids. Both the words and the images are evocative, do not make each other impotent, and have achieved a unity of presence. The images are not illustrations in the conventional sense, although Callaghan does see the text and the image sharing a similar sensibility. They are, after all, from the same hand and mind: "what is at stake in the hand is the very nature of the psychic investments which are bound up in it."[8]

The Victorian critic John Rushkin published a long treatise on wood engraving entitled *Ariadne Florentina* (1876).[9] In it Rushkin proposes that both writing and drawing have the same source in the *first* scratch on a surface to make a design and that all such signs participate in labyrinthine assemblages to express "in one way or another love, war, death . . ."[10] The primordial scratch is an illuminating cleft, in the manner of the fissure or rift fundamental to Heidegger's notion of the work of art. When we ponder the work of art we obtain a sense of it as the concealing-revealing oscillation of Being itself, *a lighting.*

The suggestion that writing and drawing share some common character is entertained, too, in recent scholarship addressing "the question of the relationship between written text and its timid counterpart, problematical opposite, and unacknowledged twin: drawing."[11] Martine Reid, the editor of *Boundaries: Writing and Drawing* (1984), affirms that critics who study the development of texts from their origins in manuscript and draft form through revisions to the final printed volume often seem preoccupied with concerns of an aesthetic kind. They examine and analyze the figurative activities of the written letters and words, their layout on the page, characterizing the lazy pen or the energetic pen by the hesitations, jots, scribbles, doodles, and deletions found in the hand. Here is genuine evidence for the presence of the author so unceremoniously declared dead by Barthes and his followers. By offering the categories of *legibility* and *visibility,*[12] Reid is able to suggest another way to look at the relation between the written word and the image. Writing, as a communications tool, is more or less effective as it is more or less legible. Illegible writing is a demonstration of the erosion of the sign by its own figurative nature, always lurking close beneath the surface, ready to bring the figure back to the

status of a drawing. Drawing gives precedence to visibility over legibility. By conceptualizing the categories of
legible and visible, Reid has evoked the possibility of a
liminal space where transformation can take place:

> In the hazardous limbo between the legible and the visible
> . . . the illusory barrier between one domain and another
> is erased. And graphic representation appears: it appears
> during the pauses and hesitations in the thought process,
> when the pen can be caught accomplishing other gestures:
> additions, scribbles, and excessive embellishments of let-
> ters, the transformation of words, lines, and ink blots into
> head, animals (reviving some mimological effect) . . . [13]

In many of the Hogg pages, Callaghan's longhand shares
the field of the sheet of paper with the drawing (admittedly added after the writing), presenting the
reader/viewer with an opportunity to oscillate between
the legible and the visible. This dynamic movement
between the familiar signs in the text and the alien
superimposed images heightens the effect of the introduction of "sensation into the heart of the cognitive
process,"[14] – another *lighting*.

What of the poet's drawing process? How does he go
about it?

> Until there is pain, pain, all the muscles seizing, and I wait
> for it, the pain, to speak, picking up my pen, cross-hatch-
> ing the paper, cramped fingers, lines discovering bulbs of
> bodies, welded centres of stress, feet, toes, cunts, fingers,
> cocks, legs, I listen to how I have hurt them, a low
> whistling narrow gloom, a silence but a speaking as I watch
> my hand follow the pen, the lines dance . . . [15]

It is evident that the drawings are executed after the text
has been written and revised. The poet's first premise is
that the visual experience is equal to the verbal experi-

ence. In his poetry (as evident from his revisions on some of the pages) he attends to the positioning of the words on the page. Callaghan draws without a model; untrained, he works from the imagination, believing that the drawing process is "impelled from within, a line impels another line, a colour impels another colour."[16] There is no premeditation at all; the process is rather more like "the intuited discipline of a jazz player." When starting a drawing, he has no idea of what the image will be, but works with the black and white structure of the text of the page toward some formal visual coherence of text and image: "intuitive on the foundation of practice," the way jazz is played. There are no erasures, no revisions. What is put on the page is drawn with a surety that precludes change. This is not unusual. "There . . . emerges a sort of ethics of drawing, which forbids the use of an eraser, and which requires drawing to show everything without dissimulation."[17]

Drawing the image is seen as a filling-up of the space on the page, a "form of visual completion."[18] Callaghan believes that he has an ability to understand how space works, that he possesses a *spatial eye*, which accounts for his unfailing positioning of the line and the progress of the drawing down the page from the top in an unpremeditated way, both a veiling and an unveiling.[19] "The genesis of the text, as of any written mark (particularly that of drawing), must be considered from the viewpoint of the original spatial play which the hand stages."[20]

When the pages are examined in the light of the above, it becomes clear that there are some genuine differences between the image and text. Most notably, the texts are subject to extensive revisions, time and time again; they signify temporality, the "very duration that presides over their elaboration."[21] Lines are moved around in the same poem; words, phrases, lines and whole stanzas, are drafted and revised in longhand adjacent to a typewritten version (a text immobilized). The appearance of similar fragments in different poems shows the poet's quarrying technique, deleting and excising lines here and there, maybe later to be inserted into another poem. Unlike the drawings which are not changed or revised, recognition of the traces of the texts provides the traces of creation, leading to the printed poem.

On the sheet the text serves as a matrix for the drawing to *install* itself, seeking the organic formal relationship with the textured objects, most often, especially when typed, occupying the centre of the page. Longhand versions tend to flow more organically over the whole page. The open peripheries of the typescript are filled in. Apparent randomness is belied by writing's own aesthetic impulse. The poet's web of self-editing lines, linking one section to another, splitting a line here, centering a stanza along a vertical linear axis at another point, becomes integrated into the overall design, achieving a unity of presence. The poet takes advantage of the mobility of the line to inflect the static visual composition of the typescript.

Some drawings Callaghan has enhanced with colour. "In its relation to drawing, colour is mere ornament – superfluous, but also necessary, added to drawing as a type of supplement."[22] There are drawings in which colour is paramount, and these are often seen by the poet as series with strong formal and thematic relationships. Here, I want to introduce the *heads*, occurring in several journals (particularly in the one from 1986) and a sketchbook (1986-87), independent of the *Hogg Poems*, but related. Executed in oil pastels, richly characterized and entirely imaginative, Callaghan often identifies one or another with the personalities in the *Hogg Poems*, especially the cast of characters in the Third Book, who participate in the dark underside of Toronto life: "every face has a story; immortality is in the story." For Callaghan, the heads evoke associations with St. James, who lost his head to Herod Agrippa I, and the Cult of the Head, a Celtic phenomenon that resonates with his Irish heritage.[23]

The poetry and drawings differ in their mode of realization. The profound disparity between the unstable, revisionary presences of the texts, and the "permanence of the line laid down, nothing to be added or taken away" of the drawings, recalls distinctions Carl Jung made in his two papers on psychology and poetry.[24] Jung proposes that poetry is of two kinds: the first, works that derive wholly from the poet's intention to produce a particular result; the second, works that subordinate the poet, by forcing themselves in their own form upon the writer.[25] When we examine the fuller description of the first kind, we find there are parallels with Callaghan's mode of writing poetry:

> There are literary works, prose as well as poetry, that spring wholly from the author's intention to produce a particular result. He submits his material to a definite treatment with a definite aim in view; he adds to it and subtracts from it, emphasizing one effect, toning down another, laying on a touch of colour here, another there, all the time carefully considering the over-all result and paying strict attention to the laws of form and style. He exercises the keenest judgment and chooses his words with complete freedom. His material is entirely subordinated to his artistic purpose; he wants to express this and nothing else. He is wholly at one with the creative process, no matter whether he has deliberately made himself its spearhead, as it were, or whether it has made him its instrument so completely that he has lost all consciousness of this fact. In either case, the artist is so identified with his work that his intentions and his faculties are indistinguishable from the act of creation itself.[26]

On the other hand, Jung's description of the second class of works parallels Callaghan's drawing mode in which images:

> Flow more or less complete and perfect from the author's pen . . . These works positively force themselves upon the author; his hand is seized, his pan [draws] things that his mind contemplates with amazement . . . Here the artist is not identical with the process of creation . . .[27]

In the second essay, "Psychology and Literature," Jung sets out another informative pair of categories: the psychological and the visionary. In the psychological mode of artistic creation, the artists – poets, painters, etc. – find their materials for their creations in their conscious life: "with crucial experiences, powerful emotions, suffering, passion, the stuff of human fate in general." There is no doubt that the Hogg poems are inspired by the poet's everyday and commonplace experiences. Elevating them to the poetic, he makes us ". . . vividly aware of those everyday happenings which we tend to evade or overlook because we perceive them only dully or with a feeling of discomfort . . . Such themes constitute the lot of humankind . . . they fully explain themselves in their own terms."[28] In the visionary mode the reverse occurs; Jung should speak for himself:

> Here everything is reversed. The experience that furnishes the material for artistic expression is no longer familiar. It is something strange that derives its existence from the hinterland of man's mind, as if it had emerged from the abyss of prehuman ages, or from a superhuman world of contrasting light and darkness. It is a primordial experience which surpasses man's understanding and to which in his weakness he may easily succumb. The very enormity of the experience gives it its value and its shattering impact. Sublime, pregnant with meaning, yet chilling the blood with its strangeness, it arises from the timeless depths:

glamorous, daemonic, and grotesque, it bursts asunder our human standards of value and aesthetic form, a terrifying tangle of eternal chaos . . . the primordial experiences rend from top to bottom the curtain upon which is painted the picture of an ordered world, and allow a glimpse into the unfathomable abyss of the unborn and things to be. It is a vision of other worlds, or of the darkness of the spirit, or of the primal beginnings of the human psyche . . . We are astonished, confused, bewildered, put on our guard or even repelled; we demand commentaries and explanations. We are reminded of nothing in everyday life, but rather of dreams, nighttime fears, and the dark, uncanny recesses of the human mind.[29]

There is no reason why the poet cannot combine both modes in his work. The poet need not be exclusive.[30] The visionary mode, as Jung encapsulates it, is most significant for our understanding of the drawings. This is a pattern we have seen before, in which the text and the drawings seem to manifest strikingly different qualities: text is unstable, controlled by the poet, and inspired by the conscious world; images are stable, uncontrolled by the poet, and are rooted in the unconscious.

II
From couplings of incongruities . . . discovery is born.[31]

The automatic nature of Callaghan's drawing and the apparent source of the imagery in the unconscious necessitates a foray into the labyrinths of Surrealism, the literary and art movement that splintered off from Dada[32] under the leadership of André Breton in 1924, and grew to include the *verists* like the painter Salvador Dalí. Callaghan might be described as a verist, too. It has been noted that Surrealism ". . . upsets in the most spectacular way the old imperatives of differentiation"[33] between the word and the image. For Breton, "The essential discovery of Surrealism is that, without preconceived intention, the pen that flows in order to write and the pencil that runs in order to draw *spin* an infinitely precious substance."[34] Categorically, the *Hogg Poems* are not Surrealist in process or intention, although the often shocking juxtapositions of images may be received that way. Callaghan as a poet is too rooted in the history of the poetic form to follow a movement that made denial of aesthetic conventions one of its central tenets; the seeds of the *Hogg Poems* occur in a courtly love sonnet.

What I want to note here is a pattern. Callaghan makes the parallel of drawing with jazz. Jazz is disciplined, yet intuitive.[35] Surrealism advocated the primacy of the irrational or what may be more properly called the anti-rational. Recent scholarship has demonstrated that the Surrealist worked within a framework of conventional logic[36] to establish the field within which he (or she) could consciously choose a method like automatism ". . . to make discoveries he regarded as revelatory only so far as the automatic method allowed access to things his principles incited him to invest with significance."[37] Automatic responses are made "within a framework set up, in advance, so as to give a definite orientation to the inquiry in which all the players find themselves engaged."[38] There is a resonance here with Callaghan's understanding of how jazz works, and how he understands his drawing process.

Having established this affinity, do the *Hogg Poems* possess any of the characteristics associated with Surrealist images? Surrealist visual images are informed by a number of principles that are present regardless of the diversity of styles practised. An inventory of them would include freedom from imitation or arbitrary use of imitative devices, illogical juxtaposition of diverse visual elements, and spontaneous application of drawing procedures. Surrealist visual art manifests metamorphosis, transformation, distortion, and modification, disorder, fusion of forms, all of which can be found in Callaghan's drawings. The prominence of eyes, mouths, feet, toes, and fingers in company with breasts, vulvas, and penises, sometimes in grotesque and humorous fusions of body parts, sometimes floating disembodied on the page, often oriented by a cursory landscape with semicircular moon on a horizon line, would have a strong affinity with many surrealist paintings and drawings.

Callaghan is conscious of the organic nature of the body, the interconnectedness of the parts which become his vocabulary. Those parts are the extremities of the body. The extremities are the most vulnerable parts of the body and the most subject to pain. His egalitarian view of the parts of the body – *"cock and cunt, toes, head-bones, fingers, eyes, nipples, etc."* – is patently evident in the drawings; and the eyes – "The eyes [I's] are who you are."

Here, yet another difference between the *Hogg Poems* and drawings is highlighted: the poems are almost all predicated entirely upon gender differentiation, most notably, the heterosexual love affair of Book I. The fusion of the penises, breasts, vulvas, and other body parts in the drawings suggests a sort of "unification"[39] in a single amorphous form, potentially the focus of disgust and eros, often captured in the gaze of a head emerging from the labyrinth of lines or in (a) mislocated and genderless ironic eye(s) located somewhere in the form, not necessarily accompanied by the other expected features of the human visage. In the poetry, the unifying moment is "The Gift of Tongue." Here is a profound statement of organic oneness in which the whole patriarchal core of the Judeo-Christian belief in the separation of the flesh and the spirit is called into question: the moon-muse swallows the sun-poet in the presence of the minaret: "that stone shaft into / the mouth of god."

These drawings call to mind the excessive visions of Georges Bataille, who found himself dismissed by Breton for his repugnant, base, and excremental obsessions. Bataille wrote a novel *Histoire de l'Oeil (Story of an Eye)* (1928) and a shorter piece titled *L'Oeil (Eye)* in 1929, the same year *Le Gros Orteil* (The Big Toe) appeared in print in *Documents*, a somewhat luxurious art review, which he helped found. The ugly big toe, a "phenomenon of base seduction," part of a foot which leads an "ignoble life" in the mud, and when injured is "psychologically analogous to the brutal fall of man – in other words, to death," is "the most *human* part of the human body."[40] The seductive big toe, with its phallic associations, sums up ins short Bataille's project, the creation of "a vivid and disturbing image of a reconceiving of the human body, which dramatically violates the boundaries of gender."[41] In *Eye*, Bataille dwells upon the eye in nightmarish contexts: a cannibal delicacy, an eye of conscience, the hideous scene in the *Andalusian Dog*, and a mid-nineteenth century J. J. Grandville illustration of the *Dream: Crime and Expiation*, in which a criminal is pursued by a large disembodied eye in the sky.[42]

In *Histoire de L'Oeil*, Bataille's literary eye[43] is transformed by a series of metaphoric substitutions for the globular object – eggs, testicles, the sun, etc. and fluid contained – yolk, tears, urine, sperm, etc. The interaction of the two series of images activates a machine-like production of yet another, infinite series of images; e.g., tearful eggs, sunny sperm, pissing sun, etc. These images are not the result of chance meetings, the characteristic that would make them Surrealist. This conclusion is founded upon the conventional understanding of Surrealism as wholly irrational, an understanding we have seen to be insupportable. But if irrational is replaced by anti-rational, then it can be argued that the metaphors may indeed be Surrealist.[44] The presence of the two series of metaphorical substitutions serves as a rational framework for the game of producing the third series, a never-ending relay of images, combined and recombined, "a perfectly spherical metaphor."[45] The round eye,[46] thus, lacking a point of origin in the real world, deprived of a beginning, stands for a perfectly ambiguous identity – a round phallicism – which collapses the differentiation between what is properly masculine and properly feminine, permitting "transgression" and the destruction of "meaning/being." Recall the unifying moon-sun, minaret-mouth imagery in "The Gift of Tongue."

Callaghan's focus in the drawings on the body extremities serves as an analogue of the rational framework set up by the Surrealists when they carried out one of their projects. He can achieve countless different combinations of the parts. The forms in the drawings make up one series of potential metaphors (e.g., the eye as I, the toe as the phallus, moon as the muse, sun as the poet, etc.). The poems in their various revisions and final form are made up of other series of unstable metaphors (e.g., the eye as rolling wheel, the eye's tears as "stones," boiled eggs as eyes, stone as heart, stones as testicles, stones as horses, Jerusalem as the sea of stone, etc.[47]). The interaction of the two series offers the potential of a third series, an infinite number of associations and parallels, a never-ending relay of images, combined and recombined, "a perfectly spherical metaphor," made possible by Callaghan's union of text and image on the page.

But contrary to the appearance of disorder in the drawings and the destruction of "meaning/being" inherent in the transgressive interaction of the drawings and the Hogg poems, the goal of the poetry is the reconstitution of lost meaning/being: descent (a state of loss) is followed by ascent to a state of atonement and unity.

The drawings, "periods of silence and mediation locked in stone," and the texts form a whole.

Bataille was a medievalist, and in this fact there is a clue to a shared sensibility or temperament. Callaghan has read St. Victor and facsimiles of medieval manuscripts. He has translated the poetry of Robert Marteau, a French poet who lived briefly in Quebec, and who has a propensity for griffins, other fantastic creatures, and alchemy (as do the Surrealists and Jung). Callaghan acknowledges a predilection for what he terms "gargoyle humour" when some of his images were compared to the kinds of monstrosities medieval illustrators and sculptors found to populate the margins in the codices of the faithful and to teach the unlettered as they passed through the cathedral entrances. Single-footed creatures that hopped around on one foot (not unlike one of the drawings published in the first edition of the *Hogg Poems and Drawings*) using their oversized foot as a sunshade, one-eyed Cyclopes, headless creatures with the facial features in their torsos, big-eared creatures that used their ears as blankets when sleeping,[48] all wondrous grotesqueries from the margins of medieval European experience.

Marteau persuaded Callaghan to make the pilgrimage to Santiago de Compostela, a major destination during the Middle Ages for the faithful who wished to prove their faith.

Callaghan's empathy for the medieval leads to the grotesque.[49] The grotesque as an aesthetic category has attracted the attention of the likes of Ruskin, Schlegel, Kant, and Hegel among others. The grotesque compels human attention. Its characteristics according to Hegel include the unjustified fusion of different realms of being, excess and distortion, the unnatural multiplication of one and the same function, the presence of numerous arms, head, etc.[50] For one critic, the fusion of animal and human forms reduces the grotesque to the fantastically comic,[51] although if a body part makes itself independent we have a genuine grotesque. Callaghan's figures fall somewhere in this spectrum. And there is some inkling that Hogg himself might be on the border-line: *The Temptation of St. Anthony* is one of the root motifs of the fantastic grotesque signified by his attribute, a pig. The same critic believes that Surrealism rejected the quest for the grotesque, basing his position on the conventional idea that the Surrealists were intent on the destruction of logic. We have seen that this is not entirely an accurate assessment, and that the Surrealist mind, more precisely described as anti-rational, works within a framework established by reason and logic: ". . . the surrealists' experiments aimed at prospecting the irrational are particularly revealing of their attitude toward poetry and of the conduct it imposes on surrealist poets intent upon retaining and using faculties that the mad patently have lost"[52] – logic and reason.

To be anti-rational is to locate oneself somewhere between the irrational and the rational, a middle zone where we, in our naïveté, encounter the grotesque, "our attention . . . arrested, our understanding unsatisfied."[53] Composed of fragmented, jumbled, and corrupted monstrousness, familiar forms that should be kept separate are shuffled and fused in unfamiliar, illegitimate, and repulsive ways to achieve the grotesque. This could be a description of Callaghan's forms. The intensity of our experience of the grotesque is conditioned by the degree of our naïveté. The grotesque spurs us to interpretive activity, turns us into instant exegetes. We seek closure in explanatory metaphor, analogy, or allegory, but such closure is costly since the mind is poised between "death and rebirth, insanity and discovery, rubble and revelation,"[54] between heaven and hell, a dynamic and unpredictable mid-region where actual transformation or metamorphosis occurs.[55] This location and its attributes echo the *Wall of Paradise* which, concealing God from human sight, Nicholas of Cusa described "as constituted" of the "coincidence of opposites," its gate being guarded by the "highest spirit of reason, who bars the way until he has been overcome." The pairs of opposites (being and non-being, life and death, beauty and ugliness, good and evil, and all the other polarities that bind the faculties to hope and fear, and link the organs of action to deeds of defence and acquisition) are, according to Joseph Campbell, "the clashing rocks (Symplegades) that crush the traveller, but between which heroes always pass"[56] in the mythic quest for the Self; that is, Jung's process of individuation.

> The process of individuation is the search for a pragmatic individual interpretation: steering the dangerous course between chaos and sterility for direct contact with the unconscious. In effect, the individual "in search of effective images" – symbols to satisfy his need for "wholeness" – recapitulates in his own development, now undertaken consciously, the structure of the unconscious development of the histories of cultures.[57]

The central premise of myth is Protean, a perpetual metamorphosis of a thousand faces in a cosmic passage, the stories of which mediate inherent contradictions, or what anthropologist Edmund Leach termed binary discriminations: human/superhuman; mortal/immortal; male/female; legitimate/illegitimate; good/bad.[58] Accordingly, all realms of being (visible, invisible, past, present) are equally accessible and mutually interdependent, following the "law of infinite metaphor," by which everything is potentially identical with everything else, [and which] ". . . illuminates all of mythic thought, and thus the sources of our response to the grotesque . . . mythic thought, which begins with an intuitive perception of metaphor, not in the sense that myth uses figures of speech, but in the root sense of the word – 'carrying across' established boundaries, perceiving a unity of essence . . ."[59] in what reason would find absurd, in the grotesque. The double motion of resisting and inviting interpretation, common to both metaphor and the grotesque, is likewise what enlivens, but does not replace, art of all kinds.

III

Holy Holy Holy
He went to Jerusalem.[60]

The quest itself is . . . understood as the manifestation of
a primordial or archetypal urge or drive.[61]

Poets come in the evening into the Old City
and they emerge from it pockets stuffed with images
and metaphors and little well-constructed parables
and crepuscular smiles from among columns and crypts,
from within darkening fruit
and delicate filigree of hammered hearts.[62]

Hogg the hero is a pilgrim Everyman, repeating the perilous journey to the Holy City undertaken by countless others before him, descending into the "crooked lanes of his own spiritual labyrinth"[63] – "lean alleys," "Ramla Road," "26 the Avenue of Suleiman the Almsmenor," "The Street of Chains," "Agan Lane,"[64] – in quest of the Self: "the totality of the psyche embracing both the conscious and the unconscious, including the individual's rootedness in the matrix of the collective unconscious."[65] Callaghan took the first step, withdrawing from his disintegrating external world into the internal world, to engage the symbols of the dominant mythology in a renewal of life, a rebirth.

Hogg was born on Swimming Snake Island, named for the occasion when the poet found himself swimming beside a snake. The primordial imagery of the collective unconscious cannot be ignored by our pilgrim, for anyone of the symbolical figures he encounters may swallow him, although symbolism "has gone all to shit. It's not felt any more. It's just idea."

Callaghan has cast Hogg in the Christian mode.[66] The poet uses imagery drawn from the language and the incident of the life of Christ (in the tone of the Douay and/or King James Version) commencing with Hogg's allegorical crucifixion. "Christ-quisling" on the "killing floor;"[67] the crucifixion will lead to a resurrection.[68] Hogg, the pilgrim sets out for Jerusalem to seek the answer to the paradox of art not living up to reality. Even the earliest pilgrims endured "an intensely ambivalent experience: the real destination, the celestial Jerusalem, is unreachable, and the arrival at what might have come to seem, from far away, sacred territory would only make more vivid the absence of sacred events and presences from the mundane world of which, after all, it is a part."[69] Hogg moves through the hero's progress in the quest, marking off the stages from the encounter on the Abu Gosh Road with the archetypal Wise Old Man, redeemer, helper, "a man taking names, who had the enamelled eye of the mole who never sleeps,"[70] to rescue by the community of monks, to meeting the beautiful woman who offers him gifts.[71] But the promise of Paradise, "East of where Eden was,"[72] comes to a wrenching end in "At the Lazarus Stone": *"And the swine, though he divide the hoof, and he be cloven-footed, yet he cheweth not the cud; he is unclean to you."*[73] "The meeting with the goddess (who is incarnate in every woman) is the final test of the talent of the hero to win the boon of love (charity: *amor fati*), which is life itself enjoyed as the encasement of eternity."[74] But the test is aborted, not because Hogg "refused to admit the fullness of that pushing, self-protective, malodorous, carnivorous, lecherous fever which is the very nature of the organic cell,"[75] but rather, the lover, ultimately was unable to betray her tribe. Burdened with the baggage of a patriarchal "puritanical, world-negating ethical system" that radically transfigures all the images of the myth, "the goddess of the flesh [became] the queen of sin"[76] in her own mind and rejects Hogg. Hogg must begin the quest again, now into the belly of his birth city, Toronto, "A Whale of a City."[77] The Toronto subway is a fissure, a rift in the Heideggerean sense, and essential condition of the work of art, both a concealing and an unconcealing, and serves as a figure of the light of Being – a Lighting. The thunderclapped Hogg regains consciousness at Sheppard[78] (not *Shepherd*) Station, and commences to do the stations, not of the *Cross*, but of the Yonge Street subway, where he meets a cast of characters fitting for a contemporary "divine comedy": jazz pianist Sweet Meat Manzone; Dorado, the dwarf disc jockey; Canned Heat, the hermaphrodite; Medusa among the Moochers; Hell's Belle; Sisyphus the Crack King; Doctor Ded; Momma Anno; John the Conqueroo Decatur; Bad Blood Jeremiah Stuck[79] . . . are only the ones recorded.

Will Hogg achieve atonement? "Behold the whole Hogg."[80] And what is the boon? *The Hogg Poems and Drawings*.

Conclusion

The progress of the work becomes the poet's fate and determines his psychology.[81]

The whole Hogg: the *cleft* parts have been rejoined. Contrary to the dominant belief in the Christian church,[82]

Callaghan believes that the flesh and the spirit are one. Image and text share the unity of the page, proffer a unity of presence. Surrealism is concerned fundamentally with the pursuit of a unity: "one of the basic characteristics of the surrealist mind is its uncompromising will to find a foolproof unity in the universe."[83] The Surrealist alliance of poetry and visual art demonstrated the fusion of art and life, denied their separateness. Such a fusion could occur because Surrealism aimed for the "total recovery of our psychic force by a means which is none other than the dizzying descent into ourselves, the systematic illumination of hidden places and the progressive darkening of other places, the perpetual excursion into the midst of forbidden territory."[84]

Mythic thought in all its manifestations seeks unity. All things, in all realms of being – visible, invisible, past, present – share continuities and are connected in labyrinthine ways: "equally accessible and mutually interdependent . . . Spirit and the flesh are one interdependent. Distance between the natural and the civilized is abolished."[85] By drawing upon the Christian myth, Callaghan brings Hogg into a state of oneness, paralleling the condition in which "Christ [does] not merely *symbolize* wholeness, but as a psychic phenomenon, he [is] wholeness."[86] Unremarked until now, there is a series of drawings showing multiple profiles or three-quarter views of heads joined together. The Janus heads recall the theme of betrayal in the poems, but may also be viewed as the faces of love and loss (the fertility/fatality complex). "Faces of a single force that annihilates individual identity, absorbing it into the flux"[87] – birth death, rebirth – without beginning, without end. The mythic manifestations of the collective unconscious are, according to Jung,[88] compensatory to the conscious attitude, in effect bringing a dangerous, one-sided condition of consciousness into a state of balance or equilibrium:

the male animus (paternal *logos*) is compensated by the female anima (maternal *eros*). The unity of presence of the manuscripts of the Hogg poems *(logos)* and drawings *(eros)* is a material manifestation of a search for the middle way, the equilibrium necessary for atonement in the flux of infinite metaphor.

Notes

1. Gombrich, Ernst, *The Heritage of Apelles,* 64, cited in Harpham, Geoffrey Galt, *On the Grotesque: Strategies of Contradiction in Art and Literature* (Princeton University Press, 1982), 176.
2. This is Callaghan's preferred *poetic* term as opposed to Self.
3. Reid, Martine, "Legible/Visible," in Reid, Martine, ed., *Boundaries: Writing and Drawing,* Yale French Studies, 84 (1984), 1.
4. Republished in 1997 in a new edition including poems from *Stone Blind Love* (1988) as *Hogg: The Poems and Drawings,* Hayden Carruth, intro. (Toronto: Little, Brown and Company (Canada) Ltd., 1997). References are to this edition. The drawings divide themselves into three groups: 1) finished drawings without manuscript, many of which were published in 1978 and exhibited at Isaacs Gallery; 2) unpublished drawings, both with and without manuscripts of poems; and 3) a series of heads dating from 1986-87.
5. Froula, Christine, "Modernity, Drafts, Genetic Criticism: On the Virtual Life of James Joyce's Villanelle," In Contat, Michel, Denis Hollier, and Jacques Neefs, eds., *Drafts,* Yale French Studies, 89 (1996), 114.
6. Miller, J. Hillis, *Illustration* (Cambridge: Harvard University Press, 1992), 73.
7. Ibid., 67.
8. Tisseron, Serge, "All Writing is Drawing: The Spatial Development of the Manuscript," in Reid ed., *Boundaries: Writing and Drawing,* 29.
9. Ruskin, John, *Ariadne Florentina. Six Lectures on Wood and Metal Engraving* (Sunnyside: George Allen, 1876).
10. Miller, 75. A scratch is a cleft. Cleft has as synonyms "fissure" and "rift," terms that establish connection with Heidegger's essay "The Origin of the Work of Art," in Heidegger, Martin, *Basic Writings,* Krell, David Farrell ed. (San Francisco: Harper San Francisco, 1977), 143 ff. This is a slightly abridged version.

11. Reid, 1.
12. Ruskin introduces visibility as a category. For the engraver "Visibility is quite essential to your fame as permanence," 29.
13. Reid, 7.
14. Ruskin citing Jacques Leenhardt, "See and Describe: On a Few Drawings by Stendahl," in Reid ed., *Boundaries: Writing and Drawing*, 81 ff.
15. Callaghan, *Hogg*, 63. See Ruskin for a different view of drawing. "The quality of a pen drawing is to be produced easily – deliberately always, but with a point that *glides* over the paper," 30.
16. This and all other unattributed quotations are from an interview in Barry Callaghan's home 17-18 February, 1997.
17. Roque, Georges, "Writing/Drawing/Color," in Reid ed., *Boundaries: Writing and Drawing*, 47-8.
18. See for comparison Gaudon, Jean, "One of Victor Hugo's Discarded Drafts," in Contat, et al, ed., *Drafts*: "Hugo's drafts are visual compositions as well as verbal ones, and are often organized according to visual needs . . ." 139.
19. Miller, 78.
20. Tisseron, 29.
21. Viatte, Françoise, "Weaving a Rope of Sand," in Contat, et al, eds., *Drafts*, 87. This study focuses upon the changes artists make to *drawings*, likening a change to a *repentance*. "An exhibition on repentance in drawing might amount to a chronicle of effacement; it is the secretly audible sound of a writing taking shape, of a voice that is willing to correct itself...It seems that the strictly moral sense of repentance, as an expression of the regret inspired by error and the will to rectify, to "do penitence," can be applied by analogy to the idea that correction is attached to expression. Repentance, in its most undifferentiated form, could simultaneously include constant transformation in the incomplete, the unfinished, and rapid accumulation of ideas that would lead, paradoxically, to a kind of 'fixed idea,'" 88.
22. Roque, 55.
23. The head rather than the heart was the home of the soul for the ancient Celts. According to Diodorus Siculus, the Irish "cut off the heads of enemies slain in battle and attach them to the necks of their horses. The blood-stained spoils they hand over to their attendants and carry off as booty, while striking up a paean and singing a song of victory; and they nail up these fruits upon their houses, just as those who lay low wild animals in certain kinds of hunting. "They embalm in cedar oil the heads of the most distinguished enemies, and preserve them carefully in a chest, display them with pride to strangers, saying that for this head, one of their

ancestors, or his father, or the man himself refused the offer of a large sum of money. They say that some of them boast that they refused the weight of the head in gold; thus displaying what is only a barbarous kind of magnanimity, for it is not a sign of nobility to refrain from selling the proofs of one's valour." Cited in Ellis, Peter Berresford, *A Dictionary of Irish Mythology* (London: Constable, 1987), 141.

24. "On the Relation of Analytical Psychology to Poetry," 65 ff. and "Psychology and Literature," 85 ff. in Jung, C. G., *The Spirit in Man, Art, and Literature* (Princeton: Princeton University Press, 1966).

25. Jung names these respectively *introverted* and *extroverted*. See Jung, "on the Relation of Analytical Psychology to Poetry," 72 ff.

26. Ibid.

27. Ibid.

28. Jung, "Psychology and Literature," 89.

29. Ibid.

30. Given the importance of the love affair in Callaghan's life at this time, we can probably see it serving as the stimulus for the visionary aspects of the Hogg poems. See Jung's discussion of Goethe's *Faust* and Dante's *Divine Comedy*: "It even seems as if the love-episode had served as a mere release, or had been unconsciously arranged for a definite purpose, and as if the personal experience were only a prelude to the all important 'divine comedy.'" "The creator of this kind of art is not the only one who is in touch with the night-side of life; prophets and seers are nourished by it too." *Ibid.* 95.

31. Harpham, *On the Grotesque,* 29.

32. The international movement, based in New York and Zuich, dating from 1915-1923, that encoraged "discarding a certain mental attitude and ensuring that we were not influenced, either by our immediate environment or by the past...ridding ourselves of clichés . . . freeing ourselves" (Marcel Duchamp, 1946).

33. Reid, 5.

34. Breton quoted in Poling, Clark V., *Surrealist Vision and Technique: Drawings and Collages from the Pompidou Center and the Picasso Museum, Paris* (Atlanta: the Michael C. Carlos Museum, 1996), 23.

35. Intuition: immediate apprehension independent of any reasoning process.

36. The Surrealist projects were arranged to "give rational minds the impression of having explored the irrational." Matthews, J. H., *Surrealism, Insanity, Poetry* (Syracuse: Syracuse University Press, 1982), 117. See page 121 for his distinction between irrational and anti-rational.

37. Matthews, J. H., *The Surrealist Mind* (Selinsgrove: Susquehanna University Press, 1991), 37.
38. Matthews, *Surrealism, Insanity, Poetry*, 114.
39. ". . . the great Neoplatonic philosophers of the Renaissance . . . for whom the most perfect form was that of the divine androgyne or "divine hermaphrodite" – a form that was perfect because it was complete (man and woman) and autonomous or self-sufficient, capable of procreating and parturating at one and the same time, creator of its own self." See Gandelman, Claude, "The Author as "Traumarbeiter": On Sketches of Dreams by Marcel Proust," in Reid ed., *Boundaries: Writing and Drawing*, 131.
40. Bataille, Georges, *Visions of Excess: Selected Writings 1927-39* Stoekl, Allan, ed. (Minneapolis: University of Minnesota Press, 1985), "The Eye," 17 ff., "The Big Toe," 20 ff.
41. Poling, *Surrealist Vision and Technique*, 44.
42. Callaghan, the aficionado of gambling, informed me that this is the name of the watchdog of the gambling tables.
43. Krauss, Rosalind, "Giacometti" in Rubin, William, ed., *"Primitivism" in 20th Century Art: Affinity of the Tribal and the Modern* (New York: Museum of Modern Art, 1984), 513-15, recapitulating Barthes' "The Metaphor of the Eye" in R. Barthes, *Critical Essays* Richard Howard, trans. (Evanston: Northwestern University Press, 1992), 239 ff.
44. Barthes, "The Metaphor of the Eye," notes that "here we encounter the law of the surrealist image, formulated by Reverdy and adopted by Breton (*the more distant and accurate the relations of two realities, the stronger the image*)."
45. Krauss, 513, citing Barthes' commentary on Bataille's *Histoire de L'Oeil.*
46. The drawing is unlocated, but we reproduce the image from the 1978 edition of *The Hogg Poems and Drawings.*
47. Callaghan, *Hogg*, 59, 24, 49, 36, 46, 47, 17.
48. All with wondrous Latin names, often the result of monkish errors in transcription from one manuscript to another. See Friedman, John Block, *The Monstrous Races in Medieval Art and Thought* (Cambridge: Harvard University Press, 1981) for a full inventory of the *Plinian races.*
49. Callaghan brought Sherwood Anderson's "The Book of the Grotesque," the first story in *Winesburg, Ohio* (1919) to my attention: "It was the truths that made the people grotesques. The old man [a writer] had quite an elaborate theory concerning the matter. It was his notion that the moment one of the people took one of the truths to himself, called it his truth, and tried to live his life by it, he became a grotesque and the truth he

embraced became a falsehood." The Viking Critical Library Edition (Penguin Books, 1996), 25.

50. Kayser, Wolfgang, *The Grotesque in Art and Literature* Ulrich Weisstein, trans. (Gloucester, Peter Smith, 1968), 102.
51. *Ibid.*, 103.
52. Matthews, *Surrealism, Insanity, Poetry*, xii.
53. Harpham, *On the Grotesque*, 3. The following is derived from Harpham's discussion.
54. *Ibid.*, 18.
55. Callaghan would propose here that he is poised between the racial "black and white." See "The Wrong Shoe," *Hogg*, 113.
56. Campbell, Joseph, *The Hero With A Thousand Faces* (Princeton: Princeton University Press, 1972), 89.
57. Philipson, Morris, *Outline of a Jungian Aesthetics* (2nd ed., Boston: Sigo Press, 1994), 8.
58. Cited in Harpham, *On the Grotesque*, 53.
59. *Ibid.*, 52.
60. Callaghan, *Hogg*, "Inside His Wooden Suit," 15.
61. Laszlo, Violet de, "Introduction," xxv, C. G. Jung, *Psyche and Symbol: A Selection from the Writings of C. G. Jung* R. F. C. Hull, trans. (Princeton: Princton University Press, 1991).
62. Amichai, Yehuda, *The Selected Poetry of Yehuda Amichai*, Chana Bloch and Stephen Mitchell eds. And trans. (Berkeley: University of California Press, 1996), 53.
63. Campbell, *The Hero With a Thousand Faces*, 101.
64. Callaghan, *Hogg*, 39, 49, 26, 21, 49.
65. Laszlo, "Introduction," xxvi, C. G. Jung, *Psyche and Symbol.*
66. Christian imagery reaches its symbolic climax in the Eucharist with the image of wine and the wafer (Callaghan's persistent moonlike wafer), consumed by the faithful. The fullness of the imagery is seen also in Joyce's *Portrait of the Artist as a Young Man.* Joyce's villanelle conjoins the imagery of sexual desire with that of the Eucharist. Joyce, James, *Portrait of the Artist as a Young Man* (London: Palladin Books), 1988, 221-8.
67. Callaghan, *Hogg*, 13.
68. "If we see the traditional figure of Christ as a parallel to the psychic manifestation of the self, then the antichrist would correspond to the shadow of the self, namely the dark half of the human totality, which ought not to be judged too optimistically." Jung, "Christ, a Symbol of the Self," in *Psyche and Symbol*, 42.
69. Campbell, Mary B., *The Witness and the Other World: Exotic European Travel Writing, 400-1600* (Ithaca: Cornell University Press, 1988), 40.
70. Callaghan, *Hogg*, 16.

71. *Ibid.,* 19.
72. *Ibid.,* 59.
73. Leviticus 11:7.
74. Campbell, *The Hero With a Thousand Faces,* 118.
75. *Ibid.,* 121.
76. *Ibid.,* 123.
77. Callaghan, *Hogg,* 83.
78. *Ibid.,* 84.
79. *Ibid.,* 86, 88, 90, 95, 97, 101, 106, 115, 119.
80. *Ibid.,* 133.
81. Jung, "Psychology and Literature," 103.
82. "In the Christian concept...the archetype is hopelessly split into two irreconcilable halves, leading ultimately to a metaphysical dualism – the final separation of the kingdom of heaven from the fiery world of the damned." C. G. Jung, "Christ, a Symbol of the Self," in Jung, *Psyche and Symbol,* 42.
83. Matthews, *The Surrealist Mind,* 19 quoting Anna Balakian, *Surrealism: The Road to the Absolute* (1959).
84. Breton, André, *Manifestoes of Surrealism* (Ann Arbor: The University of Michigan Press, 1972), 136-7.
85. Harpham, *On the Grotesque,* 51.
86. Jung, "Christ, a Symbol of the Self," in Jung, *Psyche and Symbol,* 62, note 75.
87. Harpham, *On the Grotesque,* 58.
88. Jung, "Psychology and Literature," 89.

HOGG

An Introduction

Hayden Carruth

Barry Callaghan of Toronto originally created *The Hogg Poems and Drawings* during the 1970s and published them in 1978. It was an event of signal importance, registered as such in the consciousness of readers throughout North America, although not on as large a scale as it merited. To say the least, the very least, Hogg is an extraordinary cultural personage in our conspectus. A few years later, in 1988, Callaghan published *Stone Blind Love,* which was soon recognized, by him and others, as pure Hogg, in spite of its ostensible topic – a dying mother. Now Callaghan has combined the two, edited them, revised them. The result is the present volume, which gives us the entire text and a good section of the drawings; in other words, the entire vision of Hogg, this momentous lyrical and epical triumph.

Who was Hogg? James Hogg was a settler in York, as Toronto was called then, in the early years of the nineteenth century. He built a cabin and began to build a church in an area north of the main community, an area which became known as Hogg's Hollow, as it is still called today. During the rebellion of 1837, Mackenzie's Rebellion, James Hogg became aware of rebel forces approaching from the north, and he hurried south from his cabin along Yonge Road to warn the Tory officers – and that is all one needs to know, that is, that Hogg sought and found his destiny in betrayal.

Years later York became officially Toronto, but the city is still known across the country as Hogtown. Yonge

Road became Yonge Street, reaching, as Torontonians like to say, from the shore of Lake Ontario into the nowhere of the North Pole. Along it the city's first subway line was built. Its northern terminus was just above Hogg's Hollow, and the name of the station is Sheppard Station. And the southernmost stop is, significantly, Union Station, near the Lake.

Hogg, having come up for air, so to speak, in a cold dark country, feels driven by remorse, paranoia, and who knows what else? He sets out to seek redemption, such as he may hope to find it in our world and our time. Traveling toward the sun, he goes to a city, Jerusalem, where he hopes the word will be Holy Holy Holy. (One must note that when he was younger Barry Callaghan was for several years a correspondent in the Near East, reporting on the Black September War to Canadian newspapers, radio and television.) What Hogg finds is not redemption, of course. He finds a surreal melange of displacement, desecration, and violence. He also finds prophets hawking old bones and a desert woman with whom he has an intense but anxious and somewhat mysterious affair, only to be rejected by her ultimately when she returns to the isolation of her own people.

Back in Hogg's Hollow, Hogg is devastated and falls into silence. The unspeaking stone of the desert, replete in its anguish, has returned to him. Yet Hogg's silence is an articulate silence because he begins to produce his drawings. Hogg the poet becomes Hogg the imager when his writing hand fails to come up with words. Instead he finds a nightmarish imagery of sexual and religious violence in his inner consciousness. His hand delineates not merely despair but the forms of the unspeakable, in which he nevertheless finds ultimately a way back from silence into poetry again, into the city. And so begins his final journey, the subway trip through the stations of the city's underground from Sheppard Station to Union Station, like Jonah in the whale's belly; this is Book Three, the concluding book, of the poem.

Throughout one encounters an astonishingly rich amalgam of symbolic images from religious, sexual, cultural, and even geographical contexts. The surreal sensibility of the entire twentieth century, so resolutely metaphysical, from Kafka and Dali and Buster Keaton down to the Bread and Puppet Circus of today, is recapitulated – synthesized and harmonized. But in addition one recognizes the conspicuous intermixture of the sensibility of the North American underclass – Irish, Jewish, and especially African American. The wry accommodation to hardship and inequity, so characteristic of the blues, is evident in both the attitudes of the poems and in their language, which is heavily rhythmic and full of street idiom. Some of the poems sound like rap, with its concentrated rhyming and propulsive beat, until one stops to think that the poems were written years before rap became a specifiable genre; both rap and Callaghan's poems have a common source in the music of the 1940s, 1950s, and 1960s. But the most astonishing thing to contemplate in these poems is the way all these elements, from the haute monde and the demi-monde and a dozen other mondes as well, are combined in one work without the least forcing.

And beneath it all one discovers the Christian, even Catholic, even Irish Catholic ethos transplanted to Hogtown and the twentieth century, and significantly revised in an epos of betrayal. Judas, the existentialist anti-hero par excellence, is seen to be in covert co-conspiracy with Jesus, the two bound in the myth and meaning of betrayal. Only this view permits Hogg at last to emerge into light and communion.

No one could be better suited to accomplish this than Barry Callaghan. He has lived in Toronto all his life but has traveled extensively and from time to time has sojourned in Jerusalem, Rome, and Paris. His other writing – novels, poems, essays – is well known. He has been close to the roots of international literary and philosophical consciousness through his work as publisher and editor of *Exile*, the literary quarterly, and Exile Editions, the book-publishing house. His television documentary on the blues, featuring such friends of his as Brownie McGhee, Sonny Terry, Muddy Waters, and Otis Spann, remains a classic. He has performed his poetry in concert with blues and jazz musicians in Toronto, New York, and Europe. He is as thoroughly cosmopolitan as anyone in the jet age can be, and yet at the same time he has the humane recorder's eye for the suffering and degradation of ordinary men and women everywhere.

Hence we have the poems and drawings of Hogg. They comprise an existentialist epic without equal, though such other anti-heroes as Beckett's man in the trash can, Berryman's Henry, or the drummer boy created by Günther Grass may come to mind. The more you attend to Hogg, the more you see and understand the twists and turns, connections and combinations, of his mind. And of course the whole work is wrought in a remarkably original texture of expression, classic and classy, unforgettable. Like other supreme works, the poems and drawings of Hogg have the quality of being immediately indispensable in their moment of existence – which always is now.

Callaghan Powerful

George Elliot Clarke

Barry Callaghan is Anglo-CanLit writ large. The far-sighted publisher of Exile Editions and avant-garde editor of the literary journal *Exile*, he is also a damn good writer. In *Hogg The Seven Last Words*, Callaghan gives us a verse-novel, mainly about Hogg, who finds himself in Leningrad, pondering much, but especially Russian and Soviet history and literature.

Hogg's odyssey begins, appropriately enough, with an epigraph from Charles Baudelaire, whose Dark Romantic vision suits an era containing gulags and the Holocaust. No wonder the first poem casts Hogg as a "soldier [who] knee-deep / in blood bled to death." Early on our hero understands, post-Dachau, "Love is a caveat" and "All light seeds the dark."

This poem-novel is really a discourse on the lousy twentieth century, where death, in many cruel and bloody Aprils (and other months), "undid so many" (to refer to T.S. Eliot). Hogg ambles the wasteland of fatal ideologies, looking for love, but finding the memory of stacked-up corpses: "He saw / ice inlaid in light / along the canal // and old men / fishing / for their sons // under birch trees / hung / with the severed tongues // of bells tolled at Lubyanka // where bodies were laid out / pearled with blood . . ."

Callaghan employs free verse and rhyme to narrate Hogg's emotions and insights, but the poems all share one fact in common: every line is centred on the page, whether one is eyeing quatrains or stanza-less poems. The device allows for a balancing of traditional and post-modern esthetics.

Callaghan's imagery is smart, tough, beautiful and believably suffused with Russo-Soviet life. It is also accurately feeling: "he saw her turn naked / from washing her auburn hair // to ask if true love / ever comes true."

Hogg The Last Seven Words is so good a verse-novel that it reads hauntingly like a combination of Derek Walcott and the movie, *Casablanca*. Its superiority is found in the righteous juxtapositions of story, wisdom, images: "They / can hang / light bulbs / by / a / vinyl / cord // but / the poet / hangs / by / his / spinal / cord."

FISHING FOR HOGG
IN THE MIDNIGHT SUN

David Sobelman

For here were men and women intent upon
The mystery lying hid beyond the tomb.

W. W. E. Ross

Dear D.,

After forty years of reading poetry, and "reading" those who write it, I feel confident enough to let this letter speak for itself. Make of it what you will.

I'll write about, as well as question and analyze, the character radiating brightly from the work of a poet who calls himself Hogg, for two simple reasons: 1) I know the poet, I've been reading his work for twenty-five years, and 2) you said, "you *never* read poetry but you *always* enjoy reading my letters." So be it, then. If while reading this letter "the graces of poetry" do become apparent to you, no one would be happier than I. I will focus my letter mainly around two of Hogg's books, *Hogg The Poems and Drawings* and *Hogg The Seven Last Words*.

More specifically, I will use two poems, "Prologue" from the first Hogg book, the book of Hogg's youth, and "Ice Fishing" from Hogg's second book, the book of Hogg's last days.

Prologue
In this
land of eelgrass
and ice drifts and snow, how does a
man live through an endless winter of endless
nights, and how does he stay sane while sitting

squat hour after hour by a seal hole in the ice,
waiting for the snout of the seal, for the one heave
of the harpoon that he can make into the dark
water, and then groping in the water under the ice,
feeling for the dead bulk of the seal body, hauling
it home, the moment of triumph as brief as the
arctic summer in which the sun shines
all night, exhausting itself in a last
lunge against the dark
and then the cleft
of light
closes

"Prologue" frames the birth of Hogg as a man concerned about his sanity while ice fishing for a seal:

. . . how does he stay sane while sitting
squat hour after hour by a seal hole in the ice

The seal can be read as a symbol for the poetic truth
Hogg seeks to "harpoon" and bring back home:

. . . hauling
it home, the moment of triumph as brief as the
arctic summer in which the sun shines
all night . . .

Why are these lines so revealing? They seem to say that
articulating his *singular* poetic existence, *his truth*, is
central to Hogg's vision. He wants us to behold him as
he is, as he makes clear in Hogg's "Epilogue," the last
poem of his first collection:

when his search for singularity
was done, he'd be no hang-dog
sour with self-pity,
but crying, "Behold the whole Hogg."

In other words, Hogg tells us clearly his poems are devoted to his search for singularity. Singularity of voice (intent, meaning, tone, musicality, and metaphoricity) being the essence of modern poetry. But perceiving "the whole Hogg" also means recognizing how the poet's quest for his singularity comes to life.

So how does Hogg go about his search?

First by announcing who he is.

In the second poem, "The Hatching of Hogg," the poet reveals himself as not only fishing for seals, but also as the seal himself. "The Hatching of Hogg" begins with the line: "Hogg came up for air./ Before he was half out of his hole they got him," and it ends with, "HERE HANGS THE KING OF THE HATCHING DEAD."

So who are the "hatching dead?" The dead who "hatch" the living? As Hogg tells it, "they got him" like a seal coming up for air and hung him out to dry, his crown "a dead pig's tit." He cries out, "Christ-quisling," but no one hears; no one, that is, but the hanged king. The king of what? The King of the Dead, hatching eggs to be born again?

In other words, to paraphrase Yeats, Hogg, the poet's alter ego, is giving birth to himself, as he hangs amongst the "hatching dead," that is, the royal realm of poetry, where poets are alive-in-death.

Being alive-in-death is of course a symbolic way of identifying Hogg's poetic soul (within a living poetic tradition). It tells us that the poet's body *is in the moment*, writing his poems, but his soul belongs to the eternal, that is, the essence remaining alive-in-death (and the reason we read the poetry of the dead poets we still read).

Also, please notice how in the movement from the first poem ("Prologue") to the second ("The Hatching of Hogg"), the poet gives himself to us, as a King, a royal ruler of a sovereign realm, the realm of poetry, the King-

178

dom of Hogg. This is a vital point, since all of the Hogg poems, as well as the stories in the poems (not only their meanings, but also what they are in and of themselves), emanate from, and continuously develop, this narrative device – *the metaphoric exposition of a poet who calls himself Hogg.*

Since little else is known about the poet before the publication of his first book of poems and drawings (more about drawings later), I propose the following observation: Hogg's poetic identity arrives "on the scene," so to speak, as a *fait accompli.* By mythic association, I suggest to you that Hogg could have been born, like Pallas Athena, fully formed from the head of Zeus.

Be that as it may, the poet certainly presents Hogg to us as a questing figure, given to versifying about his search for singularity and the mystery of life and death, as well as the truth of being that he encounters along the way.

In other words, Hogg appears to us as a poet by birth, not by profession. His life and times, as defined by the poet, exist in two complete Hogg books of poems, each book the poetic record of a voyage Hogg undertakes.

Each of the two Hogg books contains a Muse, she is both a lover and – as Goethe called her in *Faust* – "the eternally feminine," drawing Hogg forwards and upwards. The first muse figure is an unnamed lover, a "daughter of Jerusalem," a Jewish woman he meets in "Hotel Tarshish."

The second book's Muse is identified by name, Marina, in one of the poems ("Hogg in the Land of H."). But she is also (by name association) Hogg's poetic spirit guide. "Marina Ivanonova Tsvetayeva is the woman's namesake," as the poet indicates in Hogg's Notes.

The first journey (in the first book) is motivated by the desire to escape the mundane, to go on a pilgrimage, to find himself or to define his spiritual ground, "Inside his Wooden Suit." To that end he decides to travel to Jerusalem:

> . . . there had to be
>
> one place where the last words
> on the dice were
>
> Holy Holy Holy.

Hogg's second voyage of discovery (*Hogg The Seven Last Words*) is to Leningrad, in the U.S.S.R., also known in the old and new Russia as St. Petersburg, a territory that appears to be Hogg's literary, as well as spiritual, home.

The second poem (in the second book) is called "Air, Air, Air," and in it Hogg's love for the dark heart of Dostoievsky becomes the book's *leitmotif*:

> . . . Hogg limped on alone to Leningrad, Number 7,
> Pergevalsky, sat down to tea spiked
> with homebrewed alcohol
> in Raskolnikov's yellow room
> where Dostoievsky, playing double solitaire
> with the pawnbroker for the axe, cocked
> an eye and said,
>
> All light seeds the dark,
> total darkness is irretrievable and so too
> despair. All men need is
> air, air, air.

In the Notes (at the end of *Hogg The Seven Last Words*) – notes which are equally as meticulous and equally as necessary as T. S. Eliot's notes to *The Waste Land* – our peripatetic poet reveals that Number 7 Pergevalsky is where Raskolnikov's room was located in *Crime and Punishment* and where Dostoievsky lived for a time.

In many ways, "Number 7 Pergevalsky" is the dark symbolic room, the imaginary space, the interior landscape in which *Hogg The Seven Last Words* is written. One could say, as the poet does in a poem called "At Dostoievsky's Grave," that the author of *Notes from Underground* (and *The Idiot*) is Hogg's spiritual progenitor. Trying to console the "girl in his arms" at the Aleksandr-Nevsky Laura cemetery where Dostoievsky is buried, Hogg remembers his own father telling him that,

> . . . love is a silent prayer
> sung for the living
> by the dead.

This is the love that prevails in Hogg's realized eschatology, it's not the love of ideology or power or religion, but a love for the dead who live in our silent prayers.

By the way, the other side, the light side of this "hatching" consolation, is found in the line, "Ice is only rain yielding life again." A line of seven words that represents Hogg's natural philosophy, as well as his own last seven words (in the poem "Seven Last Words"). In my opinion, both "sevens" allude to one or all of the seven last statements made by Jesus on the Cross; "O Father why hast Thou forsaken me?"

So, I ask myself, was Hogg forsaken by his father?

The answer is in the poems, as you shall soon discover. But for now let me just add that nothing is ever as it seems when it comes to Hogg and his poems, least of all his relationship to his father.

> *The essence of art is poetry. The essence of poetry, in turn, is the founding of truth.*
>
> Heidegger

As I delve deeper into Hogg's poetic substance, the oceanic undertow in which he swims, let me ask myself again, "Who is Hogg and why does he write the poetry he writes?"

To behold "the whole Hogg" is to sense the essence of a poetic mystery. Here is a poet who not only calls us, his readers, in his own unique voice, but he also provides us with ample evidence that he sees himself as a travelling poet *per se.* The epigrams of both Hogg books indicate as much.

The second epigram (in the first book) is by Henry Miller. It announces the poet's pilgrimage to "the belly of the whale" (more about it later).

The epigram in the second book is an invitation to join the poet on his journey, taken from Baudelaire's "L'Invitation au voyage." So who is Hogg? Hogg is a poet who goes abroad, he travels, he lives high off the Hogg, so to speak, as he visits foreign places, encounters strangers on their own turf and writes poetry about it, his experience. But to what end? Well, I think, first to know himself and then to *reveal* himself, as he is in his own skin(s). As Hogg states clearly in "The Note":

> . . . What gives value to travel is fear . . . There is no pleasure in traveling, and I look upon it as an occasion for spiritual testing . . . Travel, like a greater and graver science, brings us back to ourselves . . .

"The Note" is taken from Albert Camus, as Hogg's Notes indicate. Not only are Hogg's travels a "spiritual testing," but his persistent transience also suggests a being who feels exiled (or alienated or abandoned). In other words, Hogg is an existential spirit using the classical *metaphoricity* of a hero's journey (an *anti-hero's* journey in this case) to establish his authenticity by and for himself. First in his own mind, and then in the minds of his readers "back home," as the poet indicates in "Hogg, Eight to the Bar":

Hogg was home, with no song
of woe and bone to be sung
to the dong of the bell,
but home, home out of hell.

This aspect of Hogg's dialogical rhetoric, once one has read both Hogg books, reveals a lyric voice responding to actual events in a public manner. Hogg is no wall-flower, no! He's a poet who understands the living poetic tradition to which he sets out to link himself. This poet's public lyricism is integral to the poetic vision revealed by Hogg. It is his unique strength as a poet, especially when one remembers that his home is, "a land of eelgrass and ice drifts and snow," and "an endless winter of endless nights."

One of the several reasons I return to the Hogg poems often is because, as I said before, he is not a professional or academic poet, but a writer of Hogg poems when he's "on the road." His virtue, as a poet, is a decision he makes to sing his singular songs, his *Hogg Songs*, in the same way every bird is born to sing its vocal part in the avian symphony we hear during our early morning walks through the woods. So, again, who is Hogg?

As the poet indicates in "Hogg in Space," he is not who he is in the mirror, he's not his mirror image, no,

he's a hand reaching for a hand
sealing the space
between
face and face
in a silent word,
the I am
who Am.

Beauty aside, this sublime little poem is first about Hogg as he sees himself, and then (sub-textually) about the art of writing poetry, as well as fiction. But it is also a deceptively simple metaphor for the Old Testament God, the "I Am (who I Am)," the God of History. This history Hogg recognizes as the essence of his poetic ground, as well as the figure of his poetic being, his substance or existence.

So who is Hogg? Well, this much is clear, he is a being, that is, he's a poet, as he sees himself in truth, and he's a poetic vessel, that is, a metaphoric extension of the poet.

But pray tell, who knows how to write about a being that *is* and at the same time a being that *is not?* A question that belies the first Aristotelian principle of non-contradiction. (Was it not Baudelaire who wrote, "contradiction is the poet's eleventh commandment?") But this too is inherent to the graces of poetry, a realm where, as Robert Musil wrote, "[anything,] an idea or a person – anything in the world – can be simultaneously true and false, existent and non-existent."

Frank Kermode, commenting on Musil's statement, wrote: "When you think about it, this oxymoronic habit, this determination to find *a* and *not-a* in a fruitfully suggestive relationship, arises from a generous reading habit, a recognition that poetry is capable of such acts of philosophical defiance . . ."

Only a true poet, only a master of metaphor, would risk contradiction to bring us – from across the Abyss – the contours of his eternal soul, suspended between "the silent word" and his poetic speech. In fact, I say, Plato's damnation of poets be damned. Hogg is a poet, as well as a "philosopher king" – *Ecce Hogg* – at the heart of the history of his times:

> *Everything profound loves a mask.*
> Nietzsche

Ergo: I assume Hogg must also be the mask of a poet who does not want to *simply* tell us the profound truth

184

he has found in his being. Why is that so? And can I prove it? That's what I intend to show you by the end of this letter.

Meanwhile, however, hear a few revealing lines about this aspect of the masking process, described in "Tell It Slant" (a wonderful homage to an Emily Dickenson poem):

> . . . there is
> no wafer
> of light, no light:
> we drool over light
> in our dreams, seize the day
> in the dark
> and try to live

> . . . We atone, we
> atone, persisting in the sin
> of doing nothing
> but exist
> and we inoculate
> our lives
> with alcohol.

Of the 200 or so poems the poet has published in his two Hogg books, Hogg appears by name in about forty of them. But he is the observing presence and voice in all.

Each of Hogg's poems is either about an *encounter* (sometimes loving, sometimes not) or about *a place in which an encounter occurs* or about *a certain state of mind*. That's all. There are no poems showcasing his poetic "know how," as Americans call it. There are no Hogg poems about objects *per se* or sunsets or daffodils or some such sweetness. Each poem is grounded in the objects around the poet, as the event or the encounter described in the poem reveals itself.

Furthermore: each of Hogg's poems has its specific purpose in the book's overall narrative structure (like the Stations of the Cross) because the poet wants to be clear about his unfolding pilgrimage or journey, and thus reveal to us Hogg's dark view of reality. Even the lighter poems are suffused by the blackened surround of a midnight sun, that is, the ice cold arctic summer "in which the sun shines all night."

In overview, Hogg's poems appear as a series of short (poetic) stories connected by a central character (Hogg) and by the poet's abiding passion for the existent, and for justice; and for the truth of selfhood and freedom.

Even a poem called "Hope," the last poem in the second Hogg book, is really about death and the disappearing of the light:

Death,
like the night,
only
darkens
the
door
of
day
at dawn
long
enough
to disappear.

In other words, even Hogg's hope is but a revelation of what Sartre called the life we live between existence and nothingness before we "disappear."

Nearly all the best Hogg poems are either *lyrical* (song or song-like) or *symbolic* (signifying a state of mind or a mood, mostly dark and brooding) or they are a *short narrative* (prose poems) set to the musicality inherent to the art of poetic line breaks. That's it: either one engages with Hogg and his historical narrative on his own terms or one is left on the outside looking in. There's another metaphorical implication in the "Prologue" that needs to be addressed because it is a theme that evolves throughout Hogg's *oeuvre*. The seal (the singular being the poet is fishing for) is also the dark matter the poet sets out to harpoon and bring to light, even if it means the light of a midnight sun (a light that is found beyond epistemological knowledge, that is, the light of wisdom):

> waiting for the snout of the seal, for the one heave
> of the harpoon that he can make into the dark
> water, and then groping in the water under the ice,
> feeling for the dead bulk of the seal body, hauling
> it home,the moment of triumph as brief as the
> arctic summer in which the sun shines
> all night . . .

In other words, the subject matter to be "harpooned" could be both food for the body and food for the soul. (To paraphrase a notion Jung suggested often, as long as we don't bring to consciousness what is buried in our dark unconscious, we shall be haunted by it.) Or it could be, as Pablo Neruda wrote, that, "[t]he poet [is giving] us a gallery full of ghosts shaken by the fire and darkness of his time." This poetic concern for the buried truth, the ghosts of our past, is returned to over and over again in Hogg's poems, revealing itself as a second *motif*. (I'm using *motif* rather than *theme* here to stress the musicality in Hogg's poems.)

> . . . so a diviner
> wearing a striped yellow and grey cap
> had circled the house
> criss-crossing his track.

Hogg's circling and criss-crossing and returning constantly to his (interior and exterior) landscape feels sometimes like the work of a compulsive obsessive child. A child who was betrayed by some long forgotten events. Events that keep him alert to his poetic vocation, the profound truth he was born to sublimate into poetry.

I happen to have known the poet's father, who confessed to me one day — in front of a formally executed and highly expressive painting, painted by his teenage son — that one of the great mistakes he made as a father was not supporting his son's evident talent for drawing and painting. " I didn't encourage him then and now it's one of my regrets," he told me.

As the drawings in the middle of Hogg's first collection reveal, our poet also possesses a keen eye for colour and composition, as well as a natural way with line and perspective. He could have become a painter, but instead he became a poet, a versifier who uses words to paint poetic-story-images of his being in the world.

In the shadow of this poet's story (told in his poems), a man reveals himself as Hogg, his poet's identity of choice. This man, this Hogg, shows himself to us (his readers) as a travelling man who is sensitive to human affairs, to love and death, to truth and lies, and to the hypocrisy and compromises we endure in the name of power or survival.

In many ways, Hogg is a true Liberal poet, as I hope to show you by the end of this letter. His ultimate concern — ostensibly with his own singularity — is for the freedom of the individual and freedom of speech, i.e. the freedom to breath, and speak, and write one's truth. ("All men need is air, air, air.")

In his truth, Hogg is a poet of people, places and power (dynamics). He is a poet who goes out to celebrate life abroad and discovers that life is actually a cruel struggle to keep body and soul alive. There's no justice in power and love is but a cautionary tale because, as Hogg says, it "has too many endings."

Hogg's only "heavenly graces" (as Shakespeare called it) are suggested in two or three love poems, like "To Turn Again":

Her
eyes
as dark
as
a
starless
night
were
stars
that led
him
in to
the
light.

Hogg's true light, his brilliance, however, is found in his poetic descent into the heart of human darkness and in the never ceasing expression of the sorrows of being human (that is, being a *mensch,* as they say in Yiddish). His genius is for the constant, unrelenting, poetic articulation of the agony some people feel, when observing the atrocities, the evil, we humans perpetrate on each other. It is a unique perspective in the poetic landscape of Canada.

Taking a quick structural overview of the subjects and patterns in Hogg's poetic landscape, we find a Totemic-Animistic-Judeo-Greco-Roman-Christian world rising into history (*"one day the age will rise/ like a corpse in a spring river,"* we are told in "The Wound"). But, as it turns out, irrespective of the personal failures we experience in love, *"only love is holy"* but it's a holiness found in being true to one's deepest darkest desires, as the poet writes in a darkly uplifting poem called "Rasputin":

> I haunted the holy ghost.
> I sacrificed myself to sin.
> The scourge, the rutting was all for Him.
> Just as He chose to die for me
> cankered in my skin,
> I chastened souls till they became His sluts
> I repented and am consoled.

What kind of love is this? you ask.

It's the Holy Roman Love of the Word made flesh, but it is also a love of abandonment.

Now, to continue building on the evidence, here's a brief summation, Hogg on Ice: *a taxonomy of the poet's motifs*. Snow. Ice. Stone. Water. Air. Fire. Sleepwalking. Fathers. Mothers. Sons and daughters. Judges. Cops. Crooks. Lawyers. Junkies. Holy men, and Christa, Christ's sister. Evil brothers and lost cousins. Drinking. Eating. Singing. Music and making love, *La Petite Mort,* and loving one's dead ancestors. Visiting foreign places and meeting other writers, living and dead (like Yehuda Amichai, A.B. Yehoshua in Israel. Osip Mandelstam, Isaac Babel, Marina Tsvetayeva, and Anna Akmatova in Russia, to name a few), and always, always, holding on to the freedom of his selfhood (*"I am who Am"*), the freedom to be himself, to be Hogg. That's the genius in these poems, the genius of the two Hogg books, and the reason they'll survive long after the poet is dead and buried.

Now, I must repeat, clearly, there's no one like Hogg in the imaginary landscape of Canadian poetry. That's a boon to his originality, but, so far, it has not helped him as a public presence.

Three people I talked to about the poet found him either too "hermetic" or too much of "a prose story teller" or too "narcissistic." My answer to all three was: "Rubbish."

And so, sadly enough, Hogg is better appreciated in France, Spain, Italy, and Eastern Europe, than he is in his own back yard. Go figure! Well, actually I have. The poet's foreign affairs and the implied transience he chooses as his poetic ground indicates a sense of self-banishment, a going into exile to return home renewed or reborn, like Jonah was from the belly of the whale, or "transfigured," as in "The Transfiguration," to cure the "spiritual blindness" of his people back home. But most of the good folks back home (Irving Layton and Anne Carson being exceptions) are too caught up in defining their cultural identity to recognize the transcendent spirit, the *anti*-hero's mythic journey, represented by Hogg's pearls of perception. (Love is love no matter where we love; evil is evil wherever it rears its ugly head, etc.) Hogg has certainly been "seen and heard" in his home land, but, as is well known, seeing and hearing is not understanding; and so they do not (yet) perceive him as a rarity, a poet singularly devoted to the truth of death and metamorphosis.

A few years after the poem was published in *As Close As We Came*, I showed the poet a short alchemical story I was writing, also called "Seven Last Words." My story used "Ice is only rain yielding life again" as its epigram. When the poet saw it, he decided there and then (on January 9th, 1999) to use it as the title of his next book. A few years later, it became his definitive poetic master-piece, *Hogg The Seven Last Words*.

On December 14th, 2003, the poet and his *covivant*, Claire, an artist and a wise woman, invited me for supper. At the end of the evening, we ended up discussing the nature of evil. To cap our discussion, I asked the poet to read me his "Promise of Rain," if only to remind myself of the historical fact that

> . . . men like Stalin, Himmler, Beria, not only
> know the evil they do
>
> but find it wryly amusing
> in all its intricacies of device,
> the way pulling the wings off butter-
> flies is ferociously funny
> to queerly strung choir boys.

"Promise of Rain" will live *in me* because this poem captures the utter self-consciousness of those who find the means to rationalize evil:

> What else could their defiant sign
>
> WORK MAKES FREE
> over the gate of a death camp be
> but a joke that only
> killers could enjoy.
> They knew, they knew, they knew
> and they laughed, he said,
>
> as they laughed at
> work, work, the dignity of work
> in the work camps of Siberia.

Many of the poems in *Hogg, the Seven Last Words,* are remarkable in their descriptions of Hitler's heinous Final Solution and Stalin's purges, concentration camps and gulag camps *("I did a tenner / in a gulag work gang, on six ounces of bread a day"),* mass killings and mass starvation, and the slaughter machines we humans invent to become efficient killers.

The only way Hogg himself can deal with such a horror ("the horror, the horror, the moral terror," as Brando's Kurtz cries out in *Apocalypse Now*) is by writing a masterful poem, like "Stigmata." It begins as the trial of a simple shop assistant:

> Boris Samoilov, look
> how indolent in his own defense,
> . . . kneading . . .
> . . . the open
> abscess of accusation in his hand,
> eager to verify every lie
> he testified to as true,
> trying not to die, not to die, not to die.
> Preposterous . . .

And it ends – as an existential lament – with King Lear's despairingly absurd cry on the heath (emphasis of final line mine):

> It's all the same to me.
> Burning, scalding, stench, consumption,
> fie! fie! pah! pah!

In a poem called "Himmler's Law," the poet uses an epigram by Heinrich Himmler, ". . . it was a merciless morality . . .," to set up a poem about Lot's lot. This epigrammatic line, however, is also the poet's lot. In their own way, every poet adheres to it, to this "merciless morality," in the name of truth, that is, the truth Hogg sublimates into his poetry and the reason I return to his poems in times of self doubt.

> *All art, as the letting happen of the advent of the truth of beings, is as such, in* essence, poetry.
> Heidegger

To my mind, Hogg is not just the mask of a poet determined to bring his truth to light, but also the totem image of a rational animal. Hogg is both a "cover up" and a poet "breaking cover" to show us his true self. In simple words, Hogg is the master of his own creation, as we hear in "Hogg at Prayer":

> The devil
> dances in our eye,
> creature
> of our own creation.
> And God,
> also in the image of the race,
> wears our face.

So who is Hogg?

Well, he is a man fishing for a truth we humans can only utter in poetry. His poetic life, as revealed in the Hogg poems, is historical, but his existence is a mystery. Take "Ice Fishing" for example:

Ice Fishing

> He saw
> ice inlaid in light
> along the canal
>
> and old men
> fishing
> for their sons
>
> under birch trees
> hung
> with the severed tongues
>
> of bells tolled
> at
> *Lubyanka*
> where bodies were laid out
> pearled with blood
> beside

skinning bowls
made from the silver spoons
of those

who died
looking for
air holes

in the ice
filled with the blue
sky and hooks.

There's something about this poem that speaks to my
curiosity and invites me to read it as a key to the poet's
oeuvre. Who is fishing?
    A bunch of old men, as seen by Hogg.
    What are they fishing for?
    A profound truth that can only be revealed in poet-
ry? What kind of a truth? The truth of

. . . old men
fishing
for their sons

under birch trees
hung
with the severed tongues

The sons these old men are fishing for have had their
tongues cut out? Why? Because

. . . bells tolled
at
Lubyanka

where bodies were laid out
pearled with blood

These bodies belong to sons killed at Lubyanka, the secret police headquarters and a legendary prison in central Moscow. And why did they die? Because they were searching

for
air holes

in the ice
filled with the blue
sky and hooks.

In other words, it seems to me, the sons were trying to escape the police state their fathers had created, but, at the same time, their fathers are "fishing" for ways to help them; they are seeking "air holes," seeking a way to help them escape the cold hard frozen surface, the repression containing them, that is, the oppression of a society where the freedom to "blue skies" is in a deep freeze and where many "hooks" have tried and failed to save those who are caught by it. Still, I ask myself, the deep freeze of what? Could it be a rational life balanced by faith – as Hogg writes in "The True Believer":

redeemed
through Christ's cry.
Goodbye, goodbye to the slaughter.
They know not

what they do
with these rows of empty shoes
and so forgive them
Little Father.

Nothing, however, is ever as it seems in Hogg's poetic world. The Old Believers, we are told in "Hogg's Notes," are members of an old Russian religious sect founded in the late seventeenth century. But in the

U.S.S.R. of the 1920s and 1930s religious education was a political crime under Article 58-10 of the Code. The poet Tanya Khodkevich got ten years for writing:

You can pray freely
but only if God alone can hear.

That's not all, not in Hogg's poetry: Little Father also turns out to be a name of awe and affection for Stalin among ordinary Soviet citizens. This is but another example of how Hogg, the poet, manages to invoke in his poems a *metaphysics* that exists beyond what his words describe. The mark of a great poet, as "Prologue," "Ice Fishing" and "The Old Believers" reveal.

MARGARITAS ANTE PORCOS

ROBERT MARTEAU

Ran cow and calf, and eke the very hogges.
Chaucer, *Nun's Priest's Tale*

Yes, it's true, I'm back in Montreal again, Côte des Neiges, 1977-78. John Montague, an Irishman exiled in Toronto, has sent us a man, a decisive man to say the least, a sweet talker, free as the air (or so it seems), a player of ponies (for sure), his veins still full of the savage blood of his ancestors from ancient kingdoms by the sea, kings risen from cowherds, perpetuated in the movies of John Ford, his indispensable John Wayne sometimes coupled with Maureen O'Hara. Bards, raids, heroic cowboy kings with emerald crowns and wives dressed in the green of grass and sea, they all came back to me carried by the eloquent voice and gestures of Barry Callaghan, carrying his saga all the way from a Jerusalem drawn from the seedy bowels of Toronto, of which I've since had a cinematographic overview in *L'année du Dragon*.

So Callaghan set about initiating me to the arcane of this first testament, introducing me to his hero, a man named Hogg. What are we supposed to read into the name: hog, pig, *porc, cochon,* swine, piglet? Should we see a distant cousin of Monsieur Cuine, one of Bernanos' creatures? If we look at the drawings that are the context Callaghan gives to Hogg, would it be fair to see him as a refugee from German expressionism, the urban expressionism of the 1920s? Hogg's eruption seems more like the leaps and pirouettes of an acrobat than a coming out in the world of belles-lettres.

Translating all of this turned into an expedition through regions seldom or barely visited, with the pilgrim finding refuge in nothing but dumps built on the edge of swamps, places where you can only take shelter if you know the password. But what we have here is not that kind of mocking modernity that anyone can lay claim to with a little back-handed moralizing; no, and neither is it the rejection of all antecedent, all tradition, or the pathetic ferocity of humour. I was perfectly aware, as I walked along clutching a stick in one hand and my guide's fist in the other; yes, I was instantly and perfectly aware that this wasn't just a question of off-colour jokes, of a more or less obscene farce, but that under all this apparently foul language hid an unspoken modesty. The rough language bespoke a shame that dared not speak its name, and we were much closer to what Unamuno called "the tragic sentiment of life" than we were to pornography.

Could it be that Callaghan has given us the key in his recent memoir, *Barrelhouse Kings*? It seems that Hogg may have taken shape during Callaghan's first stay in Jerusalem and that this is indicated in the episodes that refer us to Luke 8: 26-39, Matthew 8: 28-34, and Mark 5: 1-17, where the demons beseech Jesus in these words: "If thou cast us out, suffer us to go away into the herd of swine," and Mark goes on in this way: "And forthwith Jesus gave them leave. And the unclean spirits went out, and entered into the swine; and the herd ran violently down a steep place into the sea (they were about two thousand) and were choked in the sea." All three evangelists agree that the people who witnessed what had happened "began to pray Jesus to depart of their coasts." So it appears that in this act Jesus follows Jewish law that prohibits pork – as Islam would do later – a malediction that appears at least once in the gospels, in the parable about not casting pearls before swine.

Compare this with the pig as seen by the pagan people of the north: it is the most basic food, especially for the agricultural class, and later on among the converted pagans, in every house the pig was fattened on scraps, leavings and refuse from the table and became the indispensable host to be sacrificed, hung, butchered and prepared in order to become nourishment to sustain the body, a sacrifice and consummation fundamentally and profoundly a mirror image of the crucifixion and Eucharist.

That which is elevated is the same as that which is low, and that which is low is like that which is high: an annunciation found in *The Emerald Table*. That doesn't mean one is the same as the other, but we must confront necessity if we are to go beyond it and attain the spiritual. We all know the old adage: "In every man there is a sleeping pig," or "The fish begins rotting at the head." Far from avoiding these two realities of existence (which come from our having been expelled into matter), Callaghan's work is designed to force them together, perhaps even with a certain glee, but I would also suggest that he does this without hypocrisy, and with a generous heart.

Yes, exactly: yes, that's just the word I was looking for: generous. You can't enter into Callaghan's work if you haven't found the key. And the key has a name: generosity. And it is this quality – truly the only thing required – that connects him by the golden chain of poetry and the filigrees of the *Book of Kells* to the spiritual plane without any contamination, ever, by any sort of intellectualism or ideology. "I am not he who does not sing," sang the Welsh bard; and at the same time, or before or after him – I don't know – it was also this shaking of the soul to its deepest voice which has allowed us to hear the chant and the song of the troubadours that Ezra Pound had the gift of making green once more. And if you could lay your hand on the songs of Guillaume de Poitiers you might very easily guess that they could harmonize very well with verses from the epic of Hogg.

I write this as I'm reading Barry Callaghan's marvelous *Barrelhouse Kings,* where the genesis of the Hogg poems is more-or-less explained. But my reading of the book doesn't in any way trouble my first "inspiration" or intuitions concerning the poems. Nor am I convinced that Hogg has anything to do with a pig or a swine, though at the same time I tell myself he could also and just as well be an avatar of Monsieur de Poureaugnac, the hero of Molière's three-act comedy ballet in prose (1669), a bumpkin who comes to Paris to marry a pretty girl and is the butt of ridicule by wits who have taken the side of his rival (to quote almost exactly the *Nouveau Petit Larousse Illustré,* sixteenth edition). The similarity obviously lies in the fact that Hogg is also a comic and picaresque character. The situation is too grave to be taken seriously!

I'm rereading the "Seven Last Words" spoken on the Mount of Skulls, at the ninth hour, the supremely tragic moment that, once and for all time, abolishes tragedy through traversal and transgression while the Son of Man says in the same breath: "Father, why hast thou forsaken me?" and "Father, why have you glorified me?" as he hangs on the tree of the world which is also the tree of the axle of the millstone that grinds the grain of the harvest that we are.

So could it be that Hogg is the indelible figure of Christ scripted in all of us, whether we know it or not, a figure soiled by existence, by EX-PULSION, THE FALL, EX-ILE, TERRIFICATION, a figure obsessed by bestiality linked to the survival of what we call the human and humanity? And suddenly I become aware of what Callaghan's Hogg gains by adding a "g" to the "hog" of the swineherd and the butcher. I see it as something like a genesis, an act through which a man is created, but two days after the fish and the birds, and another day after the other animals, the ultimate creature who is said to have been made *man and woman*.

Translated by Ray Ellenwood

THE SEVEN LAST WORDS

David Wevill

. . . and I wrote poems of dread about men I had met the
year before – I had been in Moscow and Leningrad – who
had stainless steel teeth, who smiled as ink fell on a blotter
and a name disappeared, and I learned from a woman I'd
met along the ice-locked canals that

> we know what love is
> when it's over
> the trail of two people
> bending into the echo of their own laughter
> across a lake fresh with snow.

This brief passage from Barry Callaghan's memoir
describes the genesis of *As Close As We Came,* published
in 1982. The poems tell of encounters the poet had during his time in the Soviet Union: stories of bureaucrats,
war survivors, women, children, ghosts, the living and
the dead, past and present. At the core of the book are
more intimate poems, poems of a man and a woman,
who are together for this brief time in wintry Leningrad,
an environment cold to love.

Then, almost twenty years later, that narrative
sequence was reborn as Hogg re-emerged in *Seven Last
Words*. It is a longer, much fuller narrative, and it
includes ten pages of detailed, idiosyncratic background
notes, a choric book, as the drawings are a choric book
in the first Hogg. Almost all of the *As Close As We Came*
poems have been revised or rewritten, and many new
poems have been added. What had been essentially an
elegy is now a darker, sardonic indictment of a system
and a world, a powerful work of humour and imagina-

tion. The woman's voice tells her story more fully, and she is now named, Marina, and the man is plainly identified as Hogg. The world that surrounds them is more overwhelming and oppressive, and their intimacy more muted.

As we know, when the figure Hogg appears, nothing remains the same. Hogg is more than the poet's alter ego or persona. He is a trickster, like the Winnebago Wakdjunkaga, a kind of ur-force on the loose, albeit an educated one, eloquent in his power to both disrupt and create. He is "a wise fool who's seen in a scarecrow's pod, god," an adventurer, a scourge, a witness, a stranger and a fellow sufferer who, in a note concerning travel, quotes Albert Camus: "What gives value to travel is fear . . . There is no pleasure in traveling, and I look upon it as an occasion for spiritual testing . . . Travel . . . brings us back to ourselves." In some ancient cultures, to be fear-struck was taken as a sign of awakening consciousness, of a new sense of reality, perhaps the beginnings of conscience itself. So it is with Hogg: "Curiosity plus dread was his curse," and here, along the ice-locked canals of time-frozen Leningrad, Hogg lends an ear to fear and gives voice to the harrowed, the comic and tragic inmates of this territory hostile to the self.

Seven Last Words begins:

Since
all light
seeds
the
dark
total
darkness
is irretrievable
and
so too
despair.

The next poem announces Hogg's presence, "sleepwalk-ing / in Noah's muddy shoes" through wintry Leningrad, visiting the cramped yellow room where Dostoievski lived, where he placed his axe murderer, Raskolnikov, archetypal figures in the terrible, magnificent, mean past of Russia that suffocates the present: the present where, as Dostoievski said, "All men need is air, air, air," an echo of despair.

"What is love?" asked the poet Marina Tsvetayeva. "It is a flower / flooded with blood." She is one of the ghosts that accompany Hogg and Marina as they wan-der the winter streets. There are others: Dostoievski, Isaac Babel, Osip Mandelstam "dead in the grave, teeth / singing in the zero," Andrei Voznesensky, Yevgeni Yev-tushenko. The living and the dead share one world. Love, like time, does not stand still here but is always sliding back into the past, which is the future. As Mari-na describes it,

We alone, we
alone, persisting in the sin
of doing nothing
but exist . . . We are laconic, erect
on the grave's lip.

In their wandering, the pair drift between memories and strange human encounters, the poems throwing off an uncanny light blend of realism and fantasy, especially in the memory-voice of Marina, her troubling images of her father,

who played chess, alone
and accused himself of cheating.

Some of the strongest poems in *Seven Last Words* address Russian history, politics and society, poems that expose, with sardonic humour and sharp detail, the cruel, dulling absurdities of policy and daily life. This is where the dark satirist in Hogg has full play, and the mocking force of these poems contrasts with the more lyrical Marina and Marina/Hogg poems. There is tragedy here, too, and bitter indictment. The Hogg of these poems is no domestic prize porker (the wild boar is the third incarnation of Vishnu) but a spirited witness and scourge.

Most memorably, perhaps, we meet Cousin Smerdikov, ex-sharpshooter and present-day thief, who "kept a live sparrow / in his breast pocket, both wings broken." Smerdikov is a cynical, street-wise opportunist, ex-soviet Army and now "tomorrow's man," predictive of the new free-market Russia of gangs, killings and drugs. "I'm in it for the *plantchik* and whatever else I can nick," he tells Hogg. "Socialists to a T, we don't believe in private property."

And wandering among the legs and around the boots of all these inmates are children, street urchins, orphans. They, too, are forced to live in the past, in an unending history that offers no issue or hope and eventually the separation of love.

The ten last pages are background notes in the voice of a third choric figure, and so ends this wonderful book in which Barry Callaghan has succeeded in bringing together the dimensions of satire, political comment and intimate personal lyric. The book is one of tenderness and rage, dark humour and sadness, subtlety, grace and power. The creator of the poems has a talent both massive and precise, a large figure, Hogg, who walks on delicate feet. Forty years ago, I stood by the Irrawaddy in Burma, watching a water buffalo amble up out of the brown river onto the muddy bank. There the huge creature paused, slowly raised a hind leg, bent its head around, and, posed on three legs, picked, with perfect delicacy, something off its eyelid with its hoof.

Ice is only rain yielding life again.

The seven last words offer a note of hope, and beg, too, the question of what kind of life it is that will be yielded, after such a history, after such a century.

A SLAVICELTIC CIRCUS POET

Gale Zoë Garnett

In Barry Callaghan's *Hogg The Seven Last Words,* the two primary tones are a *Celtic* joy of language, his patrimony, and the *Slavic* – specifically Russian. The Russian is there less for the obvious reason (the poems are set in the KGB-riddled Brezhnev years of the former U.S.S.R.) than because Callaghan has always been intoxicated by the sounds and images of the Slavic world. This rare and interesting combination of cultural influences and affinities has created both a filmic and symphonic poetry; a unique, multi-dimensional and dynamic circus.

In conversation, Callaghan says, "the 40s and 50s films of Sergei Eisenstein (*The Battleship Potemkin, Ivan the Terrible*) had an enormous effect on me, on my generation. For those of us who loved those films, they changed the way we see. Eisenstein's films are the visual equivalent of Schostakovich-operatic Slavic symphonies. He cut his films like a poet, leaving out the conjunctions. As if life is a dream. There are severe dislocations of place, *film noir* lighting – lone surreal images; cuts of meat filled with maggots the size of fists . . . In my early childhood, I'd listen to Schostakovich's *Leningrad Symphony* over and over . . . and singers too. John McCormick, the great Irish tenor, and Chaliapin. I sang at school. What could be sillier – and at the same time, more poignant – than a boy soprano singing the bass solo of *The Song of the Volga Boatmen?*"

The Callaghan engagement with Slavic imagery and sound goes beyond film and music to the purely tonal. Once, when he thought we might do a radio-reading together from his Leningrad poems, he wanted me to read using the Russian *"myakiznyak"* – the particular liquid "L" of the Russian language. When he writes in English of things Russian, that sound is part of how the jazz-infused Callaghan hears the riff. Without the sound, the speaker would be doing what studio musicians call "playing footballs" – metronomic, soulless and orderly tones – devoid of persona. Accordingly, the letter "L," in its soft Russian double-tone, fills many of the Hogg poems:

> We all *live* with a *lie* up our *sleeves*.
> ("Tricksters")

> There was a knock on the door
> and the *lock* un*latched*. A *lean* man
> in a *longshoreman's leather* coat,
> eyes embedded in ash,
> told them they had to go.
> ("The Leningrad Evening News")

In reading Callaghan, it is also helpful to know that one of the writer's childhood ambitions was to be a painter. It is impossible for any visualiser to read Callaghan without receiving the painting-become-poem-scenes that transmute into moving images into complete films – nowhere more so than in "Mon Grand Guignol":

> "Then there was my acrobat.
> Tall and double-jointed, he could bend his body
> in a circle backwards and hold onto his heels
> so that a clown wired like an angel
> with little wings could jump hoop through him.

> He'd call to me upside down from between his legs,
> 'One day we'll wheel within a wheel into the sun.'
> He skipped rope too, on a high wire,

double-dutch, cavorting with the clown,
but the army plucked him out of the air

and parachuted him into the Afghan hills.
He blew off a lèg to a land mine and came home
looking for himself in our bedroom mirror
but got lost in the silver lining.
Out of sight, he went out of his mind,

tried to tighten the letter O around his neck, his rope
his skipping rope, but then crawled into an asdic hut
salvaged from an arctic submarine hunter
that sits rusting under Petrovski bridge where Rasputin
had been wormed half-dead through a hole in the ice.

Every morning he stands there on his hands
And talks down through the crust to the beard,
bared gums, and crazed healing eyes of the holy man jacking
the ice with all his might, trying to come up for air.
On clear days the acrobat bends his body backwards.

He holds on with two hands to his one heel. He waits.
But the circle is broken. 'O,' he cries. 'O.' The clown never
comes.
Sometimes he stands on his good leg
like a crane and wheels his out-
stretched arms, trying to take off."

The Irish hurl words at their pain. Slavs do the same,
only, as I've noted, more slowly, to the jigless rhythms of
late-night gypsies or the vodka-blooded Vladimir Visot-
sky. Callghan-time is, picture after picture, d-minor after
d-minor, somewhere between the two speeds. The wan-
derer-fusion of a Toronto-based man who calls his literary magazine "Exile?"

"Fire and Water," a shorter work than "Mon Grand
Guignol," is equally filmic:

"My lonely mother said the sun is a fire wheel
and leapt through the hoop,
fleeing on snowshoes
over snow thirty feet deep,
tangled her feet in the tops of trees
where she died
and was found in the spring
reaching for the earth,
her bones glazed by the wind.
My father gave up sulking in the dark,
asked for more vodka and marzipan.
at two in the morning,
and quoted Mandelstam:
'The shy speechless sound
of a fruit falling from its tree,
and round about the forest's
silent music, unbroken. . .'
He went out and reached for the moon
reflected in a quarry pool
and drowned
believing he was born again."

Where "Mon Grand Guignol" is a Fellini film, "Fire and Water" evokes the subtler, quietly violent cinematic grief-evocations of the Soviet, Andrei Tarkovsky. Both poems make me wonder what paintings they might have been if Max Ernst and Leonor Fini, once a marriage, had also painted together. Or if the Russian surrealist, Alexander Tchelichev, had painted the creatures and tales of *The Seven Last Words*.

Yet, for all the surrealist-seeming imagery, these poems are about a specific time and entirely real place (the Leningrad of Leonid Brezhnev's U.S.S.R.). In his notes for the poem "Ice Fishing," Callaghan writes that "Lubyanka (was the) secret police headquarters and prison in central Moscow. Before the 1917 Revolution, the building housed the Rossiya Insurance Company. Hogg was told that the Company's motto was 'We are With You to the End.'"

In stop-frame between Fellini and Tarkovsky, there is the wry Callaghan contemplating the brutally anti-human late middle period of that which had begun as a Utopian dream. He looks at the Stalin-crushed, the death-stalked dreams and dreamers. The decay of buildings, of souls. The downwardly spiraling bureaucratic rules and regulations. He evokes these in image after image, striated like marble throughout the book:

> Was it a rat? Or the squeal
> of a misshapen shoe?
>> ("The Leningrad Evening News")

What else could their defiant sign

> WORK MAKES FREE
> over the gate of a death camp be
> but a joke that only
> killers could enjoy.
>> ("Promise of Rain")

And those who know the work of Anna Akhmatova and Osip Mandelstam will find not *echoes* but empathic harmonies, sometimes in the form of aching homage:

> as they took me naked to the final
> genuflection and fed my legs
> through the scaffold's door of sprung light,
> a footloose gaiety just
> like Godiva's dance of ankle bells
> up the stairs in Leningrad,
> O Godiva, goodbye, I'd forgotten,
> even when I can't breathe I want to live . . .
>> ("Osip Mandelstam Moves His Lips")

The will to live. The mending, often times crookedly, of both real and metaphoric broken bones. The turning of blood to wine – even with real blood. Uprooting, one within another, the *matyoschka* dolls, looking for secrets within secrets, of prisons and poverty until the joke, however dark, is found. The transmutation of the grey banalities of reduced options into a filmic, paint-streaked, verbal circus of colour and energy – these are some of the tensile threads that hold *The Seven Last Words* together.

The title phrase belongs to Christian liturgy, to Christ's last phrases on the cross. The last of these seven phrases, spoken after Jesus ("I thirst") seeks water but is given parching vinegar, are "It is finished." Jesus then gives up the ghost. However, Callaghan's more mortal earthbound protagonists continue to believe that if you keep pushing toward your possibilities, the living through the push may be brutal and horrific, but it is *never* finished. The seven last words of the book's title speak to Barry Callaghan's unflinching understanding of quotidian horror, and to the persistent lyric hope of a northern Slaviceltic poet: *Ice is only rain yielding life again.*

AGAINST FORGETTING

Notes on Barry Callaghan's
Hogg The Seven Last Words

Janice Kulyk Keefer

1. On the Appearance of Hogg The Seven Last Words

With this volume Barry Callaghan gives us two hugely welcome gifts. The first is an exceptionally fine collection of poems on the subject of History – recent Russian history – and on the power of Memory. The second gift is as important as the first: with his allusions to and quotations from Akhmatova, Mandelstam, Tsvetayeva, Babel – all of whom were perseucted, and two murdered by Stalin and the apparatus of State Terror he controlled – Callaghan encourages us to reread or perhaps to discover some of the greatest of Russia's twentieth century writers. He also conjures up for us more recent Russian voices, including those of Voznesensky, Solzhenitsyn, and Yevtushenko, while slipping in some masterful translations of poems by writers whose sensibilities have been shaped by afflictions similar to those undergone by the Russians.

The Seven Last Words is many things. It is an account of a journey into an infernal region of ice and snow which is at one and the same time the city of Leningrad and the crazed, corrupt human heart. It is a record of the powerfully sensual and "spiritual" love between Hogg and the Russian translator Marina, whom the volume links to the great poet and occasional translator Marina Tsvetayeva. It is also the evocation of a great city which has undergone several politically motivated metamorphoses, from St. Petersburg into Petrograd into Leningrad and now again into St. Petersburg. But Callaghan refuses to bracket off the sufferings of this city from the other horrors of twentieth-century history, particularly the mass terror and genocidal slaughter of Shoah. The *gulag*, in Hogg's eye, is the twin of the *Lager*.

The scope and ambition of this volume of poems will inevitably raise, among a certain class of readers, the question of authorial arrogance or good old-fashioned chutzpah. What right does a non-Russian – a Canadian, for Christ's sake – have to write about a subject as morally and historically huge as Russia? And if one is going to tackle such charged and complex ground, why send Hogg as an ambassador – Hogg who is neither mystic nor philosopher but *l'homme moyen sensuel* with a brain – hardly the Messiah.

The title of this volume might indeed seem to suggest that Hogg is putting himself in the place of the Redeemer, providing equivalents to the last utterances of the crucified Christ as revealed in the Gospels. Other writers have referred, directly or obliquely, to the seven last words: Gerard Manley Hopkins in his seven "terrible" sonnets, Joyce via *Stephen Hero*, Ted Hughes in "The Seven Sorrows," and, most pertinently for Callaghan, perhaps, Samuel Beckett "in his insistence upon Good Friday as his birthday and his declaration that his 'birthmark' is his 'deathmark.' In the 'single sentence' of the spiritual biography gradually unfolding in his magnum opus, 'flesh becomes word' only to degenerate through a series of 'last words' into sound, 'a stain upon the silence'" (DBT, 702).

But what are the seven last words, as harmonized from the passion narratives of the four gospels? 1) "Father forgive them for they know not what they do"; 2) "Verily I say unto thee, today shalt thou be with me in paradise"; 3) "Woman behold thy son! . . . Behold thy mother!"; 4) "Eloi, Eloi, lama sabacthani" ("My God, my God, why hast thou forsaken me?"); 5) "I thirst"; 6) "It is finished" and 7) "Father, into thy hands I commend my spirit" (DBT, 701).

In the context of Hogg's journey into the hell of Leningrad and pre-glasnost, pre-perestroika Russia, the reference to paradise is a brutally ironic one, while the omnipresence of vodka there puts an unexpected gloss on "I thirst." And Beckett's famous characterization of human speech as a stain upon the silence resonates powerfully against our knowledge of the incomprehensible number of victims of a revolution-gone-direly-wrong: those exhausted by famine or slave labour or by torture in prison cells which became an obscene parody of the confessional.

The God of *The Seven Last Words* is a Father who has forsaken his Son, and does not merely appear to do so; He is the counter of sheep that keep on coming to the slaughter, the disposable victims of an overcrowded earth. But Hogg is no victim: he comes through this book not as Christ but as someone who works more in the spirit of sauve-qui-peut, "Sleepwalking / in Noah's muddy shoes" (SLW, 2), and having more than a passing acquaintance with the dove from the ark. And that dove is the symbol of the hope which features so precariously in *The Seven Last Words*, fighting for space with the various dogs which figure so ominously in the poems. Hogg's dove is the dove released from the ark, returning with an olive branch, the promise of humanly habitable space in a waste of waters. It is the dove of a cynic turned Holy Fool, who believes that "total darkness is irretrievable" (SLW, 3) and that "Ice is only rain yielding life again" – those seven last words with which Hogg takes his farewell of his lover Marina (SLW, 128). In speaking out as he does, wherever he finds himself, whether Dachau or Leningrad, Callaghan's Hogg is no poseur but a witness, cursed by "curiosity plus dread" (SLW, 2) and driven to speak of what he hears and feels and sees in a time and place in which silence, as Nadezhda Mandelstam's memoir *Hope Against Hope* informs us, is tantamount to a crime against humanity.

2. The Question of Context

Although the Notes to *The Seven Last Words* give us some idea of the historical context by which the poems are shaped and in which they resonate most fully, it is left to Callaghan's readers to learn what they need to know, both about the history of St. Petersburg in its various incarnations, and about the history of modern Russia. Hogg's Notes are as arch, in some places, as Eliot's to *The Wasteland*; they are prefaced by an epigraph from Margaret Atwood's "Notes Towards a Poem that Can Never be Written," a phrase concerning the foreignness of any home ground. These Notes are a coda to Hogg's journey, and though they identify or clarify some of the "characters" and incidents in *The Seven Last Words*, they point us, inevitably, to the part we need to play in the struggle for the survival of memory.

We need to inform ourselves, for example, of the continuum between Tsarist and Soviet autocracy; of how censorship in both cases led to the writing of texts with double meanings, set in foreign climes and earlier times, yet functioning as critiques of the present. We need to know that if the Leningrad which Hogg encounters is infernal, then the St. Petersburg/Petrograd which immediately preceded it was no less hellish for the majority of its citizens. I am speaking here of the massive numbers of peasants who fled to the city at the turn of the twentieth century, abandoning the Russia, in Trotsky's phrase, of icons and cockroaches, for a world illuminated by ideals of reason and progress, and human liberation. And while these pesasants turned workers may have cast off the dark superstitions of the village, the cockraoches were rather more tenacious. The new factories of St. Petersburg were located in the middle of that beautiful city, spewing toxic waste into the canals and rivers that formed the city's supply of drinking water. Landlords agitated against the construction of suburbs and public transport, insisting that workers be housed in whatever accommodation they could find in the centre of the city, with predictable results: massive overcrowding, lack of sanitation, contamination of the domestic water supply, breeding cholera and typhus, so that "The death rate in this City of the Tsars was the highest of any European capital, including Constantinople, with a cholera epidemic on average once in every three years" (PT, 112). In the winter of 1908, just three years after the first Russian revolution, which had forced the Tsar to give some power to elected representatives of the people, and nine years before the cataclysmic October revolution, 30,000 citizens of St. Petersburg were struck down by cholera.

While the formation and development of a Communist State extended the pool of human suffering into the middle and upper classes of Russia, it is worth remembering how acutely miserable the lives of working people were under the last tsar: "'One cannot help but note the premature decrepitude of the factory woman,' a senior doctor wrote in 1913. 'A woman worker of fifty sees and hears poorly, her head trembles, her shoulders are sharply hunched over. She looks about seventy. It is obvious that only dire need keeps her at the factory, forcing her to work beyond her strength. While in the West, elderly workers have pensions, our women workers can expect nothing better than to live out their last days as lavatory attendants'" (PT, 113).

It was in St. Petersburg, or rather Petrograd (as the city's name was Russianized and de-Germanized in WWI), that the October revolution broke out in 1917, leading to the seizure of power by the Bolshevik party and, shortly thereafter, the Dissolution of the Constituent Assembly. The consequences were civil war (1920-1) and famine in the cities (1921-22). (It was during this famine that Tsvetayeva's younger daughter starved to death in a Moscow children's home.) Emma Goldman described Petrograd in 1920 in terms of dirty, deserted streets, neglected houses, and emaciated people searching for crusts of bread and sticks of wood; the population was reduced from a pre-war 2 million to 500,000 so that the cultural capital of Russia resembled a ghost city. Gorky's description of Petrograd at the same historical moment speaks of dogs eating dead horses in the street; of canals crammed with rubbish. In other words, the pre-revolutionary conditions which prevailed in the workers' district – for example, excrement piled high in the back yards and collected by wooden carts at night – were replicated in the poshest parts of the city. Squalor and suffering were no longer the exclusive province of the "lower classes."

In 1918 Russia's capital was relocated from Petrograd to Moscow, a defensive move made by a vulnerable revolutionary government. By 1921, this government was under pressure from within as well as without. Peasant revolts against grain requisitioning had led to a massive shortage of food staples for the cities; with workers and soldiers starving in the streets, strikes became urgent and numerous. In Petrograd and Moscow, workers demanded an end to privileged rations for members of the communist party, restoration of free trade and movement, free re-elections to the Soviets or workers' councils, and a convocation of the Constituent Assembly dismissed by the Bolsheviks. The city that saw the outbreak of the

1917 revolution with the firing of the guns of the battleship *Aurora* witnessed an attempt by sailors in the Kronstadt garrison just to the north of Petrograd to reclaim the revolution in 1921 – a mutiny savagely put down by the Bolsheviks. Tragically, "Russia in the 1920s remained a society at war with itself – full of unresolved social tensions and resentments just below the surface. In this sense the deepest legacy of the revolution was its failure to eliminate the social inequalities that had brought it about in the first place" (PT, 771).

The bureaucratization of the Communist Party under Lenin created the foundation for Stalin's consolidation of power after Lenin's death in 1922. The disastrous effects of collectivization and of the ludicrous goals of the various five year plans are well-known, as is, one hopes, the appalling constructed famine of 1932-3 in Ukraine and Kazakhstan. Yet what had the greatest effect not only on Leningrad but also on the Soviet Union as a whole was the reign of terror unleashed by the staged assassination on December 1, 1934 of Sergei Kirov, Leningrad's Party Boss. Kirov's murder served as a pretext for massive purges over the next four years, purges facilitated by the NKVD, formed out of the former Cheka, the heir of the Tsarist secret police. Show trials were held in which leading members of the Communist Party – perceived rivals to Stalin and his apparatchiks – confessed to crimes against the state and to harbouring extreme reactionary goals. Gulags were built – rather as St. Petersburg itself had been – using slave labour, this time of political prisoners forced to exploit mining and logging resources in the far north and east of the U.S.S.R.

The zenith of the terror was reached in 1937-8. It claimed not only high-fliers such as Bukharin, the editor of *Izvestia*, and Rykov, the former prime minister, whose attempts to halt the terror ended in their arrest and abduction to Moscow's main prison, the Lubyanka, but many less prominent victims, as well. As historian Orlando Figes has observed, railway workers, engineers, anyone seen talking with a foreigner or who had been abroad, members of national minorities – all were targeted on charges of espionage or counter-revolutionary activity and worst of all, of being "a member of the family of a traitor to the fatherland." One of Stalin's most lunatic moves was the 1937 purge of experienced army officers – precisely the men most wanted when the 1939 Nazi-Soviet non-aggression pact was scrapped on June 22, 1941, when the Germans launched a surprise invasion of Russia. The enormous suffering of the people of the U.S.S.R. during WWII is, or should be, well-known, with the most horrific event of that war for the Soviet people being, arguably, the 900 day siege of Leningrad. Perhaps the only blessing of the war for Russians was the suspension of state persecution of artists. By 1946, however, Zhdanov, the notorious Commissar for Culture, was clamping down brutally on, among others, the writers Akhmatova and Zoschenko, and the musicians Shostakovich and Prokofiev. And just as artists were prevented from publishing or performing their work, leading scientists were sacked and forbidden to advance new theories and paradigms.

Stalin's death in 1953 and the resulting power struggle between Malenkov and Khrushchev, in which the latter, of course, prevailed, led to the Twentieth Party Congress of 1956, in which Khrushchev delivered his famous report "On the Cult of Personality and its Consequences" to a closed session of 1500 delegates. Rehabilitations of the purged, imprisoned and disgraced began immediately: millions were released from the gulags. But censorship was alive and well, as proved by the harassment of Boris Pasternak who, in 1958, was forced to refuse the offer of the Nobel prize for his novel critiquing the revolution, *Dr. Zhivago*. He was also brought to recant in *Pravda* in order to protect the safety and livelihood of his lover, Olga Ivinskaya – a translator, as is Hogg's Marina. (In 1949, after Pasternak had read parts of *Dr. Zhivago* to a Moscow audience, Olga Ivinskaya was arrested and interrogated at the Lubyanka, where she miscarried, only to be sent to a labour camp.)

Khrushchev was ousted in 1964, replaced by the geriatric crew of Kosygin, Andropov, Brezhnev, and Chernenko before Mikhail Gorbachev rose to power. His attempts to save Rusian communism by introducing the policies of glasnost ("openness') and perestroika ("restructuring") facilitated the collapse of the moribund Soviet Union in 1991. Hogg's visit to Leningrad can be assumed to have taken place in the period of stagnation after the ousting of Khruschev: a reference to "the Afghan hills" in "Mon Grand Guignol" (SLW, 59) dates his sojourn in Leninville as being post 1979, when the Soviets invaded Afghanistan and pre-1985, the year when Gorbachev became General Secretary of the Communist Party.

To read *The Seven Last Words* without even this amount of potted history in one's grasp would be as puzzling a task as watching the recent film *Russian Ark* without a notion of who Peter the Great, Pushkin, Catherine the Great, or the family of Nicholas II were, and what role they played in Russian history. It can be done, of course, but at the risk of impoverishing both the art and its impact upon us. It would be, you could argue, like an amnesiac reading the memoir of a life he doesn't know to be his own. Once more, it is not the poet's task to "supply the background," but rather, to so pique his or her readers' interest that they search out this history for themselves. What, after all, is a knowledge of history but the training of memory?

3. Against Forgetting

"Let no one forget; let nothing be forgotten!"

Extract from a poem by Olga Berggolts, inscribed on the belatedly erected wall of the memorial at Piskarevsky Cemetery, Leningrad (SL, 518).

Works like the W.G Sebald's *Austerlitz* and *The Emigrants*, Mavis Gallant's *The Pegnitz Junction* or Barry Callaghan's *Hogg The Seven Last Words* are written against the act of forgetting. They are not records of, or memorials to, horrific events but reinventions, reinscriptions of the fact of those events in a way that insists on our recognition of their impact upon us and our responsibility for them – not necessarily or increasingly our implication in the genesis or perpetration of those events, but our responsibility for remembering that they happened and for wanting, like Walter Benjamin's Angel of History, to undo the massive damage, or at least, to keep such horrors from happening again.

It may be useful to make a distinction, at this point, between moral and historical memory. Moral memory may be construed as having a primal source and trans-historical import. It consists in an awareness of the human capacity for inhuman behaviour: man's inhumanity to man, or, if you prefer, the souring, to the point of poison, of the milk of human kindness. (I use this last word not as a synonym for 'niceness' but in the Shakespearean sense that we are all of the human kind or species; I would further suggest that to inflict injustice and cruelty, needless suffering or death on another is to break a taboo that should be as absolute as those against incest and cannibalism – the latter having been practised in Leningrad in the terrible winter of 1941-2.)

Historical memory is as collective an entity as moral memory; it can be understood as our knowledge of how lapses and occasions of moral memory have occurred on a mammoth scale throughout recorded time. Events such as the practice of the African slave trade, the genocide against the Armenians or the Tutsis, the use of atomic bombs against Hiroshima and Nagaskai and, on the angels' side, the Emancipation movement of the nineteenth century and, in the twentieth, the overthrow of Apartheid, should form part of the historical memory of the species, without which we are doomed to repeat our catastrophic errors and malignant actions until we have effectively destroyed ourselves as a species. With the practice of moral and historical memory, foreign territory becomes home ground, and home ground is recognized as foreign territory, to refer to the epigraph Hogg takes from Atwood.

In the context of moral memory, one of the most powerful themes of *The Seven Last Words* is the cruelty inflicted by parents upon children: the psychological as well as physical/sexual abuse of Marina by her father, for example, and the lethal surveillance by the "man with silverfish eyes" of his son's desires in "Amputated Love." "How," the father asks Hogg, "do I apologize before he dies?" The question is an example of the revival, the very functioning of moral memory. In this context, too, Hogg himself is "rattled" by anger at a cinema audience's reponse to the plight of a physically and psychologically trapped man. What infuriates Hogg most is not the audience's delight in the man's being literally sunk by his predicament, but rather their roars of laughter as the glassed telephone booth in which the man's been hiding vanishes, and "the waters settled into an absolute stillness" (SLW, 40). It is this double erasure – from the moral horizon of the audience, and from historical memory, as though the man, his predicament and the forces which set it into motion had never existed – that devastates Hogg and drives him to exorcise his anger by "making wordless love standing up by the sink until

[Marina] cried out, her mouth twisted by joy, his anger swealing away" (SLW, 40).

The exercise of moral memory, which involves the activation of curiosity as well as conscience – in itself a particular form of imagination – enters the realm of the historical with the details supplied by a poem like "Amputated Love," in which those whose dreams transgress the borders of desire set down by the state find themselves "queuing for aminazine / in psychiatric jails" (SLW, 41). The condition of Russia – and the events of the twentieth century, for that matter – subverts "any optimistic view of history" (SLW, 147). But where optimism fails, irony flourishes: hence Callaghan's inclusion in both poems and notes of such details as the fact that it is to Fritz Haber, a German-Jewish chemist, that we owe the invention of chemical warfare in WWI and the idea of using Zyklone B gas to exterminate European Jewry during WWII (SLW, 121, 149-50). Or the fact that when, during Stalin's terror, it became clear that those denouncing friends and neighbours would make themselves liable to arrest and imprisonment, the volume of denunciations did not diminish but actually increased (SLW, 146).

Much of what *The Seven Last Words* remembers concerns how Soviet power, as turned against its own citizens, produced a world of betrayal and abuse of trust, in which corruption, spying, blackmail, suicide and murder in its official and unofficial forms, proliferated. The consequence, as Hogg discovers to his cost, is that personal relations are hopelessly compromised; thus in "Sour Grapes," Marina reminds Hogg not to trust anyone who befriends him in Leningrad – not even herself. In a world where everyone is out to save her or his own skin from an army of knife-happy flayers, memory becomes a matter of the most urgent self-interest.

Finally, Callaghan's insistence on the act of remembering in *The Seven Last Words* must be understood in the context of such obscenities as the official forgetting of the Leningrad blockade. This involved gross understatement of the sacrifices made by ordinary citizens as well as members of the armed forces, the minimizing of the death toll, the closing of the Museum of the Defence of Leningrad, the arrest of its director and confiscation of its archives, all for the purpose of preventing negative political repercussions for those in the Soviet elite most responsible for the city's wartime suffering (SL, 518; RE, 158).

"Nothing in the chamber of Stalin's horrors," it has been observed, "equaled the Leningrad blockade and its epilogue, the Leningrad affair. The blockade may have cost the lives of a million and a half people. The 'affair' destroyed thousands of people who survived the most terrible days any modern city had ever known" (SL, 582). The Leningrad affair involved politically motivated charges that the Council for the Defense of Leningrad was part of a plot to deliver the city to the Germans, charges used to "exterminate all Zhdanov's lieutenants and thousands of minor officials. They were shot or sent to prison camps" (SL, 582). Interestingly, it has been said that Stalin was prepared to sacrifice Leningrad to the Germans, who intended to raze the city to the ground, as they did, more or less, to Warsaw.

4. Portrait of a City

In 2003, to enormous hoopla and at enormous expense, St. Petersburg celebrated the 300th anniversary of the founding of Russia's "Window on the West" by an autocrat who had been powerful enough to get away with the murder of his own son. It seems entirely appropriate that a westerner, the eponymous Hogg, should gaze through the window offered by his own social, cultural, and political formation, onto the city of Peter the Great.

St. Petersburg has always been a city brutally scarred by history. It was built on the bones of the slaves who transformed marshland into what would become the Venice of the North. It was the scene of "Bloody Sunday" (1905) when the city's abject poor marched peacefully to the Winter Palace only to be fired upon by mounted cossacks, resulting in the death of a hundred people. It was the birthplace of the revolution of 1905 and the February and October revolutions of 1917. It also withstood, at a staggering human cost, the 900 day siege launched by the Germans in 1941. During the first winter of the siege, it is estimated that 1000 Leningraders died each day of cold and of starvation in a city deprived of electricity, fuel for heating, and anything like adequate food supplies. (As Marina tells Hogg in the poem "Hunger," "our soldiers / ate cattle cakes and boiled carpenter's glue / and froze to death in antitank ditches / refusing to cut ancestral trees for firewood" (SLW, 79). Wood for coffins became almost nonexistent: bodies were dumped on the streets or, if the bereaved possessed the strength, lugged on children's sleds to the burial grounds. Often the bearers of the bodies would collapse and die of the effort involved in simply reaching the cemetery.

Appropriately, Callaghan's Leningrad is haunted by ghosts both native and foreign, from Tsar Peter to Rasputin to the dissident Vladimir Bukovsy, from Dostoevsky to Apollinaire and Paul Celan. Even the streetscapes of *The Seven Last Words* resonate with the phantoms of past events. The Astoria Hotel, where Hogg and Marina attempt to escape surveillance while making love, is the very hotel to which top Party bosses moved during the civil war, and where they lived luxuriously, being addressed, it is said, as "Comrade Master" by the "comrade servants." It was also the locale in which a principal convalescent station was set up at the end of December 1941, to try and keep some of the population's "elite personnel" from starving and freezing to death (some of the elite had been evacuated at the start of the siege – Akhmatova was one of these lucky ones, though she bitterly regretted her exile from her beloved city). The journalist Nikolai Markevich described conditions at this "convalescent station" thus: "The hotel is dead. Like the whole city there is neither water nor light. In the dark corridors rarely appears a figure, lighting his way with a . . . hand-generator flashlight or a simple match. The rooms are cold, the temperature not rising above 40 degrees. Writing these lines my hand is almost frozen" (SL, 493).

Appropriately, one of Hogg's orientation points in Leningrad is the Troubetzkoy Bastion of the Peter and Paul fortress, St. Petersburg's most ancient prison (SLW, 87). Moscow's infamous Lubyanka prison becomes a powerful, if borrowed, part of the ambiance of Leningrad, as is the sweep of the gulag, in the references made to Kolyma, for example, the far north-east corner of Siberia, where living conditions, climate and isolation were harshest (SLW, 10). Stalingrad makes an entrance in the same poem as "the work camps of Siberia" (SLW, 27). Marina's address off Glinka Street is associated with the siege, during which her "'grandmother's ivory-inlaid metronome / was propped by one of the symphony's second violinists / before an open microphone / at the radio station / so if Shostakovich stopped / the nation would know / we were still alive by the / *tock tock tock*'"(SLW, 47). The Petrovski bridge marks both the site of Rasputin's murder and the resting place of a cold war "arctic submarine hunter"(SLW, 59). It is from this rusted hulk that a former lover of Marina's, a crazed, maimed verteran of Russia's Vietnam in Afghanistan, makes a shelter for himself. On the most famous street in St. Petersburg, Nevsky Prospekt, black marketeers, *zeks* or survivors of the gulags, and madwomen parade, along with "guttersnipes, deadbeats, leeches / who say they only steal because Stalin stole their lives" (SLW, 78).

It is a city of winter, of scraped ice, snow – cold fleece on a black day" (SLW, 30) – death by drowning, and mass graves of the machine-gunned (SLW, 83): not, one imagines, the most auspicious season or city for a love affair. Hogg and Marina meet in grimy cafés invaded by the police, and in a restaurant made from a converted battle cruiser and frequented by the KGB (SLW, 102). As for the Mikhailovsky Gardens, it is the scene not of kisses but of screams, not of dalliance, but of furtive commerce – it is outside the gardens that Hogg encounters the small boy selling wooden scarecrows whose souls glow in the dark (SLW, 14). The flowers in this wintry city are dried or plastic – or malevolantly alive, like the "black poppy" microphone in a bedside vase (SLW, 31). Hogg promises to find his lover 'real flowers . . . perhaps /a pot of eyebrights" (SLW, 51) but we never learn if he has been able to achieve this miraculous feat – as difficult in this city, one suspects, as it was for the heros of fairytales to find strawberries in the snow. Perhaps the closest one comes to a living flower in *The Seven Last Words* is Tsvetayeva's famous description of love as a flower flooded with blood (SLW, 66).

In the run-up to the 2003 tricentennial celebration of St. Petersburg's founding, ordinary Russian citizens were to be heard remarking on the injustice of so much money being spent on fireworks and circuses in a city stricken by an acute shortage of affordable housing. The immense gap between hyper-rich and degradedly poor remains as obscene as it was in Dostoevsky's time, it seems, or in Akhmatova's, when she and her lover Nikolai Punin had to share an apartment with Putnin's former wife. *Plus ça change.*

5. *Love, Lust, Mistresses, Muses*

The violence of cruelty and destruction in *The Seven Last Words* is opposed by the violence of desire and the "production" of ecstasy – ex stasis, the power to free oneself from the prison of time and space, from the executioner's shadow, as, for example, "the Master" and Margarita do in Bulgakov's eponymous novel. For those trapped in the terrors or endless daily frustrations of Soviet Russia (see "Stasis," SLW 68), the achievement of ecstasy, spiritual or sexual (or à la Bernini's St. Teresa, the two in one) is a mode of deliverance all the more precious for its rarity and transitoriness.

For Love, in *The Seven Last Words*, walks hand in hand with Terror. (In Stalin's time, Terrora was a popular girl's name – perhaps replacing Lyuba, which means love.) In the infernal city which Hogg explores, "Love is / a caveat" at worst, at best, "a silent prayer / sung for the living / by the dead" (SLW, 3; 111). As for Eros, the play of desire, it gets short shrift, ambushed as it continually is by suspicion, fear, and the inevitability of betrayal: each time Marina embraces Hogg she is taking into her arms the "crook-backed" spies who overhear every whisper and shadow every movement (SLW, 18). Perhaps the most eloquent expression of eros ambushed by terror is the poem "Wishboned": "At midnight she made a wish on his body / and began to dream / of sleeping till the end of time: the drip drip / of blood / in the hourglass stopped, / whipping stalls stood empty, / only the stain remained / as men ladling stars / from root cellars / saw aureolas appear / around their eyes, a promise of rain, / and fear big as sails / took flight. / In still waters / she lay waiting / to never wake up. / It was unbearable, / like waiting / for a child to drown. / At dawn, / she began to scream" (SLW, 58).

Hogg's lover Marina owes much of her fascination to the two great poets Anna Akhmatova and Marina Tsvetayeva. The latter, after a period of exile in France and Czechoslovakia, returned to Russia in 1941, only to hang herself shortly thereafter (her husband and eldest daughter were both in a gulag at the time). Tsvetayeva is a poet identified with Moscow, the city of her birth; she is famous for her intense love affairs as well as her hugely original poetics, and for such works as "Poem of Leaving" detailing, with spirit and fierce energy, the unwelcome end of a love affair. Ahkmatova, who outlived Tsvetayeva by some twenty–five years, was often referred to as the "Muse of Tears" for her many poems dealing with the loss or failure of romantic love. Yet it is Akhmatova who is synonymous with St. Petersburg/Petrograd/Leningrad, with, for example, Fontany Dom, a former mansion in one of whose rooms she managed to live off black bread and unsugared tea. Or the Stray Dog Café located in the basement of a building on Mikhailovsky Square, where the new wave of Russian poets met to read their work in the years leading up to WWI. And it is Akhmatova who wrote the finest public poem of her epoch, the famous "Requiem," which grew from her experience of lining up, with hundreds of other women, outside Leningrad's prisons, waiting for some news of their menfolk who had vanished within.

Hogg's affair with Marina becomes, in fact, a kind of *ménage à quatre* with her and the ghosts of Tsvetayeva and Akhmatova. Both poets spent extended periods with lovers who curtailed their writing, either through outright hostility, or through their inability to provide the means of support that would have released the women from the heavy tasks imposed on them by domesticity in conditions of extreme poverty. And though Hogg is no Shileyko or Efron to his lover, burning her work or endangering her life through his bungling, Marina is the kind of "wounded" worshipful lover that both Akhmatova and Tsvetayeva represented themselves as being in their poems. For both poets, it was possible to have an intense relationship, through the written word, with persons they had never met; for Hogg this is also true. Tsvetayeva and Akhmatova often function as Muses in *The Seven Last Words*. Thus "Himmler's Law" owes not a little to Akhmatova's "Lot's Wife," just as "Promise of Rain" invokes Tsvetayeva's "Poems for Blok."

Certainly, Hogg's Marina is worshipful of the man she describes as the sun that rises between her thighs (SLW, 25); "I love you like I love God"(SLW, 47), she declares. Hogg's fascination with Rasputin's fabled sexual powers and privileges, which included whipping the "wife of a Petersburg general, / as a concertina played and she held him / by his cock, crying out, 'You are God!'" (SLW, 52) may, in fact, be mistaken. According to Orlando Figes, Rasputin's assassin and alleged homosexual lover, Felix Yusupov, claimed that his prowess was explained by a large wart strategically situated on his penis, which was of exceptional size. On the other hand there is evidence to suggest that Rasputin was in fact impotent and that while he lay naked with many women, he had sex with very few of them. In short, he was a great lecher but not a great lover. When Rasputin was medically examined after being stabbed in a failed murder attempt in 1914, his genitals were found to be so small and shrivelled that the doctor wondered whether he were capable of the sexual act at all. Rasputin himself had once boasted to the monk Ilidor that he could lie with women without feeling passion because his "penis did not function" (PT, 32).

Whatever the case with Rasputin's – or Hogg's – sexual prowess, the point to register is that eros cannot help but be a dead end in the kind of police state which pre- and post-revolutionary Russia were. In "Puppy Love,"

Marina confesses to Hogg that she has lied to him throughout their affair: "I lie and lie / Even about lying. It's how / I made love to you, / in love, like a blind / puppy being drowned, / swallowing the dark / as if it were air, / choking on air, / crying, / I'm free, see, see, / there's no despair, no prayer, / only you. Yes, you, and no, / I was not afraid, no I'm not, / it's true, / everything else I said to you was a lie" (SLW, 123). Love, then, is no deliverance, but only another form of labyrinthine betrayal in the cause of self-preservation.

Another fundamental mode of deliverance from the horrors of the here and now is absent in Callaghan's text, or rather, is available only to the visitor, the witness, becoming the poems we read in *The Seven Last Words*. I am referring here to the ecstasy of creative activity experienced, for example, by Boris Pasternak's Yury Zhivago, writing for the first time in years, in the compromised paradise of Varykino. Surrounded by howling wolves and yet buoyed by the comfort and peace of his lover's presence, the "happiness and life" of the stillness pervading the house once everyone else is asleep, Zhivago writes poems into the small hours of the night:

> After two or three stanzas and several images by which he was himself astonished, his work took possession of him and he experienced the approach of what is called inspiration. At such moments the correlation of the forces controlling the artist is, as it were, stood on its head. The ascendancy is no longer with the artist or the state of mind which he is trying to express, but with language, his instrument of expression. Language, the home and dwelling of beauty and meaning, itself begins to think and speak for man and turns wholly into music, not in the sense of outward, audible sounds but by the virtue of the power and momentum of its inward flow. Then, like the current of a mighty river polishing stones and turning wheels by its

very movement, the flow of speech creates in passing, by the force of its own laws, rhyme and rhythm and countless other forms and formations, still more important and until now undiscovered, unconsidered and unnamed.

At such moments, Yury felt that the main part of his work was not being done by him but by something which was above him and controlling him: the thought and poetry of the world as it was at that moment and as it would be in the future. He was controlled by the next step it was to take in the order of its historical development; and he felt himself to be only the pretext and the pivot setting it in motion.

This feeling relieved him for a time of self-reproach, of dissatisfaction with himself, of the sense of his own nothingness.

At three in the morning Yury looked up from his papers. He came back from his remote, selfless concentration, home to reality and to himself, happy, strong, peaceful. (DZ, 389-390)

Hogg's Marina, as previously noted, is no poet, but a translator. The poet's voice in Soviet Russia is a posthumous one, as we hear in "Osip Mandelstam Moves His Lips": "Now I'm dead in the grave, teeth / singing in the zero" (SLW, 29). The explanation for this is whispered to Hogg by the poet Voznesensky: "They / can hang / light bulbs / by / a vinyl / cord // but / the poet / hangs / by / his / spinal / chord" (SLW, 55).

6. Technicalities

What are the most striking features of the poems Hogg brings back from his *saison en enfer*? Perhaps it is the fact that these poems come to us in a host of different voices, not only Hogg's and Marina's, but also those of a variety of Russians, exemplary and noxious. In "Stasis," for example, we hear ordinary Russians describing day to day experiences and rituals, lining up for "sugar, squeaky rubber shoes . . . toilet rolls . . . a single lemon" (SLW, 68). In "Tomorrow's man," Smerdikov the "shiv," thief and general opportunist, denounces Yevtushenko for being in the pocket of the apparatchiks, then declares: "This country's history is a breathing // corpse. I'm the left hand in its right pocket / Watch me pick it clean" (SLW, 108-9).

The Seven Last Words is, in fact, a patchwork of translations, monologues, conversations, quotations and explanatory notes that, in many cases, function as prose poems in their own right. Russian proverbs and fairy tales, or versions thereof, bureaucratic forms ("Classification of Apartment Claimant [para.26. sect.16.16]" (SLW, 32), "legal fragments"(SLW, 42) and trial notes (SWL, 92) are interwoven into the tissue of Hogg's and Marina's declarations and confessions. The effect is Bakhtinian: no one authoritative or magisterial voice is allowed to emerge; the collection as a whole resists the temptations of any easy order and wholeness.

Most noticeably, this sequence of poems is distinguished by the frequent use of rhyme, perfect and imperfect, and lilting rhythm, which often create the effect of nursery rhymes recited in Hell, as in Lady Macbeth's "the thane of Fife / had a wife / where is she now?" A poem such as "Her Potato Song" is written in the idiom of a playground chant (SLW, 117); "Letters," in the singsong of a nonsense rhyme (SLW, 22). Some of the most haunting poems in this volume are the small collages of reported speech, proverbs and authorial witness – as in "Snowflake": "It began to snow. / 'You suspect my silence, / but it is the way I keep my head clear, / wiping each thought / like a small mirror / or antique angel or candlestick. / The small things / men kill for I clean: / it's all we can do, especially with wounds.' / A child took a snowflake on his tongue. / He's swallowed a tear, / his life has begun" (SLW, 36).

Hogg The Seven Last Words is too rich and complex a work to be summed up by anything so sketchy as a series of notes. It is a work that repays repeated rereading, one that demands its readers learn as much as they can about the world it describes, a world both inspiring and repugnant, and all too human. With its combination of power, beauty, rawness, and something that might be called prayer, it leads us through a labyrinth that can only be negotiated through the passionate practice of memory.

Works Cited and Abbreviations Used

Callaghan, Barry. *Hogg The Seven Last Words*. Toronto: McArthur & Company, 2001. (SLW)

Figes, Orlando. *A People's Tragedy: The Russian Revolution 1891-1924*. London: Pimlico, 1996. (PT)

Moseley, Virginia, "Seven Last Words" in D.L.Jeffrey, ed. *A Dictionary of Biblical Tradition in English Literature* . Grand Rapids: William B. Eerdmans Publishing Company, 1992. (DBT)

Pasternak, Boris. *Doctor Zhivago*, tr. Max Hayward and Manya Harari. London: Collins and Harvill Press, 1958. (DZ)

Salisbury, Harrison E. *The 900 Days: The Siege of Leningrad*. New York: Harper & Row, 1969. (SL)

Note: I have used Callaghan's spellings of transliterated Russian names throughout.

THE FICTION

The Black Queen Stories, The Way the Angel Spreads Her Wings, When Things Get Worst, and *A Kiss is Still a Kiss*

BARRY'S LAMENT

Douglas "Dougie" Richardson

THE BLACK QUEEN STORIES

TIMOTHY FINDLEY

In writing *The Black Queen Stories*, Barry Callaghan has kept the Queen of Spades well hidden up his sleeve. In most of the stories, he only shakes her down to lay her shadow out across the page – a thing he does with the kind of finesse you expect of a good magician. When the Black Queen makes her actual appearance, the result is surprising, comic and startlingly sad. Callaghan deals her neither from the deck nor from up his sleeve, but snaps her out of the air and slaps her hard of someone's forehead: gluing her there for everyone to see. He parades her like an announcement: "Look, everybody! Look who I am!" After which, he fades her out of sight. But she hovers over all the stories until, at last, we discover she is neither sinister nor lethal, neither capricious nor prejudiced. She is simply there in all our lives – and we have to learn how to cope with her.

Reading through these stories, there is an odd familiarity which, for a while, remains elusive: not about the tales themselves but about the kinds of people and the places they describe. At last, it becomes clear that Callaghan's people and the places in which they live have something in common with the people and the places found in the books of Marian Engel. There – as it should – the analogy stops. Engel and Callaghan are certainly writing about the same city streets and houses. Each has clearly witnessed the same parade, but each has come home with a different set of notes and each has offered a unique observation of the parade and the streets through which it winds.

There is, nonetheless, an awareness in reading *The Black Queen Stories* that just around the corner there's a row of houses known as Lunatic Villas. This – though it might appear to smack of comparison (with Engel) – does nothing of the sort. It is just a comment, made important by the fact that – *at last* – an identifiable place is beginning to emerge: a place that exists beyond its concrete self, as Paris does because of Dumas and Zola and Gertrude Stein and London because of Boswell and Thackerey and Virginia Woolf; a place whose people have achieved a literary dimension – readable and recognizable because of books such as Engel's *Honeyman Festival* and *Lunatic Villas*, Margaret Atwood's *Life Before Man* and Callaghan's *The Black Queen Stories*.

Here, in other words, are a place and a people taking that first and vital step toward maturity – which is to say, their existence can be *imagined*: they can be overheard and spied on – yearned for – laughed at and grieved over – seen without actually being beheld. And this, of course, is precisely why this country and its people have been such a long time in coming to grips with what and who we are. We could, none of us, imagine one another – let alone ourselves. Well – those days are over, done with, gone. And here we are, in *The Black Queen Stories*.

The book is magical. Much of this magic lies in the tales themselves. The rest is in their presentation. Callaghan's voice is always on the verge of that unmistakable Irish rhythm his name suggests – but the stories forbid that it be constant. The people here are Jews, Italians, Chinese, French; some from France and China, Italy and Israel – others not, being born in Canada. This way, the book abounds in the dialects of those for whom English is an acquired and foreign language and also in the dialects of class and color and lifestyle. It speaks in the voices of blond and boy-thin girls come up from California and in the voices of blacks whose lives have been lived without a glimpse of daylight; of neon-spangled transvestites and jet-set, garter-belt monosexual ladies; jazz musicians and history teachers; men and women who meet in art galleries, waving from a distance, never speaking except to themselves.

Like all good books of stories, there's a unifying theme – but it's not obtrusive, not insistent – more like the pulse you hear alone in the night than a drum or anything else that beats outside yourself. This theme is darkness; not, however, the darkness lying at the edge of all our lives brought into focus and identified: the darkness of things not done, of loves that have never been declared and of hatreds not acted out and left to fester, relationships that might have been but weren't achieved.

All the stories seem to begin or end with twilight and in almost every story there are faces seen through mirrors, windows, glass in one form or another. Nearly every conversation is only half recounted, interrupted by a memory of something else being said in someone's mind – or the thought of something wanting to be said aloud, but silenced out of fear or shyness. And out of these half-said, half-seen images, thrown against a screen of vividly recounted whole events, Callaghan leaves us with the unmistakable news that, if we reached a little further, we could touch, and if we turned the noises down inside our heads, we just might hear the voices of our lovers and our friends.

Why are these called *The Black Queen Stories*? Perhaps because, if we hadn't given up on love or walked away from life and other people, the Black Queen wouldn't be there waiting to be dealt into all our lives. It is not, these stories tell us, just mindless fate that hangs her above our heads. She is avoidable. The trouble is that we seek her out, insisting the Queen of Spades is a part of the human condition, a kind of blind acceptance that we have to fail.

But Callaghan knows better than to let us wallow in this news. Instead, he leads us – in stories of great maturity and beauty – into worlds where children, born to fail, succeed by outwitting the failure of others; where impotence becomes a man's defence against achieving a dream relationship he would rather keep as a dream; and where, in a truly masterful story called "A Terrible Discontent," an old blind woman succeeds in trapping her tormentors into reliving her own failure to connect with other human beings – a story in which failure itself is a kind of triumphant success.

THE SHORT STORY AS MINIATURE

Barry Callaghan's "The Black Queen"

MICHAEL TRUSSLER

In *The Genesis of Secrecy*, Frank Kermode sympathetically refers to Wilhelm Dilthey's notion of the "impression-point," that incisive moment of a life or a text which "gives articulation to the whole" (*Genesis* 147 n. 4). Concerned primarily with the "impression-point" as an aspect of reading, Kermode is attentive to the provisional nature of such moments. He maintains that this particular exegetic approach may involve either "discovery or choice" (*Genesis* 16); that is, these openings need not be determined solely by textual guidance, but can instead be generated by the reader. While it is irresolvable whether a life or a text offers the unity necessary for an interpretation that relies upon the revelatory impression-point, it is readily apparent that the short story fundamentally solicits (and critiques) the hermeneutic examination of the relationship between part and whole. Traditionally, the genre has engaged the notion of the impression-point through its propensity for the epiphany, but one can expand this observation to say that short fiction generally activates a version of the hermeneutic circle. It is surprising that no short story theorist, to my knowledge, directly acknowledges hermeneutics as part of his or her methodology since it is clear that the discipline's early principles have generally influenced the scholarly and popular discourse surrounding the form.

There seems to be something intrinsic to the genre that impels numerous writers to speak of it in holistic terms. Formalist criticism has furthered Edgar Allan Poe's dictum that a short story should strive for "a single *effect*" (47) by analyzing the form's dependence upon imminent endings, which would be an instance of a textually directed impression point (see John Gerlach and Susan Lohafer). For Nadine Gordimer, to write a short story is to create "the life-giving drop – sweat, tear, semen, saliva – that will spread an intensity on the page; burn a hole in it" (*Selected* 15). Invoking the reciprocity between the body and its constituent parts, this cellular imagery parallels the metaphor underlying Dilthey's thinking; the very small intrinsically accommodates a larger whole. In their content, both classic and contemporary short stories thematize existential identity, implicitly asking the question with which A.S. Byatt begins her review of Alice Munro's *The Love of a Good Woman*: "Do we experience life as a continuum or as a series of disconnected shocks and accidents?" (16). Although especially germane to Munro's writing, this inquiry is relevant to most short fiction, given the genre's overall accentuation of epistemological and ethical crisis. Complimenting Munro by comparing her work to Gustave Flaubert's *Trois Contes*, Byatt declares that Munro's short stories "contain whole lives . . . in the brief spaces of tales" (16). Byatt's high praise tacitly sets up a generic ideal: the short story should strive to compress the meaning of an entire life into a single incident or brief series of events. But how can we think through this generic correspondence between part and whole, this notion that the short story somehow extends beyond itself?

Terry J. Martin proposes that John Barth's "Petition" is "a paradigmatic example of the short story as microcosm" ("Barth" 79). Although Martin's use of the Greek term is quite general – to him, Barth's story "forms a microcosm of all human conflict" ("Barth" 79) – the notion of the microcosm offers a preliminary means of understanding the short story's engagement with a larger totality. However, to call upon such an obsolete epistemology is immediately to be plunged into difficulties. Consider George Boas' definition: "The idea indicated by the couple, Macrocosm-Microcosm, is the belief that there exists between the universe and the individual human being an identity both anatomical and psychical" ("Macrocosm" 126). Because few individuals would admit that an "identical" concordance exists between the human subject and the cosmos, perhaps it would be simplest to say that when contemporary writers use the word "microcosm," or refer to microcosmic correspondences, they are only speaking loosely. Or perhaps we should follow Hermann Lotze who, in *Microcosmus*, speaks of "the mind's tendency always to seek for connection and order" (666); this system thus testifies to our ancient horror of chaos as much as it announces our joy in making associations. While our use of the term doesn't entail the intricacy of systematic connections mapped out by Renaissance Neoplatonism, the concept that the local gives rise to the global remains a potent one. To speak of literary manifestations of the microcosm, however, becomes limiting because these aesthetic objects are thereby denied artistic selection and particularity; if the microcosm shares an exact accord with the universe, then all literary texts presumably reiterate this identical relationship.

Gottfried Wilhelm Leibniz's metaphysics suggest an initial way out of this problem. His *Monadology*, the most sophisticated development of microcosmic thought, describes individual monads as expressing totality while retaining singularity:

And as the same town, looked at from various sides, appears quite different and becomes as it were numerous in aspects [*perspectivement*]; even so, as a result of the infinite number of simple substances, it is as if there were so many different universes, which, nevertheless are nothing but aspects [*perspectives*] of a single universe, according to the special view of each Monad (*Monadology* 248).

A specific short story, then, if seen as one of Leibniz's monads, maintains a unique bond with the larger totality to which other short stories also refer (though the analogy is complicated by Leibniz's belief that the monads are windowless, an issue to which I will return later). To say that all short stories immanently contain the same "universe," and that they maintain an intrinsic ratio with each other, however, contravenes the pluralist tendency of contemporary thought; most people would be skeptical of Leibniz's unifying theological principle of "pre-established Harmony," the divine grounding that underlies all monads.

Let us therefore abandon the rationalist metaphysics in Leibniz's thought, and, follow Theodor Adorno, who keeps the monad as an aesthetic model, owing to its substantial descriptive power. To him, "Artworks synthesize ununifiable, non-identical elements that grind away at each other" (*Aesthetic* 176), "and yet in their hermeticism, they represent what is external" (*Aesthetic* 179). Perceived in this manner, short stories depart from "reality" by condensing often incommensurate elements from the larger world in a monadic fashion, while simultaneously, they point beyond themselves; each in its own way "strain[s] toward the whole" (*Aesthetic* 178). Different from Adorno, who compares all art objects to the monad, let me posit that the short story is a genre that particularly reveals a residual monadology. Part of the reason that so many writers employ organic or microcosmic imagery in their discussions of the short story is that, as we shall see, the form itself contains persistent traces of this pre-modern world view.

Unlike the novel, described by Barth and others as being "a cosmos itself" (*Friday* 17), the short story is closer to Leibniz's model; instead of actively creating a world, the short story is a monad that immanently, although tentatively, reflects one. "Writing stories," remarks Grace Paley, "I wanted to get the world to explain itself to me, to speak to me" ("A Conversation" 1527). Paley's use of the philosophical conception of "the world" suggests how, for her, national associations need not necessarily define short fiction. Certainly Paley's stories reflect New York City, but paradoxically, her strenuous historicity implicitly moves beyond the local in a microcosmic manner. Much Canadian fiction operates similarly; as we shall see, stories that are based in Canadian culture raise questions that go beyond national boundaries. Prodding "the world" to speak, then, the short story writer *reverses* the usual direction of microcosmic progression. Rather than moving from the small to the immense, Paley's phenomenological project is one in which totality contracts itself into the fragment, an important distinction.

The extreme brevity of Barry Callaghan's "The Black Queen" – only three pages in *The Oxford Book of Canadian Short Stories* (1988), making it the briefest in the anthology – recommends the text for an examination of the genre's monadic qualities. By emphasizing the assembly of a stamp collection, "The Black Queen" self-consciously evokes the dynamic reciprocity of part and whole. All collections create an internal autonomy as much as they point to those elements that are as yet missing from the set. Although Callaghan's story depicts rage and love, and closes with one character making an astonishingly gentle gesture to another, "The Black Queen" is constrained in its turbulence, aware of itself as a minute literary object.

Thinking about the story's keenly polished realism, its penchant for Victoriana, and its dependence upon the local, made me choose the word "miniature" for my title, rather than "microcosm." The miniature shares the microcosm's urge to go beyond itself; the miniature too demands an abstract totality to grant it cohesion, but it is also so much more apparently something created, something almost clumsily secular. In *The Poetics of Space*, Gaston Bachelard suggests that "the *causality of smallness* stirs all our senses" (*Poetics* 174). Short story enthusiasts are drawn to this "smallness." Part of this attraction, I think, entails our desire to make the story connect to our larger private worlds while, similar to our experience of the miniature, we happily, sometimes gratefully, acknowledge that the story quite clearly exists apart from our projections. "The Black Queen" is a literary miniature that contains, among other things, the notion of the microcosm; the story is founded, like the microcosm, on the mysteries of the human body.

I

Part of a short story cycle that resembles James Joyce's *Dubliners,* in as much as the collection delves into a particular time and place, in this instance Toronto in the 1970s, the story "The Black Queen" can also be read on its own terms. Because the story is more likely to be familiar to readers in its anthologized version, I will ignore its place within the original volume, other than to say that Callaghan uses the figure of the "black queen" as a unifying motif, among other things, that floats throughout the stories: a postage stamp in the title story, it becomes a playing card in "A Terrible Discontent." To continue further the *Dubliners* comparison, "The Black Queen," like the "The Dead," warrants being pondered separately for the especial power it gains when read as an autonomous text.

Specifically mentioning that a week passes during the story, Callaghan foregrounds the experience of temporality. Hughes and McCrae, a gay couple undergoing a crisis resulting from the onset of middle age, are falling victim to rampant decomposition. Their once up-scale neighbourhood is no longer attractive, the culture of their youth isn't current anymore, and their bodies' aging has taken them by surprise. Painstakingly bourgeois, they maintain their dignity by daily ritual, irony, and stamp collecting. Quarrelling with each other because they can't alter these larger changes, they hold their customary Mother's Day party during which McCrae startles Hughes. He's secretly purchased "an elegant black stamp of Queen Victoria in her widow's weeds" ("Queen" 60) that he pastes on his forehead and then he serves the hors d'oeuvres, winking at his lover. Gently depicting these two "fastidious men," Callaghan takes care to catch the reader unawares with McCrae's unanticipated frivolity; nothing in his characterization leads one to predict he'd make such a self-effacing, yet thoroughly orchestrated, gesture – one old queen displays another. In fact, this unexpected romp with Dada is at odds with the story's rich, though strangely selective, elaboration of setting and psychological background.

For a story of this concision, the narrator at first seems overly meticulous in providing textual detail. Some of the description is coded to provide psychological insight; the couple's picket fence is "painted pale blue" ("Queen" 58), which presumably indicates their Camp response to that conventional mainstay of the North American middle class. But the narrator's delineation of their stamp book, also blue, as having "seven little plastic windows per page" ("Queen" 59) is noticeably calculated. Callaghan gives the impression of being deliberately spurious in this descriptive exactitude. The characters' moods are presented with equal nuance; depressed by the unpleasant appearance of aging flesh, Hughes and McCrae wish "to yield almost tearfully" ("Queen" 59), the adverb rendering a distinction that recalls Henry James in its circumscribed intensity. Viewing the story as a verbal miniature clarifies these fine differentiations; unlike a physical miniature in which the diminutive is made visibly apparent, the literary miniature must communicate the sensation of having one's attention drawn to the infinitesimal. This scrupulous style exactly suits the story, not so much because the couple are "fastidious men" ("Queen" 58), but for the reason that such an idiosyncratically precise approach atomizes the particularities of this fictional world, sets it apart, makes it, in effect, a miniature.

By making his characters philatelists, Callaghan reinforces the text as miniature; stamps themselves are metonymic of geographical locations, political systems, historical occasions and the like. The fact that the stamp McCrae purchases is designed with Queen Victoria's image juxtaposes the present with the past; more important, this detail implicitly contains a return to the origins of stamp collecting. "Postage stamps, long taken for granted," Asa Briggs points out in *Victorian Things*, "were one of the first Victorian inventions" (*Things* 328). Philately was also a Victorian creation, and as such, participates in a much different ideological horizon than that in which collectors like Hughes and McCrae find themselves. Dr. J.E. Gray, Keeper of Natural History at the British Museum, and author of the first systematic handbook on stamp collecting, upheld:

> The use and charm of collecting any kind of objects is to educate the mind and the eye to careful observation, accurate observation, and just reasoning on the differences and likenesses which they represent, and to interest the collec-

tor . . . in the history of the country which produces or uses the objects collected . . . Hence a collection of postage stamps may be considered . . . an epitome of the history of Europe and America for the last quarter century; and at the same time . . . they will show the industry, taste, and neatness of the collector. (qtd. In Briggs 353-4)

A mirror and a teacher, the collection typifies order, progress, and the positivist love of hierarchies. For Gray, this new hobby can cultivate virtues useful for living in the present, whereas Hughes and McCrae depend upon their collection to furnish a bastion against contemporaneity.

The men delight in handling their stamps, agreeing "that there was something almost sensual about holding a perfectly preserved piece of the past, unsullied, as if everything didn't have to change, didn't have to end up swamped by decline and decay" ("Queen" 59-60). But what is this "past" that the stamp incarnates? Do they find the stamp to be metonymic of Gray's passions for order, the Victorian period in general, or does this piece of gummed paper primarily signal the possibility of survival? Taken as a textual impression-point, this passage crystallizes Hughes and McCrae's sensibility. The new world in which the present continues to engulf them is intolerable, so they encounter each other through the private intimacy of their collection, though they revealingly decline to collect recent stamps: "holding a stamp up into the light between his tweezers, [Hughes] would say, 'None of that rough trade for us'" ("Queen" 60). Entirely different from Gray's approach to collecting, which operates through an imagined extension into the sociopolitical world, Hughes and McCrae assemble their collection not only to retreat from this reality, but also to repress the physicality of their bodies.

Walter Benjamin's remark that "the collector's passion borders on the chaos of memories" (*Illuminations* 60) aptly identifies the refuge from melancholy and mutability that the stamps afford the two men. That they are nostalgic for a past that they didn't experience, a past that would, in fact, have been hostile to them as homosexual men, suggests the vigor of their need to forestall their steadily accruing defeats. Collecting in "The Black Queen" isn't simply an activity; it becomes a mode of being. In *The Volcano Lover*, Susan Sontag offers a cogent analysis of this state: "The collector's world bespeaks the crushingly large existence of other worlds, energies, realms, eras than the one he lives in. The collection annihilates the collector's little slice of historic existence" (*Volcano* 233). Collecting is therefore double-edged; it forms a thin defense against chaos as much as it hazards the loss of individuation. Put in terms of the earlier microcosm-macrocosm discussion, the collection is a microcosm that is menaced by the utter magnitude, indeed sublime immensity, of the macrocosm's potential totality.

All of these uncertainties are eclipsed by McCrae's Mother's Day performance. Exhibiting the stamp on his forehead, he seeks to communicate as much as he desires attention. The action is iconic and carnivalesque, a swaggering defacement of time. After licking the expensive stamp "all over," McCrae slips "on the jacket of his charcoal-brown crushed velvet suit," and announces to his guests "`My dears, time for the crudités'"("Queen" 61-2). Delighting in Camp, returning to physicality, McCrae winks at Hughes. He still speaks to his lover in the code that they've established, but the stamp's importance as a unit of exchange – both in terms of its market value and as a private fetish – has been transformed; now it is a living message, silently restoring McCrae's availability as a partner.

Emmanuel Levinas' account of the subjective experience of the Other is useful here. Accepting Leibniz's concept of the self-enclosed monad, Levinas states: "It is by existing that I am without windows" (*Time* 42). But it is possible to become aware of one's solipsism. Solitude can be grasped, though; strictly speaking, the Other cannot. Instead, meeting the Other reveals the "plurality" basic to existence. McCrae's gesture to Hughes approximates what Levinas calls "the encounter with a face that at once gives and conceals the Other" (*Time* 78-9). Storyness, at its most basic level, perhaps entails such a meeting; the activity of telling a story is an offering that both creates and displaces subjectivity. But this ambiguous offering demands that it be accepted as such. McCrae's greeting requires acknowledgement; it is a request as much as it is a gift. Up to this point in the text, each man had been existentially invisible to his partner. The last line of the story describes Hughes "staring at the black queen" ("Queen" 62). For Levinas, such a display is an exposure and concealment simultaneously. Ending by showing Hughes gazing at the stamp while, we infer, McCrae looks at Hughes, the story doesn't tell us how this gesture will affect the couple's relationship, if it will at all.

Callaghan makes the reader face a different kind of problem than the immediate existential one in which the characters are enmeshed. The Victoria stamp is a "dead-letter stamp from the turn of the century" ("Queen" 60), which, apart from identifying it as being Canadian because the British didn't use stamps to seal dead-letters, leads to a hermeneutic dilemma that threatens to undermine hermeneutics. How are we to interpret the detail that this stamp was originally intended to mark an undeliverable message? Perhaps we are meant to understand that the past is mute. More difficult, perhaps the past was never "addressed" to us at all. The stamp exists, but only as an object in the present; its "pastness" is so alien as to be wholly eradicated. If the story has allegorical components, are we not placed in Hughes' position, mesmerized by the Queen in her widow's weeds, but perhaps unseeing the Other bearing this image? Callaghan offers us no aid here. Classical in its plot structure, generously providing compelling characters, "The Black Queen" nonetheless brooks the possibility of epistemological nihilism, summons unanswerable questions. If the entire Victorian age dissipates into a gesture at a dinner party, does Callaghan mean that our immediate present exists only to become the future's whimsy? What does it mean to see another person? If the text is allegorical, how do we respond to the world as McCrae does?

"There are no miniatures in nature," Susan Stewart observes, "the miniature is . . . the product of an eye performing certain operations" (*Longing* 55). "The Black Queen" accentuates vision as a physical experience with existential dimensions. Callaghan's story is a literary miniature that spirals inward, finally resting on the elemental situation of two people looking, perhaps at each other, perhaps not.

II

One practical use of the microcosmic model made in the Renaissance was Guilio Camillo's memory theatre; imagining he could oversee the cosmos, Camillo declared that human divinity allowed him to remember the universe. Commenting on this "stupendous claim," Frances A. Yates comments: "the microcosm can fully understand and fully remember the macrocosm, can hold it within his divine *mens* or memory" (*Art* 148). "The Black Queen" is not so bold in its assessment of human comprehension, but it is no less concerned with the impulse to take an isolated phenomenon and place it against a larger totality in order to understand both more completely. What authors articulate, Mavis Gallant claims, "is that something is taking place and that nothing lasts" (*Paris* 177). The short story is a mnemonic device of sorts, though of a phenomenological rather than pragmatic nature. Short stories are miniatures, which, manifesting the sudden experience of temporality, force the world to speak. These miniatures are also utopian in that, like Hughes and McCrae, they often defy what the world insists on saying. Describing art in general, Adorno could be speaking of Callaghan's story: in it "is the resistance of the eye that does not want the colors of the world to fade" (*Negative* 405).

Bibliography

Adorno, Theodor W. *Aesthetic Theory*. Trans. Robert Hullot-Kentor. Minneapolis: U of Minnesota P, 1997.

———. *Negative Dialectics*. Trans. E.B. Ashton. New York: The Seabury P, 1973.

Bachelard, Gaston. *The Poetics of Space*. Trans. Maria Jolas. New York: The Orion P, 1964.

Barth, John. *The Friday Book: Essays and Other Nonfiction*. New York: Putnam's, 1984.

Benjamin, Walter. *Illuminations*. Trans. Harry Zohn. New York: Schocken Books, 1969.

Boas, George. "Microcosm and Macrocosm. *Dictionary of the History of Ideas: Studies of Selected Pivotal Ideas*. Vol. III. Ed. Philip P. Weiner. New York: Charles Scribner's Sons, 1973. 126-31.

Briggs, Asa. *Victorian Things*. London: B.T. Batsford, 1988.

Byatt, A.S. "The Stuff of Life." Rev. of *The Love of a Good Woman* by Alice Munro. *The Globe and Mail*. 26 September, 1998. D16.

Callaghan, Barry. "The Black Queen." *The Black Queen Stories*. Toronto: Lester & Orpen Dennys, 1982. 58-62.

Deleuze, Gilles. *The Fold: Leibniz and the Baroque*. Minneapolis and London: U of Minnesota P, 1993.

Gallant, Mavis. *Paris Notebooks: Essays and Reviews*. Toronto: Macmillan, 1986.

Gerlach, John. *Toward the End: Closure and Structure in the American Short Story*. University: U of Alabama P, 1985.

Gordimer, Nadine. *Selected Stories*. Markham: Penguin, 1978.

Kermode, Frank. *The Genesis of Secrecy: On the Interpretation of Narrative*. London and Cambridge: Harvard UP, 1979.

Leibniz, Gottfried Wilhelm. *The Monadology and Other Philosophical Writings*. Trans. Robert Latta. London: Oxford UP, 1951.

Levinas, Emmanuel. *Time and the Other*. Trans. Richard A. Cohen. Pittsburgh: Duquesne UP, 1987.

Lohafer, Susan. *Coming to Terms with the Short Story*. Baton Rouge: Louisiana State UP, 1983.

Lotze, Hermann. *Microcosmus: An Essay Concerning Man and His Relation to the World*. Vol. 1. Trans. Elizabeth Hamilton and E.E. Constance Jones. Freeport: Books for Libraries P, 1971.

Martin, Terry J. "John Barth's `Petition' as Microcosm." *Short Story*. 4.1. (Spring 1996): 79-88.

Paley, Grace. "A Conversation with Ann Charters." *The Story and its Writer: An Introduction to ShortFiction*. 5th Ed. Ed. Ann Charters. Boston: Bedford/St. Martin's, 1999. 1526-9.

Poe, Edgar Allan. "Review of *Twice-Told Tales*." *Short Story Theories*. Ed. Charles E. May. Athens: Ohio UP, 1976. 45-51.

Sontag, Susan. *The Volcano Lover: A Romance*. New York: Farrar Straus Giroux, 1992.

Stewart, Susan. *On Longing: Narratives of the Miniature, the Gigantic, the Souvenir, the Collection*. Baltimore and London: Johns Hopkins UP, 1984.

Yates, Frances A. *The Art of Memory*. London: Routledge and Kegan Paul, 1966.

TWO JEWS' BLUES

Norman Snider

> *Most people are other people.*
> Oscar Wilde

The last thirty years have borne witness to what Stanley Crouch has called an "ethnic narcissism that prevents us from speaking to each other across categories." Under this prissy dispensation, it's been decreed that literature must restrict its scope to self-referencing ethnic enclaves. That is, African Americans must only write in the light of slavery and Reconstruction, Anglo-Saxons restrict themselves to depicting the pinch of propriety and sexual frustration in small towns, and Jews confine themselves to writing under the long shadow of the death camps. To venture out of your category and onto somebody else's turf, it is said, constitutes "appropriation of voice." The phrase itself evokes a picture of the colonialization and exploitation of memory and experience: minority groups standing helplessly by while the evil conquistadors of publishing, wearing Panama hats and penny loafers, rob and loot them of their precious literary birthright. Barry Callaghan, a Toronto boy of Celtic blood, has written two remarkable stories about Jewish life – "Our Thirteenth Summer" and "The Cohen in Cowan," both exploring the moral and psychological confusions caused by the flight from ethnic and religious identity. "Our Thirteenth Summer," from the collection *A Kiss Is Still A Kiss,* is a forcefully original depiction of a boy's introduction into the fallen nature of adult life, not in a ritual or ceremonial sense but in an existential one. The unnamed narrator, clearly Callaghan himself, is looking back from the vantage of his adult self at his

258

boyhood in Toronto of the wartime 1940s. His family live on the upper floor of a duplex in a mixed downtown neighbourhood which is also not named but is clearly the Annex around Walmer Road in Toronto. The family who lives in the apartment below are troubled by the times. The father's name is George Reed. He's an expert in explosives, working in the Canadian war department. His Jewish wife is a recent immigrant from Nazi Vienna, a refugee from "Hitler's town" as Callaghan's father calls it, and she is understandably still terrified after a flight from such annihilating violence. Even though she and her orthodox father have found sanctuary in Canada, she has lost her inner moorings, "gone strange." The mother's ordeal under Hitler has so twisted her psyche that she thinks safety consists in making the world believe that she and her family are not who they are, Jews, obviously since her devout old father, given to afternoon strolls on the street, still dresses in rabbinical black, complete with skull cap and dangling side curls.

Callaghan and the son of the Reed family, Bobbie, play with tin soldiers and airplanes on the front lawn of the duplex, taking different sides, each sometimes being Germans, sometime being the Allies. When Callaghan, in his innocence, declines to believe Bobbie's denials concerning his family's religion, he's rewarded with a hard punch to the chest. Debacle follows. Callaghan has been taught by his pugnacious father how to box; Bobbie hasn't, even though his father is an expert in TNT. Consequently, Callaghan bloodies Bobbie's nose. Bobbie's mother, hysterical that violence has found her family out again, emerges screaming from the house and flattens Callaghan. His father goes downstairs and tells Bobbie's dad, "If either one of you ever hits my boy again, I don't care how big your bomb is, I'll knock your block off." If all this isn't nasty enough, and confusing to the young Callaghan, there's another Jewish family down the street named Asch, more at ease with their Jewishness than the Reeds. As with most immigrants, sports and pop culture has been their bridge into the larger society. They listen on their front porch to Mel Allen broadcast Yankee games on the radio; the daughter is a fan of Frankie Laine's. Callaghan has an affectionate relationship with the mother; Mrs. Asch holds his head to her huge maternal bosom. Callaghan pitches baseball; the family's son, Nathan, his close friend, is his catcher. The family Asch detests the family Reed for denying its Jewishness and treats them with contempt. They literally spit and jeer at the devout old rebbe as he passes by their house. The grandfather, however, despite these callous provocations, maintains his enigmatic silence concerning his family's background. Not unnaturally, this wacky situation further bewilders young Callaghan, especially when his friend Nathan shouts at the old man from the porch, "You might as well be from Mars." All this cultural confusion in the Annex of the 1940s comes to a head, in this carefully constructed story, during the summer Bobbie and Nathan turn thirteen, traditionally the age of manhood and confirmation by the tribe. When Nathan becomes bar mitzvah, he is told by his family that he can no longer associate with Callaghan. He says, "You're unclean, you eat unclean food." This ancient Jewish insistence on singularity and self-exile, of being Chosen, not only distinguishes Jews from other minorities, but, as Philip Roth has pointed out, it can also result in a sense of moral superiority attached to the shame and pain of perennial alienation, and therefore to misunderstanding and bruised feelings. If Jews were pushed to the margins of Toronto society in the 1940s, they returned the favour, albeit out of a defensive stance. Callaghan, lonely, now excluded by his neighbourhood Jewish friends, plays more and more by himself. He realizes that Bobbie's father is attempting to teach him how to box. Callaghan's father has taught his son how to take a punch. He says: "That's so he'll understand that getting hit never hurts as much as he thinks it's going to hurt."

Then Callaghan learns to his dismay that Bobbie's father expects his boy – now oh-so-WASP-ily re-named Robin – to fight him again in a front lawn rematch. Unless he puts on the gloves and boxes him once more, poor Robin or Bobbie will not be allowed to enter manhood, he will not have a thirteenth birthday party with cake and sodas. At this moment, Callaghan, looking back from maturity, zooms in for a moment of vivid emotional insight, a veritable Joycean epiphany. He writes:

> For the first time in my life I just suddenly felt all tired, like my whole body was tired. And sad. I was laughing while the two of us stood there with great big gloves hanging off the ends of our arms, but I felt so sad I was almost sick, and though I could tell right away, as soon as Robin put up his gloves, that he was the same old Bobbie, that he didn't know how to box at all . . .

The boy Callaghan, for the first time at the age of thirteen, has had a glimpse of the black absurdity, the tragic laughable pain-ridden farce that is life. It is this realization, more than any bar mitzvah or first communion that propels him into manhood. He's relieved that his own father is not home; then the demands of family pride would have forced him to beat and humiliate Robin. Instead, in an extraordinary act of generosity, he lets Robin or Bobbie hit him with a knockdown punch. It is here that the story takes an exhilarating turn. Since the destruction of the Jerusalem temple, certainly since Maimonides, it has been the self-declared note of the Jew – as he has been beaten and persecuted – to take that persecution on behalf of Jew and non-Jew alike and in so doing redeem the world, becoming " a light unto the world," and this, ironically, is exactly what the young Callaghan, who has been taught to take a punch, does at the very moment Mr. Reed and his Jewish son become the perfect goyim, fists raised in triumph. Just as before, when they were playing with tin soldiers, the roles have been exchanged. The bar mitzvah can now begin! The only person who understands what the young Callaghan has done is the enigmatic rabbinical grandfather:

> "It's not so easy to hurt you," he said.
> "Nope," I said.
> "You would make a good Jew," he said.
> "How would you know," I said, real sharp, "you're not Jewish."
> "No, that's right," he said, smiling a little more, and then he leaned down and whispered, "I'm the man from Mars."

This moment in this exceptionally well-told story does not point towards appropriation. This is not experience appropriated but the experience of being Jewish felt from the inside with considerable conviction by a non-Jew.

"The Cohen in Cowan," from an earlier volume, *The Black Queen Stories,* is a Christmas tale in a lighter vein, yet it too cuts to the quick of what it's like to be a Jew caught in flight from culture and ethnic identity. This time Callaghan puts himself in the skin of a Jewish bookie named Adrian H. Cowan who, like Bobbie Reed, is also ambivalent about who he is. Callaghan shares a taste with Isaac Babel and Damon Runyon for raffish Jewish types. Cowan is a near-relative of both Babel's Odessa gangster, Benya Krik, and Runyon's Nathan Detroit; his story is a comic monologue with definite Borscht belt overtones. Some say the greatest Jewish contribution to American popular culture is the Broadway tune as practiced by Gershwin or Harold Arlen; others make claims for the Hollywood movie as practiced by Billy Wilder or Steven Spielberg; my nomination would go to the comic monologue as practiced by standup performers like Mort Sahl and Lenny Bruce, or in literary form by Philip Roth in *Portnoy's Complaint.* That novel's title, suggesting both the whine of kvetch and the lament of the medieval complainte reveals standup's essentially poignant nature. There would be nothing funny about Job getting onstage and telling you about all the good things that are happening to him.

Callaghan's story's distinction, not to mention its charm, lies in the headlong freedom of its language. Cowan's very syntax, breathlessly slipping and sliding, reflects his ambivalence. Here is the climax:

> . . . and my only regret was he couldn't call me by my real name which is Cohen 'cause my name is Cowan, which lets you know right away where I stand except standing there at center court I didn't feel that I was me at all 'cause I don't exactly know who I am but now I know I'm not nothing.

Cowan the bookie, with his street argot, occasional Yiddishism, and syncopated line of patter, is a direct descendant of Ring Lardner's faux-naif pitcher, the Busher, L'homme moyen sensuel, and cousin also to rabbinical comedian Jackie Mason.

Adrian H. Cowan is a thriving bookie and small time t-shirt entrepreneur who has changed his name from Cohen and long left his religion behind. "I used to be Jewish," says Callaghan's character in one of his few cringe-making lines, "but now I'm successful." He has a nice house, a long black car like an alderman, a dapper suede coat with a fox fur collar. Life is sweet. Yet there is a vacuity and a vulgarity at the heart of Cowan's entrepeneurism. He will even sell lampshades on which the customer's own face is silk-screened. His motto: "Let the light that lights up your room light up your life." In Cowan, a very bad Jew, Maimonides' "light of the world" has descended into appalling kitsch. He has married a sexy, doting gentile wife; even she is appalled by the death camp echoes emanating from these lamp-shades. As in "Our Thirteenth Summer," sports are closely tied to religion. Cowan not only takes bets on games, he shoots baskets at his local "Y." For Callaghan, luck is a function of God's grace. Cowan knows he has the winner's touch when, in tune with the ball, he can effortlessly sink baskets; the touch carries over to his gambling. When he can envisage "things hanging togeth-er in a framework" the hand of God touches his hand. When he refuses to countenance a Christmas tree at home, everything goes out of tune and Cowan's luck takes a savage turn for the worse. His wife won't sleep with him, all the putz losers in town start to win their bets, he can't sink a basket to save his life. All the sweet-ness goes sour. When Cowan, defenceless because he is defending so little, caves in and buys a Christmas tree, he finds that his wife has done the same. Cajoled by a priest on the phone, he donates the tree and a turkey dinner as well to a poor Catholic family. He thinks he's solved his problem. "And it's a fine, Christian thing you do," the driver from the Cathedral tells him. For a sec-ond, it looks like Cowan will be saved by a Christian act of giving. But Callaghan is too good a writer to end his story that way. The poor family's ramshackle house is in Cowan's old neighbourhood. When he drives down there and sees it, memories of his upbringing, when his father was a Cohen, flood back. He feels trapped by the circumstances of his generosity and understands that the family would be humiliated by his presence. Despite his disappointment, a small miracle occurs: ". . . almost without thinking I lifted my hand like I was saying goodbye, and it was only when I was back driving alone in the car that I saw my hand in the air like it was a blessing the way my father used to bless me." This blessing causes Cowan's touch with the ball to return; luck, God's grace, mysteriously descends into his life once more. A small man, he has a small moment of redemption. He is not nothing, after all; all his negatives add up to a positive. This is not an ethical matter; God's grace is powerful enough to descend even onto a sinner like Cowan; he perhaps knows enough about right and wrong to stay out of jail, but that's the limit of his moral compass. A man like Cowan is not going to be won back to faith by subtle theological argument or by a need for ethnic solidarity. He is purely a creature of sensation. The warm feeling – the moment of inadvertent blessing – associated with his holiday generosity is possibly the noblest sensation he's ever had.

After "The Cohen in Cowan" was first published in Punch in 1979, several local Jewish authors set up a parochial howl and complained about its publication in Canada. Graham Greene can write all he wants about bad Catholics; *The Sopranos* and *The Godfather* can show the world thuggish Italians forever. But all Jews must be seen as paragons. Bad enough that Jewish bookies hustling tasteless lampshades exist at all, worse that they should be exposed to public view for the goyim. A harpa and a shonda! A scandal and a disgrace! Mordecai Richler was bad enough but how much worse when insightful writing on Jewish themes is done by somebody called Callaghan! In his Jewish stories, Callaghan's intonation is absolutely flawless. This is not appropriation of voice, this is not stealing fruit from the tree, this is a good writer placing himself persuasively inside the category of the Other, making tribal narcissism irrelevant.

FULFILLED EXPECTATIONS

PAUL WILLIAM ROBERTS

Few first novels have been as eagerly awaited as this one. Barry Callaghan has long been regarded by many as one of the most extraordinary talents this country has produced – a one-man cultural force comparable to Ezra Pound in generosity, scope and potency.

As a publisher he has consistently championed the work of lesser-known Canadian writers as well as drawing attention to the presence of exceptional talents in other countries.

As translator he has published poetry from all over Europe, besides doing more for Quebecois writing in Anglo-Canada than anyone in Quebec. Editor, journalist, teacher, media shaman . . . the list is daunting. But until now his most distinguished accomplishment has been his poetry.

While his collection *The Black Queen Stories* (1982) certainly proved he could master the short story form, his prose fiction never fully expressed the confluence of sensibilities he contained. But with *The Way the Angel Spreads Her Wings* Callaghan has more than fulfilled our expectations, with a first novel that is as surprising as it is almost frighteningly good. Wedding the power and beauty of his poetic style to a prose that is resonant, balefully evocative and irreducibly precise, he has produced a work that is not so much a love story as a story about love.

The Way the Angel Spreads Her Wings is classical in form, a journey into the heart of a darkness within which are concealed the seeds of light, of new life. Like any great quest it is about return and not departure, about seeing the place from which the journey started as if for the first time.

The protagonist, Adam Waters, is a war photographer who has spent his life recording images of a world in agony. This time, however, his mission is not to seek out objective horrors but to find the woman he has loved and who has mysteriously disappeared, making his own life a horror.

The antidote to pain is love, without such love he is nothing, yet to earn the right to love he must first make sense of his entire life.

As Adam searches for the lost lover, Gabrielle, in remote corners of a planet tearing itself apart with greed, ignorance and war, he is forced to reflect on what it was that made him who he is. Like the "spots of time" in Wordsworth's *Prelude*, he finds moments that have remained from the past to exert a fructifying virtue on the present. Images – an abandoned shoe, an Uzi machine-gun – recur with increasing significance until Adam's moment of revelation comes in a scene in which, like the first man, he is caught in a monsoon rainfall.

The rich texture and the allusive subtlety of Callaghan's writing are such that on finishing the novel one is obliged to start again, sacrificing the exhilarating drive of plot for the more refined pleasures of a style that is Joycean in its range of tone, its ability to seek out the extraordinary in the ordinary, to see heaven in a grain of sand.

From meditations of a profound and soaring nature to snatches of blues songs and the streetwise banter of city lowlife, the book is frequently bewildering in its ability to capture the voices of this world. They speak; you listen.

In his short stories, Callaghan generally seemed to be struggling to hide the poet, providing he could exchange passion for form and content – proving perhaps, that he could even take on his father in the arena of choice. No one could ever battle Morely Callaghan on such terms. Finally, however, his son Barry has transcended such Oedipal concerns, fashioning a voice, a style that is utterly his own. There is nothing trivial in this book. Each conversation, each account of reality is packed with the kind of resonant meaning that Morley Callaghan's work would reject as unrealistic.

Yet this density is not oppressive – in fact it has a liberating effect. Adam Waters, through excavating the past, arrives at the present with new eyes. Through being loved and loving he understands love; and through the life or lives he has lived he also understands love.

From the edge of life or the edge of night, Callaghan's writing is breathtaking. His book will either hurt or enthrall. No one will be indifferent to it, however, and it was certainly worth waiting for.

COMPLEXITY, CIRCULARITY, AND DISTANCIATION

Notes toward a reading of
The Way the Angel Spreads Her Wings

Alef Graf van Steijn

1

"[R]ows of soft-faced paratroopers stood in attention in battle dress, young boys being inducted, while on a platform, under the huge paratrooper insignia, set on fire in the night sky . . ."

Adam had sent that transparency . . . to his magazine with a note: "You collapse, yet everything is normal. *Man kann sich tosiegen!*" It was never printed.

"You've got more balls than brains. And," she said picking up the photograph, "what is this *man kann sich tosiegen* shit?"

"It's true . . ."

"Don't fuck my head. I had it translated. *'Drive yourself victoriously into the grave,'*" and she laughed and said, scowling, "Look, you're one of the best in the world, you know the name of the game, gimme a paratrooper helping a refugee girl across the road, maybe we'll run them both. Balance. There's got to be balance, you know that."

"Balance is a lie."

"We got responsibilities, responsibilities to more than what you spy with your little eyes."

There's supposed to be such a thing as the truth inherent to objectivity. It's an old argument in journalism, and in *The Way the Angel Spreads Her Wings* Adam comes eye to eye with this argument as soon as he returns with his images from Jerusalem.

Waiting for him is his angry editor.

She thinks the image she has in hand, together with

Adam's inscription, is biased. He knows it's what he saw in front of his eyes and that the irony of the German inscription under an image of Israeli paratroopers is inescapable.

She argues for balance (that is, objectivity).

Adam believes balance is a lie.

One can argue that – at its still center – this novel is about the way we use linear, so-called objective story telling to mask (or obscure) the fact that balance (as a cultural, social, editorial, ideological force) is a lie.

Balance is personal choice, a subjective choice that has nothing to do with so-called objective truth. A balanced point of view aims at smoothing over contradictions, at creating a false harmony, at idealization, while an unbalanced view takes aim at inherent contradictions, it refuses to idealize and it recognizes the critical unity (or natural harmony) between opposing forces.

The only basis for balance (and unbalance) in art is aesthetic.

In *The Way the Angel Spreads Her Wings*, Callaghan uses this philosophical truth (that is, the binary proposition: balance/unbalance) to tell his story in a complex, non-linear, circular form. What becomes obvious is that he intends to achieve – in tone and effect – what Brecht called the "distanciation effect" (or the *Verfremdung* effect, also called the "alienation effect"). I use the hermeneutic "distanciation" here to signify a positive form of (critical) alienation. In plain words: the reader is constantly asked to step outside the narrative and think about what its author is constructing.

2

[H]e could not escape a dream that dogged him year after year . . . an anxiety that bored like a bit of light through the blackness of his sleep . . . a faceless old man with big bony hands, bony shoulders in a loose jacket . . . luring him underground into a parking garage . . . and cracking an iron bar across that faceless skull, a tire iron . . . and as the dream light shed itself on the shoulders of the unknown man, Adam woke up deprived of the face yet seared by the act, by the belief he had killed him . . . the dream came back time and again, the face almost clear, and though he knew he was innocent, he was afraid he was guilty.

From this point in the story, Adam's dream demands that the reader confront the novel's structure.

1. As a reader, I shall attempt to suggest the reason why this story is not told in a linear style, a style that easily accomodates balance.

One doesn't have to be a Freudian to know that the recurring dream is either about Adam's own death wish or about some buried unconscious psychic residue in which Adam felt he had to kill himself to survive (that is, when he was still a young child).

From the dream scene onwards, the reader must accept that complexity, circularity, distanciation, and fragmentation are inherent to the experience of reading this novel. The circular structure aims to signify the musicality of the modern mind or modernity. Modernity dictates the complexity, and the emerging need for the literary distancing effect.

How?

By making transparent the technique behind "best-selling novels," and by challenging writers to play with conventional form.

The Way the Angels Spreads Her Wings sets up its story, Adam's story, in the first few pages. Then it begins its arresting process of distanciation. It cuts, inter-cuts, parallel cuts, and fragments to build its arc and the image of its intended meaning.

Why?

Pierre Teilhard de Chardin suggests that every biological and cerebral process tends to complexification over time. This idea is evident in the history of the novel and the reason for it, I think, is aesthetic – to reflect the complexity of the modern mind. The fragmented, inter-cut, narrative of *The Way the Angels Spreads Her Wings* must be integral to the way the author sees the world.

After his seeing and our reading are done, the meaning of the story is clear: love and war have not only taught Adam to know good and evil but he has learned how to believe in what he sees.

What he sees is a world complex in every moment – as in a suffocating jungle of luscious greens, where the living feeds of itself, where disease is an evil incarnate, where there is no perspective possible except of the Self.

3

Note: the reader is not allowed to settle into the story and forget about authorial techniques (of production). Brecht was right, and I paraphrase: if you want political engagement you'd better make sure that your audience is estranged, kept at a distance. In *The Way the Angel Spreads Her Wings*, that distancing effect is achieved with a style all its own.

The story is told thematically, not linearly. Its five *leit motifs* are:

Florence (mother), Web "Sweetwater"(father), Adam Waters (central figure, protagonist); his experience of them as his family.

Even here we are not allowed to completely identify. Mom is Florence. Dad is Web. Adam is a figure in two environments – a) home, a usual Catholic community spawning the unusual, and b) abroad, an unusual, war-torn, jungle-casino-leper environment spawning the usual, that is, the absurdities of the modern world, or modernity.

2. Adam's adolescent/adult encounter with Gabrielle O'Leary and her sexual abuse; she's a runaway, from her

family, from Adam. But she also represents Adam's quest for love – as Eros and Thanatos.

Death note: the epitaphs used as compositional exit points from section to section. These are also reflected in the tone, as well as being a reminder of our final exit, our final "purpose" in this world. Courage for Adam signifies a purposeful "stillness," a keeping calm in the face of despair.

Also note that we are given Adam's own epitaph as an epigram: the kind of gesture Tristram Shandy would make: *Here I lie, taken from life.* "Lie" could be read as a modern ambiguity, as in *I lie in the ground, no longer alive,* and as *here I lie through my teeth, to get at a truth taken from life.*

3. Adam's profession: he is a photojournalist with a literary mind. (Description is his way of "picture tak-ing." Observation: Adam is *I am a camera*: a figure in the landscape he "describes." He doesn't talk about lens-es, angles, film speeds; he talks about what he sees.)

4. War as ground – in Beirut, in Amman's Black Sep-tember War, and in South West Africa. Adam is the fig-ure in that ground: we see it through his eyes and the story becomes his search for perspective, and given a perspective, his search for love. We come to know this through his "word pictures" rather than his "photo-graphs."

Only halfway through the novel, in the scene with his editor, quoted above, do we realize that "he is one of the best in the world."

In other words, again, it's not a linear story about a photojournalist on a quest but a circular, polyphonic, story about how the observer is witness to his own mind at work.

5. A constant conjunctive juxtaposition of inner/outer mind. Thoughts and exterior dialogue are intercut; per-spective is fragmented (to create a narrative cubism). In

effect, Callaghan insists that his readers keep all these aspects going in their mind – if they are to "see" (that is, discover) what is in the end, a) the compositional musicality inherent to the protagonist's mind, and b) the reader's own ability to pull together scenes into the mosaic the author has laid out – to tell us a true story, as authentically as possible.

These 5 *leit motifs* are interwoven as in a musical composition; they are the narrative notes forming the dream structure of this novel.

Freud, in his *Interpretation of Dreams*, tells us that "the dream . . . shows the real, if not the entire nature of man, and is a means of making the hidden psychic life accessible to our understanding."

If one accepts the dream sequence, quoted above, as a clue to the dream structure of this novel, then this story lends itself to a most revealing psychoanalytic session about its author's state of consciousness.

4

Dispositio (arrangement), the second division of classical rhetoric, is key to the way the author wants us to read this narrative spread of his angel's wings.

Why?

Because (I think) he means to alert us to the polyphonic aspects of the conscious mind.

But why?

Perhaps because he is weaving a most complex tale to represent his life, *his sweet Sheherazade*, rather than approach himself, and us, through the conventional "bourgeois" novel.

(Note to potential film maker: segue into Rimsky-Korsakov's symphonic suite of Sheherazade, use it as a set-up for narrative polyphony, and then quote Walter Pater's "All art aspires to the condition of music.")

5

To paraphrase Jacques Lacan, this novel is using/abusing narrative technique to reflect political intent (for example, not allowing the reader to settle into the bourgeois comforts of the classical – linear – novel).

Circularity is oral, and oral is hip-talk, dream talk, you stay with it through the jump cuts to hear its meaning.

But linear is classical narrative, and that is straight talk, formal talk, respectful of narrative continuity and the bourgeois reader.

A case could be made that Morley Callaghan, the father of the author, could only write linear narratives and that Callaghan *fils'* dream sequence (as represented autobiographically through Adam) is indicative of the rebellion of the son and the reason he, the son, became a master of the circular (and far more complex) form of oral storytelling.

This is especially evident if one reads *The Way the Angel Spreads Her Wings* as a thinly disguised rebellion against the linear tradition (that is, the father) and the reason Adam believes he is guilty of murdering a man.

The author is innocent, of course, but only because he figured out how to sublimate his rebellion into his fictions.

6

Dispositio (arrangement of the subject) is used in this novel as a rhetorical distancing effect. But the interior logic between its *leit motifs* is musical.

The Way the Angel Spreads Her Wings is not literally (or formally) a fugue, but it has a similar quality of short melodic attacks (that is, the subjects he tells us about), being introduced, one by one (as five intertwined themes), and developed (non-linearly).

The spine of the story is Adam's quest to know and understand his love for Gabrielle and why she ran away – that's the leading voice, the central through line, we keep returning to from beginning to end.

To be properly a fugue, the themes would have to reveal themselves taken up by the other leading instruments, the other voices, but that doesn't happen: Adam is the only lead instrument in this story.

The fugue-like interweaving of themes and motifs is the author's way of reminding the reader that memory recollected in tranquility does not come to us chronologically but circularly (polyphonically). In that sense, the composed dream-like structure is perfectly "balanced" (that is, written/told) and the "unbalancing" (the distancing effect) is an aesthetic choice made in the name of an authentic experience, a writing/reading experience that acknowledges the role of critical (or political/moral) distanciation.

7

Why the distancing effect? Why is the author consciously bringing about narrative estrangement?

To be relentlessly convulsive and thus *force* the reader to think – to engage with the scenes – not to identify passively or sentimentally but to think about the scenes and hear the voices critically, as they are presented on the page, in the moment.

To avoid having the reader read the novel as a "best-selling" story. To reflect the habit of mind that is not about commerce, but about living one's life with a sense of perspective, discovering meaning.

In the market place of ideas, the bourgeois reader associates linear narratives with so-called traditional economics and nonlinear narratives with so-called complexity economics: that is, Third World economies, the underground economy, the black market exchange rate, etc. In *the Way the Angel Spreads Her Wings* both the story and its structure reveal a protagonist who is completely aware of the absurd divide between those two economic, hence narrative, forms.

Cyclic patterns of thought are associated with orality because that's the way we talk, the way we sing, and the way we come to compose music. Linear patterns of thought are associated with the traditional nineteenth-century novel and established, conventional, literacy. Because *The Way the Angel Spreads Her Wings* is also about the fragmenting, destructive, impact of twentieth-century wars and their absurd means of ruination (that is, the military industrial economic complex to which both sides of the ideological fence are addicted), its form is a logical extension of its meaning and its narrative content.

Finally, as we pull together the pieces of the mosaic in our own minds, we discover that the novel is also about the pestilence loose in the world. A world where Self and mercy, as Gabrielle shows us, can only find rest in the selfless act of nursing lepers in the heart of dark Africa or in the particularity of a singular character revealed to us – in his stillness – through the pieces of the mosaic.

The author of *The Way the Angel Spreads Her Wings* wants to engage the reader in the world of ambiguity, circularity, and the absence of the absolute. He wants to tell us about the insanity, and the absurd that has entered reality via relativity (of which Cubism is a visual manifestation). We, the readers, are to note and deal with the inside that is outside Adam and the outside that is inside his cubist view of the world – a world in which he is the lead character, leading us through the modern world as he sees it.

This is the novel as an art object, representing itself as a reflection of the modern mind and reflecting back to us how consciousness really works when it is "taken from life," that is, with all the mordant humour appropriate to such a life, mourned even before it is begun.

WHEN THINGS GET WORST

ANN DIAMOND

I read *When Things Get Worst* with the overwhelming feeling that is was not about what it claimed to be: a first-person account of the life in hard times of a young woman living in southwestern Ontario. This is a novel that, whatever other criticisms may be leveled at it, leaves a strange residue in the mind.

It put me in mind of a hitchhiking trip I took to Niagara Falls, Ontario, with my boyfriend back in 1972. It was a trip that changed my life, because it taught me that there is much in our so-called country that remains unspeakable and unspoken. There is even, in Canada, an undercurrent of "evil" that rarely surfaces in the public consciousness. True evil is also in short supply in Canadian fiction, as if it were someone else's problem. But I think all that is about to change. Despite the efforts of certain judges, evil is creeping into our national consciousness.

Evil is, after all, contagious. After reading this novel, I felt an irresistible compulsion to get friendly with the author. We met furtively in a bistro on Toronto's Bay Street, and I saw immediately that Barry Callaghan is the kind of guy who wears sunglasses when entering a restaurant at night.

Our conversation was also shady. I asked him why he wrote this novel in the voice of a young woman named Anne, who is married to a man named "Evol." Is Evol evil, or is he "love" backwards? Is that why Anne's perspective on the world grows out of a shattered innocence? Is it also why she speaks in a tide of imagery owing much to Pentecostalism, describing a world of complete hopelessness and desolation?

Religion is the oral literature of the poor, but these days even the poor have stopped believing in it. Callaghan claims he has always identified with people who desperately want to believe in something. In Anne's speech we hear dim echoes of prayer and confession. All that's missing is the exhortation to come home to Jesus. In fact, however, this novel is really a kind of poetic crawling back to a female Christ. You could say that our heroine discovers she is Christ when she picks up a rifle and points it at the other man in her life, the religiously inspired Lute, short for Luther, who is about to blow up a dam and inundate her family. The spiritual revelation, if there is one at the end, is as dark as the scenario that preceded it. One reviewer has said that the book suffers from a "poverty of spirit," but I disagree. This is a spiritual book about poverty.

It's only fair to mention, as other reviewers have, that Callaghan has trouble with plotting. He often writes brilliantly, but having exhausted his feelings for a character he tends to lose interest in what happens next. Perhaps that's why this darkly lyrical jeremiad seems to swirl in a profusion of public stillbirths, headlong acts, and meaningful deaths: what Callaghan himself calls "the reverse of the mystical assent."

Here's a guy who believes in nothing, for whom women are gods in human dress. Remember "Crow Jane" in *The Black Queen Stories*? A clear-cut case of voice theft. Appropriating a voice that he claims dictated the book to him at the race track, Callaghan comes on like the Virgin Mary with armed response. Between the lines, though, it's all "Give up, go home, have a good cry, the race is over, there's nothing left of the human enterprise." In other words, friends: repent. And kill that vulture circling our heads.

"When things get worst," opines Evol, "how are you?" Adding later on, "The more sin grows, the more grace abounds." This is a spiritual viewpoint, not to be confused with literary posture or a mere imitative nod to twentieth century "swallowing the darkness whole."

Outside Quebec, few Canadian writers have even tried to enter this terrain. I can see why Barry Callaghan hangs out in a certain Bay Street bistro, disguised as an Irish gangster and surrounded by French-Canadian waiters. What better place to practice his secret religion?

TELLING STORIES

An Appreciation of Barry Callaghan's When Things Get Worst

Kathleen McCracken

The highlands and the lowlands of western Ontario's Grey County can be trying territory. Sweltering in July, a wind-cut deep-freeze from November to March, these are places as soul-destroying as they are soul-making. A mere 100 miles north of Toronto, society and sensibility in this rural pocket remain remote from those of the urban cosmopolis. Few writers, however, have attempted to give a voice to the historical realities, much less the cultural idiosyncrasies, of the region. Among those who have, Barry Callaghan is characteristically original in his approach to and acute in his understanding of the freighted stories and peculiar lifeways of the inhabitants of the townships of Proton, Luther, Egremont and Glenelg.

Barry's 1993 novel *When Things Get Worst* is at once a hymn to hard-won farmlands in ravaged decline and a Breughelesque depiction of a world as skewed and grotesque as it is noble and enduring. His evocation of the trials and tribulations of a loosely knit group of poor white "trailer trash," many of whom bear some significant physical deformity (a sixth toe, a missing arm, a hunched back), stands as a northern counterpart to Flannery O'Conner's gothic South, or Cormac McCarthy's southwestern borderlands. Here, a menagerie of complex, frequently bizarre characters, whose lives are beset by misfortune and despair, yet punctuated by moments of intense joy and rare insight, enact a darkly humourous tragicomedy which begins with one murder and ends with another.

First and foremost there is Evol Dewan, a man "who had all the grit and good looks in the world but no special skills," and who "had this doom thing in him." Evol's Christian name is an anagram for "love," so is in keeping with his inherently contradictory personality, a personality expressed in his conviction that "the more sin grows, the more grace abounds." Alternately cruel and sensitive, an egocentric pessimist and an intuitive realist, each of his moods laced with a trenchant wit, Evol epitomises the human condition. As capable of killing a man in cold blood or shooting a bottled foetus to free its ghost as he is of charming cattle with his fiddle playing or discoursing on the nature of love, he is the narrator-protagonist's lover, muse and nemesis. Faced with imprisonment for a crime he did not commit, Evol chooses suicide, leaving her and their ill-fated infant daughter Loanne to fend for themselves. A descendant of Catholic Irish horse traders who became boot makers, Evol's cure for "done feet" (the gem in a litany of eclectic folk remedies) is one of many indelible passages in the book:

> that was to sit down and do absolutely nothing and drain your mind of all distraction, an entire draining until this light that was not a light you could see anything by began to well up in your body, a light like you get when you close your eyes completely shut, shut tight on a bright summer day and you stare up toward the sun, and all that heat is full on your face and there's suddenly a bright light inside your eyelids but you can't see anything except your own little veins across the light. You just know there's heat alive in you, the same way Evol came alive in me . . .

And stay alive in the narrator Evol does, arguing from "the endless whiteness . . . the mind of God" against

Luther Alm, also known as "Lute the map-man," a hardware salesman and "come-by-chance" preacher in the Chapel of the Abandoned Apostle. Unlike the philosophical Evol, Lute is a man possessed by a "raw, mulish vigor" who speaks "strange words full of forked talk, furious." He and his pick-up truck seem to be "intended," appearing on the very day the narrator loses her only child to the effects of pneumonia on a "too small" heart. He stays long enough to swindle her out of the title to her land and leave her pregnant, his seductive courtesy masking a charlatan whose grasping capitalism seeks to exploit the failing farms for what little gravel they may yield.

The rivalry between Evol and Lute, and by extension the tragic gap between the living and the dead, the past and the present, the transient and the immutable, is at the core of *When Things Get Worst*. It governs the lives and the deaths of Sabina and Wishbone Tullamore, the narrator's parents, who survive a marriage blighted by "contrariness" and a "rancour of the heart" to be snatched from a ferris wheel during a freak tornado, as it does the two brothers exhibited in a travelling carnival's Temple of the Exotics, their lizard skins reputedly turning to stone, or drunken uncle Ambrose, a hunchback who on a December night crept into the Carlson lime kiln for warmth, his skeleton found the next morning "sitting bolt upright, the arms upraised, all the flesh gone and the bones glowing red in the kiln darkness." These and a catalogue of other liminal figures struggle against harsh environmental, economic and personal circumstances. None, however, fights so tenaciously and ultimately overcomes with such conviction as the narrator.

Perhaps Barry Callaghan's greatest achievement in this novel is his rendering of an authentic female voice. Indeed, the young narrator (she is no more than twenty-two years of age), through whose telling the others' stories are filtered and refracted, is so convincingly female that she rivals Molly Bloom or, more recently, Paul Durcan's Haulier's Wife or Chuck Palahniuk's Shannon McFarland. That the narrator is never named might be taken to mean that she is effaced by the decidedly patriarchal social structures which seem to enclose her. On the contrary, hers is a fluid consciousness which encompasses and connects all the characters, which firmly refuses to be named. The free-flowing, stream-of-consciousness style is its own *écriture feminine* – broken, digressive, distinctly oral – fleshing out as it goes not only the experience of one woman (though it does that beautifully) but charting the soulscape of an entire community. The narrator's accounts of love-making and childbearing, like her synaesthetic apprehension of words as colours – "when I said the word child I saw honey, a dark honey colour, almost an ochre, the same colour that was in so many of the leaves dying on the trees" – attest to her individuality and her gifted imagination. Despite her losses of family and "the sweet land," other passages emphasise her strong sense of inherited continuity and her deep association with home places:

> This farm was nonetheless the nearest I could come to the breathing lives that were lived and long since forgotten around here, and when I wanted to get close to those who were forgotten I walked back through the woods following the markers in the map of my mind, walking a branch of the Saugeen in the shallows, flushing chipmunks and flickers and a hare, until I got to a closed-off stand of gleaming white dead elm trunks in a marsh that Evol had found for me . . .

When Things Get Worst is essentially about "re-membering," about not forgetting and knowing how to keep the past alive, not in any physical form, but through the spoken word. The settlers' village of Hole-in-the-Woods may be "long gone and ploughed under for the government placing of a hydro," but their efforts are preserved in the narrator's telling:

> back in the olden time when loggers had come from Fergus village along the Garafraxa Road to the lumber camps, and the road was a crooked trail of corduroying through the swamps, all cut and slash through the close bog, and those sweet tough boys had carried the seeds they'd known they'd need in their cuffs, and their pockets were stuffed with sprigs of lilac rooted in potatoes for the moisture . . .

Likewise at the end of the novel, when the dead appear to rise and "come home" in order to aid in the purgation of the scourge Lute from the land, their efficacy and their release is made possible through the narrator's words.

One of Evol's favourite sayings is, "When things get worst, how are you?" In the course of the five chapters which constitute *When Things Get Worst*, the narrator is on a quest to discover her own response to his query. The close of each 'movement' brings her closer to total eclipse, *and* nearer to what in a different context might be called 'enlightenment'. For the narrator, life is an endurance test, it is about finding ways to survive against the odds. But it is also, and most importantly, about communication, and the strength that is gleaned from spoken words.

From the outset of her story, the narrator possesses a strong sense of the spiritual world which permeates and outlasts this corporeal one. With her daughter in her arms, she runs down Pandora Road, thinking "the sky full of pollen and seed flecks floating thick in the air . . . must be the souls of all the angels come to see my baby die." Among Evol's first words to her are, "I want to talk to you." Talk – language, words, communication – was and continues to be the foundation of her relationship with Evol, and when he dies it is his voice she desires to hear again. Whether born of longing, guilt, memory or madness, the narrator finds herself able to hear the dead Evol "talking his whisper talk" and Loanne "talking back to him, quiet, confiding, as if I wasn't there." These perceptions begin the first time she makes love with Lute, and experiences a pain "like my soul escaping out of my body." While the consummation signals a final, physical break from her departed family (and has Evol "talking a blue streak," though her daughter is less direct), it paradoxically enables the birth of a more profound connection with them, one that is oral and aural, that counters the Word of the "holy" con-man Lute with an intuitive language that is the provenance of the poet-mother. Once opened, that channel of communication between the living and the dead, the past and the present, between muse and writer cannot be curtailed. It is the lifeblood circulating between generations, and allows the narrator – and with her Barry Callaghan's readers – that final illumination:

> I knew why Loanne had not spoken to me through all these months. She was waiting, waiting to be the word in the ear of my coming child, as Evol has been the word in my ear.

For the narrator, when things get worst she is more than simply able to survive. She is able to tell stories.

"WHEN ONE PART BEGINNETH AND THE OTHER SINGETH THE SAME"

Re-reading When Things Get Worst

Seán Virgo

The voice of *When Things Get Worst* elaborates on a chord which, once sounded, dictates the whole shape and substance of the book.

That's true perhaps, or ought to be true, of any first person narration. If the voice is authentic then what the speaker chooses to remember and tell (share) – and when, and how, and from what point in time – will be authentic too, and the book will be structured accordingly.

Personality, memory, cadence – they collude precisely in the unfolding of this story; but Barry Callaghan has achieved something more ambitious and original here than the fusion of character and chronicle.

This voice is at once the mind of an unnamed woman[1], the dialect of a moribund township, and a sustained hopscotch with time, back and forth across three generations.

There's a moment of revelation one third of the way through the book. It forms the climax of the second of five chapters which comprise *When Things Get Worst*. And like most elements in this intense and complex, though seemingly artless, novella, it works on several levels and radiates implications.

It is, for a start, a climax in more ways than one. Not-Anne Tull, the narrator, finds herself on the parlour floor, *"under the overhead wagonwheel lamp with two of the candlebulbs burned out"* wrenched open by convulsive pleasure, with Luther Alm – the "come-by-chance

preacher" and future devastator of the Tull family home-
stead – *"slumped on top of me and breathing in my ear
like he was about to die,"* and she hears, overhears, the
voices of her dead – her child and its father – in conversation *"out in some loneliness, maybe along with the
loons."*

That is not-Anne's revelation: that the dead are still
there, somewhere, even if out of her reach.[2] But the revelation for the reader – this reader at least – is that nothing gets left behind in this story. The dead, as it were, are
not alone in this. What was accomplished in the first
chapter was not "just" the telling of a grim, ironic and
mischievously compelling story[3], but the laying down of
motifs that begin to reappear at this crucial point in the
composition, and will recur again in new combinations
and contexts. It's at this moment, as readers, that we
realise[4] that a pattern of variations is already under way
and that our memories (of what we have read so far) are
being co-opted by the memory of not-Anne, drawing us
into an intimacy not just of being confided in but of
responding.[5] So we embark on the third chapter[6] prepared for fresh variations, and our involvement with the
unfolding plot is concerned at least as much with the
past as with the future: they are equally freighted with
suspense and familiarity.[7]

The language of music has crept in here because I've
realised that *When Things Get Worst* is best understood
and appreciated as a fugue. That climactic closure to the
second chapter was what alerted me to this, and I want
to explore the scene and its implications in more detail.

Writers like myself, who don't sub-define themselves
as critics or scholars, tread carefully when discussing the
work of another writer. There's a wish to preserve its
"innocence" and that of the reader: to honour its unan-
alyzed affect. Simultaneously, though, an insider's
assessment of craft is always at work. When confronting

something marvellous, our initial response is one of gratitude for the increasingly rare enchantment of being caught up in a book (for that experience is what led us to the calling in the first place), but two questions follow almost at once: *How did he/she ever think of that?* (we know the answer but we ask all the same); and *How did he/she make it work?* (which can sometimes be answered).

The scene is a marvel of imagination[8] for me, its truth underscored by the unpredictable notes (the counterpoint of dissonance) – the burned out light bulbs, the *"hacking for air,"* the *"pain to my own backbone on the floor,"* and the comical shock that ignites their passion in the first place: not-Anne's yell of *"Talk to me, why aren't you talking to me?"* to the offstage whispering ghost of her dead love, that startles Lute out of his almost drowsy state as he leans back against her.

Far from reducing sex to ungainly lust, these discords intensify not-Anne's ecstatic astonishment, and set in relief the tenderness that draws her and Lute (each of whom has divined that the other is somehow "intended") into each other's flesh. Dissonant notes are the spice to not-Anne's voice from the first page of *When Things Get Worst* and they govern the novella's whole tone and structure.

"Realism" is not at issue here[9]; for not-Anne's voice *is* the whole world of the book, and there are no intrusions from outside her world[10] to invite or justify comparisons with "normal" speech, or assessments of "authentic" dialect.[11] Nor is Barry Callaghan addressing the problem that has always bedevilled writers of Naturalist novels: how to render inarticulate people articulate – not-Anne is articulate as all get out. All the same, the voice does embody a perspective that is characteristic of the socially or culturally deprived – that of seeing and describing oneself as if in the third person, with a detachment, almost dispassionate and often laconically humorous, about even the most traumatic events.[12] In that sense, the voice is simultaneously naïve, dramatic and poetic.[13]

Not-Anne's voice – fluid and insistent – functions as a fugue in action on the page. Psychologists commonly use *"fugue"* to mean "dissociative fugue" – a coherent flight from someone's actual life into a decodable (so they say) alternative reality. But there are *associative* fugues too – flights towards and through the essence of an actual life, governed by the random logic of memory: shaped by patterns and couplings of image and obsession (by association, in short) and quite indifferent to linear organisation. Molly Bloom's solliloquy in *Ulysses* is exactly such a fugue, and *When Things Get Worst* is one, it seems to me, in its totality. What fascinates me about this associative memory-flight as a mode for storytelling is that in its apparently unplotted flow it is actually a sophisticated vehicle for the most basic of pleasures – suspense. Events, already understood (or known, at least) by the speaker, unfold in ways that keep the reader guessing, without any of the artifice or archness of the mystery writer. The outstanding example of this game-with-our-expectations is the death of not-Anne's parents at the little country fair which closes the third chapter. Even if we expect their deaths to occur here (they are first mentioned on page 17 in chapter one, and nudged closer to our curiosity with increasingly suggestive allusions in the next 100 pages) we clearly anticipate a mechanical accident to befall their ferris-wheel ride, and are not prepared for an act of God – the tornado which comes ripping across the township *"like one of those stingray fishes in the air."* Just as we reach the climax of this particular episode[14], after the prolonged tease of suspense, we realise that a trick has been played on us, all the more effective if we believed we were ahead of the story.[15] But in fact the feeling of completion-at-last is itself a tease – the suspense is over, the reader relaxes, but the real ambush comes 30 pages later, with the washing of the bodies and all that that triggers, and forms the climax of the following, fourth, chapter. What is most remarkable, though, about the actual description of the parents' deaths, is that it is just one part of a whole cluster of motifs, themes and images which look backwards and forwards in the novella's structure – the fairground catastrophe is in fact interwoven with other progressions altogether, and is part of a memory-within-a-memory of the doomed marshlands, and the spectral image of a flayed horse, set up mysteriously over the dark waters like an Iron Age sacrifice. And even this doesn't do justice to the complexity of this seven page sequence, since the real context of the scene is not-Anne's realisation that Lute's mystic babbling about the "stone seeds," and his handfuls of gravel samples, have translated into the flaying of her own ancestral land. *"The back-hoeing and scraping . . . the gouging out of the gravel"* have just begun.*"Death,"* to appropriate Ihab Hassan's epigram, *"takes the measure of every change and inspires its metaphors."*[16] I may seem to have wandered from the scene which closes the second chapter to the one that closes the third (alluding en route to the one that closes the fourth) but the seven pages I've just described are an elaboration of the variations in motif, theme and image which, as I've suggested, the coming together of Lute and not-Anne sets in motion and prepares us for. That scene and chapter end with the faint voices of Evol and baby Loanne sounding inside not-Anne (as they also do in the very last lines of the novella): "the two voices being born again in me with their words so hushed I could hardly make them out, words that went on for a long time till I fell asleep with Lute already sleeping the sleep of the dead in my arms, listening to the loons laughing the devil's laugh."

It's a resonant ending in more than its cadences.[17] It echoes, with poetic distillation, motifs and associations that we have already heard and that we shall hear again – more clearly but with more complication – as the novella unfolds:

> The loons and the devil's laughter (counterpoint to the trance-like pallor of God's mind) have recurred already in the first and second chapters, along with Evol's redefinition of that laughter as the "opening up of a place somewhere beyond words . . . where the dead wait to talk to you," and the other deaths and entrances that are the lynch pins of the novella.

By this stage we have learned all but one of the motifs, the images, the voices and the themes – each not just stated, but elaborated already at least once – that will braid with each other through the rest of the book.

We know the deaths, the histories, the pioneer ancestors, the sectarian divide. We know the despairs, the buried infants, the suicides by hanging. The junk heaps and trailer parks are as much the landscape as the marshes and the first homesteads. The fighting dogs and the horses are as vividly present as the smoke-eyed Indians (who are also the carnies at the fair). The rifle is there already, blasting one of the stillborn infants into further oblivion. The stones above ground and the crystal web of waters beneath it are essential adversaries, and will become even more so. We have Evol's voice, and the mother's and father's, and (the main function of chapter two) the "counter voice"[18] of Lute.

And the theme of desolation, of entropy, of the tacky materialist exploitation that writes *finis* to the so brief three-generation history of Hole-in-the-Woods[19] simmers in the urgency of not-Anne's speech with all of Blake's "honest indignation." A composer could take these elements, and their initial elaborations, and – with musical equivalents – know almost exactly how to proceed from this point.

For though I've described not-Anne's story as an associative fugue I'm also using "fugue," as I suggested earlier, in its primary sense. With none of the rigidity or obtrusive control that would signal self-conscious intent, Barry Callaghan has created a structure and dynamic in *When Things Get Worst* that function exactly like a musical fugue. The initial motifs and elaborations, the alternating "expositions" and "episodes" are all in place by the end of the first chapter, even if it takes the "counter voice" in chapter two to make this pattern clear to us. There follows the longer stretch of the three central chapters, where, in musical terms, *"the remaining voices do whatever fanciful things enter the composer's mind"*[20] as inventiveness fleshes out the texture and population of not-Anne's world – again through exposition and episode – all the time knitting the motifs, images and events closer together in preparation for the last chapter, the coda.

A new counter voice appears in this coda – that of Killjoy, the mocked outcast of not-Anne's schooldays, who will be the last-minute redeemer of all that has poisoned the township and who literally removes the first counter voice, Lute, by blowing him up and releasing the waters that not-Anne and Evol had dammed, along with the (literal) ancestral ghosts. In fact, though, Killjoy has been there all along – he is not new, he is just revealed. He is meek Albert Easley, whose wife, like not-Anne, is pregnant by Lute, and who repeats his childhood pattern of violence against oppressors. That pattern unites the other patterns of the book – with this final trick on the reader, the whole drift of not-Anne's apparently formless story comes at last into focus, clarity and a human as well as formal satisfaction. This is the point from which not-Anne has been telling her story all along.

To get there, though, she had one other strand to tie in. She achieves this at the end of the fourth chapter after which the coda, the resolution of her story, can proceed.

There are grotesque elements in *When Things Get Worst*, as there are in almost any hillbilly or trailer trash world,[21] but there is only one Gothic scene in the book, despite what some early reviews of the novella claimed. It is the killing of the horse (so many horses in the story, all of them dead) and the implanting of its heart in not-Anne's breast by Wishbone Tull, her father. *"It was terrible to be loved by my father . . ."* she says, and she is remembering this as she washes his dead body, and her mother's, after they've been brought home from the fairground: "there was blood on my bedshirt and in the bed from the tiny cut between where my breasts were going to be and daddy was standing looking out the window saying that he'd put the horse's heart inside me . . . and that if I was ever untrue to him the heart would burst and I would die."

This sequence, act and image, does startle – it is as though an oboe has been quietly playing its descant among the woodwinds and then suddenly bursts out, declaring its own theme, while the orchestra momentarily falls silent around it. For the theme is not an ambush on the reader, though it functions with the force of one – the moment was prepared for in several references to the stigma, sometimes bleeding, between not-Anne's breasts; in the opening bars of chapter three (*"Where me and Momma are from, it's what Evol called daughter-fondling country . . ."*) and in that crucial closing scene to the second chapter, just a page earlier, which begins with Lute sinking back into not-Anne's arms, *"his head between my breasts . . ."* That stigma, like the cry of the loons which ends the love scene, is an *"opening up of a place somewhere beyond words . . ."* for it is at this moment that the voice of dead Evol starts whispering inside her. This is not the deep dark secret which decodes and then overshadows and reduces the rest of the novella (*When Things Get Worst* is not a book about incest or child abuse, and not-Anne's love for her father, like her love for Evol, is deep and unjudgemental). It is, though, something that has to come out in her story, a last ghost to lay before she can move through the coda and into the unknown future, where only one chord still lingers. That is the "whisper talk" of her unborn child and her faithful dead lover, Evol.

Notes

1. She's not named, as I say (though her family name *is* Tull), but I won't saddle her more than once with "the Narrator" (or "Ms Tull"). On page 12, following his greeting, "'Lo Anne!" (from which she will name their child, Loanne), she tells Evol, "My name's not Anne." I've taken her at her word.

2. Their actual location, the "white coldness" of God's mind, is another one of the motifs that recur and are redefined against the foreground of trailer-trash rapture and religiosity.

3. Though that story did exist, and was published independently, before the novella was written.

4. Though in the "innocence" of reading to which I'll shortly refer, this realisation may be – in defiance of dictionary definitions – unconscious, intense and delightful.

5. With recognition at first, but then with increasing empathy.

6. Though the novella's sections are called "chapters," I've come to think of them as "movements" because the structure of *When Things Get Worst* has more in common with musical composition than with most literary forms.

7. Relationships in the actual world evolve in this way too, of course, through a language of private references; while in a novel like Russell Hoban's *Riddley Walker*, for instance, the process of learning/sharing a language is the essential dynamic.

8. Imagination" signifying, always, invention fleshed out by human complexity.

9. "Realism" being merely each generation's antidote to idealism – situated, as one postmodernist wag put it, *"somewhere between academicism and kitsch."*

10. This is essential to the novella's integrity (the police who appear in chapter one have a catastrophic effect but little actual presence). By contrast, in Callaghan's extraordinary third-person novella, *Never's Just The Echo Of Forever*, the private and visionary world of Albie is not only contrasted with, but is destroyed by, a "normality" that is wholly lacking in imagination and speaks a different language.

11. If memory serves me right, some reviewers indulged in exactly these inanities, one suggesting the voice was an invention based on the dialects of Appalachia.

12. Anyone who has spent time in a Native community in the last fifty years will recognise this as the usual narrative mode.

13. Like the voices, for instance, in William Faulkner's *As I Lay Dying*.

14. "Episode" in the musical sense, too.

15. A combination of bamboozlement, admiration and, perversely, trust (at being outwitted by a writer, but through no cheap trick) is one of the most rewarding experiences for a reader. John Fowles' *The Magus* and John Banville's *The Book of Evidence* unfold in much the same way and also lead me to ask, *"How did they think of that? How did they do it?"*

16. In my unscholarly way, I transported this luminous sentence to my notebook without chapter or verse.

17. Beyond the scope of this essay, are the stylistic grace notes (within not-Anne's distinctive voice) that Callaghan executes; like the liquid "L" played with here – perhaps the only consonant that can repeat alliteratively and atmospherically without the blatancy that mars, for instance, Joyce's "The Dead" in its final lines.

18. "Counter voice" or "counter subject" as defined in *The Art of Fugue*.

19. Applicable to almost every part of Canada where the forests were cleared, the prairie broken, the minerals hoisted, the waters dammed.

20. Chapter and verse here: *Hofstadter, Douglas R. "Gödel, Escher, Bach . . ." NY: Vintage, 1979.*

21. *As I Lay Dying, The Double Hook, Cold Comfort Farm . . .*

A COMPLEX BEAUTY

Joan Thomas

Barry Callaghan caught my attention on the first page of
his collection of short fiction, *A Kiss Is Still A Kiss*, by
depicting a Canadian poet driving an Audi. Callaghan
never entirely accounts for this anomaly – his subject is
the importance of art, not its usual meager compensa-
tion. "Because Y Is A Crooked Letter" recounts a season
in the life of the poet and his partner Marina, who write,
sculpt and entertain in a renovated house full of antiques
and art treasures from around the world.

Art in Callaghan's story is not interior decorating. It's
the sensuous and spiritual centre of his characters' lives,
their connection with the past, their affirmation of life.
The mahogany grand piano on the main floor was a gift
from Marina's father, a man who'd been gassed in a rat
infested trench in the First World War. "Always listen to
music, no matter what," he'd said. But the poet has
begun to hear "the whisper of malevolence and afflic-
tion on the air," and one summer day the house is broken into and ransacked – tapestries slashed, sculptures
smashed, fires lit. This is the pillage of the barbarians,
and Callaghan sets it in a wider context: the cop
assigned to the case doesn't catch the poet's allusion to
Macbeth, the Crown Attorney doesn't know who Queen
Esther is. The poet and his partner might find the
resources to deal with the disaster, but the cultural
treasures of the past are still in peril.

This story, published under the title "A Motiveless
Malignancy," won a National Magazine Award for
Callaghan. The piece is autobiographical: Callaghan
endows the two men who were convicted in 1988 of

ransacking his Sullivan Street home with literary immortality by naming them in the story. We usually cast our eyes demurely down when we recognize the sources of a story in an author's life, but in this case, Callaghan's open treatment of his own experience makes the reading richer. "Because Y Is A Crooked Letter" is a fascinating personal statement from a man who, as poet, novelist, publisher, translator, has made the creation and celebration of art his life.

The sensibility that Callaghan articulates here is borne out by the stories in *A Kiss Is Still A Kiss,* by the effortless, almost profligate beauty of their surfaces, and by their emotional intelligence and accuracy.

One of the things that distinguishes the collection is its unity, although it's a unity that's not immediately apparent. There's a novella of over 100 pages, and a story comprised of one short conversation in a bar, and Callaghan uses a range of styles and tones, from the realistic coming of age story "Our Thirteenth Summer" to the playful "But Nobody Wants to Die," in which a man contacts his dead wife by walkie-talkie. The stories have no characters in common. And yet I'd be tempted to call them linked short stories, because the author so deliberately weaves them together by common themes and especially by imagery.

Blind men, as representatives of inner vision, shuffle through one story after another. ("I can't close my eyes to what I see," says the blind man in the first story, as he picks the winners at the race track.)

War is another motif, and its substitute – men playing with model planes or boats. There are songs from the forties or fifties, or children's rhymes in almost every story – I started to hear them as a sound track to the collection.

Seagulls on city streets, train whistles, cemeteries, crippled men, hanging men . . . Like a jazz virtuoso,

Callaghan uses these ideas as riffs, playing with their tone and colour, using them to reveal and deepen and tie together the meaning of the stories.

This technique is especially apparent in "Up Up And Away With Elmer Sadine," a story about a Vietnam vet that begins in a postmodern vein. When Elmer Sadine's parents are killed in an explosive collision with a truck carrying watermelons ("gave up trying to get watermelon seeds out of their bodies," says the mortician), a twitching eyelid is as close as Elmer can come to emotion. Elmer eventually settles into a life of flying model airplanes in the park, where he is joined by a man named Mellens, a Holocaust survivor who carries a cane with a handle carved in the shape of a grub.

Gradually, through their relationship, and through images of earth, ice, worms, seeds, Callaghan takes us closer and closer to the meaning of Elmer's experiences. The movement in this story is wonderful, subtle and inescapable, like long-repressed feelings thawing.

For all the images of physical decay, Callaghan's real interest is in the living dead. Death-in-life is represented in one story by a man who's had a stroke, in another by a woman's gangrenous feet, but more often Callaghan writes about quasi-lives bounded by loneliness, fear, emptiness and self-contempt.

Henry in "Intrusions" has come home to live with his mother. He feels "a terrible sense of being cheated," but the story touches on his own inability to take hold of happiness. "Even men who have two good legs dream they are cripples," says the gardener. Callaghan's eye for dramatic gestures is superlative: "In the bleak light from the bay windows, [Henry] saw that a large painting on the east wall was hanging crooked and when he straightened it there was a clean slash of white left on the wall. 'We can't have that,' he said. 'It looks like a scar.' He moved the frame so that it was crooked again . . ."

Henry is afraid of his sexual impulses, and not without reason. He and the headmaster of the school where he taught have just agreed that he should not be working with boys. The fear of sex for other reasons – its reminder of the flesh and of death – runs through the collection.

In "Mellow Yellow," Marie-Claire has her first sexual experience in a cemetery, "In the long tufted grass lying between the stones," but her boyfriend is so frightened "of the dead and her white body in the falling light of dusk" that he scrambles up and runs away. In "Buddies in Bad Times," Arthur and Jeff meet, flirt and plan a date virtually over the body of Arthur's friend as he lies in an open casket in the funeral home. But when Arthur finds out that Jeff is the undertaker's assistant, he bolts: too close. In "Up Up and Away With Elmer Sadine," an object as neutral as soap becomes an index to Callaghan's themes: Elmer associates soap with a prostitute's rituals in a prairie hotel, and Mellens remembers it as a symbol of the death and degradation of Jews in a concentration camp.

The final piece, the wonderful novella, "Never's Just The Echo of Forever," is the story of Albie Starbach, crossing guard, caretaker and urban cowboy. Albie finds intimacy where he can, renting rooms to strippers and hookers, for example, and sitting in the furnace room with an ear pressed to the air ducts listening to them weep on the telephone.

But there's a kind of desperate pride in Albie, an insistence on proving his worth to the gun-toting desperadoes who populate his inner world. With his genius for resonant images, Callaghan weaves the motif of drowning fish through the story: creatures who, like Albie, are dying in their own element.

Callaghan's picture of the contemporary urban world is tragic, at times highly ironic, but still surprisingly affirmative. In the characters in the title story, there's a sense of sturdy adaptation to a world that has lost its connection to the beautiful and the sacred. Cindy Witchita describes her spiritual rebirth, standing in front of her window in the sunlight with "the shadow of the cross from the crossbar on the window on me, on my boobs, and like, I felt full of joy. I knew right then that I was saved, that I had the mark of the cross on me . . ."

An hour after meeting in a park, and an hour before going to bed together, Cindy with her yellow Mohawk haircut and Abner Deerchild in his stolen cowboy boots stand at a kiosk in a mall and plight their troth. They buy a purple plate with a Polaroid picture of the two of them reproduced on it. Somehow, in the wasteland of the barbarians, the fundamental things apply.

NEVER'S JUST THE ECHO OF FOREVER

LEON ROOKE

Not for Barry Callaghan the summons of the paltry, timid, hardly-beating heart. His is a big roar in affirmation and celebration of life, never mind that the route he often takes, in his life and work, sees him charting those depths where sharks and charlatans, snakes and fallen saints reside.

He not only feeds this mad assemblage, he jumps in and says, "If nothing else will suffice, brothers and sisters, then feed on me." He refuses to be hedged in by the trivial or depleted by the commonplace. All evidence to the contrary, a many great people go on believing the world is flat. Not Callaghan. He gets in there where deadly lightening bolts flash and every breath courts disaster, yet no hand is raised in surrender. He hammers home Paul-Emile Borduas's ringing call-to-arms: "Together we will undertake the extravagance of living under a sharpened consciousness" because how otherwise may we assault the demons? Gusto, a spirit of this rare order, is demanded when a writer commands to the page a justly-celebrated work like the Hogg poems. Ditto, the stories. Ditto Albie, his desperado, guiding little children into the echo of forever. Callaghan loads his ore with wit: his angels frequently spread their wings: he lays down a beautiful line.

*

Toward the end of Albie's story, *Never's Just The Echo of Forever* – Callaghan's immensely powerful novella – a sleazy photographer snaps a *pic* that will later appear with a newspaper report whose headline is: THE CROSSING

GUARD NOBODY KNOWS. The unwilling subject, the novella's hero, has recently lost his job as a crossing guard for school children but he can't stop doing what he's meant to do, so now he helps assorted other stragglers and old folks to get safely to the other side: "Stopping traffic, helping people all day just for the sake of helping them, it's a terrific human interest story," the newspaper says. "It'll cheer our readers up."

The chilling banality of that term aside, a terrific human interest story is exactly what *Never's Just the Echo of Forever* is. For all the pain and terror encountered it should also cheer the reader up – and stop our traffic just to hymn its praise – to experience this gorgeously wrought, profoundly tender piece of work. This may well be Barry Callaghan's best story, and certainly it is one of the most perfectly accomplished and haunting Canadian fictions that I know. The central character, this Crossing Guard nobody knows, this man always on the brink of never, is known in the end by Callaghan so deeply, with such vast compassion, that by rights he ought to go on forever.

Albie Starback is twenty-nine, a caretaker for a Toronto rooming house and caregiver for his crippled mother as well as a crossing guard: thus, thrice over, marked as one who gives. For much of the story the word "grief" haunts Albie; later a second word, "give," becomes its companion. Together they go to the heart of Albie's achievement as a human being, and the truth of that achievement persists despite the violence that overtakes him. For all that he has lost or never had, for all the torment and craziness he seeks to hold at bay, he is a man of great sweetness, true generosity.

Albie is haunted also by a constellation of obsessive images and by a pair of old "desperados," invisible to others, sad-eyed gunslingers out of the cowboy myth that he lives amid the steel and glass canyons of Toronto streets. This is very much a poet's novella; Callaghan is, of course, a brilliant poet as well as a powerful story-teller – part of the strong Canadian contingent of genre-crossers that includes Margaret Atwood and Michael Ondaatje. Like them, he uses image patterns of great complexity and tensile strength to build his fiction and to make it sing. Interestingly, there is a strong similarity at the level of image and in the handling of insanity and violence between Callaghan's novella and Ondaatje's *Coming Through Slaughter*, especially at the stunning close of each. The two heroes are wildly different men, but each comes through slaughter (inner torment, his own violence, and the ugliest of external realities) to a place where he can no longer be touched by it; each crosses over safely to a place that only those who enter the character fully with the author will know is one of beauty. The world of this novella is dangerous, an explo-sive Desert Storm both in the microcosm of Albie's mind and in the geopolitical surround reflected by his moth-er's TV viewing of the first Gulf War. Spectral gun-slingers hang from the trees, a train will come at High Noon to a town with only one defender, the gift of sex-uality goes dark, and in a furnace room the voices of the doomed are channeled through air ducts to the danger-ous, gentle man who waits at the centre of it all. But Callaghan also maintains for Albie and for the reader, on the other side and sometimes here, an alternative world of natural beauty, tenderness, and spiritual peace. And this is conveyed not only through the imagery of a yearning imagination but by the reality of the characters.

Best of all is the lovely relationship of mother and son, through which the balm of humour also comes into play. Astonishing Emma Rose, her palm bleeding stig-mata-like years after being nailed by a knife-thrower lover's errant blade, lifting barbells so that she "looked like a fugitive from the law practicing to surrender at gun point," walking on her hands in the basement apartment, her poor crippled legs dancing in the air, or refreshed by the breeze during outings with her good son on a Toronto ferry boat, is a magnificent creation. There is also wonderful Sebastien, the boy who loves and wants to be like Albie, who puts lipstick on so that the face of his lost mother in the mirror can assure him that she loves him. And there is Yuri, substitute father and lover of Emma Rose when Albie was nineteen, who put cowboy boots on his feet and taught him what he learned himself in a Nazi concentration camp – the need to concentrate.

The rich theme of the lost father is central here. Albie has never known his father, but he is a thorough mensch in spite of that: eminently trustworthy employee and good family man to his mother, the lonely dwellers in the rooming house, and the children on the street. The lost father, Yuri, and the old desperados merge, and are linked to another lost father who is "WANTED, DEAD OR ALIVE: GOD." Albie wonders if god (who "saw all there was to see with the freshness of vision in which nothing was hid") wasn't in him, together with "God's words, because out of nowhere, the dark waters at the back of his mind would part and he'd see with utter clarity…a crease in the face of a weathered old man, or an unlaced shoe, and wings, white wings, and flying fish." But the angels, he would know in his heart – though "they had lived and flown and fought with each other in the sky" – were gone now, "scissored out" of a picture that has been left full of holes.

In the end, Albie eats the words of God in a beautifully ambiguous act – and the anger inside him shrivels, so that "there was not an angry bone left in his body," and the words from *Apocalypse* that Callaghan uses as the epigraph for this beautiful work are fulfilled: "*And I went unto the angel, and said unto him. Give me the little book. And he said unto me. Take it, and eat it up; and it shall make thy belly bitter, but it shall be in thy mouth as sweet as honey."* So it is with the transformative power of Callaghan's little book.

THE ART OF DISASTER

Notes on Barry Callaghan's "Because Y is a Crooked Letter"

Rosemary Sullivan

As I finished reading Barry Callaghan's "Because Y is a Crooked Letter," I felt the enormous satisfaction that only a story can provide. A story moves in vertical time, swirling around one incident. It offers the pleasure of a perfectly enclosed, self-contained aesthetic object. What a satisfying story, I said to myself, and wanted to leave it at that. But the story sat in my mind. Why is it such a perfect model of what a story can be?

It all begins with the narrative voice. I realize I know a lot, cumulatively, about this narrator, and yet how do I know it? I discover him, as I would a stranger, by the asides he lets drop. He does not entice me with intimacies, but he does not push me away either. I know that he is a writer, but not one of those romantic, self-congratulatory writers. He tells stories because that is what he does. He watches, "detached," and very little gets past him. "A writer is someone on whom nothing is lost," Henry James used to say.

I know from the outset that this man, who is telling me a story, has a passion for racetracks and playing the horses. But I begin to think that for him, life, too, is a game of chance that requires skill and panache, and that it involves, by definition, winning and losing. This is a man who has trained himself "to stand back and look at things." "Ah, but what things?" I ask. People – at their best, in the work they produce, whether art, music, or training horses; in the love they are capable of. And people at their worst – in their inherited hatreds, their pettiness, their wars. A chance comment lets me know that this writer has worked as a reporter, has been to Israel and to Belfast; not out of vicarious curiosity, but rather because these are the things a writer must know.

But this is all very well, I say to myself. I would expect no less. There is something else that astonishes me and I need to put my finger on it. It is the self-observation of this narrator. He speaks of "a dark rankling alertness" that he feels as his story builds, but I realize that he turns this not only on others, but also on himself. I watch carefully as he rings the changes of his own emotions and I immediately admire his resistance to self-pity, to sentimentality, to letting himself off the hook. "There is a little larceny in all of us," he says. He has pulled me in with this laconic, detached, and yet passionate voice.

Still, the narrative voice is not everything in a story. I think that what makes a story great is how it builds: what I would call the arc of expectation, an expectation whose fulfillment is continually extended or deferred. I think this narrator would call this a jazz improvisation since jazz, and the Blues, are part of his intimate spiritual repertoire, going as far back as childhood.

As I read, I think his song, his story, is going somewhere, only to discover I am wrong as he compels me to enter again, somewhere other than I expected. Just when I think the story is over, there is a new riff. That's the mastery. This narrator, this writer, has invited me to enter a simple story, an incident, and in a few pages, he has managed to wring every implication from it, until I stand exposed to a "motiveless malignancy" and then he spins me back into the light. It is a trajectory that imitates life itself.

Now, I suppose, is the moment to tell you what this story is about, though the word "about" is misleading since a story is never *about* something. It simply is. Still, the story does have a plot. It is very simple. One day, while this man and his wife are away, a number of thieves break into and vandalize their home. The thieves smash personal possessions, write graffiti on the walls, and set seven fires throughout the house. The implications are obvious and most writers would find them: the violation of the sanctum of privacy, the desire for an explanation, the need for revenge.

But the power of this story is that it begins before the incident and resonates long after it. The language is precise and exquisitely controlled:

> It began over a year ago. I was going to drive to the foothill town of Saratoga to stay for two weeks in a rambling, spacious house and try to have lunch every day at a table under the tent at the old gabled racetrack. I had renegotiated the mortgage on the house and bought a new pair of tinted prescription sunglasses so that I could read the racing form in the glaring sun. Marina had packed several oblong dark bars of wax and her slender steel tools. She is a sculptor. I am a poet. We went out the back door of our house, through the vine-covered and enclosed cobblestone courtyard, and decided to move the car forward in the garage, toward the lane. I turned the key and the Audi lurched backward, breaking down the stuccoed wall, dumping concrete blocks and cement into the garden. I looked back through the rear-view mirror into an emptiness, wondering where everything had gone, and I heard the whisper of malevolence and affliction on the air. I did not heed it.

The language has been so lean and unadorned until the last two sentences that these sentences seem staged and exaggerated, but the story will earn their timbre. This will be a story about malevolence and how it catches us at our most vulnerable because we are mostly distracted. We walk casually, but there is always a fault line just at our feet waiting to trip us up.

Early in the story, we meet the house that will be broken into. It becomes almost a character. The narrator recalls its walls, filled with "drawings, paintings, tapestries – all our travels and some turbulence nicely framed." Such an exquisitely economical way to encapsulate the lived-through tensions of a marriage. We are reminded that a house is not a structure, but an articulation: of imagination, feeling, memory, "all the bindings of love," all the things that make us what we are. What, then, does its violation mean? For this house is totally violated.

Vandals have not just stolen objects. They have broken the house's precious mementoes; torn up its memory in books and written documents; and, most brutally, destroyed its connection to the ancestral past. Fires have been set. The destruction is so total it seems that the thieves must have had a motive; they must have been on some kind of personal vendetta.

Now comes the real beauty of the story. This writer will resist the easy comfort of rage or blame. "I felt only the torpor that comes with keeping an incredulous calm in the face of brutality," he tells us and by doing so he violates the rules that society imposes on victims. There is always a *why* to malevolence and those responsible must be punished.

Other characters enter the story: the detective who investigates, the police who dust for fingerprints, carrying with them all the paraphernalia of justice that insists that human acts are rational, explainable, containable, and must be punished. This writer, they insist, must have enemies. And beneath this statement is the implication that he somehow provoked this violence; this must be his fault.

The story moves past the destruction of the house to the court case where all the participants sit: the lawyers, the judge, the criminals, the victims. Of course the writer is not a sentimentalist; he wants the criminals punished since they have committed a crime. But "vengeance," he says, "is a second-rate emotion." He suggests that the realm of the criminal is a necessary and parallel world that imitates that of the powerful. There is always the "uptown swine" who feed off the junkies. The whole judicial process moves as if by rote, as if by formula, and nobody asks why.

Feeling hollowed out inside, the narrator and his wife begin the process of "life as repair." They will make it. They have lost time and the future, the things they might have created had this malevolence not entered their lives. But the house is resurrected and laughter re-enters it.

The story ends with a stunning image. The narrator recalls a childhood game when he used to leap from the protective and anonymous darkness through the spotlight in his back yard, back into the darkness. He and his wife have been exposed to that light, but as the story ends, they have recovered their "secret selves."

How astonishing that mere words can invent a character who becomes less ephemeral, more intimately known, than many of the actual people we meet. But this happens only if the language holds up. I will remember some of the phrases in this story indefinitely. This linguistic trick is the final magic of fiction.

Sometimes stories find you when you need them. I am writing these notes to "Because Y is a Crooked Letter" in the Spanish town of Portbou, just across the frontier from France. I have come here with my husband for the second time to film the memorial to Walter Benjamin. It is one of the most evocative monuments I have ever encountered. On September 25, 1940, guided by a young German woman, Walter Benjamin crossed the Pyrenees on foot. He was fleeing from the Nazis. In Portbou, the guardia civil apprehended and imprisoned him for the crime of being a stateless refugee. Threatened with the prospect of being transported back to a concentration camp in Germany, Benjamin committed suicide the next day.

The monument to Walter Benjamin is an iron shaft that cuts like a wound into the mountainside. As you descend its sixty-two steps, the dark shaft opens suddenly to the light, to the looming mountains and the open sea. On a glass wall are written the words: "This site is more to honour the memory of the nameless than the memory of the renowned."

This morning I climbed down the shaft to the glass wall and then immediately climbed back up. As I emerged from the darkness, I said to my husband: "Something terrible has happened since our last visit. Vandals have shattered the glass." He is Chilean and knows about these things. "That's what it is," was all he said. And yes, I thought, that's it: "Motiveless malignancy."

ORPHEUS IN RETIREMENT

Love, Myth, and Questions of Audience in Barry Callaghan's "Nobody Wants to Die"

Priscila Uppal

C.S. Lewis' *A Grief Observed*, a poignant meditation on the death of his beloved wife, begins: "No one ever told me that grief felt so like fear" (5). He goes on to add, "And no one ever told me about the laziness of grief" (7). The book is a harrowing journal: brief, yet far-reaching, passionate yet oddly calm, doubtful yet faith-driven, honest yet embarrassed; its psychic and physical territory is the territory Willard Cowley occupies in Barry Callaghan's short story, "Nobody Wants to Die."

Much of Callaghan's work is infused with a consciousness of death, how much actual living means when it can be stolen from you by death at any second. Like most with a Catholic upbringing, Callaghan is obsessed with the idea of resurrection, but frequently, in both his fiction and poetry (and even in his literary journalism), contrary to the traditional Catholic consciousness, his men and women can only achieve resurrection through a stubborn and violent personal act of will, not through the grace of God. It is the individual outside mainstream society who possesses a creative, even destructive, energy that can sometimes outwit life, at least for a little while, and can achieve secular redemption, most often through a transcendent encounter with artistic genius or the love of a great (not "good") woman.

The short story, "Nobody Wants to Die," fits this Callaghan rubric, yet deviates from this narrative in specific, un-Callaghan-like ways. First and foremost, this story explores the dynamic of grief and the possibilities of resurrection as experienced by an old widower caught between the states of fear and laziness.

The most famous death in Catholicism is, of course, the crucifixion of Jesus Christ, and Callaghan's revisionist imagination has taken up the story of Christ on a number of occasions (see Hogg *The Poems and Drawings* and Hogg *The Seven Last Words*). Likewise, many other biblical figures and stories interest Callaghan: Cain and Abel, Exodus, Veronica, Lot, and the Last Supper, to name a few. As Callaghan explains in his 2002 philosophical non-fiction piece about storytelling, "True Stories" (since republished in *Raise You Five*, 2005), he deeply respects the "official" versions of these biblical tales, but his interest lies primarily in how even the most "official" versions are revisionist in nature, that they all contain powerful, potent, and imaginative lies. He assures his readers that even though he might be challenging biblical stories as representing historical truth, in doing so he is not "inviting a laughter that belittles the story," but, rather, he is pointing out, as Aristotle observed, that "chronological detail . . . is a low level of awareness" (126). For Callaghan, the story need not be "literally true in its factual details" in order for "its great truth to be trusted"(126).

As Willard Cowley will reveal in "Nobody Wants to Die," as he walks the streets, grief-stricken, unsure of where he is or where he belongs, longing to hear his recently deceased wife's voice: "the truth was that all the great myths were based on lies" (200). Although Willard is thinking of the Exodus from Egypt (since it takes only three-and-a-half days to walk across the Sinai, it seems implausible that the desert migration of the Hebrews took forty years), the main myths that Callaghan revises in this story are the Judeo-Christian story of Adam and Eve in the Garden of Eden, and the Greco-Roman story of Orpheus and Eurydice.

The first striking revision Callaghan makes to both myths is his insistence of their relevance to the experience of old age. Adam and Eve are rarely, if ever, in either pictorial or literary representations, characterized as older people, senior citizens, because the bucolic Garden of Eden represents the beginning of human creation and ancestry, our first parents, certainly not our last, as they are initiated into an awareness of mortality. But, as Callaghan is acutely aware, a ritual initiation into mortality is not the same thing as the ritual initiation into grief and/or mourning. Grief is not an easily definable state; it's an experience, somewhere between fear and laziness (Lewis intends the word to encompass numbness and inactivity), and our awareness of mortality changes as we age. What happens when you are no longer afraid of your own death, but the death of another? When you are afraid that the one who possessed all the knowledge you sought has drifted off into another plane of existence, leaving you behind, ignorant, bewildered, alone, bored, scared? This struggle is not so much with mortality itself as it is with the nature and meaning of grief and how to survive those painful emotions through what Freud termed, in "Mourning and Melancholia" (1917), "the work of mourning" (253). How does one perform the work of mourning when there is no lush and inviting garden to return to, only an empty bedroom with the lights left on and a house that has ceased to console. And the apple? The apple was thrown out long ago. You can't find it, and even if you could, you wouldn't recognize it as the knowledge of good and evil, but only as food you no longer like to eat.

Then there is Orpheus and Eurydice, another myth about young people in love, and, I would argue, the prevailing myth that is explored and revised in "Nobody Wants to Die." Orpheus is the "quintessential mythical singer" (*The Oxford Classical Dictionary*,

1078), and model for elegiac poets, the passionate artist who is able to turn his grief into song and beauty though he loses his wife not once, through a snakebite (a connection to Eve), but twice, when he ascends from the underworld and, against terms set by the gods, looks back to see her before they have reached the light of earth. He sings her praises and sings of his grief when she dies the first time, and he continues to do so with renewed fervour a second time, after he's lost her for good. In several versions of the myth he is even decapitated, castrated, and cut into tiny pieces, but that stubborn head keeps singing and founds new poetic cults (see "Orpheus" in *The Oxford Classical Dictionary* for various versions of the myth as represented by classical writers). As several studies of the English elegy tradition point out (see Peter M. Sacks' *The English Elegy: Studies in the Genre from Spenser to Yeats* [1985] or Melissa F. Zeiger's *Beyond Consolation: Death, Sexuality, and the Changing Shapes of Elegy* [1997]), the entire tradition from John Milton's "Lycidas" through Alfred Lord Tennyson's *In Memoriam* to the twentieth century is modeled on the triumph of Orpheus, the triumph of the singer in the face of death, and as a figure he is a favourite of poets from antiquity to the present (I note that the very last poem in Czeslaw Milosz's final collection, *Second Space*, is called "Orpheus and Eurydice"). I would also argue that the Orpheus and Eurydice myth continues to interest poets, especially Judeo-Christian poets, because the Bible, while jam-packed with stories of intrigue, violence, retribution, and moral lessons, contains almost no moving love stories of the earthly variety. Couples pair up with each other, not out of love, but to beget future generations. Although spiritual devotion is a favourite topic among many poets, so too are our worldly loves, our sexual pairings. Even

Callaghan cannot make Adam and Eve a compelling love story without a little help. He must invoke that lover-mourner of Greek myth.

Yet in "Nobody Wants to Die" Callaghan inverts the classical Orpheus and Eurydice: in his version, Orpheus and Eurydice have lived with and loved each other for decades; they are old when Eurydice dies; and though he might be said to "sing," Orpheus has lost his audience; his grief is passionate, but also ignorant and one-sided. Furthermore, Eurydice dies of a disease that is quick, but not immediate; Orpheus watches her die while he keeps vigil at her deathbed, and then he must sleep, not in a new, uninitiated marriage bed, but in the bed where she also slept; he must live in the same house and recall the conversations they engaged in during their marriage. Eurydice has had more than enough time to make many profound and intelligent statements about the nature of life, love, and death, and Orpheus puzzles as much over her words as he does over his own. This is not an Orpheus obsessed with his own mortality, but, like C.S. Lewis, with the *meaning* of his wife's death and how best to mourn it, not only for his own sake, but eventually for hers.

"Nobody Wants to Die" begins, by its very title, with the knowledge of death and our common attitude towards it. Despite whatever tales or myths we've been told, whatever religious or spiritual upbringing we might have experienced or might subscribe to, Callaghan claims that the totality of the human race has no interest in dying. Therefore, it is no wonder that Callaghan begins his own tale by invoking chronological time and realistic place, but also cyclical time and the eternal space of the myth or fairytale: "Willard Cowley lived with his wife Kate in a sandstone house. There was a sun parlour at the back of the house and the windows of the house opened on to a twisted old apple tree" (189). In a subtle manner, Willard and Kate appear both as a realistic couple living in the late twentieth-century Rosedale neighbourhood of Toronto, and as a mythical couple clearly linked to the Adam and Eve story by the reference to the apple tree and, later on, because of Willard's reactions to Kate's death, to Orpheus and Eurydice. Willard, as Adam, is older, wiser than the younger version we are accustomed to: "Everything alters," Willard often told Kate, "under the apple tree. One by one we drop away." At first we might think that Callaghan's Adam has no need to be seduced into knowledge through his Eve; Willard is "a well-known scholar" who informs students that it's his job "to tell the young all about tomorrow's sorrow" (190). He is, like Orpheus, a speaker, a singer, a "teller," and yet, as Kate points out in the sweetest yet still most striking of ways, Willard has acquired very little wisdom about the most important things in life, least of all death. When Willard retires from teaching and can spend more time walking and talking with his wife, she starts to point him in the direction of profound and meaningful knowledge. "Someday you'll take death seriously" (190), she tells him. "I do. I do," he protests. Nevertheless, although Willard has considered his own death (he hypothesizes that he might like to die in the desert rather than in the city), we soon learn that he has not genuinely considered the death of his wife as a real possibility. He often wonders about the calm she exudes while sleeping, and is amazed that she has transformed from a woman who woke up screaming in her youth to one who has achieved control and dominance over her fears.

However, Willard does not ask Kate about how she has accomplished this mortal feat; instead he talks, talks, talks, about the recent discoveries made by archeologists that confirm "the Bible was not history" (192), that the whole narrative might be based on lies, or "theological dreaming" (192), and that maybe humans created their own gods:

> We create them and then they turn around and taunt us. Maybe Christ on the cross is really a taunting dream of death and redemption, a dream in which Christ has to stay nailed to the cross because we don't dare let him come back and live among us like a normal man because then there'd only be a dreamless silence out there without him in it, a great dark silence. (193)

But though the intellectual, studious Willard makes interesting theological and philosophical arguments throughout the short story, pondering whether "ignorance" is, as Joseph Conrad's *An Outcast of the Islands* suggests, a man who "knows all about himself," or whether he is experiencing the opposite problem and maybe doesn't know anything about himself (197), he is far too caught up in presenting his theories to his one-woman audience, Kate, to wonder too long about her half-promise, half-accusation, "someday . . . I'll tell you what I really think" (194).

I do not intend to suggest that Willard is cold or blind or sexist; he isn't. He's obviously good-natured, dedicated, passionate, and well-read. When he retires from public life, he proclaims: "Kate, you're my whole life. Thank God" (193); but he does not appreciate, nor explore what this declaration actually means until Kate dies. He has questioned and examined philosophies regarding the nature of humankind, one's relationship to God, to other humans, to history, mythology, literature, and art; yet rarely has he thought in concrete terms about his relationship to love. Or to grief. Here Willard is lost. He must become initiated into his own myth; which isn't one of god versus humans, or one of struggle at all, but of eternal love. In fact, the most astonishing thing about Callaghan's short story is that very little conflict occurs at all. This is not typical Callaghan as represented by other stories in *A Kiss Is Still a Kiss*, his novels and novellas, or his poetry where his poetic persona, Hogg, of *Hogg The Poems and Drawings* and *Hogg The Seven Last Words*, suffers more physical beatings from thugs and officials than he does love affairs. In "Nobody Wants to Die" there is no underworld violence. No starvation or excess drinking or drugs. No crimes committed. No priests attacked. No tough talking. Not even a single volatile argument. But in this story, the lack of conflict makes the grief that much more poignant and believable. The conflict is emotional and spiritual, not told with passion but with understanding, the wise voice of an experienced, but never condescending storyteller imparting a truth understood only in retrospect, over time, as if pulled out of deep memory, the collective memory of the imagination, or what we sometimes refer to as myth.

Unlike Orpheus who gains an audience after the death of his wife, with Kate gone, Willard loses his. At the funeral, we are told, only "a few old scholars came and none of his former students" (199). As someone approaching retirement from Toronto's York University after thirty years of teaching when he wrote this story, Callaghan was likely drawing emotional insight from an approaching understanding of what it might mean to experience a dwindling live audience as a teacher and lecturer and as a public intellectual. He was also likely drawing further emotional insight from the previous changes in audience he has witnessed and experienced in his long career as literary journalist and writer. Like many other 1960s and 1970s CBC journalists and their audiences, Callaghan has lived through and has been deeply affected by a cultural news transformation from the days when the CBC was a vital presence and forum for the Canadian public (pre-24 hour cable news stations, pre-digital television, pre-internet) to a news culture where tabloid journalism and consumer agendas rule. In addition, the Canadian literary marketplace has severely changed too over Callaghan's literary career, harmed by international takeovers and books as commodities sales forces, and bestsellers lists dominanted by entertainment-driven fantasy novels and Chick-Lit. So, what happens when Orpheus outlives his fame and lacks an audience? When his use to society has been served and he is no longer considered vital to culture or society? As a widower in "Nobody Wants to Die," Willard is poignantly portrayed as a man who deeply grieves the loss of his beloved wife, but what Willard experiences after Kate's death highlights mythical and artistic consequences as well. Can the artist without an audience live on? What does immortality mean in such a context? Can it even be achieved?

Unlike Adam, Orpheus' search for knowledge does not lead him into paradise to eat of the fruit; he ventures into the underworld to question the gods, find the dead, and ultimately, to convince the gods to grant his beloved Eurydice resurrection. Willard also heads underground, into Toronto's St. George subway station (St. George is the patron saint of England, a martyr from the third century who acquired mythical status nearly one-thousand years later when a dragon-slaying story was attached to him – see "George, St." in *The Canadian Oxford Dictionary,* 584), sure that he, too, is "on to something big, a simple truth, so simple that he knew he had seen it, and the truth was that all the great myths were based on lies" (200). Callaghan insists on a mythical structure for Willard and Kate's narrative, and on mythical resonance in much of his fiction and poetry, perhaps, because, as an old man in "True Stories" affirms, "If someone else told the same story, then it must be even more true" (129). Willard descends, and like Orpheus, he does not gain

Eurydice's resurrection; his narrative story is one of failure; yet, "Nobody Wants to Die" is the recognition of the great story of our failure. The title, and the blues song by Albert King that acts as epigraph for the short story collection *A Kiss Is Still a Kiss*, the collection in which "Nobody Wants to Die" appears – "Everybody wants to go to heaven/But nobody wants to die" – remind us that we all desire immortality; no one is satisfied with the inevitability of death. Where Callaghan's version of the Orpheus and Eurydice myth is most satisfying is in his recognition that this dissatisfaction is not just Orpheus'; it is also Eurydice's.

And so Eurydice seeks her own recognition from Orpheus; but, as he is unaccustomed to being the listener in their relationship, though he searches for her voice throughout their home, he cannot hear her singing. Significantly, he bans himself from their bedroom, allowing a reading lamp to remain on until it burns out; and consequently, he chastises himself as a "coward" (202) awash in overwhelming, pitiful grief. Then, the once-failed Orpheus returns to the underworld yet again, to "the Hudson's Bay underground shopping mall" (203). Here Willard learns, like a good student of McLuhan's, that the medium is indeed the message, and he must adopt a new instrument to deal with the new times, the new circumstances of his audience-listener relationship. The eureka moment is achieved when he notices several people talking away on cell phones as they shop or walk through the city, and he arrives at the conclusion, "maybe they're not talking to anyone" (203). Considering that *A Kiss Is Still a Kiss* was published in 1995 ("Nobody Wants to Die" previously appeared under the title "Willard and Kate" in *Toronto Life* in 1986), Callaghan had the good fortune to hit on a medium that was only making its first steps to superstardom, and to recognize the potential use of the mobile phone – as a prop to link the material world of the living with the spiritual world of the dead *sans* hassle from the general population – offering us a prescient moment, a moment of near genius that satisfies both the fictional realism of the story and its magic realism and mythical counterparts. Willard, however, remains "on to something big," rather than immediately aware of the ramifications and potential uses of his great discovery; he decides to purchase a single child's walkie-talkie, but the Uruk Sound Systems salesperson will not let him do so, insisting, wisely, that he must buy two: "You can't talk to no one. Someone's got to be on the other end" (203). The name Uruk is an ironic, yet fitting allusion in the story to the setting for the *Epic of Gilgamesh* where another mythical figure ventures into the land of the dead, not to beg for the resurrection of a loved one, but to seek eternal life for himself. From the salesman Willard buys the pair of walkie-talkies, but he only uses one, hitting the *Send* button to resume his talking to Kate. Talking keeps Willard alive. But the question is: does it keep Kate alive?

The walkie-talkie is a practical medium that allows Willard to deal with his grief in public; he can speak aloud for hours and hours, wherever and whenever he likes, to his missed wife. Yet in the hands of a talented storyteller, the technology is also an artistic outlet, one that might be seen here as equivalent to Orpheus' poetic expressions, though Willard tells his dead wife jokes in addition to stories and philosophical ponderings. While standing on the footbridge over the Toronto ravines (for those who know Callaghan, this bridge alludes to the one near his home in Rosedale which is now named after his writer-father, Morley Callaghan), Willard is bothered by the fact that he's never descended into that wilderness, and therefore has no knowledge of what "goes on down there" (205). Because Willard as

Orpheus has failed yet again to retrieve his lost wife, the ravine appears as a third underground in the story, but Willard resists the urge to visit this other-world, as he is now genuinely bothered by the apparent discrepancies between the Judeo-Christian biblical stories and the archeological factual histories. Here, we encounter Willard struggling with the potential consolations for death art attempts to provide. Is Kate alive, in another form, in another world? Such a narrative is attractive, perhaps even essential, for many to believe. But is such a belief *true*? And does it not then cut off the mourner from communication with the dead? C. S. Lewis also ponders these questions in his meditation on grief: "Time and space and body were the very things that brought us together; the telephone wires by which we communicated. Cut one off, or cut both off simultaneously. Either way, mustn't the conversation stop?" (14). Furthermore, can the consolation artistic imagination provides actually equal and potentially transcend the experience of mortality? Is this achievement *fair* to the dead? Critics like Melissa F. Zeiger argue that "an identificatory fixation on Orpheus and his poetic success is all too compatible with a repressive, death-denying, and self-canonizing masculinist compulsion in elegy *and* its reception, which now calls for critical re-evaluation" (3).

C.S. Lewis laments that, as time passes regardless of his sincere and devoted grief, he is aware that his beloved wife will become "more and more an imaginary woman" (17), a composition of his own making rather than a representation of who she was as he continues to write about her. I have argued elsewhere (see *Recovering the Past Through Language and Landscape: The Contemporary English-Canadian Elegy*, PhD Dissertation, York Univeristy, 2004) that English-Canadian elegists, agreeing with Canadian poet Earle Birney's declaration: "It's only by our lack of ghosts/we're haunted" (138), have sought to reconfigure the traditional Orpheus and Eurydice elegy template in order to actually accomplish what Orpheus initially set out to do: recover the dead and live and speak with them again. Callaghan's short story also destabilizes the prominence of Orpheus and the consolation of his artistic powers in favour of active and renewed dialogue with Eurydice, re-evaluating the myth in ways that suggest a contemporary and even feminist reorientation. The misrepresentation of the dead is a real concern for Willard, who at this point in the story has only utilized the one-sided *Send* function of his walkie-talkie set, and who misses the real Kate of his marriage who *chose* to listen to him rather than this void that he might simply be calling Kate for his own grieving purposes.

Fittingly, Willard witnesses Kate's resurrection on noon of Easter Sunday. Taking out his walkie-talkie and crossing the footbridge to Bloor Street, he is consumed by a revelation he thinks he is having about the expulsion of Adam and Eve from the Garden of Eden, that the new Eden is the one that Cain cultivates "on the edge of the world," and this is significant because it was the first time man took "his own word for everything" (207). While Willard continues to pontificate, a woman in "owl-glasses" (207) – an important physical detail because owls are frequently associated with death and the underworld, with the "Crone Goddess, who embodied wisdom as well as mortality" ("Owl," *The Woman's Dictionary of Symbols and Sacred Objects,* 404) – agrees with him, but Willard wants no one else to enter his space, his garden, and he shoos this potential knowledge-bringer away. Nevertheless, as he does so, the incident acts as a catalyst for the real revelation to occur. In his initiation, Willard's hand slips along his walkie-talkie and he hits the *Receive* button, surprised, finally, into conversation. Our Eurydice scolds Willard for his inability to hear her singing over his own: "Can you imagine what it's been like listening and listening and I couldn't say a word . . ." (208). She also reinforces the connection between speaker-singer and audience-listener as a necessary two-way contract crucial to survival, to living. Kate claims that Willard's ignorance of her presence and his inability to acknowledge her voice is what nearly killed her for good: "I was yelling so loud at you I thought I would die. I was hoarse for two days, I lost my voice" (208). Callaghan's revision of the Orpheus myth suggests that just because Orpheus turns to look at his wife, consequently causing her to disappear from his view, this appearance of absence does not necessarily mean actual absence; Orpheus might simply be lacking the ability to see Eurydice and, more importantly, to hear her.

With his wife returned to him, Willard is now eager to stop bickering about lost time and is desperate to know what Kate, as promised, really thinks. The reader, as audience, pauses; we know that Kate has always possessed more crucial knowledge than Willard; we know that it is she, not Willard, who is "on to something big," and we desire her wisdom. Perhaps Willard has come to realize that this desire for revelation is why grief occupies a space that travels between the states of fear and laziness. Both emotions, as described by C. S. Lewis, are associated with fundamental qualities of narrative, and particularly with narrative "suspense": "And grief still feels like fear. Perhaps, more strictly, like suspense. Or like waiting; just hanging around waiting for something to happen. It gives life a permanently provisional feeling" (29). Kate has returned and we too want our promised ending; we want to hear her voice. This is a ghost story, but not a traditionally gothic one. Gothic ghost stories scare us, not necessarily because the dead return – though, as

Roger Grainger writes regarding burial rituals, "A wandering ghost is a dangerous kind of entity, because he or she might decide to wander *back*" (29) – but because in these tales the ghosts are unhappy and unsatisfied with the living. Is Kate unhappy? What does she really think? As in all great myths, and like Willard, the wisdom we think we are going to acquire is rarely the one we do acquire; in "Nobody Wants to Die" we do not eat of the apple of good and evil and come to knowledge about death; instead, we learn about love. Kate tells Willard: "I can't imagine living without you. I hang on every word"(208). Although even Willard questions whether or not she is being truthful in her response, we allow ourselves to trust in the great myth of love as Kate insists: "I would never lie to you"(209). We also revel in her resurrection, in her utter defiance of death, as she, not Orpheus, is given the last line of the story, a line that Willard must listen to in his new position of audience: "Nobody wants to die"(209). This is knowledge we possessed from the beginning, from the title, but we too were far too selfish to realize its essential truthfulness to life, and to fiction and myth, until Eurydice expressed it for us from the other side.

In "Nobody Wants to Die," Kate embarks on the most mythical of all migrations, the journey of death, without Willard. Willard has to find a way to journey with her, to catch up in his understanding. Fiction then becomes a sort of "mourning play" (144) – as Freud termed tragedy in "Creative Writers and Day-Dreaming" (1908) – and accomplishes similar aims as the *fort-da* game, described in Freud's "The Pleasure Principle" (1920) as a game of pretend that allows a child to practice grief and take "an *active* part" (16) in the process by throwing objects away and then facilitating their return when the displeasure of their absence becomes overwhelming. Mourning play is one of the reasons that stories exploring grief, like this one and C.S. Lewis', help us learn about how to cope with grief when it arrives. For those who know Callaghan, it is hard not to read into this story the mourning play of a man entering his own retirement from the university and potentially eventually from artistic production, but also of a man deeply in love with his partner, a great woman, the painter and sculptor Claire Weissman Wilks, writing out the fear inherent in loving someone for decades who will die before or after you and with whom you seek eternal two-sided conversation. Love is no lie; "Alone into the Alone" (14), as C. S. Lewis cites his wife quoting before her death, is not an acceptable answer for Lewis in the end, nor is it for Orpheus and Eurydice, nor for Willard and Kate, nor for Callaghan, who through the rewriting of myth also tells us a truthful and transcendent story of his own love, and what Eurydice has taught him.

Works Cited

Birney, Earle. "Can Lit." *The Collected Poems of Earle Birney*. Vol 1. Toronto: McClelland and Stewart Ltd., 1975. 138.

Callaghan, Barry. "Nobody Wants to Die." *A Kiss Is Still A Kiss*. Boston, Toronto, New York, London: Little Brown and Company (Canada) Ltd., 1995. 189-209.

——. "True Stories." *Exile: The Literary Quarterly*. Vol 26. No 2. (2002): 120-133.

Freud, Sigmund. "Beyond the Pleasure Principle." 1920. *The Standard Edition of the Complete Psychological Works of Sigmund Freud*. 24 vols. Ed. James Strachey.
London: Hogarth Press, (1953-1974): 19: 227-232.

——. "Creative Writers and Day-Dreaming." 1908. *The Standard Edition of the Complete Psychological Works of Sigmund Freud*. 24 vols. Ed. James Strachey. London: Hogarth Press, (1953-1974): 9: 141-153.

——. "Mourning and Melancholia." 1917. *The Standard Edition of the Complete Psychological Works of Sigmund Freud*. 24 vols. Ed. James Strachey. London: Hogarth Press, (1953-1974): 14: 243-258.

"George, St." *The Canadian Oxford Dictionary*. Ed. Katherine Barber. Toronto, Oxford, New York: Oxford University Press, 1998. 584.

Grainger, Roger. *The Social Symbolism of Grief and Mourning*. London; Philadelphia: Jessica Kingsley Publishers, 1998.

Lewis, C. S. *A Grief Observed*. London, Boston: Faber & Faber, 1966. (First published 1961.)

Sacks, Peter M. *The English Elegy: Studies in the Genre from Spenser to Yeats*. London: The John Hopkins University Press, 1985.

Uppal, Priscila. *Recovering the Past Through Language and Landscape: The Contemporary English-Canadian Elegy*. PhD Dissertation. York University, 2004.

Walker, Barbara G. "Owl." *The Woman's Dictionary of Symbols and Sacred Objects*. San Francisco: HarperSan Francisco, 1988. 404.

Zeiger, Melissa F. *Beyond Consolation: Death, Sexuality, and the Changing Shapes of Elegy*. Ithaca: Cornell University Press, 1997.

THE NON-FICTION

Barrelhouse Kings, Raise You Five
and *Raise You Ten*

HOMAGE TO B.C.

John Montague

A large young man appears at my studio door.
"I'm from Toronto, Barry Callaghan,
Come to Paris on my honeymoon!"

His ample voice, as he strides before
With my wife, while his new bride
Strolls along the Seine, by my side.

Dark-avised, blue-eyed as Elvis,
You tutored me in the Blues,
Old Stewball was a race horse

Flowing into afternoons at Woodbine
He never drank water, he only drank wine
With George Yemec, that princely Ukrainian,

While I tried to prescribe for you
The two sides of our Celtic coin,
Flahool (or extravagant), versus Skinflint,

Which never seemed to be your bent,
Lavishing largesse wherever you went,
Your motto, like Forster, *Only connect*.

With Pavlovic in sombre Belgrade,
Mystic Marteau in Mont Réal,
Miron blasting on his mouth organ.

Master of the monologue, in prose and verse,
With a lavish talent almost too diverse:
Hogg meets Judas on the same bench!

Suppers on Sullivan with artist Claire,
Then climbing the picture-lined stair
To her studio where images flower.

Or Scotch-and-soda at 20 Dale,
Disputing everything with old Morley,
Tough-shelled as a tortoise.

So much, half of it cannot be told,
Though most of it pans out pure gold
So here is a paean to friendship foretold.

A FEW WORDS
ABOUT *BARRELHOUSE KINGS*

ANNE MICHAELS

Barry Callaghan has written fiction that reads like memoir (the stories in *A Kiss Is Still a Kiss* for example) and memoir that reads like fiction. Over the years he has unerringly navigated the boundaries between genres and mediums, to powerful effect.

Barrelhouse Kings, his memoir, is spring-loaded. Wherever it falls open, life leaps out. All the risks of love are in these pages. Many times I paused as I read: does he dare to go there? And yet there? Writing, as Marguerite Yourcenour said, with open eyes. The content is full tilt and convulsive with living. Again and again we careen into the most intimate moments, only to have words leave off. In this way, the reader's own depths are plundered. It is this restraint, this courtesy that brings us so intimately to the heart of the moment; no amount of disclosure could be as effective. Callaghan knows that intimacy is always a privilege, never a right. Especially the intimacy between parent and child. *Barrelhouse Kings* is steeped in this courtesy, and this gratitude. It is not only the privileged courtesy of son, brother, father, husband, but it is also the novelist's intimacy and the novelist's restraint and that is the book's mastery.

A SON'S LAMENT

PAUL WILLIAM ROBERTS

I remember, many years ago, being invited to dinner at
Barry Callaghan's house on Sullivan Street in Toronto. It
was an intimate, elegant affair, and besides myself there
were only two other guests, one of whom was Barry's
father, Morley Callaghan. I'd met Morley several times
previously, but I'd never experienced father and son
together. And quite an experience it was. Some time
before anyone arrived, the two had begun a discussion
of whether Canada in general and Toronto in particular
possessed a provincial sensibility. Veering from quirky
anecdotes, through a sort of arcane social history, to
shameless declamations of what was loosely described as
"fact," the two-handed debate – conversation it was not
– proceeded on throughout the entire meal and beyond.
No one else said a word. Far from boring, however, it
was entertainment of the highest order: two refined,
erudite, eloquent minds sparring verbally, not to win,
but for the sheer joy of it.

I recall thinking: this is how they show their love for
each other. I add that recollection because I also had the
misfortune on many occasions to witness the relationship
between another famous literary father-and-son team,
Kingsley and Martin Amis. It was anything but loving. On
Kingsley's part, at least, it was often cruel and vindictive;
and for both it was highly competitive.

Fathers have always intrigued me – perhaps since I
never really knew mine – and so it was possibly with some
sort of vicarious objective in mind that I began to visit
Morley Callaghan on my own. We lived near each other,
both of us then alone, and many nights I would go over

for coffee to see how he was, only to find myself boozily stumbling back at 3 a.m. You don't meet many people who can recount an evening spent with James Joyce and who tell you that "Jimmy was a little guy, see? But Nora, his wife, was massive. It was she who'd kick us out, saying 'You've had enough, Jim! Tell your friends to go.'" I noticed that Morley had grown tired of people asking him about that famous summer in Paris – the time he'd spent with Ernest Hemingway and F. Scott Fitzgerald during the early 1930s – so I studiously avoided the subject, finding that he would naturally reminisce about famous acquaintances – Wyndham Lewis, Edmund Wilson, William Saroyan, Sean Connery, etc. – if it fit the conversation at hand. What conversation it was, too! His mind was as sharp and bright as a straight razor, though gentler; and whether commenting on Tina Turner's legs (he frequently watched MuchMusic) or a new biography of Ezra Pound, he invariably elicited from the subject something wise and insightful, something salutary.

I also understand now a little of what his son means when, in the Author's Note to *Barrelhouse Kings*, he writes: "I cannot describe the silence in the night of my life without that voice, without that talk since he died."

Barrelhouse Kings is a staggeringly great book, and something quite unique in our literature. Subtitled *A Memoir*, it might be more properly called, "A Meditation on My Father." Beginning as a biographical sketch of Morley – a veritable diamond mine of anecdote drawn from Callaghan *père's* papers and Barry's memories – it suddenly also becomes, somewhat astonishingly, the autobiography of Barry. Accustomed to the one-pointed narration of a biographer, we are unprepared for the words: "A few years later, Mother had a Caesarean section. I was born." Enter the book's second subject: the growth and gradual flowering of one artistic sensibility in the benevolent shadow of another.

Barry loved his father and, far from trying to super-sede him, was ever solicitous of his welfare and career. Indeed, Morley made it easy for the talent of others to co-exist with his own. Quoting his father, Barry writes that he could convey "an intransigent honesty," but it was nearly always in the context of a "corresponding humility . . . together with a ready friendliness toward the whole world. This friendliness was not, however, rooted in humility. He had long since decided that he, in his heart of hearts, could be close to almost no one and therefore friendly to all."

Morley taught his two sons to stand their ground with him, to say their piece, and hold to their own con-victions. But "There was a problem. If we could be our own men in our own house in relation to our father, we believed we could be our own selves anywhere . . . Michael and I got into much trouble outside our private world, outside the house. Morley was much cleverer about the outside world than we were."

Indeed he was. A lawyer in training, Morley remained shrewd and canny to the last – and careful with a dollar to the point of miserliness. Whereas Barry, a positive spendthrift, tended to wear his heart, and much else, on his sleeve. This could come across as rudeness – indeed, it has appeared as such to me – but one comes to see, as this huge, mesmerizing family saga unfolds, that Barry does not believe he can be close to almost no one, yet a condition of his closeness is an almost brutal form of honesty.

Barrelhouse Kings is nothing like as straightforward as it first seems. The book gradually turns into a kind of non-fiction novel, in which Barry Callaghan the author writes about another Barry Callaghan, also an author, incorporating parts of his father's own novels that cor-respond to real life. It is a devilishly ingenious and sub-tle device. Barry reveals himself to be almost painfully aware of his perceived shortcomings – or how others misperceived them – while constitutionally incapable of changing or adapting himself.

It struck me profoundly, reading this, that our degrees of separation from one another are complementary, not contradictory, and are, furthermore, the very meaning of life. Or the lack of it.

It has always been very un-Canadian – or so it has seemed to this immigrant – to strut your stuff on the world stage, to befriend Titans, to dine often in Paris or Rome, to entertain at home on the grand scale and to be fêted in foreign countries. This, curiously enough, was the substance of what the two Callaghans had been debating over dinner on that night long ago: the difficulty, or undesirability, of making a noise in this country. It's often said of Morley that he'd have been far more famous if he'd abandoned Toronto for New York back in the 1930s. But it is a fact that in many European countries Barry Callaghan is better known than Margaret Atwood or Michael Ondaatje; and it is also a fact that in Russia Morley Callaghan is compared with Chekhov and Turgenev – as no less an authority than Edmund Wilson suggested he could be without absurdity. Fame and the opinion of posterity are really beyond the whims of western media, whether they like it or not.

Barry writes as objectively about that other Barry's successes as he does about his failures here, and to accept the latter is to accept the former, too: it is not grandstanding. That house on Sullivan Street, as I came to find, was famous the world over as a place where writers were welcome. The same is probably true of the house where Barry now lives – the house where I used to talk with his father. I haven't been there since Morley died. It may seem odd to call a son's memoir of his father a love story, but that is what *Barrelhouse Kings* finally reveals itself to be. A great love story.

"THE TRUTH WAS ALWAYS
IN THE TELLING"

Storytelling in Barrelhouse Kings

Dennis Lee

1

Let me digress.

I want to celebrate *Barrelhouse Kings*, Barry Callaghan's shaggy-baggy marvel of a memoir. But where to begin? There's a whole hubbub of books between the covers. One creates a Toronto of the imagination – and what a tour de force it is: a roll-call of pimps and philosophers, of bishops and strippers and bluesmen. Another records Callaghan family history. Then there's a thick file of political and cultural reportage from around the globe. And a whole gallery of men and women who lived with abandon, beyond the limits. With all these sub-books being stitched more or less comfortably into the account of Callaghan's own progress, from roaring boy to witness to his times.

Throughout this bursting-at-the-seams variety, *Barrelhouse Kings* is first and foremost a treasurehouse of stories. Which is what I want to pursue: the storytelling, concentrating more on the craft than the content. But before I do, I need to digress, to rummage through its predecessors. What had Callaghan learned about telling stories before he sat down to write *Barrelhouse Kings*?

2

Perhaps because he has played so many different literary roles over the years, Callaghan's four books of fiction stand as a batch of discrete outings, rather than a full and coherent body of work. But some elements recur in a resonant way.

His imagination is most deeply engaged when it deals with characters on the margins, outside the respectable middle class. Misfits, ne'er-do-wells, hustlers, loners, scrambling not so much for money or social position as to achieve gestures of a larger, freer, more passionate life. Or at least to keep that dream alive, in the face of personal limitation, brute circumstance, or the life-denying ethos of old Toronto. This cramping of the spirit is the point of departure in much of his fiction – a societal legacy to which characters must respond in their various ways.

Callaghan tells other stories too, tales of mainstream characters with gridlocked longings of their own. But when he kicks into high gear, it's usually the scenario of the spunky outsider that he's rehearsing. I want to examine how the story is told in those successes, and in the misfires, before moving on to the freewheeling narrative music of *Barrelhouse Kings*.

3

What Callaghan does best becomes clear if we contrast it with what he does less well. Namely, tell stories of conventional lives in the mode of well-made realism.

When a Callaghan story fails to ignite, it usually includes these elements: a third-person narrator; a plain prose style; no lowlife characters with racy, distinctive voices; and a linear plot as the structural mainspring. Then the story sits tidily on the page, competent but resonance-free. Even when it recounts a rebellion or a crackup, the story itself stays restrained and well-behaved. That is, it recreates the very conditions which are suffocating the characters.

There have been classy practitioners of this kind of storytelling. But there is no fit between what it can achieve, within its limits, and Callaghan's expansive break-the-rules imagination. For whatever reason, however, he has frequently shoehorned himself into the format. Of the two dozen pieces in *The Black Queen Stories* (1982) and *A Kiss Is Still a Kiss* (1995), there are maybe ten such stories, which never break through to the potent, irrefutable life that is the hallmark of his strongest work. As examples: "All the Lonely People" in the former, "Up Up and Away With Elmer Sadine" in the latter.

On the other hand, if Callaghan scraps even one or two elements of the genre, he's likely to achieve liftoff. "Poodles John" may be told in the third person, but the central character is a hustler with such a zesty mouth on him that the piece comes to life. And while the superb novella "Never's Just The Echo of Forever" has plot to burn, Albie Starbach is such a memorably cracked loser, and the dialogue is so wingy, that it never feels merely well-made.

4

Callaghan's only novel, *The Way the Angel Spreads Her Wings* (1989), presents a different problematic. The third-person narrative covers much of the material from his own life that sings off the page in *Barrelhouse Kings*. But for one reader at least, the book is stillborn.

It's not immediately obvious why. The content is hardly dull, and some of the local writing is strong. But the thing just sits there, a blueprint more than a living work of fiction. The doggedly programmatic flashbacks, and the character's arty, portentous pronouncements – everything bears the mark of a book willed into existence from the outside, rather than simply dancing along, at ease in its own skin.

At first I thought the opaque hero, the turgidly self-absorbed Adam Waters, was merely another problem. But given how close his external experience is to the author's, I suspect that locating the speaking centre of the book was its basic, and unresolved, challenge. In writing about himself, it was only when he turned to direct autobiography that Callaghan would achieve the amplitude and resonance of fiction.

5

When it follows the precepts of well-made realism, then, Callaghan's imagination is no more than dutiful. But when it connects with its own, very different necessities, the work comes to high-stepping, tall-talking life.

He has two uncommon gifts as a storyteller: a knack for structural improvisation, and a range of compelling voices. They're like the resources of a jazz musician, who can noodle and rage and cross-weave a melodic line till it sounds like a whole songbook; and who can bend the tone of his instrument from plangent to kittenish to hallelujah.

Callaghan can do both – sometimes separately, often at once. When he does, the results are a potent delight.

6

To sample his vocal range, you have to stretch out a little. Here's the vibrant heroine of *When Things Get Worst*, his 1993 novella-cum-hurtin'-ballad. She lives in trailer-park country north of Toronto; she and her new suitor Lute, a moody preacher and entrepreneur, are having their first fight. Listen to their voices:

> He said, "The mice are shitting on the poison," making me know that he'd been brooding all night and that he still had a hickey on his heart and a bone to pick, and that he was a real windsucker who didn't think birds tap dancing

on his glass was funny at all. Without a warning word, like he was setting out to walk a solid mile, he started tromping over the glass, trudging sheet by sheet, grim and head down, crashing and stomping his big yellow Greb work boots, and I came at him yelling and flapping my arms but he kept on till the field of glass was all broken . . .

and then with his bow-legged gait he strode down the laneway to the truck where he paused and laid his hand on the headlight and screwed up his face and hollered "And the locust shall not nestle in my heart or rest upon the stone beds that are the seed of what is to be mine, for the bookkeeping of Bilan is a precise and meticulous process," which hauled me back on my heels, gawking, because I didn't know for the life of me what he was talking about, what with locusts and bookkeeping and stone seeds, and anyway he'd been keeping his bursts of testifying to next to nothing so I wasn't used to it. As he got up into his cab and drove off churning dust down the laneway, I thought, "He's sly. He is damn well sly," because he had to mean something beyond what he was saying. All that Bilan the Bookkeeper gabble . . . (62-63)

The most conspicuous voice here is Lute's, with its whirling mishmash of Biblese. But the real achievement is the narrator's voice, especially since it sustains through the entire novella. It's earthy, tangy, cadenced, droll. A fine ear is dancing us through the same sad human predicaments as the realist stories do, with their uninflected tone. But now the voice itself creates a quirky, textured medium; the narrative space in which events unfold is vivacious from the get-go. Which is to say, Callaghan has brought the larger life his characters hunger for right into his prose.

As he does, with many changes of timbre, in all his best fiction. Here the gateway to abundant life, or at least the promise of that abundance, doesn't reside in what characters do in the plot. Or not primarily. It resides in what the words do on the page.

Callaghan's second talent as a storyteller is for structural improvisation, for narrative noodling. Unfortunately, it's impossible to show what's involved with a brief quotation, since it usually takes pages to develop.

It can swivel around within a single story-line, or jump-cut from one to another. And the rhythms of attention – the slow drag-step for a while, then the staccato changes, the loosey-goosey riffs – are something whose rightness you *feel,* long before you get an analytic handle on it. Like good jazz improv. If it's done well, it gives a sense of highly-revved buoyancy, almost of weightlessness, in the storytelling.

But while this macro-noodling can't be demonstrated in a short compass, it's possible to show how early Callaghan took to structural riffing. Here's a run from the opening story in his first book, "Crow Jane's Blues." Crow Jane, a singer past her prime, has come into the Silver Dollar tavern on Spadina Avenue, where she used to perform. As she listens to the younger singer on the bandstand, her mind starts bopping. (Here it's the darts and leaps of her mind I'm pointing to, rather than the tonal inflections.)

> I mean sometimes I lean back singing a song or lying up with another woman, all the good womens in this world, or poppin' pills, and them pills look like lemon-yellow bowling balls rolling down inside my head, an' sometimes when I get scared, when some sucker comes at me leering with the big hard-on in his eyes, I just sit there talking baby talk we used to talk, me an' EveLynn looking at each other side by side in the mirror, we used to prop the mirror on the bed, that blonde hair of yours on my shoulder an' ever since then I got all the cabbages and none of the kings, an' I been down only the long hallway, pedaling on my tricycle with the bell on the handlebar that don't work, just

goes fhzz fhzz like my daddy's old Ronson lighter that got no flint, railroad halls we called 'em, but nobody knows that no more 'cause nobody rides them trains, which is why I like the mouth harp sound, harmonica you called it, white words for black birds, lonesome trains and pain, that was my daddy since back then the onliest work a black man bagged was Pullman porter which my daddy was for a while till insomnia set him down, the clickity-clack inside his head he said, an' I mean he had the light on the whole time, he put pennies on his eyes when he went to sleep an' said I ain't dead, the light jess don't go out, and Crow Jane, listening to the voice on the stand in the small room of the Show Bar, was reminded so much of herself that she decided she wanted to talk to the younger singer, thinking she'd buy the girl a drink, hold her hand a little like she was holding hands with herself, and scribbled a note inviting her to the table. Crow Jane gave it to the waiter. The singer read the note and with a shrug flicked it back behind the piano . . . (BQS, 5-6)

8

By the time he came to write *Barrelhouse Kings* (1998), Callaghan had a combo plate of strengths and limitations as a storyteller.

He'd always been galvanized by talented people who broke loose, who said Up Yours to authority and lived with brio and unconstraint. They were his exemplary heroes, his barrelhouse kings – as was he himself, since he lived that way too. And once he took such outsize characters as his central motif, he had a template for organizing the raw material of his life and times.

At the same time, he had to *write* the thing. And that was a challenge: how to tell all these disparate yarns? Even if he could animate its conventions, the small safe victories of well-made realism – mind you, I've never discussed any of this with Callaghan – would decaffeinate, minify the grand luminescence he loved in his kings. Yet heading into a lifetime of memories with only a prose musician's resources to guide him would be iffy in the extreme.

That is, it wasn't obvious how to use the particular storytelling gifts he had. What about the narrative voice, for instance? He couldn't write his autobiography as a bible-thumper, or a black sax-man, or a Jewish lampshade salesman. He could do chunks of dialogue in those timbres, but he would have to find another voice to carry the whole thing. And then, what about structure? He could noodle like nobody's business – but could he improvise his way through his whole life-story?

Writing fiction had given him some tantalizing leads. But it was still an open question: could he write a memoir worthy of his kings? Create a book-length saga where they would be resplendently at home?

9

For a work of mastery, which I take it to be, *Barrelhouse Kings* is about as ungainly and exasperating as possible. To deny that would be to belittle the book's most substantial achievements. Yet once you've acknowledged the flaws, there is such supple grace in the narration, and such breadth and depth in the human content, that it would be churlish to fixate on the lapses. What vibrates most memorably is the music of the storytelling.

10

Kings is a cornucopia of tales – and at nearly 600 pages, a mammoth read. In this welter of yarns, the architectonics are easy to miss. But discerning the book's overall shape makes it easier to track Callaghan's storytelling strategies.

The memoir is divided into thirteen "books." It unfolds in three much larger movements, however (which don't always coincide with book divisions). And this creates a dialectical structure in the whole memoir.

Callaghan opens with a sort of prefatory drum-roll: a daisy-chain of vignettes which counterpoint the outwardly respectable Rosedale of his childhood with the demimonde to which he was soon drawn. This dazzling curtain-raiser runs from the opening to page 47.

Then the first full movement begins: The Morley section (47-120). It recounts the life of Barry's father, the most enduring of his barrelhouse kings, who toughed it out in Toronto after succeeding in Paris, and then New York.

The second movement covers Barry's own life, from his schooling in the 1950s to his coverage of the Liberal leadership convention in 1984. It stretches from Book II to the middle of Book XI (121-492). This is the longest block of material in the book, and the closest to conventional autobiography.

There's something intriguing, though. Callaghan begins the second movement partway through the period it covers – with his visits to Paris, first as a newlywed, later as a recognized writer (121-140). Only then does he take us back to the 1950s. And in the third movement (493-578), we discover why he made the detour: to strengthen "writing in Paris" as a pivotal motif. This third movement gives us Barry and Morley journeying back to the city of light in 1986. The beautifully-told episode overlays the father's writing life with the son's, as they swap stories of their Paris experiences. And in the process it carries forward the energies of the previous two movements, uniting them formally and emotionally. So the dialectic runs: part one – Morley; part two – Barry; part three – Morley-&-Barry. With writing in Paris as the lynchpin.

Part three then carries us through a sad yet joyous elegy for great ones who die – including, in the last chapter, Morley himself. This entire third movement, running from page 493 to the end, is one of the few extended passages in our literature that can properly be called sublime.

11

I spoke of the need to find a voice that would work for the whole memoir. The clipped, arm's-length tone of the realist stories would cramp the vitality. Yet the souped-up music of Callaghan's low-life outsiders was not an option (since he himself would be the speaker). And while much of the material in *The Way the Angel Spreads Her Wings* was autobiographical, it was ill served there by the third-person voice, which was both disengaged and (at times) stagily literary.

Callaghan meets the challenge of voice effortlessly. He swings into a fluent style which can go almost anywhere, equally at home with the speaker's intelligence and his cantankerous raunch. It can set up a story with panache:

> And then there was basketball.
>   I went out to the gym. It was clear who the established Varsity players were: they moved with measured aplomb, they knew the floor, the glass, the pace of the court. They had crew cuts. The slightly paunchy coach had a crew cut. My hair was long. "How are you doing, Elvis?" the coach said to me . . . (168)

It can size up public figures with a cold, analytic eye – as at the liberal convention:

> Friday night: John Turner said of himself: "What you see is what you get." Well, perhaps not . . . a private man, he had no secret life; a devout man, he seemed to have no spiritual concerns . . . "He bites all his words," a woman said to me. "How could I be comfortable with a man who told me to take off my clothes and butter my toast in exactly the same tone?" (488-89)

And it can settle into deeper rumination, as it does after Edmund Wilson's funeral:

> Though we might have wanted to weep that he was dead, his triumph made us – made me, anyway – just a little ashamed at how little I had done; yet, at the same time, we all were encouraged by what he had achieved, encouraged to go on – *boomlay boomlay boomlay BOOM* – into the outer dark – to do more, to be true to our own best talents, obstinately, with as much grace as possible, with all energy. (357)

The narrative voice stumbles occasionally – as when it lapses into the portentous, single-sentence paragraphs of think-piece journalism. Here Callaghan is speaking of his brother Michael:

> He had a habit as a child – a summer habit at Lake Simcoe, Aunt Toot's cottage. He would see the dock and toddle off onto it and keep on walking and walk off the end. I walked off to Woolworth's. He walked off the ends of docks . . .
> Michael was a dockwalker.
> Maybe we were all dockwalkers in the family. (110)

But such false notes are rare. For hundreds of pages this voice leads us through highlife and lowlife, anecdote and reflection, public and private affairs, laughter and *lacrimae rerum*. What it bespeaks is a man of enormous appetite, who wants to have it all and tell good stories too. Why? Because "It seemed to me that life at its best was when men and women came back to tell tales, some taller than others, but the truth was always in the telling" (30).

12

And what telling it often is – charged with the muscular, confident freedom of Callaghan's structural improv.

The first thing that strikes you is the narrative noodling at the beginning – the sheer hi-jinks of twirling vignette within yarn within tale. Here's a sample. Callaghan is conjuring the seedy Barclay Hotel, which he had embraced full-tilt-boogie while pursuing his higher education at St. Michael's college. He starts riffing on

> Frank Motley and His Motley Crew, featuring Frank and His Dual Trumpets. Frank was famous in the local dives for playing two trumpets at once. (He was on stage the night that Art Cuccia threatened to stick me cross-wise in the heart with a knife in the upstairs lounge of the Holiday Tavern, and Clarkie Ader – whose sister I had slept with – said to me, "If he's white I'll kill the fucker for you." When I said, "Jesus, man, I'm white," he smiled and said, "On the moment, man, I just forgot. You almost more nigger than any nigger I know." The Tavern's bouncers tumbled me down the stairs. Their logic before giving me the heave: "If you ain't here then Cuccia don't give us no trouble." Three years later the police shot Cuccia dead between the eyes during a break-and-enter into a house.) It was true that such people – such "permanent guests" – lived in the hotel and used the hotel and gave it a certain character, but the Barclay's main business was the nightclub on the second floor.
>
> I had discovered the nightclub because I'd met a young woman who was writing her thesis on John Donne's *Divine Poems*.
>
> She was double-jointed and she could – by crossing her legs behind her head – turn into a ball and roll around on the floor, singing songs . . . (30-31)

And on and on it goes. This virtuoso noodling is concentrated in the first third of the book: the opening braid of stories; the tales of Slitkin and Slotkin in Montreal (93-101); the account of Callaghan's career in the loopy world of early CBC television (184-204). It would have been bracing to dip back into this mode later on. But in any event, it rhymes unmistakably with his love for Bud Freeman's music, whose "recording, *The Eel*, was a piece of convoluted elegance worthy of the interwoven lines of monks in ancient Celtic books . . . the *Book of Kells*, the sinuous Celtic line" (346).

13

When the storytelling in *Barrelhouse Kings* bogs down, it's in parts of the 350-page middle section, which covers some thirty years of Barry's life. The material is wildly disparate, since his life itself was wildly disparate. But that's no reason why the memoir should start spinning its wheels. At times it does, however. As the reader is hauled from continent to continent, private crisis to public crisis, arts interview to political interview, the virtuoso aplomb of the earlier narrations seems to have leaked away.

There are high points, mind you, some of them glorious. Such as the portraits of the flamboyant Bill Ronald, the patrician Edmund Wilson, the mercurial Pierre Trudeau – "lives in full emotional flight, as they maintained a standard of chaos, full of the desperate yearning for love, full of duplicity, aberration, disappointment"(234). And as this long section draws to a close, there are fine extended stories of South Africa, and of the gambling life. But overall, it's hard to avoid the sense that Callaghan has not found the right storytelling mode to shape the material.

Trying to fathom this lack of fit, I'd zero in on two aspects of craft. The first is structural. In this movement, Callaghan often adopts a technique of scattershot montage – juxtaposing discrete scenes and vignettes, mostly without comment. (This might appear to be a version of the "noodling" we've already considered, but the mosaic technique is more blocky and hard-edged.) So he marches us through fragment upon fragment, hoping they'll give a kaleidoscopic image of both is fractured personal life and the chaos of public life.

In theory, I suppose it should. And indeed this is how a magazine-format television show works; Callaghan may have hoped he could carry its structural principles onto the page. But it succeeds only sporadically. When it does, we get jagged moments that hit like shrapnel. But montage in prose is notoriously a different thing from montage in film or television. It can easily become mere décor – flat, divorced from any affect. And then we find ourselves yanked from snippet to snippet, each included merely because it happened, and Barry Callaghan was there. Snagging interviews with Philip Roth or Muhammad Ali may have been a coup; but setting them end to end, even when they produced superior journalism at the time, falls short of the song of memory which informs *Barrelhouse Kings* at its best. It's tantalizing to conjecture what these 350 pages would have been like if they'd lost 50 or 100 pages, and been more deeply shaped by the dance of memorious desire.

The second problematic involves the angle from which Callaghan tells the stories. This is crucial, because he is not only the narrator, but one of the barrelhouse kings. And to tell story after story in which he himself is the hero – meaning not just the protagonist, the conscious centre of the through-line, but a luminous exemplar: fearless in combat, wise in counsel, lauded by the great, betrayed by fools and knaves – is to risk diminishing the book to an exercise in self-promotion.

Callaghan hasn't entirely avoided this pitfall. And whether you consider it a technical flaw, or a human flaw, or both, it diminishes the achievement of *Barrel-*

house Kings. It would have been strategic to position Callaghan the narrator in a subtler relationship to Barry, the recurrent hero of his stories.

But that is the hindsight of one reader, who could never have written the book in the first place.

14

And all this grumpiness falls away when we enter the third movement, the final 85 pages. Now Callaghan lengthens the rhythms of the storytelling. He no longer races us through disjointed events; he slows the sequence down, selects a few iconic episodes, and develops them like freestanding short stories. Since the material is so affecting, this leads to a kind of burnished cello sweep, a symphonic majesty in the book's final movement.

These elegiac rhythms start at page 493, with the eightieth-birthday party for Morley. And indeed the whole final section is written under the sign of mortality. But what's remarkable is how insistently the passion for life resonates. Barry's mother dies, but we're left with the image of her indomitable sexual desire in old age, and the family's life-affirming pranks at the funeral home and the graveside. An old pal of Barry's dies – Fat Saul from Yonge Street – but we glimpse the improbable bond of love between two men who couldn't have been more different. And William Ronald dies; but he goes out in such a bravura blaze of glory, painting heroically and remarrying foolishly to the very end, that his spirit seems almost to have outlived his dying.

Which brings us to the final two books of *Barrelhouse Kings.* I cannot praise them enough. Book XII conducts us through the return visit to France in 1986. As Barry and the aging Morley savour the present and swap tales of writing in Paris past, in the company of Claire and friends and ghostly memories, the bittersweet tug is very rich. And it's rendered all the richer by the narrative stringency. Callaghan doesn't go for easy heartstrings; this is warts-and-all telling, and all the more moving for that.

Book XIII is more of the same – the wild, almost liturgical last hurrah and wake of a father, rendered with heart and grief and narrative circumstance. Nobody should lose a loved one. But we should all have such a noble skirl of words to mark the passing. As one who resists any writing with palpable designs on me, I can report that I choke up every time I re-read the closing pages of *Barrelhouse Kings*. In both human and technical terms, it is a triumph of storytelling. It calls to mind other works where the old order passes, and the survivors are left to recreate the great tradition.

15

This whole third movement is an extraordinary achievement. And it sends ripples backward through the book, imparting a retro-elegiac sheen to even the slightest, most dumb-ass moments in Callaghan's life. Now all are barrelhouse; all are regal.

"The truth was always in the telling." The noblest fate of humans, in *Barrelhouse Kings*, is to find a home in quirky, majestic stories. Such transient glory.

BARRELHOUSE KINGS

Something Barry Callaghan
Left Out of his Memoir

BILL CASSELMAN

You must declare yourself at the border of Callaghan country, when about to celebrate the man and vivisect the autobiography – although some would prefer to reverse the verbs. If there be a *Festschriftliche* personal reticence, I'll have none of it. I've known Barry for thirty-five years and worked with him on and off over twenty years, usually as a CBC radio or television producer hiring Barry to talk about Canadian books or about the politics of wedging art into the dry cleft set aside for such nonsense in the average Canadian brain. Barry and I are not close friends, but friendly co-workers. What have I admired most about the man? Thistling with words, bristling with thought, he has always stepped forth.

The response to all of Barry Callaghan's work, because so much of it has been in Canada's public media since he was in his late teens, has been coloured by the response to the Barry Callaghan persona: polysyllabic cock-of-the-walk talker from a home where a Canadian father, novelist Morley Callaghan, gave his sons free rein to think aloud. In Book One, Part Ten, of *Barrelhouse Kings*, Barry writes: "Morley's fierce independence and his sense of security and the love he held in his heart for his children had led him, unafraid, to grant his children their own independence, their own fierce pleasure in being. We learned to love the sound of ourselves talking, yelling, laughing, slanging . . . and as Morley baited us, we went for him as if he were live bait."

Initial licence granted by the serene moral intelligence of Morley Callaghan has influenced every move and every word made by his son. Jealousy leaks its rancid bile wherever Barry Callaghan appears. "I hate that snot 'cause he can talk well." Barry's oratorical laissez-faire is profoundly unCanadian. It's not rare in well-schooled British kids to be able to finesse a debater's verb, but here in Canada such eloquence is scarce. In Canada consequently there remains a pioneer distrust of the person who can wield words. Anti-intellectualism teems fresh, and the loathing of accomplishment and the guts necessary to achieve it diminishes our national life daily.

Consider this assessment of Barry Callaghan. In a small Ontario town I once invited a local man, an ex-con, to paint my father's house. This man was painting the side of Dad's house that faced the back lawn. A CBC Radio show rang out from a small radio set on the top step of the back porch. Barry Callaghan was delivering a lively analysis on a program taped earlier that I had produced about Claire Martin's riveting memoir, *Dans un gant de fer*, the fanfare trumpet of Quebec feminism. Among other daughterly agonies, Martin's book, *In an Iron Glove*, confronts painfully the bad father question. The ex-con painter, his forehead pocked with puck dents, listened for a few minutes, scratched his head and got wet paint on it. Then he began to listen. Slowly a fear induced by rising comprehension spread over his face as he realized this distant female writer in Ottawa, a Frenchy to boot, why she could be writing about his life. Shee-it! Elbowing me aside, he switched off the radio and screamed with psychotic vehemence, "Load of crap! Talking about stuff don't do no good. Imagine a fellow Irishman and a Mick talkin' that shite. That Callaghan's got too big a mouth to live."

I cherish that last sentence. It is one review of Barry Callaghan's lifetime of superb art and teaching, not the most important nor the last review, true, but a response to Callaghan far more frequent and symptomatic of today's Canada than all the printed and spoken "serious" considerations of his work. That dour suspicion of eloquence, that notion that real men don't talk, oozes through modern Canadian schools and shops and playgrounds and bars and parent-infested hockey rinks. It wounds boys in their word-heart and makes it macho to be inarticulate and a bad student. Yet there was Callaghan, jock and egghead both. *Barrelhouse Kings* should be read by everyone who sets out to teach children their letters. The frowsy painter is not important, but his frightened insult is a tocsin warning us that when language fails, night falls on our country.

When the first newspaper and magazine reviews of *Barrelhouse Kings* appeared in 1998, several critics dismissed the book because of their loathing for Barry Callaghan's television image. Reading their book reviews made clear they were most upset that there had never been a medium in Callaghan's personal televisual message. On the contrary, for many of us, the Callaghan *ultimatissimum* of presence was a chief delight of his message. Barry occupies fully the space life gives him.

One Callaghan line from *Barrelhouse Kings* was singled out again and again in reviews. Early in the book, a black musician at the old Porters' Hall dance joint in Toronto tells Barry, "You almost more nigger than any nigger I know." Negative critics howled their responses: mockery and scorn. A modest whitey simply would not remember such a line. However, this imprimatur from Barry's rollicking subconscious sails over the whole wet waterfall of his memory book. Says Callaghan, let the whole be printed. A kind of sing-for-we-are-doomed

358

concision in Callaghan's best writing here in *Barrelhouse Kings* arises from his solidity of person.

His vital concision powers his written words. Callaghan is one of our best miniaturists. Early in *Barrelhouse Kings*, Barry writes of a neighbour during his childhood: "Dabney was troubled by his son, Terence, a lean, eighteen-year-old who bleached his hair and played the French horn. Late at night, he would open his bedroom window and play 'Taps' on the horn. 'That way,' he told me, 'my father knows that I wish he was dead.'"

There is not the brevity of poetic sensibility. There is prose chipped lean by dread's chisel. A trembling Callaghan quotes the kid's chop because in his own teenage years Barry felt the same way about Morley. Unlike many sunny, sonny-boy memoirs, the Oedipal binges are up front. Morley was a cheapskate, the son claims and produces the evidence. As Barry's academic marks slid to oblivion at St. Michael's College School, Morley fumed, as befuddled dads through history have done, puzzled at why their sons should be so silly as not to behave exactly as the fathers had during their school days.

Does autobiographer son get novelist father correct? The neatest thing about autobiography is: nobody can tell. Barry kills Morley only once in the book, symbolically, denying – by quoting Mavis Gallant – that his father had any sexual allure. This is convenient for the Oedipal son compelled to confront his father's power. I knew Morley Callaghan for about forty wonderful radio mornings as opposed to Barry's lifetime. So I'm no boasting Morleyphile. But Morley had all sorts of sexual allure, even as a merry elderly sprite. He had the foxy, eroto-cognitive energy of the thinker, as compelling, though quieter, as the dick-wagging stud's bray. Allure was in Morley's wonderful Canadian voice, compounded half of elf's glee and half of wise elder's public craftiness. Barry understands early on that his father is cleverer than Barry in public. To paraphrase the Bard, Morley gave every man his ear and none his heart, and so he could give all men his smile. Son Barry – for all his street smarts – boiled with more guileless Romantic urges.

Barry's lifelong trouble with cops and authority figures stems directly – not from a need to reject Morley – but from Morley having granted his son this early freedom to be. That liberty both frees and constrains one childhood necessity, what child psychologists are pleased to call "internalizing the parental censor." We all have to do it, if we are to survive: take in and keep our parents' monitory voices telling us to not cross that road, to not drink that bottle, to not ever say that word in this house again. But when there is no vivid censor, we children don't develop as strong a "deference" mechanism in the face of authority. It is good that some of us don't, but those lacking it pay a price, a cost that begins perhaps when Miss Thinlip, our Grade three teacher comments in the staff room, "That Callaghan boy was born to hang."

This flaw of not putting on a public face, not video-editing one's private face when out and about, produced Barry Callaghan's moment of opprobrium, a television interview with Golda Meir, Israeli stateswoman, one time Prime Minister of Israel, she who drew back the curtains to facilitate the Yom Kippur War of 1973 and helped isolate Israel from other nations. Golda Meir had the mien of a thug, which she was, a crude bully. Maybe she had to be. Maybe. Still she was. She liked to watch people cringe, her old crocodile eyes laughing as people writhed in cowardice before her. Golda knew most humans were despicable and she liked that, because she wasn't. Well, Golda met Crocodile Dundee on Canadian TV. Callaghan asked tough questions. Yep, Callaghan responded with jibe for jibe, did not budge, stoutly maintained his innocence and lost all kinds of future jobs for years afterward. Life lesson 6-B, fellah: Never tangle with a sacred cow.

The words "barrelhouse kings" appear in a poem published in 1913 by the American Vachel Lindsay, a popular poet who was attempting to thrust African dance rhythms into American poetry and produced a long, deeply silly, pompous, clanking, syncopated monstrosity called "The Congo: A Study of the Negro Race." Here's the opening:

I. Their Basic Savagery
Fat black bucks in a wine-barrel room,
Barrel-house kings, with feet unstable,
[A deep rolling bass.]
Sagged and reeled and pounded on the table,
Pounded on the table,
Beat an empty barrel with the handle of a broom,
Hard as they were able,
Boom, boom, BOOM,
With a silk umbrella and the handle of a broom,
Boomlay, boomlay, boomlay, BOOM.
THEN I had religion, THEN I had a vision.
I could not turn from their revel in derision.

Hugely popular later, the poem's opening verses found their way into anthologies and American classrooms. Was it set to music? Apparently. Callaghan quotes the jangly jingle but not the title, subtitle, or the poet's name, not once in the book. So how apposite is this title to Barry's memoir, a memoir far defter than Mr. Lindsay's bad poem? After all, Vachel Lindsay was a melodious mechanic whose smooth brow no thought ever creased. So identifying the title source is a minor chink left out of *Barrelhouse Kings*. I think the circumambient details of its composition embarrassed the adult Callaghan, even as its rhythm remembered from childhood delighted him.

Barry has also omitted much of how Canada reacted to his passage among us. But it's no sin of omission. He gives readers vital bounty, far more than the usual care-ful-mouthed, conservative memoirists of Canada give. Callaghan is a public man who never seems to let the jeers upset him.

How pleasing it is to watch him spread his northern peacock's tail, an act of male display much to be depre-cated in these days of equalizing mediocrity, but all the more piquant for its rarity.

Barry, I reserve for you Saint Augustine's sweetest line: *te esse laetus sum*. "I am glad you are."

JUST WHAT WE NEEDED:
A CRITIC WITH "DUENDE"

Raise You Five:
Essays and Encounters 1964-2004, Volume One

MICHAEL KEEFER

Although nineteenth-century man of letters Matthew Arnold never ventured far, as poet or as critic, from the shallow end of the pool, he nonetheless achieved one piercing insight. Arnold knew that a great literature needs, and in some sense depends upon, the co-presence of deep and passionate critical thought.

Prior to the mid-1960s, whatever one might say of isolated extraordinary writers, English Canada did not have a great literature, and showed few signs of wanting one. But since then, deservedly or not, we have had a torrent of extravagantly talented poets, short-fiction writers, novelists and, more belatedly, playwrights. This first of three volumes of Barry Callaghan's collected non-fiction writings permits a recognition – belated, but unambiguous – that we have also concurrently enjoyed the gift of great criticism.

This might seem a large claim to make on behalf of a body of work first published in what academics might sniff at as ephemeral outlets: the long-defunct *Toronto Telegram* and magazines like *Weekend, Maclean's* and *Toronto Life*. But it was precisely because the pieces collected here reached readerships of tens and hundreds of thousands that they were able to embolden other writers of Callaghan's generation into believing that there could exist a Canadian readership receptive to piercing lucidity, to uncompromising intelligence and to a depth and intensity of feeling perhaps best denoted by Spanish poet Federico Garcia Lorca's term *duende*.

A quick comparison. Northrop Frye, the great encyclopedist among critics, whose Canadian and international reputation was at its height in the 1960s and 1970s, did not have, despite his brilliant insights into the structural workings of literature and his ventures into social as well as literary criticism, the slightest tincture of *duende*. (His principled abstention from evaluative criticism may be one sign of this lack.) Barry Callaghan, in contrast, a self-described *flâneur*, or loiterer, with a bloodline that includes U.S. literary critic Edmund Wilson and political journalist I.F. Stone, has *duende* by the barrel-full. And he is in turn joyous, acerbic, celebratory and unforgiving in his evaluations.

"Duende," which literally implies a state close to possession, was Lorca's term for the unflinching awareness of suffering and morality that he found in the greatest flamenco singers and matadors of his native Andalusia. It is very clearly present in the first text collected here (also one of the most recent): a splendid meditation on the truths of story-telling and, indirectly, on the power of these truths to encompass and deflect the dark certainties of decay and death. It pervades the African landscapes that are hauntingly realized in two long travel pieces from 1979, which recount journeys to Albert Schweitzer's mission in Gabon and to Cardinal Léger's leper asylum in Yanoudé. And it overflows from a powerful sequence of texts within the first third of this volume.

This sequence includes a short account of being scornfully judged for remembering, at the Dachau crematoria, Mahler's incorporation of *Frère Jacques* into the agonized requiem of his First Symphony. There follows a translation of Andrei Vosnesensky's poem *Goya*, which encapsulates the agonies of the winter of 1941; a layered meditation on the Shoah, weaving together texts of Franz Kafka, Paul Celan, Samuel Beckett, Elie Wiesel and Eugène Ionesco; a review of Nikita Khrushchev's autobiography, "a tale of murder, decline, and decay" whose "rudderless prose" and "incoherent half-truths" are set against "a backdrop of millions of dead"; and a brilliantly concise account of one of the great novels of the twentieth century, Mikhail Bulgakov's anti-Stalinist satire *The Master and Margarita*.

History and literature are woven together with similar subtlety in the concluding section of the book. These pieces, dating from the late 1960s, begin with a finely judicious review that pairs Isaac Babel, the short-story writer who was one of Stalin's victims, with the poet Robert Lowell. This is followed by a brusque dismissal of Tom Wolfe's vacuous noisemaking, and an acid review of works by Michael Maclure, Edward Albee and Norman Mailer, whose "calculated hysteria" is judged with reference to William Wordsworth's long-distant assessment of the "multitude of causes . . . now acting with a combined force to blunt the discriminating powers of the mind."

A clever segue takes us into an extended account of Pierre Trudeau on the campaign trail in the 1968 election, climaxing with the famous St. Jean Baptiste Day riot, and to a sequence of further essays and reviews that invoke and anatomize with astonishing vividness the brief and ambiguous triumphalism of the 1967 Six-Day War, the nauseating violence of the U.S. assault on Vietnam, and the moral confusions of the antiwar resistance.

Other points of this collection include Callaghan's deliciously astute deflation of John Updike's pretensions, his affectionate and respectful 1965 interview with Margaret Laurence (published only after her death in 1987), and a finely contextualized analysis of the bilious resentments that underlie Stephen Leacock's sometimes unfunny comic prose. Add to these perceptive reviews of Hugh MacLennan, Robertson Davies and Donald Creighton, who together with Leacock embody exclusionary tendencies for which Callaghan has little patience; and the luminous account of Yehuda Amichai in Jerusalem with which the book concludes.

This book is literary criticism and cultural history of a high order. If its author has, in his own words, been repeatedly "willing to be lucky," he has also, in the full-ness of his responses to the harsh complexities of the four decades across which these pieces were written, repeatedly displayed an exemplary moral courage. Rather than flinching before the charges of aggrieved stupidity, he has leaned in over the horns and struck, with a fine blade, to the heart.

RAISE YOU FIVE

Essays and Encounters 1964-2004: Volume One

RAY ROBERTSON

Philip Larkin used to enjoy threatening to compile an anthology entitled *Utterly Useless Sons and Daughters of the Talented and Famous.* One can't help but be sympathetic. Granted, growing up in the familial shadow of an Evelyn Waugh, a Rebecca West, or a Bob Dylan likely poses its own unique problems of maturation, but coming of age without the equally unique nature/nurture benefits that such a gifted parentage bestows isn't, ipso facto, any easier. In fact, if given the choice, most people would probably prefer putting up with the racket of dad working out the chord changes to "Tangled Up in Blue" while trying to do one's homework in the other room rather than suffering through the sounds of mom watching Wheel of Fortune while munching her way to the bottom of an extra large bag of sour cream and onion potato chips. As a general rule, there are plenty of other more worthy places of spending one's pity than on the privileged. And when the end result of such an auspicious upbringing is unfulfilled promise or, even worse, mere proficient mediocrity, contempt isn't an altogether inappropriate response. Of course, one huffs, if *I* had had all the advantages that son or daughter X had had, I definitely would have . . .

That said, the Barry Callaghan of forty years ago would have warranted at least some compassion. One can only assume that, as a young man, if he had had any choice in the matter, the occupation of writer wouldn't have been high on his career wish list. Before Atwood, before Munro, before Ondaatje, there was Morley Callaghan, Canada's only truly internationally recognized writer. Someone like Auberon Waugh, at least, wasn't the aspiring scribbling son of his country's *only* writer of distinction, which was essentially the situation Barry Callaghan found himself in when he began his lengthy career as fiction writer, poet, and journalist in the mid-1960s. Of course, the younger Callaghan, like his father – like any real writer – didn't have any choice at all, he had to become a writer. That he became, along with Atwood and Richler, one of Canada's preeminent persons of letters, is as much a testament to his psychic mettle as his talents and life-long dedication to his craft.

Raise You Five: Essays and Encounters 1964-2004: Volume One gathers together, for the first time, a generous sample of Callaghan's protean journalistic output: book reviews, profiles, literary criticism, travel reporting, polemics, even memorials. Taken into conjunction with his numerous books of first-class fiction and poetry, *Raise You Five* confirms that Barry Callaghan, even more so than Edmund Wilson, America's best twentieth-century critic and one of Morley Callaghan's closest literary friends (and one of Callaghan junior's formative literary role models), is that rarest of writers, one capable of creating art out of whatever raw material he chooses or is chosen for him, whatever art form the subject matter under consideration demands.

To the artist whose medium is words, a well-written sentence – not a compelling idea, not an engaging plot, not a meaningful theme – is the marrow of his or her work. In the beginning is the word, and then another one, and then another one, until you have a sentence, and then you begin all over again. Recounting a meeting with Samuel Beckett at a Paris café in 1978, Callaghan writes: "Lean, tall, willowy, a narrow head, circular smoked-black glasses, deep eye sockets, the sinister insularity of a bird; in the glare of morning light reflected in the plate glass, he seemed to be cast in negative." Characterization as precise and perfect at this rarely appears in the majority of novels and short stories, never mind "lesser" art forms such as literary journalism.

Or, consider, from what is ostensibly a simple travel piece: "In the coastal city of Douala on the road to the local cemetery a black boy rattled a silver tambourine as he walked ahead of a small white man who was carrying a blue umbrella to shade himself from the sun. There was a hole in the umbrella and the man was staring at the sky through the hole." Not a place, but an entire *world* is evoked in just two short sentences. Reading *Raise You Five* straight through, it becomes difficult – and, ultimately, unnecessary – to keep straight which genre Callaghan is working in, the writing throughout uniformly sharp, redolent, and alive, regardless of the subject matter.

With the solitary exception of Mordecai Richler, Callaghan is also the only major Canadian writer who came of age during the *Survival* era of self-congratulatory Canadian nationalism – when it was, and, for the most part, still is, simply in bad taste, and certainly disadvantageous professionally, to criticize another Canadian writer – who wasn't afraid to say in print that some brand name Canadian wheat was really just over-hyped second-rate chaff. On culture-industry favourite Stephen Leacock, for example: "[Leacock's stories] are strangely remote in technique and temper from the literature of Leacock's time; he is no Ring Lardner; he is much closer to Thomas Haliburton and Artemus Ward than he is to Wodehouse, Walpole, Maugham, Max Berrbohm, or Wolcott Gibbs, and his work is a pale shadow of the writers he said he admired, Dickens and Twain." Hardly incendiary stuff – just clear-headed, nicely wrought criticism – but, take it from someone who only a few years ago received literal hate mail for daring to suggest that young satirists aren't riding Toronto's subways these days with copies of *Sunshine Sketches of a Little Town* tucked in their back pockets, this was an act of cultural courage when it was published back in 1971.

In the frontispiece of every issue of the still-thriving literary magazine, *Exile*, that Barry Callaghan helped found three decades ago, there's a quotation from Julio Cortazar: "The only true exile is the writer who lives in his own country." *Raise You Five* is a testament of one writer who stayed, lived, and wrote about it; this, in spite of the spectre of a famous father who did the same. Both of them are exiles we're fortunate to be able to call our own.

RAISE YOU FIVE AND RAISE YOU TEN

Essays and Encounters 1964-2004
Volumes One and Two

Diana Kuprel

Raise You Five is a book that, with deft intellectual perspicacity and integrity to the written word, snapshots, in a parabolic form, encounters with literary works, iconic figures in far-flung places and key historical events, incanting truths that transcend the contextual peculiarities of their genesis and resonate deeply with the reader in the here-and-now.

With "disinterested" but intense "curiosity" the author searches for the meaning of "reverence for life" as he converses with the ghost of Albert Schweitzer in the Lambaréné Island hospital in West Africa. He reveals the sense of *angoisse* at the core of Québécois writer Marie-Claire Blais and discloses paterfamilias Morley's act of literary betrayal. He tracks down Cardinal Léger in Cameroon and shakes hands with a leper in an embrace of life. He covers Pierre Elliot Trudeau's electric 1968 election campaign, which culminated in a riot at the Saint-Jean-Baptiste parade in Montréal, played like the finale of Jean Genet's *Le balcon*. He follows the fine line between barbarism and civilization in America explored by jailed Black Panther Eldridge Cleaver in a book of essays. He hangs out in New York's gritty desolation row. He spends Easter week in Jerusalem with Yehuda Amichai, who shares with him the true meaning of redemption. And punctuating the essays and reviews – each faithful to the experience, the whole structured not chronologically, but as a jazzy improv, wherein a motif from one piece intuits the choice of the next – are his sensual, muscular translations of poetry from Russian and French.

Volume One's ante was upped with the publication of Volume Two, titled, not surprisingly, *Raise You Ten*. Along with extraordinary portraits of literary greats like Irving Layton, Austin Clarke and Leon Rooke, poets of another ilk like Mohammad Ali and politicians Sir Winston Churchill and Bryce Mackasey, he captures places at critical historical moments: East Berlin before the Wall came tumbling down; America during the civil rights movement of the 1960s and 1970s; Canada when the *War Measures Act* was declared. Threading these disparate texts are recurring themes of gambling and crime, whether state-sponsored or against person or state. Read, for example, his no-holds-barred essay "The Simian Irish" on the State's attempt to snuff out a people's culture by snuffing out their language, wherein he cites from John Montague's soul-searing poem "A Grafted Tongue."

As these volumes exquisitely demonstrate, Callaghan is heir to and continuer of a tradition of literary journalism forged by such master practitioners as Egon Erwin Kisch, Melchoir Wańkowicz and Edmund Wilson, the latter of whom Callaghan writes an intimate, haunting portrait, reprinted in the second volume. This is a kind of documentary narrative that employs literary devices to go beyond the portrayal of the factual event as event, the end of which is accuracy or verisimilitude, in order to explore the event as meaning. While facts are the *differentiae specifica* of literary reportage, they are only the raw material, the "compass of the reporter's journey," to borrow a metaphor coined by the consummate fabulator Kisch, that serves as a catalyst for the writer's creative imagination. As Callaghan declares, "A true story is not always reportage but reportage shaped by the imagination into a lie that tells a great truth that is and is not historical."

Callaghan includes himself within the act of relating. For *Raise You Five* and *Raise You Ten* constitute no mere record of events, no mere "story about a story," no mere translation from one language into another, but a profoundly eloquent register of the author's own internal journey as a writer encountering other worlds. As works that engage the intellect, the heart, the senses and the gut, they are, quite simply, damn fine writing.

MY OLD FRIEND,
THE LITERARY JOURNALIST

David Sobelman

Journalism arose as a protest against illegitimate authority in the name of a wider social contract.

James Carey,
Columbia School of Journalism

Dear Q.,

Allow me to introduce you to a forceful, lucid, often provocative, writer: his name is Barry Callaghan, a man of letters whose work has given me much pleasure since 1981. I've been reading his latest books, *Raise You Five* and *Raise You Ten*, over the last two years and they have challenged me and inspired me to think about that rare breed, the literary journalist.

In this letter, I will, first, provide you with a bird's-eye view of his territory. Then, I'll structure an intellectual taxonomy of the categories I find pertinent to his writings and, in the end, I will draw some conclusions about how and why this literary character became the writer he is.

A Bird's-Eye View

There is no pleasure in traveling, and I look upon it as an occasion for spiritual testing.

Albert Camus

Barry's literary journey began in a Jarvis Street pub, Toronto, 1964, where he hung out after a day's work as a news reporter for CBC (his first interview was with a talking horse: they discussed Khrushchev). As fate

374

would have it, one day he was asked to "talk about books" on a morning radio program, and the rest, as they say, became *his story*.

However, we will begin in *Raise You Five* with "True Stories," a deeply moving, philosophically insightful story about the redemptive powers of fiction.

Afterwards, we'll canoe down the Ogowé river in Gabon and, later, drive to Douala in the Cameroon (where we will read about the "light" in the festering wounds of the outcasts he met during a visit to a community of lepers).

Later, at Dachau, Auschwitz and in Jerusalem, we will hear the sorrowful laughter of *Shoah* survivors and we'll recognize the sharp focus of his narrative logic, the logic of singular moments deeply seen and felt, the logic of a writer paying attention to his critical sensibility.

In Ipswich, in John Updike's shopping mall country, he will write about playing "B-Ball" with Rabbit, the most engaging profile I've read of the author of *Couples* (one of my favourite novels of the late 1960s).

He'll then drive to Wellfleet on the Cape, into a drizzly October afternoon on the dunes with writer Marie-Claire Blais, to discuss the possibility of laughter amidst the darkest gloom.

In Newark, New Jersey, LeRoi Jones – in the aftermath of race riots – will show him the shoulder of cold black rage. We'll visit mid-town Manhattan, where Muhammad Ali will sing trite Broadway tunes to him, and we will read about Washington and the Pentagon's nefarious machinations, before returning to Desolation Row on 42nd Street.

And then, yes, and then? We'll find out that he is a gambler, too, as he takes his earnings to Saratoga, to play the horses and to write about the fire storming of his house at 69 Sullivan Street by drug addicts. It is a horror he describes with a precise, moral intelligence in

"A Motiveless Malignancy." Later, we'll trot with him in *Raise You Ten* to Longchamp, the race track in the Bois du Boulogne, in Paris, visit with Samuel Beckett, and attend a conference for translators to discuss the art of *le mot juste.*

Then he'll return home and write about Irving Layton's poetry, before taking his train of thoughts to Orillia, near Lake Couchiching (a deliciously tongue twisting Chipewa word meaning "fish weir"), to unmask Stephen Leacock.

After a stretch of silence, he will be off again to Isle Grosse, a transit island for Irish "coffin" boats in the nineteenth century, to redeem the reputation of a Canadian politician.

Then a cruise ship to Glacier Bay, Alaska. Then . . . And then . . .

You get the idea, right?

His essays are like the precious stones of a mosaic slowly falling into place.

Gradually, as one reads, one begins to understand that *this* literary journalist, this essayist *extraordinaire,* is committed to reveal *the acts of barbarism that are always hidden beneath the carpet of civilization* (to paraphrase another literary journalist and cultural critic, Walter Benjamin).

In fact, *Raise You Five* and *Raise You Ten* reveal the singular voice of a devout man of letters, a journalist of ideas of the highest literary order. A writer I read for the pleasure of his text, a modern-day *feuilletoniste.*

The old *feuilletonistes* of the 1920s and 1930s set for themselves the goal that Barry has followed – to write artful stories that capture the essence of storytelling, while reporting about the culture and politics of the times (that is, his *zeitgeist*), stories that are deft parables of the human condition. But, I assure you, Q., my preamble, my bird's-eye tour, only skims the surface.

An Intellectual Taxonomy

> *A story . . . is a shaping of facts, a molding act of the imagination. And the imagination, said Jacques Maritain, approaches metaphysics; that is, it approaches first truths.*
> "True Stories," *Raise You Five*

I will identify six categories: Journalism. Literature. Poetry. Translation. Politics or Political Engagement, and Theology. These are the categories I consider vital to an understanding of Barry, the literary journalist.

The first story in *Raise You Five*, "True Stories," was written for an Italian philosophical journal, *il cannocchiale*.

"True Stories" challenges us to think about the stories we tell to beget truth. It raises a necessary ontological question, especially necessary in our time of hybrids, hoaxes and the prevailing confusion between information and knowledge: how does the telling of lies, lies that are inlaid in a story, enhance "the truth of how it was with us?"

How do lies, embedded in fact and fiction, take root in the same ground, the onto-theological substratum of storytelling? How do we end up living "the truth" that has emerged as the story – though "the truth" *per se* is countered by facts that are either false or ridiculous?

For example: the Jews know their Exodus story, and are sticking to it (though it would take only four or five days, not forty years, to walk across the Sinai); the Christians know their Passion story, and are sticking to it (though one of the three Marias, Mary Magdalene, was never a prostitute). Be that as it may, the story itself, as a story, remains. Now, to continue the taxonomy. Most of these essays were published in the popular press over the last forty years. In them, ostensibly, our man functions as a critic-reviewer. But these "reviews" have nothing to do with what we commonly understand by "book reviews."

Read the last essay in *Raise You Ten*, called "Edmund Wilson." Just as "True Stories" describes the literary-philosophical background of Barry's narrative arc, so does the essay on Edmund Wilson reveal the primary source of Barry's criticality.

Lines written by Barry about Edmund Wilson suggest, to a degree, the still center of Barry's sensibility: "[He writes by] the authority of his intelligence, in the singular authority of his voice."

A few paragraphs later, "He has gone about the saving of his soul by pursuing a solid perfection of standards."

And the aim of these standards? Well, here I give you Barry in his own words – to "convert reportage and anecdotal storytelling and portraiture into a grave, graceful stern moral act."

Barry, however, not being a Calvinist (as Wilson was), is not as stern nor as engaged in his nation's destiny. In fact, when it comes to matters of destiny – his and the nation's – he exhibits the *flâneur's* air of detachment, trusting, essentially, standards that he has forged in and for himself, standards that are the ground for his singular authority.

Lest we forget, Baudelaire, Walter Benjamin, Edmund Wilson, Roland Barthes, Frank Kermode, all followed the singular authority of their voices: a voice we read as "the pleasure of the text" (Barthes).

1. Journalism, my first taxonomical classification, is supported by one aspect of the dedication in *Raise You Ten*:

For William Kennedy, who, as a reporter, never forgot that journalism is storytelling, and as a storyteller, never forgot that he was a reporter.

I believe that Barry, as a reporter, extended a notion Edmund Wilson put to him many years ago:

> He has fought and is still fighting to impose his standards, his opinions on people by force of eloquence, by force of rhetoric – so that he might, in a modesty of arrogance ingrained in his secular Calvinism, say of his role in society, 'I have been of use.' That is what he had told me one day with disarming unaffectedness. "I want to be of use."

In "What Darkness Is For" Barry journeys to the Albert Schweitzer compound in Gabon, some years after that icon of medical Samaritans had died. There, he encounters a vivaciously strong nurse in charge of the leper's colony. She's a remarkable character (she calls herself Nurse Living Stone and she is "as unto a living stone . . . chosen of God, and precious." *First Letter of Peter 2:4-5*). Through her experience, Barry finds the means to write a "short story" that is a report on the inherent failure of Dr. Schweitzer. But it is also a story about the living disease, leprosy, and the kind of spirituality required to see into the seed of light within its darkness.

The sublime achievement of "What Darkness Is For" is in the way the writer as well as the man encounters, as a literary journalist, the ghost of Albert Schweitzer in Nurse Living Stone's story, and then leaves us to contemplate its implications when she gives him, at the moment of his departure, a "white-faced mask with long, loose straw hair and a straw beard.

"'It was here when Schweitzer was here and I'm the only one who was with him, so I can give it to you.'

"'The white face,' I said.

"'To ward off evil and *to remember why I'm here.*'"

What we have been given is fact with the narrative force of fiction. The story impels us to contemplate

Schweitzer's human failures, and therefore the failures of his myth (his story), as we rethink what the self-created Nurse Living Stone has said, who she is, and how she has become a transcendent figure in her own mind, as she lives through the actual good works she performs in Gabon.

In fact, we are shown in this story, by example, an aspect I consider essential to Barry's literary journalism, namely that the *truth* of journalism and the *truth* of literature can be one and the same truth.

2. Literature (or the literary mind), my second taxonomical categorization. But first a brief disclosure: I came to know Barry, the man, as a talk-show guest on Canada AM, and, later, as one of the hosts of *Enterprise*, a critically acclaimed talk show I co-produced at CITY TV. (The show, incidentally, won him the ACTRA award for Best Television Host of the year.) But, when I first met him, he had already been for some time the "Media Critic" on Canada AM, where I was a novice story editor.

After seeing a few of his graceful 8 a.m. performances on what Roland Barthes called "the mythologies of daily life," I volunteered to story edit every "set of pre-interview greens" for his anecdotal media stories. Many days it meant double duty for me, but I did it with pleasure. Why? Because to my mind Barry is a natural *raconteur*, a born storyteller: the first I met in Toronto, Canada, in 1981 (after having already lived here, then, for eight years).

On television, Barry told perfectly "timed" stories (usually lasting seven minutes) that were inspired by current affairs, stories that allowed him to showcase the range of his literary mind.

For example, he'd talk about the NFL Super Bowl and in the same breath, in his analogical way, allude to Tolstoy's *War and Peace* or, a few days later, while talking about the "nature" of Trudeau's characteristic shrug – how its seeming carelessness contained a stern indifference – he'd explain how Trudeau could be a stern Jansenist and a casually expedient Jesuit at the same time.

Listening to his metaphors, his parables, his allusions, his analogies, I could hear (and see) that he was both a voice for the people and a highly educated teacher, a writer as comfortable with low-lives as he was with the high-brow world of classical literature. It's this kind of paradoxical stance (one foot in the gutter, the other in the firmament) that I also found most fascinating in his own short stories (*The Black Queen Stories* and *A Kiss is Still a Kiss*), as well as in *When Things Get Worst*: a modern gothic novel that reads like a dream unfolding in the mind of a woman haunted by Ontario ghosts (seeking justice from the land!). I bring you to Barry's literary pedigree along this way for a reason: I do not want to separate his literary mind from his existential being. Literature is in his blood, it's integral to his genetic constitution. But unlike his well-known father, who mostly wrote short stories and novels, Barry has applied himself to the literary realm as a whole. It makes his literary personae difficult to define: he has not focused on a single art form or message, he has no universal agenda, yet his "brand," if you will, is as broad in scope as it is sharply focused.

Read "Piano Play" (in *Raise You Ten*), for example, and you'll ask yourself: is this a fictional account of an actual encounter or a reporter's ideational portrait of a *Mafioso*? "Piano Play" captures the essence of a Jewish gangster by describing how he came to be called "Piano." It's a simple scene: our narrator and Piano meet at a Deli, they eat smoked meat sandwiches and talk about their friend, Solly. The story is only two pages long, but it's emblematic of the kind of literary scene setting (*mise-en-scène*) and minimalist characterization that is fundamental to all of Barry's writings, journalistic or literary.

Reading through his collected volumes, you'll find similar glimpses and insights (or *aperçus*) about John Updike, Marie-Claire Blais, Alan Sillitoe, Jakov Lind, Philip Roth, Samuel Beckett, Eldridge Cleaver, Marshall McLuhan, Norman Mailer, Angela Davis, LeRoi Jones, Nathanael West, John O'Hara and Edmund Wilson.

Such an array cannot but lead to paradox. To put it in a nutshell: in "Eruption of Rage Against the Second Rate" (*Raise You Five*, written in 1968), Barry tackles the vested interests of academics. He questions their "authority," calls them "donkey researchers" and "PhD policemen," and yet, at the time, he was the Chairman of his English department at York University and a professor of contemporary literature, a professorship he held for thirty-five years.

True to form, however, as a professor of literature (now a retired Professor Emeritus and Distinguished University Scholar) he did not publish a single academic paper; instead, he inaugurated an internationally recognized Canadian literary quarterly, *Exile*, a quarterly magazine in which "the imaginative writer will not be led in by a scholarly praetorian guard," to quote Barry, its Editor-in-Chief.

Don't ask me how he did it for so long or how he got the University to support his disinterest in "the dancing scholarly horse." Just accept that to enter his literary mind you will have to discard that old specter, *logical contradiction*, and live with the paradoxical. (After all, as Baudelaire, Barthes, McLuhan and others often remind us: dealing with the paradoxical is the first requirement of the literary imagination. Baudelaire even went so far as to call contradiction his eleventh Commandment.)

I'll end this section by mentioning the love of literature Barry imbibed in at home. His father, Morley Callaghan, was a successful novelist. He possessed, in Barry's own words, "[a] curious eye, a cold eye. Not ruthless, but a lens-eye unmoved by the impediment of emotion" ("True Stories"). Without doubt, it's a *de rigueur* requirement for a novelist as well as a literary journalist.

Both writers, father and son, worked long and hard at conveying the ideas behind their literary standards, ideas sublimated in their stories. It's the reason I re-read both of them regularly; it's their ability to observe and describe the object as it is in and of itself and to seamlessly intertwine the object and subject at hand into their art of telling a story (be it a poem, a short story or a critical essay).

There's a passion for the art of narrative as reportage from the beginning of *Raise You Five*, and its first essay, "True Stories," to the end of *Raise You Ten*, and it's last essay, "Edmund Wilson." Structurally speaking, it reveals the meta-story of a writer's mind, if you will, or his character (his "moral stamina," as Barry himself called it elsewhere). But it's by no means (not psychologically or critically) a closed system, an agenda or a mission statement; there's always room for criticality and disagreement.

3. Poetry, the third category. Two years before I met Barry at Canada AM, a bibliophile I had come to know at York University, Nicky Drumbolis, had shown me a signed, hardcover, edition of *The Hogg Poems and Drawings*. The year was 1979, I didn't yet know the poet or anything about the man who called himself Hogg, but in the Hogg poems (and drawings) I recognized a voice that moved me with its narrative leap and musicality, as I followed the poet on his archetypical descent underground. (See "Fishing for Hogg in the Midnight Sun.")

Throughout *Raise You Five* and *Raise You Ten* you'll find not only poems by Hogg, but also by poets who have found their nook in his cranium: W.H. Auden, demigod amidst domestic clutter! The neglected alchemical French poet, Robert Marteau. The arcane Serbian poet, Miodrag Pavlovic, the fine and private Imagist, W.W.E. Ross, the ice-bound Andrei Voznesensky, an array of Québécois poets like the patriarchal Gaston Miron and the mystic Fernand Ouellette, as well as the tribal voice of the Latvian, Imants Ziedonis, and other moderns, Lowell and Berryman, and the steely Czeslaw Milosz, whom he met at Expo 67 and others, like the poet of a new-old Jerusalem, Yehuda Amichai, alongside excerpts from the redemptive *kabbalistic* verses of Paul Celan.

Some of these poets you'll meet in essays on their work, others you'll find quoted extensively within the body of his essays. But, be it poetry quoted in essays or essays about poets, after reading both volumes, you're left with the essential impression that this literary journalist writes with the keen, lens-eyed, focused, precision of a novelist and the heart of a poet.

His essay on Yehuda Amichai, at the end of *Raise You Five*, is a case in point. Let me quote its first paragraph:

> Jerusalem has a heart as crooked as ecclesiastical sheets, as crooked as yellow thorn branches, dry in their silence. In the alleyways there is no sound of water. By a wrought-iron window in a stone house on a rise called Yemin Moshe, looking across a gully to Jaffa Gate, Yehuda Amichai the poet sits hunched forward, solid and fleshy through the shoulders, and his face is red from the sun. "And about love?" I ask.

Aside from the beauty of the phrasing, and the cinematic descent into the scene, I point you to this paragraph because wherever you look in Barry's poetry, as Hogg, or in his prose portraits of poets and their poetic calling, you will find an over-riding *übermotif* – stone and water. In Barry's (and Hogg's) being, stone equals bread equals body and water equals wine equals soul. His world, in its concrete reality, possesses a metaphorical, almost animistic, potentiality: it is flesh waiting to be made Word.

(Incidentally, one of the most profound discussions I ever heard between Barry, the son, and Morley, his father, was about the significance of dry desert stone and scarce desert water in the shaping of the imagination of the Hebrews and the hearts of gnostic writers.)

Into this world, enters Irving Layton, the first Canadian poet I read for pleasure. He was outspoken, a selfish trickster, a sentimental clown, a follower of Eros, or as Barry puts it, a poet possessed of "a fine bawdy recklessness . . . [I]n a country whose people bought more life insurance, per capita, than any other people on the face of the earth . . . a country of sober citizens who wore good sensible shoes and were busy investing in their own deaths. In such a time, in such a place, Irving appeared . . ."

Barry's essay on Irving Layton is a portrait (by a friend and a poet) that not only reviews Layton's poetic significance with a critical tenderness, and exegetical understanding, but affirms a passion – an unrelenting passion – for the living that borders on the love of two soul mates.

4. Translator, the fourth taxonomical categorization. "Translation . . . catches fire on the eternal life of the works and the perpetual renewal of language" (Walter Benjamin). His "Black Light" essay is as insightful about what is gained and lost in the art of translation as Walter Benjamin's seminal, "The Task of the Translator." It also reveals a quality in the man not found elsewhere. The poem is as it is forever, but the translation of that poem is a living process that is never done. Translation is an acknowledgment that language is an evolving, organic, substance.

Language (*langue* et *parole*) is the erection of our contemporary sensibility and appetites, it is not a fixed notion but a *dressage*. (I'm using the word in its original French meaning – the erection or putting up of a tent or a scaffolding.)

In other words, language, spoken and written, is both a putting up of the tent-pole and the tent-canvas of our quotidian lives.

Translation, however, permits us to recognize the hidden "kinship of languages," as Benjamin called it. Translation allows the reader to approximate the sensibility of the original, not through an "alikeness," but through putting "the hallowed growth of languages to the test." Every translation tests the translator's ability to approximate the intention (tone, meaning and effect) of the original.

Barry's translation of Robert Marteau's "Claude Monet's Magpie: A Sonnet" is an English ensoulment of the spirit of Marteau's French – a *French* sonnet rendered in English:

> The magpie pecked at the snow, he spat orange
> On the black locust gate rail, sitting out in plain
> View among the black apple trees. A sheen, strange
> As any oscillating sea lamp as it sustains
> Its flame, steeps the day in coral light, a flange
> Torn along the mother of pearl that now retains,
> Now strews oriental pink and grey on the grange
> Tilted back against the sky, ashen, and its flames
> Fed not by a cold fire but the combustible
> Wintering of mistletoe, ivy, a seed pod
> Green ground to paste in someone's palm, inedible
> Except perhaps by the bird or the outcast god
> Quailing on the bottom stair, incompatible
> Among embers, out on the prowl, alone abroad.

Finally, I'll add this: Barry has translated eight books of poetry. The six I could read, from French to English, are poetic "approximations" that – to paraphrase Walter Benjamin – light the fire behind the perpetual renewal of language.

5. Politics or Political Engagement, the fifth categorization. Barry's engagement with "political journalism" became clear to me a few weeks before I actually met him. Talking about the politics of this land, I suggested to the Executive Producer of Canada AM that we should do a story about Trudeau as a literary man. That's when the Executive Producer told me about his friend, Barry Callaghan, who had been the literary editor of a defunct local newspaper. So I went to the reference library and found several of his long journalistic essays published in *The Telegram.*

In *Raise You Ten,* there's a short but powerful critical essay called "Churchill the Crisper." (Incidentally, another virtue of these essays and encounters is that they are often no longer than six or seven pages, but they pack a wallop of thought-provoking ideas and for all their clarity of style demand a thoughtful reader. Considering that they were mostly published in newspapers and magazines, they reveal yet another beneficial quality of Barry's highly literate-journalistic mind: he knows how to distill the complex into dramatic vignettes that frame journalistic, historical and aesthetic issues in a form that invites the reader to raise questions and debate the matter at hand.)

"Churchill the Crisper" is ostensibly a critical review of *The Soldiers,* Rolf Hochhuth's 1960s play about Churchill's decision to firebomb non-combatant urban areas in Germany, especially Dresden, which was "firestormed into char and cinders," not for military reasons, but to break the backbone of the ordinary German citizen and, perhaps, to help Stalin's army advance into Germany. That seems plausible enough. But hold on!

The play, he says, is "a portrait of Churchill as a mass murderer – a *good* mass murderer since he was instrumental in the defeat of that *evil* mass murderer, Hitler – but, a mass murderer nonetheless." By describing its ethical issues, Barry forces the reader, then, in the late 1960s, when the play was considered controversial, and, now, in the early twenty-first century, when hardly anyone remembers Hochhuth, to question the limits of power. It's a question that raises its historical head in Turkey, in Algiers, in Vietnam, in Biafra, in Cambodia, in Rwanda, in Israel, in Lebanon!

Barry raises *the right questions*, timeless questions, by framing the idea behind *The Soldiers* in a context that remains, and will remain, relevant for as long as the failures of diplomacy (and the failure of peaceful negotiations) lead to war.

His necessary insights, insights that originate in the milieu of aesthetics, philosophy and theology, are rooted in his pedagogical sensibility. Let me show you what I mean in a quote:

"'This world,' as Nietzsche said, and Hochhuth's Churchill agrees, 'is the will to power – and nothing besides.' As a man of such a world, Churchill is prepared – in order to defend and extend the national interests – to violate any and all conventions of war. This is Nietzsche – it is the *will* to *will* – sheer force that asserts itself as force: force that *wills* only its own *will* – force that is impersonal, incalculable, inescapable – force that is embodied in one man, the *übermensch*."

The *übermensch!* The great criminal.

This is power, all too familiar.

But then he poses a question most unfamiliar.

"There is, however, a dramatic and moral dilemma, a sin and a sorrow beyond resolution or redemption that lurks at the heart of *The Soldiers*. In deciding to bomb densely crowded cities from the air, in deciding to create a fire storm, Churchill made a choice, a choice that was made possible by the nature of technology, but because of the nature of that technology he surrendered all choice to inadvertence. In exercising his decision to kill, he left himself no control over who he was killing; this constitutes having the capacity for absolute power while at the same time lacking the capacity for any discretionary use of that power; this is the modern sin of inadvertence; inadvertent death through terror bombings; this, it seems to me, means living with a mushroom cloud in the heart." In this way, he brings the aesthetic sensibility of the storyteller, and the philosophical ground of theology, to the ethical imperatives of journalism. It's this narrative art behind the questions he asks that makes him, first, a literary journalist of the highest order and, second, a cultural critic of our times for generations to come.

6. Theology, the sixth taxonomical categorization, could also be the first and perhaps most important, *a priori*: the category of first truths.

> Where does the imagination begin?
> In memory, with the story.
> "True Stories," *Raise You Five*

First truths imply an ontological retrieval of origins and, as the above two lines indicate, the first truth of storytelling is rooted in our imagination and memories. In Aristotle's time, as Aquinas understood clearly, "natural theology" (also known as "rational theology") was a philosophical science (often called a "sacred science"). Its realm was to be known by reason alone, that is, not

389

by faith in divine revelation. Aristotle considers natural theology a practical science; "for a practical science is that which ends in action" *(Metaph.* ii). A logic that Aquinas supports: "Be ye doers of the word, and not hearers only" (James 1:22).

Later, however, in the first book of his *Summa* (first article, fourth question) Aquinas disagrees with Aristotle and points out that Theology, "the Sacred Doctrine," as he calls it, is "the speculative science of God," and that it also "includes moral theology," that is, an ethical component, because it deals with the practical science of human acts. "Still," writes Aquinas in answer to the question raised in the *Summa's* first article, "sacred doctrine (that is, theology) is speculative *rather than* practical, because it is more concerned with divine things than with human acts" [*Summa* I, 1, 4].

Though not a practicing Catholic, Barry's *habitus* is grounded in its intellectual milieu (and philosophical tradition): a speculative natural theology that knows how to raise questions of the highest order – be they theological, philosophical, literary or aesthetic.

In his sixth article, Aquinas points out the following: "He is said to be wise in any order who considers the highest principle in that order" [Summa I, 1, 6].

Throughout *Raise You Five* and *Raise You Ten*, Barry returns to an essentially onto-theological perspective, his "first truths," or, as some would say, the framework of his ethical and therefore critical standards. For example: in "Salt and Toys," *Raise You Ten*, Barry writes: "I asked myself – for one of the few times in my adult life – whether some little song might not be heard from the other side of mankind, whether God is not an impossibility?" *Nota bene*: this is not the question of a child, but of an adult, highly self-conscious writer, standing where Hitler had once stood, high in the mountains of *Obersalzberg*. It is the question, as I mentioned before, that leads all of us, who doubt our faith, to Pascal's *Wager* and to the matter "of accepting that God either exists or He does not exist." A question that, once raised, forces you, intellectually speaking, "[to] take sides, you must make the bet, because once you've asked the question you have no choice" but to answer it (*pace* Barry).

Let me now expand on how – indirectly, of course – Barry's ethical framework is based on what is (essentially) an onto-theological premise. A premise embedded (*a priori*) in his critical standards.

In the twenty-five years I've known him, he has never been afraid of applying his Catholic (specifically Thomistic) background to certain thorny metaphysical matters. I'm not saying that he is "a believer," but, since he was a one-time student of Thomism, I would point out to him – by analogy – that my silhouette of his theological sensibility is to his writing as a tonic chord is to the key of its tuning.

In "True Stories," since he's not well versed in Kabbalah and is not openly given to the four exegetical levels of hermeneutics, he deals with the story of Exodus by lifting it out of its literal level (you can walk across the Sinai in four or five days) and placing it squarely within the realm of his own metaphoric imagination.

Why? Because the Bible, as Barthes would put it, is "a text [written] like any other product of *man*," the product of his human need to tell those stories that assuage our fear of death, the unknown, and "infinitude." That need is, of course, the ontology of storytelling and the reason we know a culture by its stories:

> Like a bee, a story becomes itself.
> Like a bee, a story gets in your bonnet.
> It becomes what it is in memory. The memory of passing out of bondage is central to the being of all Jews. They

did not know who they were until they had got their story straight. Every year at Passover, by entering into memory they begin again.

"True Stories"

(Incidentally: if ever you have the time, I suggest you read Barry's poem, "Judas Priest," written long before the *Gospel of Judas* made its way out of Egypt, some twenty years ago. It will convince you of the soundness of my proposition: natural theology is Barry's philosophical ground.)

Barry knows that a lasting story is a story we created, as a single voice or as a communion of single voices, calling it our memory, personal or tribal, and that it is a story we stick to, knowing that it has to be "renovated through the ritual of re-telling, in print or orally, from generation to generation."

In "A Glass of Water Freely Given" – as renovator on the move – he goes deep into the jungle, into the heart of darkness country, to meet Cardinal Léger who is famous throughout the world as "Léger Among the Lepers." This meeting takes place at the old priest's hospital camp in the Cameroon, where, as he speaks of many things, the old priest tells Barry that a priest carries inside himself a particular possibility. In his imitation of Christ, he carries the potential for "the transcendence of . . . pain, not only through the alleviation of poverty, but through love, charity, the conviction that, as Léger puts it, 'The glass of water freely given is still the most convincing proof of the existence of God, who is present in the fevered face of the poor man.'"

It is a powerful image, a powerful idea. But, as the storyteller, Barry does not comment; he lets the image and idea be what they are.

At the end of the essay, the Cardinal sends an assistant to tell Barry – fatigued by the jungle and the heat –

that Barry cannot come to lunch (though one of the doctors working at the hospital had invited him to the common dinning table). Why? Because Cardinal Léger (like Greta Garbo), *vants* to be alone:

> "Alone?"
> "Yes."
> He handed me a plastic bottle of water.
> "I am sorry. There is nothing I can do. He's like that. You cannot come in."
> "The glass of water freely given . . ."
> He was about to ask me what I meant but then he shrugged. He was late.

He turns journalism into a masterful parable, a glass of water *not* freely given, if you will.

The fact is, you'll find many examples in Barry's essays and encounters to support my proposition that his ethics are rooted in a natural (secularized) onto-theological ground. A ground in which he, *as its figure*, adheres to the first truth of imagination and memory (and identity), as the essence of our need to tell "true stories," stories that anchor "the way it was with us" in those moments of truth and lies, those moments of achievement and failures, that beget our overriding truths. Implied in the ending of "A Glass of Water Freely Given" – in which the righteousness of the journalist is eschewed – is the idea of mercy. Not *efficacious* mercy (grace) as visited upon us by God, but *sufficient* mercy (grace) as it comes to us, as we take our stand on the line between civilization and barbarism. In another essay, his piece on Eldridge Cleaver, Barry has actually identified that fine line "as the moral awareness that allows a man to condemn without hatred and love without sentimentality."

Cogito, ergo summa

Given my taxonomical analysis, Barry is the medium of his own message: he is the ground he has tilled to nurture his truth, the figure he believed he could become. Everything he writes is integral to his being, not only as a literary journalist but – in McLuhan's definition of the term – as a modern artist: a "man in any field, scientific or humanistic, who grasps the implications of his actions and of new knowledge in his own time. He is a man of integral awareness" (McLuhan, *Understanding Media*).

It's not likely that anyone will tell you this, but his drive, his incredible "moral stamina," is motivated by a desire to articulate a simple journalistic coda: our Western freedom to pursue, through writing, the will to justice, the will to see through the false, the corrupt, the hypocritical; an absurd notion without what Aquinas called "a necessary faith in reason."

And so our journey approaches its end.

As a literary journalist of the highest order, Barry is coming out of his "forty years in the desert." After all, the subtitle of both *Raise You Five* and *Raise You Ten* is *Essays and Encounters 1964-2004*. That is forty years, *Punkt*. Over and out, but for this addendum: I often heard (in my youth) students at Oxford say of a particular man, "He is one of the Greats."

This, however, is Canada – where there was no indigenous culture, where a cultural industry had to be "instituted" (via a Royal Commission) as a defense against its British (royalist) past and the imperialistic American presence to the south; yes, it's Canada, a country where culture has never been, *a priori*, "first nature"; it is a place where culture seems doomed to remain embedded in its psyche as "second nature."

Living at the fore in such a contradictory ground, Barry's response to his situation – his relations with the public, his context – is one of sardonic merriment, best expressed in an essay he wrote for the English magazine, *Punch*, called "Canadian Wry" (a pun on the national whisky, rye). Its opening two paragraphs put it in a nutshell: "Canadians," he says, "are never what we appear to be. Deception, sometimes self-deception, is our genius. We appear to be stuporous, we appear to be boring, but in fact, we're zany and make no sense at all."

"I came to understand this several years ago . . . when I was in Leningrad trying to get to know a woman. She was watched by the secret police. I was watched by the secret police. It was grim. It was impossible. So I came home, and at the airport in Toronto, I had an epiphany. There, in front of me, was a Mounted Policeman, all in red and blue and yellow stripes. Like everyone in this world, we have our secret police, but suddenly I thought – what other people would dress up their secret police in scarlet coats, put campfire boy hats on their heads and have them ride around on horses wagging lances at the wind, calling covert action a musical ride?"

And then there was this, talking to him on the phone, Thursday, March 23rd, 2006, late at night:

"I take great pleasure in being a Canadian. I understand the duplicity we Canadians present to the world, we appear to like our privacy, above all, but only because we're in fact something different all together – we're obsessed with being recognized by the world, and with presenting our good image to the world. We want the world to know that we have a good government, that we are a peace-loving, tolerant, country of boring citizens."

I couldn't help but laugh, so I laughed.

"Do we have an identity problem? No, we don't, but we like to think we do. It amuses me to no end, because it's a non issue for me . . . I like who I am, I like what I sense, and *here* is where I am. It's *my* territory, it's where

I became the writer I am. I was born a Canadian. It is the frame of my perspective, but not necessarily the only sense I have of myself as a writer. I tell you, above all, I've enjoyed going through life disguised as a Canadian." That's it, Q., in his own words: a man whose literary contribution is not yet complete even after forty years of wandering, still in disguise, on Rue Morgue Avenue in Rosedale, Toronto, Canada.

CONTRIBUTION TO THE ARTS

The Man, The Publisher, The Mentor,
The Translator, The Teacher, The Archive

FOR BARRY CALLAGHAN

Patrick Lane

Black Irish and you know you're in trouble
with those eyes, the way they hold a country
in their grief, and you know if you go down
the road he sees, the girls and whiskey will be hard.
What to do but dance with him as hard as fists can do,
the same as when the wind comes beating on the tired
    arms
of children. He's watched us in the way that boys do,
half in wonder, half in rage. If there's an age they call
Canadian, it's him. He knows the hours spent.
I saw him touch his father's shoulder once.
He touched it the way a man turns back again
into every kind of child he might have been.
That father's dead. He led him all alone.
What bone is left to pick among the cries?
But watch what's in his eyes, such loneliness,
such pride, such loss you'd think
he'd climbed off some green island
in a sea the world forgot, the almost last man
wandering the city, half-drunk on whiskey,
full-drunk on the twist inside his chest
that is as much a laugh as a goodbye.
Black Irish, some say the only way to die.

BARRY CALLAGHAN

Marie-Claire Blais

I remember when I first met Barry in Wellfleet, New England, in the 1960s, during a visit he made to see the great critic Edmund Wilson and his family. In *Barrel-house Kings*, the fine memoir that is also a moving homage to his father, Barry gives a brief recollection of this meeting on the dunes beside the ocean, an exchange of rather gloomy philosophy between the two young writers we were at the time, worried about rumblings of war in Vietnam. But the image I retain is of an exuberant young man with unruly hair, a charmer, humorous and profound at the same time, somebody I hoped would become a friend. Barry had none of my pathological shyness, expressing himself confidently in a strong voice. He became a poet and novelist, passionate about his universal love of literature, and it's no secret how much love and energy he's put into his work as both poet and editor, spreading the word about writers and artists of all nationalities. It was through his brilliant literary review, *Exile* (which today is also an audacious publishing house, a window on the world), that we came to know poets such as Tomas Tranströmer, John Montague, Francis Ponge, Jaime Sabines, and so many others. Barry also had the courage to break the silence of the two solitudes, publishing novelists like Réjean Ducharme and Victor-Lévy Beaulieu, the poet Michel Beaulieu who died too young, and so many others. This was the imaginative young man I met in Wellfleet, the man who told me during our seaside walk through an autumn storm of windblown sand that he wanted his life to be a total exploration in writing, and he hasn't betrayed any of that youthful energy, because the passion of writing was and still is his life force, and writing for him remains the visionary art that combats all mediocrity, an art that denounces and accuses, as can be seen in his magnificent long poem *Hogg The Seven Last Words*. What an emotional trip it is to read that poem, a dantesque portrait of the hell at the heart of the last century that also plunges us into the grisly present. Barry Callaghan is the sensitive witness of centuries of cruelty and barbaric regimes. He denounces the injustice of countless murderous crimes, but doesn't he also remind us through his full-throated, inspired poetry, through words painful in their constant precision and exactness, that even today we are not beyond reliving those historical atrocities? In his harrowing poem we are reminded that Stalin, Himmler, Beria are not long gone, that their ghosts could reappear in the flesh, in the present – he knows and he predicts that the hour of the executioner can come again, any time, and the innocents are never safe from slaughter. Barry knows how

. . . the tear
in a needle's eye comes from laughter,
how men like Stalin, Himmler, Beria, not only,
know the evil they do

but find it wryly amusing
in all its intricacies of device,
the way pulling the wings off butterflies is ferociously funny
to queerly strung choir boys.
What else could their defiant sign

WORK MAKES FREE
over the gate of a death camp be
but a joke that only

killers could enjoy.
They knew, they knew, they knew,
and they laughed, he said,

as they laughed at
work, work, the dignity of work
in the work camps of Siberia.
What a joke . . .

Barry will go on astonishing us, not only by introducing us to, and showing us the talent of, a host of new artists and writers, but also through the fiery spirit of his writings so closely wedded to the anxieties of our time – writings that seem so necessary in the age we are living through, writings that seem more than indispensable.

Translated by Ray Ellenwood

THE THINKING HEART

Barry Callaghan's Exile

Alexandre L. Amprimoz

When Barry was a boy his father had a party for his old friend Jacques Maritain, the French philosopher. Barry heard his father say, "Come on, I want you to meet a fine fellow. He's the modern poet around here." Before Morley could lead the grey-bearded philosopher into the central hall of the house, to meet W.W.E. Ross, Barry heard Maritain say, "Yes, but does he have any perceptions?"

That simple, highly provocative question stuck in Barry's mind. "I have never forgotten that moment," he told me over armagnac at *La Maquette*, the French restaurant at the corner of King and Church (on that day, everything was a sign: the paintings of Michael Callaghan, Barry's son were hanging in the spacious fine restaurant and a young woman at another table happened to be reading Morley's novel, *More Joy in Heaven*. There was no lack of perspective or perception there). So, for once, I will abandon my Cartesian ways and admit that I am writing about a mentor and concede that there are cases – even in criticism – where logic and chronology must be displaced in favour of the heart's measure.

So forget about Kenneth Clark and "The Smile of Reason." It's a cold smile and rationalism even at its best – in eighteenth-century France – served only as a tool for the imagination. And Barry Callaghan could have been one of those *Philosophes*. Poet, translator and fiction writer of some international reputation; journalist and jocular acerbic presence on television, professor and war correspondent…there is a diversity in his life that is not fragmentation, that is not a watering down of talent; only narrow people with one note to their whistles think diversity excludes coherence. "One of the great lines in Yeats," he says, "is 'nothing can be sole nor whole that has not been rent.' I rend myself all the time in search of wholeness. A moment of perception, that epiphany, is a moment of wholeness that redeems."

What he writes, never predictable and always filled with the fun of discovery, he writes for profit. "I am a journalist as Edmund Wilson said he was. Whatever I write I get paid damn well for." Let's face it, Barry Callaghan is a singular journalist in this country. He has won National Magazine awards for political writing, sports, travel – and the President's Medal twice for excellence in all fields. As a former war correspondent, he knows the jails of the Middle East as well as those of South Africa and that should tell us something about his search for truth, even if it disturbs our comfortable image of the ivory-tower professor, something he's been for twenty-one years at Atkinson College, York University in Toronto. But to stay in a contemporary context, let's agree that a recent *Saturday Night* article ("The Public Ordeal of Bryce Mackasey") gives slick quipsters and slip-shod reporters like Allan Fortheringham a lesson in professional ethics while redeeming Mackasey's ruined reputation, not by making Mackasey into a saint or martyr, but simply by seeking the truth inherent in one quite ordinary man's travail. I cannot help connecting "the Mackasey affair" to "the Dreyfus affair" and comparing Callaghan's journalistic intent and integrity with Emile Zola's in *"J'accuse."* At the same time, in *Toronto Life* he was attempting to redeem – to give a wholeness to – our sense of three forgotten peoples, the Latvians, Estonians and Lithuanians. Having gone by ship to the Baltic Sea, having been threatened by a Soviet gunboat, having marched along with Vladimir Bukovsky through the streets of Helsinki, he succeeded in redeeming those forgotten peoples as only a writer can, by making them real in our imaginations once again.

But the presence of Barry Callaghan himself as either this or that is more obvious than the unity of his vocation. If I write about the founder and publisher of *Exile* and Exile Editions, it is because I think I have seen both the coherence and the central importance of the man's achievements through his apparent diversity. But, a few more dimensions before continuing: before founding *Exile* in 1972 he was the literary editor of *The Toronto Telegram*, running a book page unlike any other before or since in this country – marked by its energy and a refusal to cow-tow to the then current nationalist trend; a senior producer with the CBC – specializing in the Middle East, Quebec and political protest movements in the United States – and the independent producer of documentaries for various networks around the world. In 1978, the Isaacs Gallery of Toronto exhibited his "Hogg Drawings" and "It was not just a showing of the melancholy colours and metaphors of mind, but a celebration. A gesture. An opening night, with fine wine and fine food, the entertainment was Downchild, the blues band. None of that mean-spirited glass of sherry and a cheese-whiz biscuit. The people I love have a generosity of spirit. I try to reciprocate, I try to celebrate, to praise. To sing the blues is to sing through pain in praise of life, like a train going through a tunnel." He has also been a commentator and conversationalist on television, winning high praise and an ACTRA award in 1984.

But more than praise, homage consists of understanding and explanation. To get a grip on his generosity – and his acid animosity to smaller minds playing it safe – we need to move between the ghost of Jacques Maritain and a unique literary celebration held one night in Toronto: "Ten Volumes of *Exile*: Ten Years of Exile Editions."

It was a fine November day in 1985 at Brock University, and from my office situated on the eleventh floor of the Arthur Schmon Tower I could see the skyline of Toronto in the distance, "that city whose dream is to be a bigger boutique," as Callaghan puts it. Two enthusiastic students had dropped by to talk about reader-response criticism. One of them, a young French-Canadian woman, was holding a familiar discourse: "Professors have always made me feel that our literature is inferior. You're the first one to give us a sense of pride. I'll be able to laugh now at the colonial statements in *The Globe and Mail*. You're right, a great writer is a reconstruction of his readers and we do have great writers . . ."

The phone rang.

"Are you coming to the party?"

It is true that a poet, first of all, is a distinct voice. I certainly recognized Barry Callaghan at the other end of the line. "The party" is again a matter of perception. I did intend to go to "the reading" at Harbourfront on Tuesday, November 19th, 1985, at 8:30 p.m., but apparently there was also to be a "post-Harbourfront" meal at a chic Queen Street bistro, *Le Bistingo*. Literature is at once public and private in its making and it does not exclude the experience of vertigo when signifiers lose their referentiality to enter the network of endless reciprocal definitions. Barry would probably cross out the preceding sentence and replace it more simply by: "Literature is life in the fast lane. Emily Dickinson, when she was writing, was in the fast lane. On the edge, and on the edge is best."

On the evening of November 19th, the Brigantine Room at Harbourfront was packed with writers, poets, painters, composers – women and men in quest of perception, of the heart's measure. They had come to pay homage, to celebrate steadfastness and style. Rare were those who, at one time or another, had not found themselves knocking on Barry Callaghan's door. The mystery, for a man who is so much on the road, is how he has managed to be home so often to those who've knocked?

The reading began, after Greg Gatenby's usual announcements, with a composition created for the evening by Norman Symonds. This processional for the writers was the overture, for everything that evening was opera, in the etymological sense – a work of art. A euphoric feeling came from the openness, *opera aperta* in the words of Umberto Eco.

More than the presence of a senior Canadian composer, the work by Norman Symonds reflected the formal and yet improvisational spirit of *Exile* and Barry Callaghan's commitment to music. "As a kid I loved to sing 'Dem bones dem bones dem dry bones' and see myself dancing in the dark, even on my own grave, white bones high-stepping, and then shouting the reprise, 'Now hear the word of the Lord,' and I'm still waiting for the word. All writers do." I thought of the way he sits and waits for words at the grand piano in the front room of his house in Chinatown, and of the paintings that surround him – Meredith, Dürer, Goya, Calder, Miró, Dix, Kollwitz, Ronald, and the portrait of him by Kurelek, and all the painting that has appeared in *Exile*, and the avant-garde scores he's published over the years in *Exile*, "an artful tinkering," as he likes to call editing. "It is a serious form of play, as life should be. So I'm not a real pianist you see, I just tinker away at that. I play the piano like I translate," the deep voice of the mentor echoes in the memory. I cannot claim to know how or why the Blues claims a corner in the core of his heart (as anyone who reads his remarkable story, "Crow

Jane's Blues," can see) but I can certainly evaluate the translations while leaving his performance at the keyboard to the judgment of his neighbours. Having closely followed for years the work of one of France's great poets, Robert Marteau, I know that his outstanding English translator is Barry Callaghan, whose translations are poems in themselves. And as the *opera aperta* at Harbourfront began I thought of Marteau's *Atlante*, especially the last two lines of that splendid and mysterious long poem. In French they vibrate through the heart and they are quite apropos in Callaghan's translation:

> There's not a star you've not seen
> but new ones now are about to be.

Perceptions again. Or, as Norman Symonds put it, "Perspective" – an essay for jazz octet (1962); how do you compose jazz, how do you improvise composition? The question brings to mind another one: "How do you grow a poet?" "You see to it," Callaghan says, "that each has his own soil. That's all that Exile is: a seed box . . . and poets are like mushrooms . . . They are the bald crowd," he says, quoting Joe Rosenblatt, "incubating in the gloom. As an editor, I am a seed bed. Not everything takes. Prose cut into short lines is not poetry, it is prose in short pants. But I try to see the thing for what it is. After all, entering into another's imagination is a way to salvation."

As the pianist Diane Roblin laid down the text for the singers – Arlene Meadows and Calla Krause – the audience laughed. To most people the music seemed nonsensical, but one had to listen with what Dorothy Livesay calls "the third ear." This was no incidental music for elevators and shopping centers, this was a more strident version of W.H. Auden's "Age of Anxiety," set to music by Norman Symonds. The man who celebrated and was celebrated that night implied another question: "How do you grow an editor?"

"I don't know," he says, "but it's obviously been sandy soil in this country. Almost no editors and even fewer critics. Look, I'll tell you something about *Exile*. There are those in this country who call it 'internationalist' – as if that were a word from which we should all recoil. Can you imagine saying to the editors of the *London Magazine* or *PoEsie* in Paris – 'You are an international journal,' expecting them to hang their heads in shame. It's laughable. But anyway, *Exile* is parochial . . . not provincial but parochial. The roots are here. I'm six generations in this soil. I'm at home here. I don't have an identity crisis, I don't feel insecure, I don't feel like a mouse under the foot of the elephant. *Exile* is of this place, it's off the streets of my town. Now if writers abroad want to find haven and close-company in the embrace of *Exile*, that's fine with me. As long as they're good enough. Even so, only a quarter of the material in *Exile* is from abroad. Frankly, most American poetry these days is not good enough: tiny perfect sentences, scrupulosity . . . a bankrupt Protestantism, wherein worry over the arteries has supplanted worry in the heart, a kind of stand-still jogging on the page. But what we have now in Toronto is not the in-grown provincialism of the 1960s and 1970s . . . at least there was an ideological shadow standing in the wings during those days . . . but now it's a mean localism. It is the culture appropriate to Prime Minister Mulroney as the perfect father, the man with no sense of smell, changing diapers and unable to smell shit. So sayeth his wife, proudly. A mean localism is loose, where even the poetry of Quebec is suddenly regarded as foreign. This is the stern, vapid localism of people at the Ontario Arts Council. Do you know they just cut back the grant to *Exile* by one-third on the grounds that Exile had 'become' internationalist. They are buffoons, the Arts Council has tried to kill *Exile*, to punish it for being what it is. In so doing, they reveal what they are."

Who and what they are, history will note as asterisks on the landscape, but *Exile* – rooted in a particularly courageous awareness – is the new literature of Canada that has been with us for the past ten years. Most general readers don't know this and fewer know that its distant roots are in Paul-Emile Borduas' *Refus Global* (1948), which is not only the source of Quebec's "Quiet Revolution," not only the key to understanding the tension between Pierre Elliott Trudeau and René Lévesque, but a major influence on writers and the working classes alike. To understand how the new Canadian literature has been moving from the margin to the center we must consider the failure of the narrow-minded theme of survival that dominated a desolate realistic vision even as late as 1972 when the first issue of *Exile* appeared. At that time the survivalists of the sixties were not ready to admit that *Refus Global* was a guide to the aesthetic future of Canada. At "learned" conferences I could only find Ray Ellenwood who agreed with me on this point and it is with great anticipation that I await Ellenwood's complete edition and translation of *Refus Global* as well as his study of Borduas' *Automatistes*. Do not get confused by the ramifications, the Exile movement is immensely coherent, even in its complexity: Ray Ellenwood is one of the associate editors of *Exile*.

A quick glance at that first issue of *Exile* would convince anyone that a new movement was born and that its raison d'être was an exquisite taste for risk without which the art that lasts is impossible. Perhaps the least of Barry Callaghan's concerns is keeping his head above water. The man is a gambler: "Call me in the morning, because then I'm home; in the afternoon, I'm at the race track. That's where I do my translations . . ."

Along with the ghost of Maritain and the ghost of Pascal's wager, it is the voice of Paul-Emile Borduas, always present since that first issue of *Exile*, that best defines the Callaghan school.

"Together we will undertake the extravagance of living under a sharpened conscience, in open honesty, and we will see what happens. The worst can only be catastrophe, which is better by far than a false success" (Paul-Emile Borduas).

At *La Maquette* on that cold December day I mentioned the Borduas quotation, suggesting that since it's always been on the first page of the magazine it must be its signature. "You're quite right. That's me, that's very much me . . ."

"Survival" will not survive this new Canadian literature, and as Callaghan said in the preface to his anthology of Canadian love poems, "Survival is a small idea, contrary to any notion of love." Ten years of *Exile* and Exile Editions have already considerably eroded the power of the old school. The future holds more "open honesty" than "false success." To Ray Ellenwood's two volumes we must add Barry Callaghan's forthcoming *Alchemists in Winter: An Anthology of Canadian Poetry in French and English*. [Editor's note: this anthology never appeared; Avon Publishers cancelled it because it was too expensive.] The introduction and selections will be a stout response to the latest of the stodgy Oxford anthologies – which will certainly be remembered as a blunder by an otherwise great Canadian writer, Margaret Atwood.

Now let's get back to the Harbourfront reading. The music stopped, Joe Rosenblatt was reading. Perspective forces me, however, to leap ahead and link two readings, two books and two major literary figures. On November 19th Joe Rosenblatt read from *Escape From the Glue Factory* (Exile: 1985). On December 11th Joe Rosenblatt read from *Poetry Hotel: Selected Poems 1963-1985* (McClelland and Stewart: 1985). It was at this later reading, held at Theatre Passe-Muraille that, after a series of his distinct chanting sound poems, Canada's Kafka cum Ambrose Bierce said: "And now my friend and mentor Barry Callaghan will read from my other book *Escape From the Glue Factory.*"

Empty words? The charming tact of literary soirées? No. *Poetry Hotel* is dedicated to Barry Callaghan. In such moments it is difficult not to gear down and meditate. Joe Rosenblatt and I have the same mentor. How many other writers scattered across this country are in the same situation? How many will have the "open honesty" to admit it? How many, caught in what Gaston Bachelard calls the Promethean complex have turned against the mentor? Why is it that in this country of survival, his generosity and "open honesty" are dismissed sullenly as "arrogance"? It will hurt a few – truth generally does – but "false success" goes hand in hand with false humility. "Arrogant!" What a peculiar Canadian complaint. Just try to insult a cab driver or poet or waiter or novelist in Paris or New York by calling him "arrogant" and he will take it as a compliment.

In this anatomy of arrogance it is difficult not to be personal. Over the past ten years Barry Callaghan has edited and published three of my stories. Not only do I believe that they are among my best so far, but I also believe that if I had listened to him ten years ago I would be a better writer today.

Critical experience is only one factor that makes me realize that the Exile movement has attracted the best creative forces of the country (and elsewhere), the best aesthetic sensibilities we have. As I listened to Seán Virgo distill a mythology for our time at Harbourfront, "The Editorial" of the first issue of *Exile* echoed in the mind:

There are many excellent reviews in which the writer of imaginative prose and poetry seems to become merely fodder for the dancing scholarly horse. The writer of the critique becomes more important than the writer of the poem, especially if the critic offers a new fund of useful scholarly information. But useful for what? It is the day of the information deluge. Who sorts it all out? The imaginative writer, who can rely only on his own eyes, his own heart and sensibility for his information, is in a sense, in exile now. There ought to be a small haven somewhere for such exiles. In these pages the imaginative writer will not be led in by a scholarly praetorian guard. He will be on his own.

(*Exile*: 1972)

We totally agree, this ex-basketball star and I (ah yes! That was his first love: see his story, "The Cohen in Cowan"). The two semantic spheres in tension are information and imagination. It is either that or give in to Plato and, more dangerously, to Hegel's view of art. But I would rather try to figure out the function of the musical scores in Seán Virgo's latest fiction in *Exile* than read again, let alone teach, *The Phenomenology of the Mind*. For art might not be what Hegel thought it could have been. Today it is more a matter of perception. Barry Callaghan can perhaps best express it in concrete terms by referring back to the *vécu* experience in sports. In "The Cohen in Cowan," one of the superb texts from *The Black Queen Stories*, an "illiterate" intuitive narrator describes a mystical moment of wholeness:

> . . . 'cause when you're alone you can get this feather touch in the fingers, your whole body light like weightless, and you take off and float with the ball, looping it up off the backboard and bam it goes swish. That's as close to perfect perfection as you're gonna get, knowing you're totally in tune between yourself and the ball, and before you even take a look you see it happen before it happens . . .

There is a strong hint here about the author's sense of unity. "The Cohen in Cowan" is a story about generosity and its power of transfiguration. Perfection – illusion or reality – is the certitude of being in touch with the God(s). Grace is a gift to be discovered in metaphysics and aesthetics alike, as a lone man spins a ball on his fingertip as if it were the whole world.

But back to information: since the end of the eighteenth century the artist has been replaced by the intellectual as a social model. Information gathering is all too often wool gathering. *Exile*, perhaps the first publication in this country to shake both colonial and émigré habits, tries to give center stage back to the artist. I am not ready to dismantle the ivory tower (nor is Callaghan, who has lectured there for twenty-one years), but I am simply suggesting that its role should be that of the ever-understanding shadow of the work of art. If there is one passion still possible for today's intellectual it is precisely the understanding of living art.

After Virgo, Timothy Findley read. His seven-minute performance (and how splendid all the "performances" were that night) was worth hours of study and meditation on Louis Riel and John A. McDonald. His were not sterilized pages from historical journals, the "found poetry" of flaccid minds. Findley did not exclude the stench of death, the absurdity of murder and the evil vapours of alcohol that are present in the mind of a great man giving birth to a country. Talent is nothing without courage. The "sharpened conscience" was alive in the voice of one of our best writers, once a fine actor in London and New York.

"There's not a star you've not seen." Others read. Gestures of generosity. Pat Lane, the poet of the West, with that tough-delicate touch of his, jumped onto the stage, put his arm around Barry and said: "This man is great, he ran a magazine for ten years!"

Gratitude? No, Pat Lane just happened to be there. He had never published in *Exile*. He had been moved. Pat Lane's intervention came from the heart's measure, from a major Canadian poet who, like those published in *Exile*, has been "on his own" for as long as I can remember. A lone star.

"New ones are about to be." The line by Robert Marteau applied to Paul William Roberts, a young novelist discovered by Callaghan. His superior wry humour, his zany sense of a bizarre middle-class English family is incomparable.

And one splendid performance followed another, giving renewed vigour to Greg Gatenby's aphorism: "An unemployed actor must have spread the word that writers are very poor readers of their own work." Judith Thompson conveyed with incredible intensity the nervous black humour of her dramatic writing. Susan Musgrave was shyly subtle with her bewitching irony, and Nicole Brossard vibrated with the intellectual intensity of a woman who has absorbed feminism, the politics of language, the echoes of Barthe, into her own seemingly easy wit.

If publishing *No Birds or Flowers* and *The Optic Heart* by Diane Keating was a mark of Barry Callaghan's confidence in another young writer, it was certainly well placed. The poems that she read, love poems called "The Dead Sky Letters," show an incredible force and confirm the suspicions I have already advanced in *Poetry Canada Review*. The erotic dimension is sustained by a dark metaphysical strength and perhaps a kind of subconscious Christian fervour. I don't know of many contemporary poets who, in the midst of highly passionate discourse, are capable of such ethically responsible lines: "Set us free, cried our unmade children, beating like blind butterflies." What others take for coincidences I take for signs. It is, therefore, no accident that *Exile* has

415

published more of Margaret Avison's work than any other literary magazine in recent memory and, on the subject of "The Optic Heart," I find Diane Keating – via Margaret Avison – close to that Maritain perception:

> Nobody stuffs the world in at your eyes.
> The optic heart must venture: a jail-break
> and re-creation.

Optics, other venturing, another sign: on December 9th I went to the opening of Claire Weissman Wilks' retrospective exhibition at the Pauline McGibbon gallery. The drawings kept bringing back to mind the poetry of Diane Keating, in so far as there was absolutely no will to disconnect eroticism and motherhood in either artist. I heard Claire say: "You have come to contemplate the perversions of my soul."

Beyond the humour, I was struck again by the presence of the word "soul." I have the feeling that Claire or Barry would disagree with my attempt to see a Catholic element within the *Exile* movement, but I don't know many other influential Canadian artists or writers who are familiar with Adam of St. Victor, the theological paradoxes inherent in the figure of Judas investigated by the early church in Egypt, and what I will call a salutary Basilian influence (it was Saint Basil who articulated the theology of the beautiful devil, a seduction that can only lead to catastrophe and never to false success). In moments of perplexity Barry mumbles significant *bons mots:* "I hope God will forgive me, and if he doesn't I won't forgive him either."

What I am trying to say is that we have reached the age of ideological orphanages. Exiles in their own hearts, let alone in their own countries. My own preference goes to theological orphans rather than to Marxist or philosophical ones. As Diane Keating states: "Making love like writing poetry is a breaking apart." One thinks of Claire Weissman Wilks' *Two of Us Together: Each of Us Alone*. The sense of the felt emotional pain prior to motherhood is carried through *Tremors* and *Hillmother*. As for the religious inclination, it shines through the simplicity of Keating's line: "My eyes glimmered, you said, like icon candles in a Byzantine church." And one of the drawings from *Medallions: The Thinking Heart* comes to mind: a picture of a child-mother holding what one could see as Siamese twins as large as herself. Claire Weissman Wilks has captured an ultimate deviation of the Virgin and Child motif. In icons, the eyes are expressionless as if they were looking towards the inside. The same awareness leads the poet and the painter towards the optic, thinking heart – the only measure. So, *Exile* is not independent of a theological culture, though the culture is probably unrecognizable to orthodox theologians; it is true, you see, that choir boys go to the race track, and the song they sing in both places is *Regina Caeli*, though pictures convince me more than the words in this area and one image reappears: the late Marshall McLuhan (yes, he is in the tenth anniversary issue of *Exile*) reading the epistle on Sunday at St. Michael's Church.

In hac lacrimarum valle: The point stems from an awareness of suffering. "The bead of light in a gull's bill hook is god's only tear," as Callaghan has written in *As Close As We Came*. The scavenging pain that contains the light of god's sorrow. Pain is the reference point in the visionary drawings, *Medallions*. The pain of women on the edge of camps and prisons which leads to the realization that there is no end to the reincarnation of *Mater Dolorosa*. Michelangelo's *Pietà* was an attempt to illustrate divine suffering through human symptoms. The post-holocaust theology must also imply a post-holocaust aesthetics. Avoiding easy sentimentality, we

417

find in the Exile movement an adequate response, the coming to terms with new forms of grace. As Leonard Cholet, the old doctor in "Anybody Home?" (*The Black Queen Stories*), puts it: "You should listen to your own heart, eh? How's that for a little truth, except most people nowadays try to think with their head instead of their heart."

The Black Queen Stories is dedicated to "Claire" and these stories seem to be another form of that theology of *The Thinking Heart*. The practice of any aesthetics based on faith rather than reason requires boldness and compassion, in Kenneth Burke's logological sense. As the Illuminists stood at the origin of the Romantic movement, a Catholic culture is behind Exile's. Pragmatic survival is a serious thematic limitation for those who perpetuate and modify a stout spiritual tradition. The presence of two international literary figures as "Contributing Editors" of *Exile* confirms the metaphysical dimension I am trying to reveal: Yehuda Amichai and John Montague – who also dedicated his *Selected Poems* to Barry Callaghan. Montague has written about his own place not only in the landscape but in time – echoing Callaghan's words:

> To fly into risk,
> attempt the dream,
> cast off, as we have done,
> requires true luck
> who knows ourselves
> blessed . . .
>
> Hushed and calm,
> safe and secret,
> on the edge is best.

I return to the evening of November 19th, to recall for an instant the geological humour of David Donnell, and how Gaston Miron captured the crowd with his deeply sensual poetry and how each poem was preceded by Barry Callaghan's reading of an English version. Play and laughter and performance shared. One man founded L'Hexagone in 1953, the other founded *Exile* in 1972; editorial dedication and generosity didn't make either of them lesser poets, or presences, and both preceded that other great presence, Morley Callaghan, the dean of Canadian letters, who read a story his son had left out of the new collection, *The Lost and Found Stories of Morley Callaghan*. Lost and found, the harmony between father and son, a joshing laughter – a sign of life and hope for us all. No Promethean complex there!

These tumbling images lead back to a coherent centre, to the *intermezzo* of that unforgettable evening, because between the two sets of readings, which I have tried to evoke according to the heart's measure and not chronologically, a unique intermission took place: "The William Ronald Show."

William Ronald is a painter of international reputation, flamboyant and larger than life and closely connected to the Exile movement. He has earned for himself, like his friend Barry Callaghan, that very Canadian title: "Arrogant!" But what I saw that evening was a man full of vulnerable energy, the self-created pop art personality broadcasting at a more intense level. The man is like his paintings, strikingly colourful and rooted in abstract expressionism (his younger brother, John Meredith, is also a fine painter, and as with the Callaghans, one notices art in the family).

But it is a very special book by Ronald, *The Prime Ministers* (*Exile:* 1983), that illustrates his creative connections with the Exile movement. The book is well defined in the inside cover:

No one like the great painter, William Ronald, has tried to portray the Prime Minister of Canada. No one has taken the information about these 16 men, seeking the core of their characters and accomplishments, and then painted their portraits. The paintings, each different in size and technique, each a response to the personality and largeness of the man, are each unique – filled with mystery, humour, anger and admiration. Accompanying the painted portraits – presented in full colour – are written histories of each Prime Minister, as well as Ronald's reflections on the completed paintings, and photographs of the painter at work in his studio.

These were visions rooted in a response to actual history – orthodox history transformed so that each PM emerged as a rehabilitated orphan in Ronald's imagination . . . and it should be no surprise, therefore, that the most powerful presence and "orphan" among us – exiled between the nation's love and hate, opened Ronald's exhibition of these "portraits" – Pierre Elliott Trudeau. The book contains a page of acknowledgements that ends with a reference to the editor:

> And thanks to my old friend,
> Barry Callaghan, who always helps
> me make it through the night.

Ronald is not debilitated by what Sartre called "*esprit de sérieux.*" If one is content with superficial judgments one might dismiss William Ronald the showman, but the show is only a way of telling a large truth. Show and tell: a child's game, the artist's aim. Imagine on stage the Peter Appleyard Quartet, an exotic dancer, the George Chuvalo Boxing Club (Chuvalo: an old Callaghan friend for thirty years) and in the midst of all this, dressed like Super-Man-à-la-Liberaci, William Ronald painting "Exile" on a large canvas. Imagine the faces, the reactions and the scrupulous comments! But, in that unique moment there resided the essence of "the extravagance of living under a sharpened conscience" – the essence of the Exile movement. "Extravagance is a form of vulnerability, and all public vulnerability is an act of generosity," Callaghan says. "The problem with a crowd, the bourgeois shall we say, is that they like to understand what they should imagine and they love to imagine what they should understand." The dancer was exquisite and skilled, the boxers were very good, the Peter Appleyard Quartet was superb and the painting improvised in that euphoric atmosphere was sublime. Any man rich enough and with a minimum of appreciation for post-expressionism would have bought the painting then and there. But more important, when all was said and painted – when the boxers had punched themselves out – the crowd was completely persuaded of the authenticity of the moment, persuaded that a painting had been begun and completed before their very eyes and both catastrophe and fake success had been side-stepped, leaving us with a work of art and the memory of a marvelous gesture.

The evening ended with a special tribute from the composer, Harry Somers. As they had in the overture, the musical performers again gave a splendid interpretation to the finale – a joyful and daring piece, a coherent collage of discord that brought to mind the poster Callaghan had constructed for the walls of the city to announce the evening's celebration: the letters of the poster spelling out "*Exile* and Exile Editions" were the surrealistic letter collages of Ludwig Zeller . . . all the paraphernalia, the bits and pieces of the engraved past, shaped into the sounds of our articulate lives, so that the past ten years of publishing were alive in the promise of a future, imaginatively re-shaped, letter by letter.

This ingathering of the past to inform the future leads me to the photography of Nigel Dickson (featured in the anniversary issue). "The party" referred to earlier was not the reading. The invitation, printed on a small poster, said: "To celebrate ten years and ten volumes Exile Editions and Exile invite you to a post-Harbourfront repast of white wine, moules, dessert and cappuccino at *Le Bistingo* . . ." The illustration was particularly meaningful to me: "The bar at Lamberene Airport, Gabon, by Nigel Dickson."

The word is full of coincidences, I read them like signs. You have to know that the man at the bar wearing sun glasses is Barry Callaghan (you have to know that because he looks like a younger William Ronald). There are similar pictures in my family album in France. For about eight years my father was President of the University of Libreville. From the sparse letters and postcards he sent me during those years, I could never figure out his fascination for Africa. What I could understand however is that those years made him more aware, more intense, and I know that Callaghan himself had gone into the jungles in search of leper camps, the leper's kiss, which he accepted. Once, my father showed me the little statuettes he carried with him against bad luck. The other day Barry pulled a similar object – a goat's horn carved into the shape of a crouching figure – out of his pocket: "It is how I ward off evil. Evil is often a wound that will not heal, privation of love." Here, I can only rely on the reader's silence.

By about midnight on that November 19th, I was walking outside Harbourfront in the rain looking for a taxi. I was in Toronto not in Libreville, and convinced that I had witnessed a unique event in our literary history, certainly a moment unique in the history of Harbourfront. But of all the readings that lingered in the mind it was Barry's that echoed most surely. I was almost arguing with myself, perhaps not willing to admit that this man who can turn "catastrophes" into true "successes" could have also impressed me as one of the country's best poets. I was even ready to concede that I should start carrying a Gabon statuette in my pocket. From *The Hogg Poems* (General Publishing: 1978), Barry had read "John the Conqueroo," a monologue by a black teenager who is faster than the mechanical cowboy of our culture. It was perhaps the most difficult text that evening because of its marginality (and it was certainly outside the mainstream of Atwood's bungled Oxford book: the Hogg poem fit neither the feminist attitude of our times nor the bogus pioneer spirit of survivalism – so Callaghan's work was left out of that anthology – an insult not to him, but to readers of poetry), but John the Conqueroo had come vividly to life through the dialect and the accompaniment of Fraser Finlayson's blues harp. By the time I caught a cab a distant memory had come, not without sadness, to the rescue of my understanding. The underrating of Barry Callaghan had been explained to me when I was a student in Arezzo, by one of my Dominican teachers: "It is hard to be the best at everything, people just don't believe you!"

Finally I reached *Le Bistingo*. I sat with *Exile* editors Nora Pratt and Ray Ellenwood and that legend in our time, Gaston Miron. With Exile you can expect the extraordinary. After the superb moules – with fine white wine in silver buckets at each table – and just before rich desserts, three young women drifted away from the bar and began to sing songs of the forties. They sang *a capella* with mimetic humour. Called *The Spadina Sisters* they were better than most professionals, but are unemployed. Street singers plucked off the street by Callaghan and placed in the centre of things, already a part of history by being there.

More than anything else, what might explain the magic of the atmosphere and the conversations that evening is another "Testament of Youth" (a wartime composition by Harry Somers, a lament for the young fallen in action). Gaston Miron, as well as *Exile*, had that year lost a friend: Michel Beaulieu (1941-1985). I felt the absence, I had just reviewed Beaulieu's *Spells of Fury* for *PCR*. From the ghost of Jacques Maritain to the perception of one of Québec's greatest poets, a few lines will suffice to illustrate a permanence reminiscent of François Villon. In the fine translation by Arlette Francière:

> There is a colour missing in this hunting scene
> add some with just enough white-lead
> we don't die once but slowly
> on the spit of days and skyscrapers.

And Miron – who has seen his own death – danced. And Miron played his harmonica. And Miron drank. But in all that *joie de vivre* the epiphany came as testament. He put his hand on my arm, looked at me intensely and said: "Michel, he ate too much. His heart couldn't take it. You don't know how many times I warned him!" The extravagant warning the extravagant about the fullness of life.

Miron showed me his selected poems translated into Italian. One absence reminds me of another: the extraordinary Robert Zend who "didn't like parties," the Hungarian intellectual who, at those parties, spoke to me in perfect Italian and who one day asked me if I would translate *Oab* into French. I almost choked on my wine. *Oab* fans such as Northrop Frye, Marcel Marceau and Glen Gould – wherever he is – will understand my reaction.

The unique Robert Zend had a section, the embryo of *Oab*, in the first issue of *Exile* (1972), and the anniversary issue (1985) is dedicated to him, deceased this past summer. Two volumes, *Oab I* and *Oab II* are an ultimate "Testament of Youth," the first real break-through in the area of literary imagination since James Joyce's *Finnegans Wake*: in the words of *Oab*'s patient editor and publisher who nursed the book out of Zend over thirteen years, it is the record of an amazing "life collapsing into fullness."

But looking at the fullness of *The Hogg Poems* is perhaps the key to entering the multiple profiles of the first Canadian literary movement of real international weight. Hogg – a someone from nowhere – is at once a part of Jerusalem and of Toronto – of this world and not of this world. It was 5 a.m. and I was still walking the streets of Hogtown, trying to nurse a lifelong insomnia that has baffled my doctors. Each one of us has a different method for achieving that indispensable "sharpened conscience." I passed Union Station where Saint Hogg, after having done his subway-stations, came up for air:

> call Hogg precursor obsolete,
> but nonetheless alive to hope as more than survival,
> to prayer as more than madness, to death
> as more than a sigh.

A Catholic culture, an acute sense of the local as the mirror of the universal, a fecundation of survival by compassion and, above all, Hogg's "search for singularity" – these are the dimensions of the Exile movement.

Two very recent books confirm the coherence of Barry Callaghan's editorial vision. The first marks, I hope, the definitive return of David Wevill, a very fine poet acclaimed in England but the victim of silence in Canada. Bruce Meyer, of McMaster University, makes clear why *Other Names for the Heart: New and Selected Poems 1964-1984* was published by Exile Editions.

In 1966, the Governor General's Award Committee selected Margaret Atwood's *The Circle Game* as the poetry prize winner. That decision marked the beginning of a decade or more of an almost pro-national emphasis in Canadian verse, an era in which influences from abroad, especially from British and European poetry, became markedly less noticeable. The other major contender for the 1966 Governor General's Award for Poetry was David Wevill's *A Christ of the Ice-Floes*.

From the poem that gave the early book its title, a few lines will suffice to establish the spiritual connection:

And the ice-floes ducking downriver like drowned sheep
Or so many souls, in the mind,
Starved water, without fish rising . . .

The poet as the Good Shepherd, like Saint Hogg, passed through betrayal to reach redemption: the sacred has been brought to the profane. Christianity, even in its decline, must be experienced. We are not dealing here with ideals of secular humanism. Aesthetically and ethically the vision of Barry Callaghan, the writer as well as the editor, does not correspond to Albert Camus' "Religion without God" and has nothing in common with Wallace Stevens' "Cathedral of breath." They are not sacramentalists and, whether or not he believes in God, Callaghan is.

It was 6 a.m. and, beyond the masks, beyond the echoing of past carnivals, I found my answer. It was 6 a.m. and I was finishing Callaghan's translation of Jacques Brault's *Moments Fragiles*. It is the last of these *Fragile Moments* that touches the source of inspiration:

Like loving coming to a dead end
swollen with infantile hope
I'll carry coldness down the mountain
clattering among the shivering cicadas

and once stars shine in haste
I will shed my last wound
supine sun snake refreshed
in the course grass I will let your night settle
on my mouth   impenetrable peace?

This is a distinct discourse of orphans that leaves the reader with singular biblical hypogrammes. We are outside in the cold, in the dark, in that tenebrous space where clattering and gnashing of teeth are constantly heard. Grace, in our space, is only a memory, unless enlivened by love. As at the end of *Finnegans Wake*, there is a hint of a return to a cold "Father" and it is in the fragility of that faint suggestion that the poet will begin to search for another route to distant grace, to that "impenetrable peace." Barry Callaghan's own *As Close as We Came* – already translated into French, Serbian, and Spanish – stems from such certitude: the search always takes place out of grace and that quest is the only human possibility. Northrop Frye elaborates the point from a slightly different perspective:

> *As Close As We Came* deals symbolically with the power of love and imagination struggling to keep alive in a setting of cold, repressiveness and terror. What seem at first like prosaic statements come to resonate with repeated rereading, and become a poignant drama of the precariousness of life in a world devoted to death.

Beyond easy sentimentality, thinking remains too precious to be left to the mind alone. As for the heart, it does have other names: perception and imagination, but never sleep. "We are commanded," Barry Callaghan said to me at *La Maquette*, the walls alive with his son's colours, "to go in the dark, mouth against mouth. But I refuse. That's no tribal god of mine. I disobey. Each step we take is a sign in the light,

no matter how cold, that we are here." And he quoted
one of his own poems:

It all begins in the end,
we know what love is
when it's over,
the trail of two people
bending into the echo of their own laughter
across a lake fresh with snow.
"And this, this," you cried, looking back,
"is the whiteness of God's mind.
Without us he is nothing."

THE BIG MAN

Lauren B. Davis

Asked to contribute to this collection, I found myself thinking about a particular incident which took place at the Ottawa Writers Festival some years ago. In my mind it perfectly illustrated what I wanted to say about Barry Callaghan, who I call The Big Man, about his generosity, his kindness, his big heart. So, I began by writing up that incident, but the problem was, in isolation, it didn't tell the truth about Barry. Left alone on the page it was just a nice bit of courtesy, one writer to another. The impression I tried to convey was cramped, not doing him justice at all.

So, start again. The problem is: there's too much to say about The Big Man. He's big in *that* sort of way. The sort that is hard to contain on a page.

I remember someone once said that in literature one is always at odds to say more than what's on the page. And then there's that joke about eating an elephant a mouthful at a time. Barry's that kind of big.

Big voice.
Big personality.
Big appetites.
Big opinions.
Big talent.
Big intellect.
Big heart.

It's the size of that heart which drew me to his work in the first place. The characters in his work are imagined through a lens of compassion for the great, messy human condition. He has a sense of sorrow, as well, about the way the world works and the way we keep missing each other, about the pain we do through things done and things undone. Perhaps that is what motivates not only the compassion in his work, but also the way he lives his life, the way he has been a friend to me, and I know for a fact, to many others.

But it is very big. Big indeed, this task of reducing The Big Man down to a single essay, and the only way to proceed, I suppose, is in the tried and true methodology of chewing it over one bite at a time.

When First I Heard Him

When the phone rang I was in that deep bag-of-wet-sand-heavy sort of sleep which is decidedly difficult to shake off.

"Hello?" I probably said.

"Yeah, this is _____"

I turned on a light, tried to read the dial on my watch, but my eyes squinted shut in the sudden glare. The voice on the other end of the phone was a sort of growling rumble. I had no idea what the man (for a voice like that can only come from a man) was saying. "I'm sorry, who is this?"

"It's_____"

I still wasn't getting it.

"Just a moment," I said, rather testily, possibly. "I was sleeping. Give me a moment."

If I expected an apology from the voice on the other end of the line, I didn't get one. Just that sort of rumbly grumble. I began to think it was an ex-boyfriend who was given to calling now and again, years apart sometimes, and who expected me to know who it was simply by the depth of the murmur, a grunt he considered manly and seductive, poor dear. It would be just like him, as well, not to realize that although it might be only six o'clock in the evening in New York, it was midnight in Paris.

I was on my feet now. Blinking.

"Are you there?" the voice said, perhaps slightly annoyed. Not the ex-boyfriend, I could tell that now, but whoever it was wasn't getting the reception they intended, I thought.

"Yes, I'm here. Now, say it again, please. Who is this?"

"Barry Callaghan."

The name, I regret to say, meant absolutely nothing to my poor sleep-drugged brain.

"Barry . . ."

"Callaghan. Barry Callaghan," he repeated.

"Barry Callaghan," I repeated for what I'm sure we both hoped was the last time. Perhaps he'd think it was the telephone connection that was bad, and not my synapses. "Forgive me," I said, with a small prickle of fear starting to form in my voice. "I'm at a loss." My husband was traveling, somewhere far away. Was this Callaghan with the airline? Had something dreadful happened?

"Exile Editions. Toronto. You sent me a short story."

"Uh-huh." (Flash of sudden understanding.) "Oh, God! *Exile*. Of course, *Exile*. Tiff Findley told me to send it to you. *Exile*. Great literary journal. Barry . . ."

"Callaghan."

"Yes, yes, of course it is."

"I liked it," he said.

"You liked it."

"The story. I'm going to print it."

"You are kidding me."

"I am not kidding you."

And that was the first time I heard it: the great wide grin of pleasure in the voice. He was having, now that I understood his mission, a truly marvelous time.

I waffled on at some length, I fear, and in some continuing discombobulation. It was the first story I'd had published. Barry sounded amused, and still more pleased. He asked me if I knew Mavis Gallant. I said I knew her work. He said, "Well, when you meet her you can tell her you are published in the same magazine which has published her."

Which I thought was an odd sort of thing to say, since I doubted I would ever, even though I lived in Paris, meet the Great Gallant.

I didn't know Barry very well then. Didn't know the generosity of spirit which moves The Big Man.

The Time He Saved My Life

It was in 2000, in the autumn, at the Ottawa Writers Festival. It was the first such festival I had been invited to, and I had no idea what to expect. I was nervous and feeling vulnerable and in bad need of a friendly face, someone with a few tips on protocol and general survival. In fact, I felt very much like The New Kid on the block, the little girl who had only been invited to the birthday party because my mother had called the hostess and begged. Not really as good as the rest, a sort of charity case. (I am told, by the way, that many writers feel this way from time to time, regardless of evidence to the contrary, and I'm much better now.)

It started badly. The week before I finished reading a book by a Alistair MacLeod, *No Great Mischief*, and I thought it was wonderful. Really wonderful. The sort of book about which I would have written a gushing review, if I wrote reviews. As fate would have it, as I stepped out of the taxi in front of the hotel where all we writers were staying, Alistair was getting out of a car just behind me, with one of the organizers who had picked him up from the airport.

Without thinking, I rushed up to him. Well, all right, I probably sort of pounced on him. I introduced myself and launched into a blather of "What a wonderful book! Oh, how I loved it! Oh, you are a rare genius! Filled me with envy, but in a good way!" And more of that kind of thing. Alistair, who I have since learned is a very shy man indeed, stood mute, while his colour rose like a thermometer in a kiln, and finally muttered something that may or may not have been, *thank you* and dashed away, leaving me to fear that my first act at the festival was to have scared the headliner to death.

I went to my room, unpacked, and located to the hospitality suite hoping for a little companionship and perhaps the merest suggestion of belonging. The room was stuffed to the gills with a lot of people I didn't recognize, all of them smoking which was a problem since I am horrifically allergic to cigarette smoke. There was, as I recall, a small kitchen already littered with empty beer bottles and some cheese, turning up at the corners in the overheated air, some stale crackers, pretzels and potato chips. The food was being ignored in favour of wine and beer. There were a lot of Important Writers from other countries talking to each other in a language I didn't speak. They were also drinking heavily and since I don't drink anymore, I refused, I hope politely, six or seven times, what I'm sure was a very well-intentioned beer from a very tall man with ruddy cheeks who only looked more and more perplexed. I sat there for a while, trying to make conversation, but mostly just coughing and sneezing and at last tossed in the white flag and retreated to my room.

Suffice it to say that by the next morning I had been reduced to tears twice, once by someone who certainly didn't mean to hurt my feelings, and once, I'm afraid, by someone who did. I was firmly convinced that the best I could hope for was a weekend of doing my job, gritting my teeth and getting back on the plane for home, where someone actually loved me. Oh, I was most pitiful. I came into the breakfast room, looking, I'm sure, somewhat rumpled from a bad night's sleep and there sat The Big Man and The Lovely Claire. The only people other than me up this early, it seemed.

Other than that first midnight phone call, I had only met them once before at this stage, at a launch party for *Exile*, and we really hadn't had a chance to say much to each other. Now, however, they asked me to join them and I gratefully accepted. Within moments they were teaching the man behind the counter how to make *macchiato* rather than the oily, insipid coffee on offer. They began to tell stories about being in Italy, and then in Ireland with John Montague and the lovely dinners they'd had talking about poetry long into the night and then I told a story about Ireland, in full accent, and they both laughed and we moved on to stories of Italian gangsters and who gets to take communion at a mafia wedding and we were all doing bad accents and laughing and somehow I knew I was going to be all right after all. I had been plucked out of the turbulent waters.

We spent the weekend together and gave our readings together and went out to dinner and The Big Man introduced me to everyone who approached and then we all went to the house of a friend of my husband's, where The Big Man shot a few hoops and then he told more stories about Golda Meir, Pierre Trudeau and, of course, Morley, and I told stories about Rockhead's Paradise and living in France, and there were times I laughed so hard my sides hurt.

In fact, that weekend is when I fell in love with The Big Man and The Lovely Claire. You just can't help but fall in love with people who save your life. I told them, much later, what they had meant to me that weekend when I felt so alone and so lost and vulnerable. The Big

Man just laughed The Big Laugh and said, "What you don't understand is that you saved *our* lives!"

Which was a typically generous thing to say.

The Introductions

My husband and I were living in Paris when The Big Man and Lovely Claire, with friends, Joe and Vera Gagan, John Reeves and his partner Bev in tow, came to visit. There were lots of dinners and walks about town and a lunch I arranged with some young Canadian literary ex-pats at which The Big Man was extraordinarily gracious, even to the poet who was so nervous around him he simply couldn't stop talking. We were a big group, in mostly small rooms, such as the centuries-old stone basement where a reading was arranged and where The Big Man's head nearly brushed the curved gothic ceiling every time he stomped his foot and bounced while performing "John the Conqueroo" to a rapt audience.

We went to the horse races, of course. It was opening day at Chantilly and serious business, with all the attendant hats and frocks and Romanian pickpockets, champagne and Mongolian horsemen doing amazing things with goatskins between races, all sinew and bone and black hair and flashing teeth. We all lost money, I think, but The Big Man, wouldn't, in true gambler's fashion, disclose anything so gauche.

And then, one afternoon, Barry said, "We have to see Mavis Gallant before we go. Let's take her to tea at Lutecia. Can you call her?"

I was sure I could.

I called, explained who I was and that The Big Man would very much like to take her to tea. I learned that Madame Gallant loves this sort of thing, a big man with flowers in hand and good, gracious manners who will hold the door open and make sure there is lemon for the tea.

I did not expect to be included, since I did not know Mavis Gallant personally, was only an admirer of her work. But this was The Big Man, after all, and of course I was included. "You should know her," he said, "You should know her."

And so my husband and I found ourselves in the very grand tea salon at Hotel Lutecia, sipping Assam and Earl Grey and nibbling *petit biscuits* and listening to Mavis Gallant tell The Big Man the story of her first lunch alone in Paris, at La Coupole where the waiters gave her a very good seat, even if she was a woman alone in the 1950s and she had white wine and oysters and read the paper and felt she had found herself, at last, at home.

Madame Gallant is tiny now, her back stooped with arthritis and when in repose her face can look quite severe, but oh, when she smiles, all the chandeliers of Lutecia tinkle in admiration.

I was part of that, thanks to The Big Man.

And yes, I did tell her that we were both now published in *Exile*, although Madame Gallant has the added distinction of having published I-don't-know-how-many stories in *The New Yorker*.

The New Year's Eve parties at The Big Man's house, once the house of Morley, his father, are legendary and I'm sure someone else has written about them – the wonderful food prepared by John Henry Jackson, who used to own the much-missed Underground Railroad Restaurant, Willie Dixon on the CD player and all the interesting people, like Larry Zolf, Michael Keefer and Janice Kulyk Keefer, Priscila Uppal, Chris Doda, Daniel David Moses, Austin Clarke, Graeme Gibson and Margaret Atwood, who let me try on her fabulous Spanish shawl. All of us there and getting to know each other because of The Big Man's generosity and sense of great times. The last time I was at The Big Man's house for dinner I met Gabriela who recently married Barry's son, Michael, in Mexico. Gabriela is indescribably beautiful with skin the colour of toffee and hair the colour of a raven's wing and eyes of dark amber. She is also as talented a painter as Frieda Kahlo in my opinion. While we sit at the table she comes up behind The Big Man, kisses him on the top of his head and calls him, *Poppi*.

He melts before my eyes, becomes a Big Man of Ooze, with a silly, perfect grin that says life is good when all is said and done. Oh, but it's splendid to see.

And so we go on . . .

There is a certain weariness about The Big Man these days. He's working as fiercely as ever though, on his books of essays, which clearly establish him an unparalleled man of letters, as though there had ever been any doubt. He dedicates a copy of *Raise You Ten* to me and it says, *"We go on, to the last worn out knot of breath . . ."*

Let others talk about his art, his contribution to literature, to journalism, to Canada, and all that. I want to say something else: I want to say that beyond mattering as a writer, he matters as a man. I am not the first writer just starting out who has been picked up and tucked under the arm of The Big Man. Canadian publishing is well-seasoned with us, although, I am sad to say, not all young ambitious things understand the value of such a friendship, for true friendship it is. There have been wounds, I am sad to report, and although The Big Man doesn't dwell on them, the shadows are there now and then, just below the eyes. Isn't it even more the measure of the man, then, that he goes on, as ever, generous and excited to discover a new voice, to listen to a new story, to make a new introduction?

When we stop publishing, stop writing even, when no one remembers our names, when our reputations, such as they were, have receded into the smoke and mirrors of history, our accomplishments forgotten, when all that's left, if we're lucky, are a few scratches on the cave wall, we will be judged by what carries on after us, by each heart we've healed and each hand we've extended to the lonely, the soul-hungry, the struggling. It is the heart that matters in the final analysis, all else is, I believe, mere metaphor.

Barry Callaghan is The Big Man with a big heart, beating away in that big chest, that weary rack of boot-bruised and memory-bearing bones. I am honored to call him friend.

BARRY CALLAGHAN,
TRANSLATION, EXILE

RAY ELLENWOOD

A list of translations published in the 120 issues (and counting!) of Exile: The Literary Quarterly *magazine, as well as a tentative bibliography of book-length translations published by Exile Editions, are attached at the end of this collection. (These appendices were compiled with help from Priscila Uppal, Michael Callaghan, and Gabriela Campos, as well as Christina Sacchetti and Matt Carrington.) They show how much this subject deserves a serious study, but what follows is more reminiscence than research, more anecdote than analysis, "the Fruits," as Swift's persona wrote in his "Dedication to Prince Posterity," "of a very few leisure Hours, stolen from the short Intervals of a World of Business, and of an Employment quite alien from such Amusements as this."*

In *Raise you Five*, Barry included translations of two short Russian poems by Andrei Voznesensky: "First Ice," done in 1972, and "Goya," tried in the *Toronto Telegram* in 1968, and completed but not published in 1974. These were news to me. I'd assumed his first published translations were the first I'd seen: selections from Robert Marteau's *Atlante* in *Exile* magazine in 1977. So the practice that Gabriel Garcia Marquez called "a healthy pastime of the kind the Jesuit Fathers used to call solitary pleasures" has deeper roots in Callaghan than I thought, going back to his studies of Russian at U of T and especially to the literary pages of *The Telegram*. I also did not know that the presence in *The Telegram* of translations of international poets had a lot to do with Barry's friendship with John Montague. Montague began living and writing in Paris in the sixties with his French wife, an integral part of a circle of poets including Michel Deguy, André Frenaud, Philippe Jaccottet, Robert Marteau and others, many of whom eventually found themselves translated by Montague and published in *Exile*, probably enough to make up a small anthology (never collected for publication, to my knowledge) of some of the best poetry from France in the latter half of the twentieth century. Barry was introduced to that circle, and it's not surprising that when Marteau moved to Quebec, living there for some years, he maintained a close friendship with Barry, becoming one of the most-translated poets in *Exile*, besides translating Barry's *Hogg* poems into French. Much of the story of this circle of international and intratranslatorial poets was pre-history to me. Barry writes briefly about the scene, and about translation, in "Black Light," also published in *Raise you Five*. I'll get back to that, but first of all, some comments on *Exile* and translation strictly from my own point of view.

Hired by Atkinson College a few years after Barry, I was soon drawn into the *Exile* orbit. He showed me a translation of *Bien-être*, a short play by the Quebec poet, Claude Gauvreau. I didn't yet know Gauvreau's work, but I knew about him and the Automatist Movement through Doug Jones, the poet from the Eastern Townships whose translations of Paul-Marie Lapointe would eventually be published by Exile Editions. From the very first number, *Exile* magazine has sported, usually on the page facing its table of contents, a couple of sentences translated from Paul-Emile Borduas' *Projections libérantes*. Borduas was a painter and mentor of the Automatist Movement, and Barry was probably introduced to them by Rita Letendre, a painter enjoying a huge reputation in Toronto at the time, who had exhibited with some of the Borduas group early in her career.

Anyway, the translation of Claude Gauvreau didn't live up to Barry's expectations and he asked me to check it against the original. It turned out to be a sad deflation of some of the most audacious poetry I'd seen, so Barry asked me to do my own version, and there began a long and complex collaboration. Fresh from my studies in French Surrealism, I was eager to find out about the Automatist group and other Quebec writers, and Barry was willing to publish anything of value from all my areas of interest, even though Surrealism and its off-shoots were not really his cup of tea, and the Quebec nationalists I admired had, by this time, soured for him. Yet there he was handing me *Cotnoir*, by Jacques Ferron, surely the most erudite and incisive Quebec nationalist (not to mention anti-Trudeauist) alive. *Cotnoir* had already been Englished, unfortunately, but *Exile* eventually published three volumes of my translations of Ferron, not to mention my translations and book on the Automatists. And in the meantime, through my *Exile* publications, I was making connections with other translators and writers from Quebec (have a look at those early numbers of *Exile* — the gang's all there, and in the company of an amazing international crowd). Besides the Canadians, Barry got me to translate the Haitian-American, Surrealist-oriented poet Philippe Thoby-Marcelin (how did Barry find out about him, and why didn't we do more?), while my own contacts in France led us to do poetry and a long prose piece by the magnificent Egyptian-French Surrealist, Joyce Mansour, as well as spreads on the expatriate Canadian Surrealist artists Jean Benoît and Mimi Parent (which reminds me that we also need a serious study of *Exile* and visual arts).

I mention my own experiences and interests in order to make a few points that may seem obvious, but need emphasizing. Writers of any kind need a place to publish their work, and translators didn't have a wide choice in the 1970s. Granted, there were increased opportunities with the recent inception of Canada Council grants in aid of translation and there was a quickening interest among English-Canadians in things Québécois. The larger publishing houses felt more able to bring out translations, at least of best-selling authors like Gabrielle Roy or Marie-Claire Blais. But the translation and publication of less mainstream writers (at the time), such as Ferron, Roch Carrier, Michel Tremblay, Victor-Lévy Beaulieu, Nicole Brossard, and France Théoret were mainly left to smaller publishing houses (thus Exile Editions published Ray Chamberlain's translation of a play by Marie-Claire Blais, but her more popular prose works were done by larger houses, who could pay her more). *Exile* magazine was among the front-runners in the translation of Québécois literature, publishing not just excerpts but, in the case of my versions of *Papa Boss* and *The Cart*, whole novellas. Canada Council translation grants did not cover work published in periodicals, so translating for *Exile* magazine didn't pay, but it offered not only an opportunity of seeing your work in print, but of taking a printed page to prospective book publishers. Translations in *Exile* began early in 1972, but the first Exile Edition books didn't appear until 1976. This meant that someone like Sheila Fischman published translations of Roch Carrier in the magazine, but published the book-length versions with Anansi, while Ray Chamberlain and others, including myself, turned to Coach House Press. In fact, a certain irritation at seeing complete works he had first published in *Exile* becoming books from Coach House and Anansi was surely one of the main reasons Barry launched Exile Editions. And this little rivalry between publishers was certainly good for the translators. In the early years, many of us published with at least two of the small presses, then tended to go with one, as I did with Exile Editions, essentially because of a happy working relationship with Barry.

Publishing books in translation became a way of getting money quickly to writers who really needed it (Gwendolyn MacEwen being one), because the Canada Council grant, though modest, was paid up front, with a percentage upon signing of a contract and the rest on publication. It's hard to make a living writing poetry, and the odd translation could help baby get a new pair of shoes. The results, in Gwendolyn MacEwen's case, are brilliant translations of ancient and modern Greek literature, surely worthy of a lot more attention than they have received. Exile Editions, generally, was seen by translators as one of the better houses for respecting contracts and for acknowledging us on the covers of books, something the larger houses were slow to imitate.

It might be of interest, for the sake of comparison, to look at some information on the publication of translations by House of Anansi and Coach House Press, Exile Editions' main competitors in Toronto. (Thanks to Stephen Cain for this information.) Anansi soon recognized it had a good thing in Sheila Fishman's translations of Carrier, and brought out seven volumes between 1970 and 1981, the result being that Carrier's reputation was greater in Toronto than in Montréal. They also brought out Jacques Ferron's tales (trans. Betty Bednarski) and two volumes of Hubert Aquin (trans. Alan Brown). Concentrating early on Quebec literature, in keeping with the nationalist politics of the press, they seem to have stopped publishing translations in the early eighties, bringing out a total of 14 titles between 1969 and 1982. Coach House published a wide selection of experimentally oriented writers such as Victor-Lévy Beaulieu (trans. Fishman, Chamberlain), Nicole Brossard (trans. Larry Shouldice, Barbara Godard, Patricia Claxton, Fiona Strachan, Susanne de Lotbinière Harwood), Madeleine Gagnon (trans. Howard Scott), along with others potentially more popular, such as Dany Laferrière (trans. David Homel). Publishing exclusively Canadian translations at first, in the nineties they turned to some international writers such as André Breton (trans. Zack Rogow) and Marguerite Duras (trans. Alberto Manguel). Recently, the number of translations they have published has dropped considerably, and the total number of volumes published between 1975 and 2005 was 35. My own list of Exile translations shows 76 between 1975 and 2000. The Exile list also shows a continuing appearance of Québécois writers, but a uniquely ambitious showing of non-Canadian literature, including French, Israeli, Greek, Italian, Hungarian, Serbian, Croatian, Ukrainian, Finnish, Swedish, and German. *Exile* magazine consistently presented this very wide range, often publishing work that Exile Editions had no intention of bringing out, but which would, for example, eventually become part of Lester & Orpen Dennys' International Fiction List. At other times, publication of a number of translations certainly not expected to make money was aided by what Barry calls his "angels," people like Anton Kikas and George Yemec, who helped finance books of Croatian and Ukrainian literature in translation.

Have a look at that appended list. From any point of view, it adds up to an astonishing accomplishment. There were other periodicals such as *Prism International* publishing a variety of international literature in translation; there were houses such as Talon Books with an impressive list of translations of French Canadian literature, particularly theatre; but no one combined magazine and book publication to bring out such a kaleidoscope of national and international literature, in such a quantity. The importance of Exile Editions for the dissemination of Quebec culture was actually recognized by Liza Frulla-Hébert, the Parti Québécois' Quebec Government's Minister of Cultural Affairs at the time, in a letter to Barry Callaghan dated September 10, 1992. Here is an excerpt of what she wrote (my translation):

> I take pleasure in joining with those authors from Quebec who are privileged to be published by you, in offering our best wishes on the occasion of the fifteenth anniversary of your publishing house.
>
> The impressive list of your accomplishments is evidence of your commitment to literary creation in general, and makes clear the importance of the contribution you have made to the dissemination of the literature of Quebec. Our best writers of poetry, fiction, and drama have, in fact, been published by Exile Editions. In the past, your interest has extended not only to *Refus global*, the Automatist manifesto that had such an impact on the history of Quebec, but you have also recognized the talent of our playwrights by publishing Michel Tremblay's *Les belles-soeurs*, among others.
>
> I would also like to emphasize the exceptional contribution of translators such as Josée Michaud, David Ellis, Linda Gaboriau, to name only a few, who have collaborated in your publications. The quality of their work deserves our recognition.
>
> Please accept my congratulations and my gratitude for taking on a mission that is contributing so positively to the knowledge and appreciation of our cultural heritage.

Of course, Barry did more than bring out other people's work. *Exile* published his own first English renderings of Marteau in 1979, and from then on he became surely one of the most prolific of Canada's poet-translators. Meeting Marteau's Serbian translator, Miodrag Pavlovic, and recognizing that Pavlovic was a very fine poet, Barry began translating him as well, working from Marteau's French versions, since he knew no Serbian. Eventually, the dance card read something like this: Barry was translating Marteau and Pavlovic; Pavlovic was translating Marteau and Barry; Montague was translating Marteau; Marteau was translating Barry, Pavlovic and Montague. I hear that once in the late eighties they all got together in Beograd for a reading, each reciting his translations of the others, each solemnly declaring, following the example of Marteau, that they considered their translations superior to the originals.

In the early years, with both of us working from French, Barry and I had an efficient system of editing each other's work.[1] Because my basic knowledge of French was better, I would read his texts for literal accuracy; because his ear is so good, he would read my texts to eliminate the franglais that comes from what I call the tyranny of the source text. We'd go over the manuscripts in detail, debating every proposed change, and it was astonishing how often, as we argued various bad choices, the right word would suddenly appear, radiant, indubitable. We did a co-translation in 1989 of poems by Fernand Ouellette, entitled *Wells of Light*, where we worked so closely I can't even remember how we proceeded, though I think Barry did first versions of the opening poems, probably two thirds of the book, while I concentrated on the "Book of Hours" section. Barry left me behind, however, when he took the great road towards translating from literatures of which he could read not a word. The first examples were from Pavlovic's Serbian, as already mentioned, but the most spectacular were surely his work on the hugely popular Latvian poet, Imants Ziedonis. Unlike many who have worked in this way (I call them "the flesh of Pound") Barry never obfuscated the question of linguistic competence. In his "Translator's Note" to *Flowers of Ice*, he wrote:

I should explain that I neither read nor speak Latvian. I was given working translations by Banuta and Baiba Rubess. They quite deliberately did not seek felicity of phrase; they sought accuracy of meaning, no matter how awkwardly stated. I studied these for days, weeks, sometimes months, trying over two years to get hold of the inside of the poem, trying to feel the meaning and think the music, seeking an equivalent for the original. This is an act of faith, and hope. Once I arrived at my own versions, I consulted with several Latvians who know Ziedonis' work intimately. This was an act of trust. I am told these versions approach the original; that Ziedonis has a voice in English. I hope so. I have inhabited for a moment the mind of a man I've never met, and want to be fair to him.

This "consultation" involved reading his English texts to a table of aficionados who knew the Latvian poems by heart. It's a daring exploit, and a very complex process, not only practically but (dare I use the word?) theoretically. Barry says more about such things in "Black Light," assuming his customary "Mr. Natural" stance when it comes to literature, translation, and criticism. He tends to see them as self-evidently distinct, and quite hierarchical. Hence the announcement in the first *Exile* that "the imaginative writer will not be led in by a scholarly praetorian guard"; hence the distinction he makes in "Black Light" between poets (by implication real translators) and "the grammarians, the theoreticians, the etymologists, the guys who really knew something about language." But just as Barry knows that I know that an intimate knowledge of a source language is no guarantee of good literary translation, I know that he knows you can't render "se crosser" as "cross yourself" if you're translating a novel from Quebec (as a well-respected author and sometime translator has done).

To give a sense of the kind of work Barry does and has done in translation, let's look at a couple of examples, starting with the very first: the Voznosensky poems done in the early seventies. Here is Barry's "First Ice":

In the phone booth, chilled to the bone,
she pulls her flimsy coat close,
crooked lipstick, eyes
puffy from crying.

First ice, telephone talk.
First ice. A cold shoulder.

Blows into her balled fist.
Earrings – jet glass. Fingers – blue.
Slouching home alone, alone
along the icy street.

Frozen tears sting her cheeks –
First winter of the heart.

Here are two earlier renditions, one by Herbert Marshall, the "authorized translation," and the other by Stanley Kunitz.[2]

FIRST ICE

A girl in a phone box
is freezing cold,
Retreating into
her shivery coat.
Her face in too much
make-up's smothered
With grubby tearstains
  and lipstick smudges.

Into her tender palms
she's breathing.
Fingers – ice lumps.
In earlobes – earrings.

FIRST FROST

A girl is freezing
in a telephone booth,
huddled in
her flimsy coat,
her face stained by tears.

She breathes on
her thin little fingers.
Fingers like ice.
Glass beads in her ears.

She goes back home,	She has to beat
alone, alone,	her way back alone
Behind her the frozen	Down the icy street.
telephone.	
First Ice.	First frost.
The very first time.	A beginning of losses.
First ice of a telephone	The first frost of
conversation.	telephone phrases.
On her cheeks tear	It is the start
traces shine –	of winter glittering on
First ice of human	her cheek.
humiliation.	the first frost of having
	been hurt.
(Marshall)	(Kunitz)

Let's assume, rightly or wrongly, that the "authorized" version gives us a faithful sense of the content of the original. If so, it certainly isn't faithful to good poetry, with its prolixity and forced inversions (to help with the half-rhyming which Barry eschews). And surely the second half of line six isn't so banal in Voznesensky's original. Kunitz is better, simpler. I prefer "first frost" to "first ice," but I wonder about that sixth line, and the second part of line nine. Note the heavy alliteration in the last lines of both these translations, a technique Voznesensky loved, but here emphasizing nothing but boring phraseology. Barry pushes things. His version is even more clipped than Kunitz's. He doesn't bother writing "A girl," assuming it's clear. He actually transposes the penultimate stanza, making it the second for reasons not clear to me, and he colloquializes the phrases with "telephone talk" and "cold shoulder." I don't think "balled fist" is appropriate in line seven, but that last stanza wins the pot, as far as I'm concerned.

The same tendencies are even clearer in Barry's rendering of the other Russian poem, usually titled "I am Goya," where the title phrase, or the same structure, is repeated with hammering alliteration. But "I am" is less rhythmically powerful than "Ya," so he uses Melville's famous "Call me . . ." to get the stress he wants, and it works. At times, for my taste, he pushes condensation too far, as when he writes the sentence that Marshall translates as "I am the grim voice/ Of war, the conflagration of cities/ on the snows of '41" and Kunitz as "I am the tongue/ of war, the embers of the cities/ on the snows of the year 1941." Barry writes, "Call me the blow-horn/ of the snow-clad cities of '41" assuming that "blow-horn" is enough to evoke war, including fire. It's a risk in the name of condensation and emphatic, colloquial language, and I think in this case it's at the expense of important detail and nuance.

But look at those later translations, also included in *Raise You Five*: "Kébékanto of Love," from Gérald Godin (248-150), and Robert Marteau's sonnet, "Claude Monet's Magpie" (346), the first a gush of verbal love-juice, having fun with tacky clichés, the second a perfectly controlled, traditional sonnet with its last sentence stretching over twelve lines, and a sustained, delicate, wash of colour imagery – slow and painstaking work, as any translator will tell you. Barry can do them both. Or if you can find a copy of that most beautiful of Exile books, the facing-page translation of Robert Marteau's *Traité du blanc et des teintures/ Treatise on White and Tinctures*, a difficult, elliptical, hermetic text, full of musical assonance, deceptively simple, you'll see Barry grappling with passages like this:

Double,
le serpent parait
de par et d'autre du tronc.

Un oiseau se détache,
et brulant sur son erre
plus haut reprend sa haute errance.

A chaque arceau
se déplie un soleil,
degrés que l'humus convoite
d'une échelle ou déjà le volubilis
déchiffre par volutes
la trajectoire et l'accès.

*

Eidolon,
the serpent coils
on counter sides of the trunk.
A bird takes wing, and tacking in flames
rediscovers the high road
of wanderlust.

A flowering sun
at each arch,
and leaf mould covets the trellis slats
where scrolls of morning glory
transliterate trajectory
and re-entry.

That's good stuff, folks.

Notes

1. See my article "Bouncing Ideas: Co-operation as Process in Literary Translation," in *The Translation Process*, ed. Candace Séguinot, H.G. Publications, School of Translation, York University, 1989.
2. Barry's text comes from *Raise You Five: Essays and Encounters 1964-2004, Volume One* (Toronto: McArthur and Company, 2005), p. 195; Marshall's from *Vosnosensky: Selected Poems* (New York: Hill and Wang, 1966); Kunitz' from *Antiworlds: Poetry by Andrei Voznosensky* (New York: Basic Books, 1966), p. 23.

BARRY CALLAGHAN
AND THE INVENTION
OF CULTURAL STUDIES

Michael Keefer

On September 1, 1972 I got married – one most astonishing piece of good fortune – and several days later,
started work in my first full-time teaching position:
Assistant Master at Centennial College of Applied Arts
and Technology, one of the first of Ontario's new community colleges. The place was a converted munitions
factory on Warden Avenue, in the east end of Toronto.
Teaching load: sixteen hours per week in the classroom,
with four classes of twenty-five to thirty students apiece,
and an additional four hours weekly in the English
Department's "writing laboratory," a combined emer-
gency and orthopedics ward to which students came for
help with their deformed or shattered syntax. Add to
that whatever time I spent in office hours with students
from my four classes, plus the time required to prepare
my classes, and also, finally, the time I would have to
devote to marking my students' fortnightly writing
assignments.

On top of all this, I took on a second job, starting a
week later in that same auspicious month, as a seminar
leader in Barry Callaghan's year-long course in English-
and French-Canadian literatures and cultures at York
University's Atkinson College. I must have been insane.

But there was in fact some trace of method involved
in my decision to take on that additional work. What
did I know about teaching – or, for that matter, about
creative scholarship or creative anything? Nearly noth-

ing. Yet for reasons I'll explain I had a strong feeling that I needed to be doing something beyond just community college teaching. When I learned about an opening for a seminar leader in what sounded like a quite remarkable course at Atkinson, I thought it might be what I needed to keep the cogs turning. I was about to learn a great deal about teaching, and much else besides.

During the previous academic year, 1971-72, I'd been a freshly-minted Master of Arts looking to find out whether work in higher education could be a part of what I wanted to do with my life. I was passionate, in an immature way, about the writing of my own place and time. The University of Toronto had of course done its best to discourage any such interest (permitting, for example, just a single course in Canadian Literature to be included among the sixty-five graduate courses offered during my MA year by the Graduate Department of English). But I was not discouraged: when I wasn't on the prowl for teaching work, I was grinding out derivative verse – and, astonishingly, had a poem accepted by *Canadian Forum*, which actually proposed to pay me for the thing. (What might the princely sum have been: fifteen dollars? Fame and fortune were clearly just around the corner.)

I was able to pick up work on a per-course basis at Centennial College in 1971-72, teaching both at the main campus and in a nursing program at a hospital affiliated to the college.[1] And thanks to the University of Toronto's apparent failure to notice that I was no longer enrolled as a graduate student, I was given a lecture course in English-Canadian literature, one that I'd served in as a teaching assistant during my MA year, at the U of T's Scarborough College. That was a double stroke of luck: it helped my candidacy for a permanent job at Centennial the next summer; and as I subsequently learned, one of my Scarborough students, I. B. McAuliffe, was the incoming president of Centennial, a businessman who very decently wanted to prepare himself for the job by learning something about the humanities. (It was a pleasant surprise to hear from Lillian Frid, the director of Centennial's English Department, that when the department perhaps rather tentatively put my name forward for the job, their judgment was boomingly endorsed by the man at the top. Had I by some chance awarded him an A?)

But by the time I got that job, I'd done enough teaching of community-college business English and grammar and composition to know that if I did nothing but that – and I hadn't seriously contemplated any paying alternatives – I would shrivel up and blow away.

Though I had yet to encounter either René Descartes' formulation of the question, *Quod vitae sectabor iter*? ("What path shall I follow in life?"), or Barry Callaghan's gambler's response to all questions of this genre – "One must be willing to be lucky"[2] – I suppose I was already, proleptically, following Callaghan's advice. I allowed myself to be lucky not just in getting the Centennial College job, but also in falling into simultaneous supplemental work at Atkinson College – a happy first step, I can see in retrospect, towards severing myself from that first-ever full-time employment. (In 1974 I responded to a thirty percent pay raise and promotion by quitting my Centennial job – taking at age twenty-five what my colleagues jocularly called early retirement – and moving to England to make myself, if not a writer, then at least a scholar.)

*

But what was so special about Callaghan's Atkinson College course in 1972-73? I'm not sure that at this distance in time I could reliably remember its formal name.

(Could it have been anything as banal as "Readings in Contemporary Canadian Culture"?) And while I remember that the class met one evening every week in a giant hall in York University's Glendon campus for Callaghan's two-hour lecture, which was followed by a further hour in which the six or seven seminar leaders hunkered down in separate classrooms with their fractions of the class, I couldn't swear to the details of that format, and I have no memory at all of what may have transpired in my own seminars. What I do remember, with haunting clarity, is Callaghan's presence as a lecturer, and the remarkable power and methodological originality of his teaching.

Let me try to explain that originality. During the late 1980s and 1990s, "Cultural Studies" entered the discourses of the North American academy as one quite compelling answer to questions that had been posed during the preceding decades about disciplinarity, in literary studies and the adjoining disciplines, by feminist, deconstructive, and materialist theories and critical practices. Where, for example, are the boundary-lines between literary and non-literary texts, and between the structures, forms and social practices identified with "high culture" and those that constitute culture in general? If we're not convinced that such boundaries can or should exist, why should we disable our understanding of culture in the wider sense by enforcing its disciplinary subdivision into artificially or ideologically organized parts?

Questions of this sort reach back to Ferdinand de Saussure's early-twentieth-century vision of "une sémiologie generale," a general science of signification that he hoped might apply the insights of his structural linguistics across the whole breadth of human experience. In a somewhat narrower sense, they attach themselves to the successive formulations of something called "Cultur-

455

al Studies" by scholars like Richard Hoggart, Raymond Williams and Stuart Hall at the University of Birmingham and elsewhere in England during the 1960s and 70s – formulations that, in the wake of feminism, poststructuralism and cultural materialism, began to attract attention as evidence of a new academic "counter-discipline" that in terms both of subject-matter and of methodology held out the possibility of passing through or over the boundaries of traditional disciplines like literature, history, and sociology.

I don't mean to suggest that Barry Callaghan's teaching was linked in method or tonality with the work of the Birmingham school, or that he showed the remotest interest in such irreducibly academic discourses as the then-emergent structuralism, let alone the poststructuralism that was yet to come. But I would claim that in this course, and concurrently in his literary and political journalism of this period, Callaghan was inventing, *avant la lettre*, a specifically Canadian form of what we can appropriately call cultural studies.

I am thinking of "invention" not in a technological sense (as in the conceptualizing and assembling of a previously undreamt-of machine), but rather in its traditional sense in the discourse of classical rhetoric. In a rhetorical context, *inventio* or discovery refers to a process of coming upon and selecting out for present use and deployment the "places" (*loci* or *topoi*) – things already known and stored in memory – that are relevant to a particular situation and a particular moment. It is of course always the case that the forms and practices which come together to shape new constellations of cultural apprehension and understanding are in a potential sense already available within the culture. What is needed to activate them is someone whose cultural repertoire – or, if you prefer, whose soul – is large enough to encompass a significantly wider range of forms and

456

practices than has previously been acknowledged as possible or appropriate, and whose judgment is clear enough to enable a recognition of the most important conjunctions and contradictions within this expanded field.

What was relevant to an understanding of Canadian culture in the years immediately following the October Crisis of 1970? Callaghan's answer to this was especially rich because his store of *topoi* was drawn from French- as well as English-Canadian culture, and included not just literary, sociological, historiographic and political discourses, but also a complex array of journalistic experiences (available in the course of his lectures in the form of excerpts from filmed interviews and documentaries he himself had made), as well as constant references to wider, more cosmopolitan cultural and political contexts.

But perhaps this is too generalized a way of putting it. Let's consider in more detail the converging impressions students were given of French-Canadian culture. The intensity of the required reading in this course, and its overlay of different cultural forms and discourses, demanded a trans-disciplinary understanding. What had Quebec been in the years before Jean Lesage's *révolution tranquille*, and what was it becoming? Students acquired an understanding of the politics and cultural politics through reading essays of Pierre Trudeau from *Cité libre* in the time of the infamous asbestos strike and since, and the artists' manifesto *Refus global* (accompanied by projections of some of the great abstract canvases of Paul-Émile Borduas and Jean-Paul Riopelle), as well as through lectures that took them from the astonishing differences between English- and French-Canadian historiographical traditions up to the best-selling anticlerical manifesto *Les Insolences du Frère Untel* and Pierre Vallières's separatist autobiography-manifesto, *Nègres blancs de l'Amérique.* The gender politics of a priest-ridden, colonized culture became manifest in the anguished poetry of Saint-Denys Garneau, in Anne Hébert's equally resonant poetry and her novel *Kamouraska*, and in Claire Martin's appalling memoir *Dans un gant de fer.* And the emergence of a specifically Quebecois postmodern aesthetic, which was at the same time an angry, hallucinatory and intermittently hilarious questioning of social class divisions and linguistic divisions, and a revisionary re-imagining of a history laden with tragicomic misrecognitions, was traced in the short fiction of Jacques Ferron and the poetry of Gaston Miron, and in novels like Marie-Claire Blais's *Une Saison dans la vie d'Emmanuel,* Roch Carrier's *La Guerre, Yes Sir!* and Hubert Aquin's *Prochain épisode.*[3] Converging evidence was provided through documentary film clips – some of them Callaghan's own interviews with people like Pierre Trudeau, Marie-Claire Blais, René Levesque, radical labour leader Michel Chartrand, and student activists who had been part of the political mobilization that was shut down by the imposition of the War Measures Act in October 1970.

I'm not going to describe in parallel detail the manner in which Callaghan opened up for his students (and his seminar leaders) an equally rich and complex understanding of the cultural practices, social structures, political and historiographic discourses, initiatives towards critical self-understanding, and enduring self-delusions of English Canada. Once again we read novels and poetry, as well as the fictions of historians and sociologists, engaged with the thought of critics and communication theorists from Harold Innis to Northrop Frye and Marshall McLuhan, mulled over reproductions of art works, and watched interviews with some of the key agents and analysts of our contemporary history. Because Callaghan's literary culture is cosmopolitan (and hence by definition not merely or exclusively literary, but intimate as well with adjoining discourses), and because he had travelled in body as well as mind – his journalistic work had taken him to the Middle East, to several African countries, to Latin America and to Eastern Europe – what he had to say about English Canada was never solely and provincially just about English Canada. And once again the lectures were magisterial, witty, and compelling.

*

The brilliant critic and teacher could at times be intimidating, even cruel. I remember one conversation between Barry and his seminar leaders in which a rebellious remark of some sort from me drew forth, by way of rebuke, an oddly snobbish speculation as to the car I drove: it must be, he thought, a Chevy Vega. The point had to do, I think, with naiveté and bad taste, since the compact cars the Detroit automakers had recently rolled out to compete with the Japanese were uniformly disastrous. (The Pinto, which Ford tried to sell in Latin America without thinking that its name means, in Spanish, "sexually underendowed," was famous for its exploding gas-tank; the Vega for a more generalized mechanical ineptitude.) Or perhaps the image of someone two metres tall winding himself in and out of a small and badly designed car was by itself a sufficient marker of folly.

I confessed to driving a Vega. But the truth was much worse. What I actually drove was a wretched little English-made Vauxhall station wagon, marketed on this continent as the Envoy Epic – but epic only in its failings. Unstable, underpowered, ugly, unreliable – or rather, reliable only in that its radiator would boil over and go off like Old Faithful after two minutes of idling in gridlock traffic. Oh yes, and the heater didn't work (an attractive feature in those Ontario winters), the clutch was fussy, and the braking delicate and intermittent.[4]

*

The year 1972 was a pivotal one for Barry Callaghan. Having been unceremoniously fired by the CBC for the *lèse-majesté* of daring to put forceful questions, on camera, about the ethics of conquest and occupation to Israeli Prime Minister Golda Meir; and having concurrently lost some of the other outlets in which he was publishing literary journalism of a quality unsurpassed in that period, Callaghan launched the literary quarterly *Exile*.

The first numbers of the journal, appearing during the academic year 1972-73, added a further dimension to the aura of his teaching: here was current work by some of the writers we were exploring in that course – Roch Carrier, Morley Callaghan, Marie-Claire Blais – appearing elbow-to-elbow with work by international figures such as Yehuda Amichai, Jerzy Kosinski and John Montague. And as in Callaghan's lecture hall, the circuit of conversation was not closed: in each issue of *Exile* young Canadian writers, some of them making their first appearance in print, were being published alongside these masters.

Barry Callaghan's poetry and fiction, and his achievements with *Exile*, and subsequently and concurrently with Exile Editions (which in the autumn of 2006 published its three-hundredth title), remain available for our inspection as a material archive. And thanks to the ongoing project of a multi-volume republication of his non-fiction prose, it is becoming possible for contemporary readers to appreciate as well the scale and quality of his achievement as a literary and cultural critic.

Teaching, however, is more evanescent. The more receptive of Callaghan's students may indeed have been transformed by their passage through his lecture-hall, developing a deeper and more complete understanding of their culture and history, and perhaps also their own selves, than might otherwise have been possible. Yet however innovative that classroom work may have been, it is now preserved only in the fading memories of those who participated in it. Hence these reflections – "Though for no other cause," in Richard Hooker's words, "yet for this; that posterity may know we have not loosely through silence permitted things to pass away as in a dream . . ."[5]

Notes

1. There I had the less than brilliant idea of teaching John Fowles' novel *The Collector* to a first year class. The night before we arrived at that grim fiction of sexual predation and murder, second-year nursing students, as a prank, phoned up to the first-year floors of their residence tower the news that a sexual predator was loose in the building. By two in the morning even the original pranksters had become convinced of this terrifying fact, and students throughout the residence spent the rest of the night huddling in one another's rooms in tear-stained clusters. Two young women ran sobbing from my class that morning before I'd spoken much more than a sentence.

2. Callaghan writes of the moment at which he was offered the job of Books Editor of *The Toronto Telegram*, "Looking back, I can see that there was only one question on the lunch table: Was I willing to be lucky" – and of Harry Crowe's offer of a year's funding for a literary quarterly, "A quarterly! I didn't know anything about quarterlies. But again, I was willing to be lucky" (*Raise You Five: Essays and Encounters 1964-2004, Volume One* [Toronto: McArthur, 2005], pp. xv, xvii).

3. Students were in fact reading these texts for the most part in English translation, though it is my memory that at Callaghan's insistence the university bookstore also offered editions in the original French.

4. The literary theorist Stanley Fish has argued persuasively that literary academics – other than himself – are unrestrained masochists and drive ugly cars as one sign of their endless appetite for humiliation. See "The Unbearable Ugliness of Volvos," in Fish's *There's No Such Thing as Free Speech: And It's a Good Thing Too* (New York: Oxford University Press, 1994). Was this Epic of mine a precocious sign of professional orientation?

5. Richard Hooker, *Of the Laws of Ecclesiastical Polity*, ed. Christopher Morris (2 vols.; London: Dent, 1954), vol. 1, p. 77.

TWO-STOREY TOWN

A Song for Barry Callaghan

Jon Brooks

Imitation is not the highest compliment. Imitation is the *only* compliment – all else is insult that whispers.

Originally, I was going to provide a safely provocative essay entitled, *The Right People Know Shit*, a compliment to Barry Callaghan's novella, *Never's Just the Echo of Forever*. In particular, the story's main character, Albie Starbach – for my money, the most disturbing and thus true Canadian literary archetype since the country moved to town. Barry Callaghan's polis, his disaster, is a gridiron street plan imposed over river and ravine, a hick town of three million shopkeepers plying the bloodless practicality that is the end of compassion, and necessarily, the end of civilization. Through Albie, the spiritual homelessness of the age is revealed. In Albie's words, "The right people know shit."

I am not an academic, nor an essayist. I had a small success in Toronto in the early 1990s playing philosophically aimless songs. Thinking of Pasternak's line, *"How shameful, when you have no meaning / To be on everyone's lips . . ."* I hitchhiked through Russia, the sad-smiling Baltics, and backpacked throughout a widowed Bosnia-Herzegovina with guileless curiosity. In Northern Ireland, I asked the stupid questions that yield the profound answers. I stumbled to completion a few decent songs but I had not the *tradition* nor the *individual talent* to finish anything with sufficient "meaning." So, in 1998, I quit music and enrolled in English at York Uni-

463

versity. Barry was my first and last professor and to him I owe the return of the song.

I wrote *Two-Storey Town* for Barry a year ago. The dedication in the liner notes offered passive apology for "borrowing" Callaghan's nickname for Toronto: "a two-storey town." In class he'd complain, "Look down St. Clair, look east down the Danforth, Yonge Street, Queen: two-storeys all the way. A city of shopkeepers; store front on the bottom, apartment upstairs – once in awhile, we'll go three-storeys and make some money off the Polish border upstairs." He'd pause, as good storytellers do, throw his head back, and up, and around at York's lecture hall Brutalism, and then growl, with practiced exaggeration: "Kiddoes, this ain't the land of the James Joyces." Ours is an age plagued by literal thinking and that ubiquitous tag – before and after every movie we suffer – "Based on a True Story." Ours are illiterate times and, as Albie would say, "dangerous times."

In *Two-Storey Town* I wanted to sing out Callaghan's jab at Toronto's pretentiousness, at Toronto's unwillingness to demand for her children anything more than a playground of well-meaning, name-tagged clerks and administrators making money during the day and borrowing culture at night. Toronto gushes "yes" only after New York, Dublin, or Berlin's lead. For this reason, Barry is not as fashionable here as he probably is in Rome. And this point begs a tangent: his Exile Editions seeks, finds, trusts, and promotes what "may not be on everyone's lips."

Like a story, a song can evolve and carry within itself its own rotating list of themes independent of the writer's design. Within my song's three minutes and seventeen seconds are fragments of what Callaghan gave to me to give to you in song.

First: He gives the approval of his heart to those among us "outside of the circle of approval." Of his father's fiction, Callaghan wrote:

> His heart, he liked to say, lay with "such people, who are a little on the outside of the circle of approval on this earth . . . people who can't be approved of but who have somehow a quality of warmth in them that almost shocks us . . ."

The same may be said of Barry's work. Callaghan follows the unknown. For a self-proclaimed "fallen Irish Catholic" Callaghan ironically embraces Christianity's central tenet: that faith is only possible amid unknowing. I recall the description of Albie: "He'd become sure of himself in the dark." The light of hope shines brightest where it's needed most.

Second: The theme of complicity, and the forgotten law of opposites: that extremes meet, that opposites meet as enemies only to end in equal friendship. Boxers always embrace and sometimes kiss after the twelfth round. Jorge Luis Borges and Simone Weil were also attuned to this idea. Barry's long intrigue with the misread Judas is first found in the Hogg poem, "Judas Priest." Today's plague of literal thinkers have appointed biblical archaeology as imagination's successor. A shred of papyrus written around 160 AD in Greek and translated into Coptic breathes twenty-first-century air and, suddenly – as though anything can happen suddenly – it's as if archaeology has excavated the imagination. So what then? Was Callaghan thirty years ahead of his time? Not at all. Callaghan is among the first poets to arrive 1700 years too late.

We've tripped an inch forward since Plato. St. Francis had an idea once, and I'm pretty sure Nietzsche had one, too. But a writer seldom, if at all, has an idea. More likely, a writer builds the world by trusting what his own cruel eye sees. The scientist and mystic, Teilhard de Chardin, once suggested that the mandate was "to see or to perish." In this light, Barry Callaghan's has been a cruel and healing eye in a city that "ain't no healing town." And so, let me hazard a compliment that sings a praise I hope is pure of whispered insult.

Two-Storey Town

On a right-angled street in a right-minded time;
a gridiron named after colonist's wives:
You wore a nametag, I bummed a smoke in a two-storey
town.
Balcony flowers over neon signs,
Dignities set to terracotta and lime.
We were unplanned, like an idea in a two-storey town.

And here underneath The World's Tallest Free Standing
lie.
Ah well, at least the sun mocks only as she shines.

And you loved a guy – he had a wife and son –
it takes a good heart to betray someone.
We were reckless, like Charity in a two-storey town.
But a city of eyeless smiles and clerks,
a hostelry of souls that smirk –
we were impossible, like a God in a two-storey town.

And here underneath The World's Tallest Free Standing
lie.
Ah well, at least the sun mocks only as she shines.

Administrator 1: "La, da da da, da: da da da, da da;
La da da da, da da da, da da:
La da da da, da da, da da, da da, da da."

Administrator 2: "La, da da da, da: da da da, da da;
La da da da, da da da, da da:
La da da da, da da, da da, da da, da da."

Breathing in the second hand literal thought
under the smog of proving only what's not,
and believing in nothing but the numb great heart attack.
We were bloody, like amity in a two-storey town.
Thought we were pure, like a service charge in a two-
storey town.
Baby, your buildings are big but darlin', you're a two-
storey town.

AS THOROUGHLY AS POSSIBLE

Barry Callaghan's Papers

Christopher Doda

On two separate occasions over the past six years, I have lived in Barry Callaghan's basement. Not actually taken up residence but spent considerable blocks of time underground compiling and cataloguing his personal papers and those of Exile Editions with the intention that eventually they be donated to an archival institution. For weeks at a stretch, I arrived between 10 and 11 A.M, worked a few hours, sat down for one of Claire's generous lunches – I fattened up nicely – and back to work for the afternoon. There I would enjoy a Bartok or Shostakovich or Yardbirds CD, and a beer or two that I stored in the bar fridge, while sorting out the tangible evidence of Callaghan's life. All with the goal of someday liberating his pool table from under numerous stacks of unordered paper. At times, this would seem a Sisyphean task. Whenever I approached the top of the hill, my rolling stone in hand, I would return the following day to find another stack of paper miraculously unearthed from some hitherto unknown (to me anyway) cubbyhole in the upper reaches of 20 Dale Ave.

By the time I finished in the early winter of 2005, there were over 70 banker's boxes full of records and a condensed file list over fifteen pages in length. While predominantly textual, the records are composed of several different media. In total, they consist of:

— 40+ boxes of textual records pertaining to Exile Editions (manuscripts, galleys, and proofs for approximately 200 titles, as well as administrative and promotional material),

— 20+ boxes of textual records of Callaghan's manuscripts (drafts and research notes) for books and print journalism. Also teaching files and course syllabi for York University's Atkinson College,

— Another 10+ boxes of written correspondence with friends, family, and writers and artists from all over the world, covering a forty-year period, alphabetized by sender/recipient,

— Approximately 20+ pastel and coloured-pencil and ink drawings, of varying sizes, some rather large (up to 4' by 6'),

— Several VHS tapes of personal appearances and short films about Callaghan,

— Several reels of film (16mm) shot in the 1960s and 1970s for the CBC and others. Subjects include The Black September War, Golda Meir, John Updike, Angela Davis in California Prison among others,

— Several VHS tapes of Callaghan's television journalism,

— Several reels of audio tape interviews with Yehuda Amichai, SY Agnon, SW Hayter, George Barker, John Montague, and James Farrell, among others,

— One box of photographs from various trips abroad and some Exile events,

— One box of material pertaining to the estate of Morley Callaghan (funeral notice, naming of footbridge, newspaper articles, reprint permissions et cetera).

Because they were already in order, I was not required to catalogue them but there were an additional five dozen notebooks kept by Callaghan over the past thirty years, with photographs from various travels and festive occasions, cards, promotional notices from readings and from Exile events, glued in place. All contain the author's handwritten annotations, marginalia, drawings, and further notes and digressions, amounting to a combination of visual journal and commonplace book. Packaged up, these would amount to a further 10+ boxes of material.

In the records for Exile Editions, one finds the hard and fast evidence of what the publishing house is, what it stands for, and the principles it was founded upon writ large. Created four years after the journal in 1976, Exile followed its quarterly counterpart as a reaction against the burgeoning culture of insular Canadian literary nationalism, a nationalism spurred by Expo '67 in Montreal and the publication of Margaret Atwood's *Survival*, among others, soon after. While Exile's first book (a birthday gift produced without the artist's knowledge) was *Drawings* by Canadian Claire Weissman Wilks – then known as Claire Rumin Wilks – it was followed by poems of Israeli Yehuda Amichai and Greek dissident Yannis Ritsos. Now upon its thirtieth anniversary, Exile Editions has more than 300 titles in its back catalogue from authors, poets, playwrights, visual artists, and essayists from around the world. A national role-call of Exile's back-list reads like a meeting of the United Nations: Canada (English and French), the United States, the United Kingdom, Ireland, Chile, Russia, France, Italy, Serbia, Croatia, Latvia, Germany, Mexico, and Israel just to start. Through Exile, Callaghan's great contribution to our national culture was to champion the idea, in both theory and practice, that Canadian writing should not be raised and treated like some rare and precious flower grown under greenhouse light. The best of our writing should stand shoulder-to-shoulder with the best in the world, that Marie-Claire Blais fits alongside Michel Deguy, Atwood with Amichai, as they did in the premier issue of the journal in 1972. Moreover, he came to this conclusion twenty years before it became fashionable (and then creed) in Canadian literary circles. If the books were not indication enough, the records show the stubborn perseverance necessary for such an undertaking and the care that went into producing all those volumes.

Outside of some notable exceptions like Robinson Jeffers, JD Salinger, and Thomas Pynchon, writers or artists rarely work in a vacuum, and nowhere is this more apparent than in correspondence. Among the abundance of Callaghan's letters (which occupied more than two full filing cabinets), one is immediately struck by the care in keeping them. Not only do the individual files contain letters to and sometimes from Callaghan, but often photographs, press clippings, and other keepsakes, forming a kind of dossier on each person. Major correspondents include Yehuda Amichai, Margaret Atwood, Margaret Avison, Marie-Claire Blais, Hayden Carruth, Austin Clarke, Antonio D'Alfonso, David Donnell, Ray Ellenwood, James T. Farrell, Mavis Gallant, Greg Gatenby, Branko Gorjup and Francesca Valente, Kenneth J. Harvey, SW Hayter, Tom Hedley, Diane Keating, William Kennedy, Professor David Lampe, Patrick Lane, Margaret Laurence, Irving Layton, Gwendolyn MacEwen, Robert Marteau, Bruce Meyer, John Montague, Susan Musgrave, Joyce Carol Oates, Miodrag Pavlovic, Mordecai Richler, Alfredo Rizzardi, William Ronald, Joe Rosenblatt, Gordon Sheppard, David Sobelman, Charles Tomlinson, Seán Virgo, and Robert Zend. The tone of the letters from these writers, artists, and translators range from lighthearted and joyful to dark and despondent, from the celebration of life to bickering over royalties to missives from just this side of suicide, depending on the sender. While sorting stacks of unordered letters into appropriate files, I learned a few things. Translators, for instance, are often more bellicose about the fine details of "their" work than the actual poets are, writing in a fury if a comma is out of place or a line break mishandled in the galleys. Sometimes, confusion would reign. Callaghan has a number of correspondents with the given name of "David" all of whom simply sign their letters by first name only. After some initial frustration I was able to tell the Davids Day, Donnell, Lampe, Morley, Sobelman, Staines, and Wevill apart by signature. Examined as a collective, what this correspondence illuminates most strikingly is the level of interaction that takes place between artists of various stripes, bouncing ideas around, commenting on each others' work, asking for advice, complaining about life and lovers, and, above all, sharing stories.

Another group of files caught my immediate interest: three boxes of material for an anthology to have been titled *Alchemists in Winter*. Conceived in the mid-1980s as a comprehensive bilingual Canadian poetry collection, it was abandoned in the typeset stage when permission costs ballooned out of control. It was not the material that caught my attention per se but rather the long sheets of hand done (by cutting and pasting) typeset pages, a graphic illustration of book construction in the immediate pre-computer age. On Dupont Street, near Bathurst, in Toronto, there is a large abandoned factory building still bearing the name Mono Lino Typesetting. It is baffling to think that work performed there by a small army of skilled workers scarcely twenty years ago has been replaced by one person with a MacIntosh. The changes brought on by the widespread use of computers were also apparent in the six boxes of papers for recent years of *Exile: The Literary Quarterly* (which will join the *fonds* already held at the Thomas Fisher Rare Book Library at the University of Toronto). Outside of the usual manuscripts, proofs, photoplates et cetera I also found several thick old files of carbon-copied rejection letters from Callaghan dating back to the early 1970s. As *Exile*'s current submissions editor, I found this astounding; Callaghan used to respond to every submission personally. With the advent of the World Wide Web, and *Exile*'s presence online, it now receives 20-30 submissions a week, making such "hands-on" responses well nigh impossible.

Looking over the drafts of Callaghan's own manuscripts, it became abundantly clear that his reputation for voracious habits of rewriting and revision is well-deserved. For instance, Callaghan's sense of rhythm and cadence is relatively unique to Canadian poetry, owing more to American blues and jazz than to the Great Iambic Pentameter. He writes on the downbeat, the one and three count, not the thump, thump, thump of the two and four. Even a casual perusal of the numerous ink-laden drafts of either Hogg book reveals that Callaghan's unerring rhythm – which sounds so fluid and easy – is the product of intensive labour. When these drafts are eventually made accessible to the public, his considerable abilities as a determined poetic craftsman and technician will truly be known. The drafts of fiction, memoir, and journalism are equally subject to the massive amounts of ink-staining characteristic of a perfectionist.

Also essential are the sound and video recordings of Callaghan reading his work, including a wonderful short film of him performing "Medusa Among the Moochers" by Aaron Woodley, director of the feature film *Rhinoceros Eyes*. Much more than fiction, poetry is an oral medium. Because its essential formal characteristics are rhythm and musicality, it needs to be read aloud and listened to, not just printed and absorbed silently off the page. While a poet is alive, his voice is available to the public but recordings are the only way to preserve that unique aspect of the poet after he is gone, as all those great Caedmon tapes will attest. While many writers are abysmal readers of their own work, anyone who has seen Callaghan perform knows how his baritone animates his verse and I can think of few better acts of literary preservation than to get as much of that voice as possible on tape.

One aspect of a potential holding, institutional or private, that archivists and, subsequently, researchers prize is completeness. Are the records offered as close as possible to the whole of the records worth preserving? Irving Layton's papers, for example, are scattered across the country as he sold them off piecemeal to the, at the time, highest bidder: hardly a desirable state. Fortunately, Callaghan has kept an inordinate amount of material, and not just dealing with his public life. Full boxes of notes, assignments, writing samples, exams, sketchbooks et cetera from all levels of his education, from grade school to grad school are present in his records. Many of the other files are equally abundant. Content with financial records and family photographs, most people don't keep extensive records until they see a reason to do so; most will periodically purge out of self-censorship or the simple expedience of clearing space. (Some years ago, I happened across the collected undergraduate essays of Northrop Frye in a bookshop. Mortified at the thought that my own undergraduate observations should ever be subject to even limited public exposure, I went home and recycled the lot.) It struck me, there in Callaghan's basement in the house once owned by his father, that a desire to keep these records, to maintain the documentation of one's life so thoroughly, might be an unexpected and beneficial side effect of being the son of a famous novelist. Morley Callaghan had been a successful writer for over ten years by the time Barry was born in 1937, and he would have grown up watching Morley documented both inside and outside the family, by newspapers, magazines, even on film (the National Film Board used him to narrate a hockey documentary called "Hot Ice" in 1940). I suspect it instilled in him, from an early age, the notion that life, a life, is worth preserving as thoroughly as possible. Lucky for us it did; when the time comes for someone to write Callaghan's biography, this material will be invaluable. Furthermore, the completeness of the records reflects a quality Callaghan shares with all fiction writers of note: an eye for detail, presumably a trait of any good journalist as well. An archive is generally constituted to document the decision-making process of the institution that feeds it and if, as an extra, it keeps the papers of artists or writers it is to showcase the creative process by which art is manufactured. The completeness of these records, the succession of drafts and whatnot, is an invaluable resource into that very process.

In Callaghan's papers, like those of any other writer, we are sometimes treated to a glimpse at the events that go into making art. While I was working certain files stood out. During the 1980s, Callaghan's house on Sullivan St. was broken into and severely vandalized while he and Claire were on one of their sojourns to their farmhouse for Thanksgiving weekend. With some effort, I was able to cobble together a large file pertaining to the break-in, containing numerous photographs of the damage, victim impact statements, police reports, even a letter of contrition from one of the perpetrators written from a rehab program. In strictly literary terms, the file itself was less stimulating than some of the others, but the real event that Callaghan would spool out into an article for *Toronto Life* called "A Motiveless Malignancy" and then into the story "Because Y is a Crooked Letter" in *A Kiss Is Still a Kiss* was revealed in this record. Every stage of composition took the narrative a further distance from the reality of the original incident: changing the order of events, warping the details, leaving things out. This, of course, is how it should be. As someone who generally prefers the interpretation, the art, to the reality, I was nevertheless fascinated to look at, in a highly compact form, the raw material that Callaghan had transformed, transmogrified, into his fiction. Much has been written about the relationship between art and life: the New Critics denied it, the New Historicists drowned in it. Half in jest, Ernest Hemingway said, "art is easy, it's the living that's hard." The truth is somewhere in between. As Polish novelist Jerzy Kosinski observed, "the most essential stage of the writing process…is the process whereby the writer comes to stand outside the experience he intends to mirror in his book." As the ordeal of rebuilding his home went on for months, the incident must have been percolating in his mind for its eventual revamping into fiction, into narrative, to that instant when he stood outside the experience. The story is a record of creativity but the file is a record of the inspiration.

Pouring over the raw material of hundreds of books published, a dozen books written, dozens of essays, hundreds of letters, I felt over time a strange feeling of discontent that I could not readily explain. Inadvertently, Callaghan put a face on what I was thinking. Near the end of my labours, I came across the drafts for his inaugural 1966 essay for *The Toronto Telegram* on the venerable and prolific American critic Edmund Wilson, and then the draft of the essay he wrote after Wilson's death in 1972 when Callaghan was about thirty-five years old. It contained a phrase that shed light on my uneasiness: "Though we may want to weep that he is dead, his triumph makes a man just a little bit ashamed at how little he has done." Now, another half a life later, it is obvious that he needn't have worried. Out of love of narrative and style, he has done much more than find the fortitude to write through the ransacking of his home, much more than publish volumes of fiction, poetry, non-fiction, his own and others; he has been a passionate user and defender of the word. From my perspective, what these records demonstrate more than anything is a life well-lived, at as loud a volume as possible.

INTERVIEW

Barry Callaghan with William Kennedy, Saratoga Race Track: August 2004.

The question is complex and recurring, endlessly answered, never definitively, and the answer changes with the writer who, in this case, has worked both sides of the subject. The writer is Barry Callaghan, noted pool and horseplayer, high roller and artist, who writes powerful poetry, has reported on wars, taught literature, founded and run a literary magazine, fronted a TV show, sung the blues, and has perpetually told wondrous stories and stirring lies all through the long night as a way of life. He was born into literature, the son of novelist and short story writer Morley Callaghan. Among Barry's specialties, fiction and non-fiction loom large, voluminously, and importantly; and so we put the question to him on a day in August, 2004, at the Saratoga Race Track, under the tent, postprandially amid the fluidity of wine and trifectas, about the ultimate and defining differences between a work of non-fiction and a short story or novel, in regard to writing works that are authentic.

WK: Both forms are quests for the truest, most meaningful truth; yet both are art forms that require the writer to massively shape and reshape reality to achieve any work of high seriousness. How, then, is the truest truth arrived at, which form is more likely to produce it as art, and how, and why?

BC: Every time I report on something, as a reporter, I try to see it, with my own eye, but I know that I am, as you suggested at the beginning, shaping it; and as soon as I start shaping it, I'm putting it into a story that will have the stamp of my sensibility. Now I try not to lie about what I'm seeing but I know that there are certain aspects of human character, of even the human physiognomy, that are simply mine, imaginatively; and eventually my description of a politician will have something of the same character as my description of a character in my novel, because that's my seeing eye. It's not that it's not true, it's not that I don't see it; I do see it. But that's how I shape it or, you can say, that's how I select the information; but I shy away from the word "select" because that suggests bias, a deliberate manipulation of the detail. That's not what happens. It's just that I see things through the character of my own eye. And they're there. At least they're there most of the time.

WK: When you're looking at real history in your memory and you're turning it into fiction, what are your guidelines? How do you control the transformation? What do you leave out and what do you put in? What's the impulse to change it?

BC: This is why the story "Because Y is a Crooked Letter" is fascinating to me and to many people. That story is about the destruction of our 69 Sullivan Street house by vandals. I wrote it – and it was hard to write – in short bursts, because it was a very emotionally painful thing that happened. I wrote as authoritatively as I could about how I saw myself, and I wrote it as journalism; but I was seeing myself, accurately, honestly, as a "character" in that situation. It was a very funny moment in the actual situation, when one of the policemen took the chief inspector aside and said to him, "I think he did it." And the inspector said "Why?" and he said, "Because he's not showing any emotion! He's just watching things, looking at things," and the chief inspector, God bless him, said, "You don't understand, that's what writers do!" Well that's true. That's in the story. I reported that. So OK, that's the way I wrote the journalism.

Now, after it was done, in which I presented myself as a character in this situation, both Joyce Carol Oates and my father, said to me, "That's a very remarkable story," and Joyce told me, "There's something even Dostoyevskian about that story. Something about . . . the whole question of vengeance and guilt and forgiveness, and what you're enraged by and what you're not enraged by . . . it should be a story." So I thought, okay, it's a story. Now, you know what I changed? Claire's name! [Claire Weissman Wilks is his longtime companion.]

WK: Is that it?

BC: That's it. And some few sentences at the beginning. You can go through it. And, I put subheadings in. In the journalism piece there are no subheadings. In the fiction piece there are subheadings. But in the actual prose text I changed only Claire's name. She now says I made her fictional. Otherwise, it's the same. I was in Italy last year and people said to me, "That story, it's such a wonderful story. I wonder if a person in that situation could actually think and behave the way your character does." It's very mysterious. That means, you see, that my response to myself in that situation — as a reporter — was simply the sensibility of my seeing eye.

WK: This suggests what García Márquez said – and he has been a lifelong journalist — that there really is no difference between journalism and fiction; that the material is the same, the language is the same. And he equates Defoe's novel, *The Journal of the Plague Year* with *Hiroshima*, John Hersey's non-fiction work, and says both are great books, and that there is nothing the novel can do that journalism can't do.

BC: At their best, I agree.

WK: I disagree, and I cite García Márquez's *One Hundred Years of Solitude* versus anything he has done in non-fiction; and the novel soars over the rest, a non-pareil work of the imagination whose impact on the entire world is unparalleled in our age. But let's move on to your attitude toward works of yours that were considered both fiction and journalism. Was the work considered vastly different because it was labeled fiction? Who compared the differences between the two pieces? I think of the Borges story, "Pierre Menard, Author of the Quixote" about *Don Quixote* rewritten in the twentieth century, the character is exactly the same as the Cervantes original, yet vastly different.

BC: Half of the difference, I think, is in the anticipation of the reader. Years ago I had a column in a magazine in Toronto in which the editor allowed me to do anything. I could report, or I could write fiction, and it was in that column that I wrote half of *The Black Queen Stories*; and people thought they were reading reportage. For one column I did a little subheading saying that in a shoebox I had found the following letters, and there were five letters, and they were all written by a woman, and they were very strange and contained the story about a blind old woman who had a guinea cock, and the struggle between her and her daughter and how it came to a crisis over the head of this guinea cock – the young girl cut off its head. I mean, it was a startling, startling thing. I was at a social event and one of the best journalists in the country came up to me, took me warmly by the hand and said, "I gotta tell you, boy, what a discovery those letters were. I read them. I was spellbound, reading those letters." And since I had known him for years and I thought he'd be pleased, I said, "Well actually, I didn't find those letters. I made all that up. It's fiction," and he was outraged. I thought he was gonna hit me. He said, "How dare you mislead your readers that way?" And I said, "Wait a minute, you should be happy. You're a writer. This is an act of the imagination in which you found yourself totally spellbound. This is a triumph of the imagination." He said, "Triumph? I'm gonna punch you right in the eye for misleading me." So I realized I was in some kind of deep water there. And when it came time to do *The Black Queen Stories*, I decided to take them out of the form of letters and put them all into a monologue. I eliminated the letter form but it's the same voice, the same monologue. It's a story called "A Terrible Discontent," and many people, particularly women, love it as a work of fiction. But it was first accepted and printed as journalism. And the most outraged person in the city was one of the best journalists.

WK: You know this reminds me of Hemingway's *A Moveable Feast*, which was considered a journalistic memoir, and meticulously accurate in its detail, and it probably was, in large measure. But in his introduction he says the book may be regarded as fiction, and it seems to me that these fragments of memoir are really exquisite short stories masquerading as nonfiction because he is writing about real people and probably inventing as he goes back through his memory. So my question is: what do you trust or does it make any difference?

BC: Ah, this takes me back to a point I once made about Genesis. You see, what has come out of an experience that must have been rooted in some kind of fact is a story that has achieved the level of redemptive truth . . . certainly for the Jews. I would argue, as I have, that the story of passing over is the story, for example, of my Russian father-in-law, who passed out of Russia into the freedom of the Canadian west.

WK: You must tell your reaction to the Passover story.

BC: It's in a short piece I called "True Stories" [published in *Raise You Five*].

WK: Can you recap what you wrote? – about a man who piles up actual facts to justify a literal reading of that biblical episode.

BC: Well, it's the search for the detail in a story that on the surface is patently ridiculous, because you can walk across the Sinai desert in three-and-a-half days. Sixty thousand people couldn't have been out there for 40 years marching around. And the Egyptians, the greatest of record keepers, never saw them. So was Moses some kind of faux Bismarck marching around with his army like the invisible man of the comic books? That's irrelevant to me. What's relevant is that somehow under an assemblage of experiences, of facts, the story of some guy who must have been called Moses, has achieved a level of experience that everybody recognizes as true. And people live by it. It is irrelevant to sit around saying, "Don't you see that this fact is laughable?" There are stories in human experience that have achieved that level of truth, and it may be that it is at that level that you approach religious experience. And religious experience, I guess, as it approaches faith, must move away from the anchor of fact. If you go all the way back, there's got to be fact there somewhere, but the story has achieved its own significance, its own reality. This is another part of the mystery of storytelling.

So you speak of Hemingway, and I think you're quite right. The difference between Hemingway's *Moveable Feast* and my father's *That Summer in Paris* is that my father had a remarkable memory and, "lying" or "shaping," deliberately shaping the truth, particularly in aid of malice, or belittlement, was just not in his character. So the reason that people read *That Summer in Paris* and are persuaded that it's probably the most accurate portrait ever given of Hemingway, is that Morley seems to have had no ax to grind, nothing invested in it personally at anybody else's expense. He just seems to be tolerantly aware, generously aware, of everybody around him. Hemingway – and I agree with you – he sat down and took his experiences, very close to the experience of Morley, and made them into short stories, in their form. And, whether he embellished here, added here, I don't know, but I know that they have the effect of stories. My line in relation to this is that what a storyteller means when he says, "I'm gonna tell you the truth," is the same thing that lovers mean whey they say, "I'll love you 'til the day I die." Every lover knows that's not true, but at the moment it's true, and you want it to be true, you yearn for it to be true, but it's not true. Lovers lie to each other from day one by telling each other the truth.

WK: Let's talk about the working journalist, the news reporter, and trying to tell the truth when you're writing news.

BC: What some people call objectivity – it's very interesting to watch this work itself out on television, where all the networks now do the same thing. It doesn't matter whether it's Fox News or *Nightline* on ABC; it doesn't matter whether it's the most politically biased or the most authoritative, in the sense that Ted Koppel [of *Nightline*] is supposed to be authoritative. They all do the same thing in search of what they call objectivity. And what they do is this: they have a guy on from what they call the left and they have a guy on from what they call the right, or, if there's no left and right, they're simply in diametrically opposed positions. So, guy in position A is asked a question and he delivers his answer. The interviewer then turns to Mr. B and says, "What do you have to say?" and Mr. B says what he has to say and the two positions are in complete contradiction, and the host says, "Thank you very much," because his is the objective position, standing between two polar opposites. Now, because this idea of objectivity has to be maintained, what you never see is Koppel, for example, saying to Mr. A, "Wait a minute, I know for a fact that what you just said is patently untrue. I know that. I stand behind my authority as a reporter. I've been there. I was there. I saw the man killed. He was killed. I know that, you can't say that. That's a lie, that's a misrepresentation." No, he says nothing. His air of authority lies in his ability to abdicate. In the name of objectivity you don't get "the truth," you get two diametrically opposed positions pitted against each other. And there's just no way anybody can be sure – even while being reassured – that what we're getting has anything to do with the nature of reality. It's a really strange abdication of the responsibility of the authoritative eye on the part of the interviewer.

WK: And the consequence of this sort of reporting is the homogenizing of the meaning of the news. Because it's repeated so often over 24 or 48 hours it becomes neither fish nor flesh but rather a synthesis; and because that synthesis isn't challenged, it becomes the reality.

BC: What I used to do when I was a reporter in the Middle East, or Africa, I would go into a situation covering Rhodesia, or the Afrikaaners, or whomever, and I'd sit down and read every bit of magazine or newspaper journalism I could get my hands on. And once I was convinced that I now understood the accepted opinion, I then rejected eighty per cent of it. And this process never failed me. This ready acceptance of received opinion – which was H.L.

Mencken's definition of mediocrity – does prevail and becomes the established journalistic wisdom. I used to go into these situations and be confronted with the conventional wisdom, and I would say, "Well, no." This was how I first got into trouble in the Middle East, because I went there at a time when it was the prevailing wisdom that your average Israeli was a cross between Moshe Dayan, you know, the heroic and romantic general, and Eva Marie Saint and Paul Newman starring in *Exodus*. This was the prevalent feeling and, to a degree, it still exists. I sat down and read journalistic pieces by Israeli writers and I read their fiction and I read their poetry, and I remember going to my executive producer saying, "You won't believe this, but Israeli fiction is an extraordinarily melancholy fiction – fiction exploring moral confusion – more so than any other fiction that I know at this time." And he said, "What's the moral confusion?" And I said, "It's very simple. You can hardly pick up an Israeli story but there isn't this figure of the Palestinian walking through it, and all those fiction writers know what has happened and they all see what is coming." And he said, "Who are these people?" I said, "There's Yehuda Amichai, a young poet, there's A.B. Yehoshua, a young novelist. They tell the same story. They see themselves turning into killers. They see themselves losing what they thought was the justification for being a light unto the nations. And who reminds them of this? A lone single Arab figure they keep presenting over and over again as the figure of Abraham, because they are all walking around in their Greb boots, or drab army boots, and these Palestinians are drifting through their lives dressed in galabeahs and looking like Abraham in the movies. So I went over and made a film asking a question, which was the question no one was asking at that time because everybody was then cheerleading. I went over and said, to a general, to politicians, to writers, to poets, to anybody I could find, I said, "Listen, I find in your literature this moral confusion. I find this paradoxical. I find your soldiers are now talking about the pain of being killers, the pain of being victims who are creating victims. What's this all about?" I had a general in the Sinai, when I put this to him, break into tears. He just broke into tears, saying, "No one's ever talked to me this way about what is the truth of my life. I abhor my life. I'm now a killer. I know it. I saw all those bodies . . ." And he went hysterical. Then you look at the fiction and it's there. Look at Yehoshua's early story, "Facing the Forest." This is not to be anti-Israeli; this is not to be anti-Semitic. This is to puzzle through the situation along with those writers who really were, as Ezra Pound said, the antennae of their race. They saw what was coming. I remember talking to Golda Meir, who was a smart but crude politician, and she said to me, "The Palestinians, no one in twenty years will even remember who they are." Those were her exact words. I have them on film. Well, the writers told the truth. They knew that the Palestinians were not going anywhere. There is a bond between those two people now. They're intertwined. They're never going to be free of each other. This has nothing to do with being pro-Palestinian or anti-Israeli. This has got to do with what the Israelis themselves were seeing as their destiny, their fate, if they went ahead in the role that they seem doomed and destined to pursue. You can't take land and pretend that people aren't there. That's all. The consequences were in their own fiction. So those writers were telling the truth as they saw it. In those days Golda Meir and her boys used to shut down theater performances, used to censor fiction stories because they didn't want this truth told.

This takes us to the other role. If you switch, if you leap immediately to Russia, you know the role that the truth-tellers have played. It's no accident that when dictators take power the first thing they do is kill all the fucking writers they can find. Because there are too many writers who will not allow themselves to be co-opted, too many who will maintain a loyalty to their eye, to what they see, and will not be sucked in by the conventional or received wisdom. This is where journalism and fiction come under the gun together. You can get killed for both, because what you're really trying to do authoritatively is say what you see. In that position, what's at the other end of the hall is the gun. So some people decline to say what they see. Instead they say what will get them off the hook. Or, as happened in many of the states behind the iron curtain, they develop elaborate systems in their fiction and in their journalism through which they can tell the truth, believing that the bureaucrats can never see through the allegory or the mystification, to what they're doing. In Beograd, Miodrag Pavlovic wrote all his poetry about contemporary Yugoslavia by setting it back at the time of the ancient Serbs, the Bogomils and such tribes. What does a bureaucrat know about that? Nothing. This was true in Russia, this was true in Poland. These are the maneuvers, the devices that are used under extreme duress to tell the truth; a way of finding fictional or journalistic forms that allow you to outfox the censor, the censorious eye.

WK: So conveying the truth as you find it, whether in fiction or journalism, will very probably rely on transformation or disguise of the reality, and require a decoding by the reader to get at the truth you're offering. An oblique language or story.

BC: But you see, what will come to be understood, I am convinced, by those who are able to read – I'll use the dangerous semiotic word "signs," in this case we'll say it was allegory – what they'll come to understand is a truth that in different times would have been as simply put as Hemingway might have put it. There are times *in extremis,* when the truth, even journalistic truth, simple reporting of a situation by a reporter sent into a war, is achieved by adopting what one might say are fictional forms. I am not playing into the hands of the Post-Modernists, who say that language moves away from fact and as you move away from fact then all history is suspect; or that language creates its own reality which has got nothing to do with the truth of history and history is suspect. All of that's bullshit to me. I think that language can go rotten, but it never looses its obligation to reality. This is a distraction perpetrated by a peculiar school of French intellectuals who just don't get it, that's all. Post-modernist writers, to me, are writers who just don't know how to tell stories. I've no interest in that. I don't believe it because I know that I've achieved the same effect three different ways in my life. I've had readers tell me that pure journalistic reporting of a situation brought them to tears. That was a newspaper piece I wrote about a riot in Montreal in the time of Trudeau. I have had people tell me that the ending of *Barrelhouse Kings,* where I talk about my father's dying and his burial, brought them to tears. And I've had people tell me that reading my fiction has brought them to tears. To me, you can't argue with tears. People have taken my experience into themselves. No writer can hope for more, as far as I'm concerned. And, how did I do it? I did it as a journalist, I did it as someone writing an autobiography, and I did it as a fiction writer. Did I do anything different in any of the three operations? No!

WK: Let's talk about the implacable demand for fact, for authentic detail, as the basic and indispensable element in journalism. What happens when you override that need for authentic fact and transform it into a fictional fact? Is there any difference in value? Is there a heightening of meaning? When you create something beyond what really happened, as you know it, what is the justification?

BC: I'm sure you've had the same experience. There are things that happened to you, particularly in your childhood, that are vivid, their details are clear and you could write about them journalistically. But sometimes they become a story. I wouldn't call it of greater value, but I would say that another level of understanding takes place. And this is what is involved in one story of mine, which is becoming more and more popular, more and more translated around the world. It's called "Our Thirteenth Summer," and it's a story that comes out of my childhood. And it's all true; all the details are true; it's the house that I lived in. The people who lived downstairs were exactly as I describe them; the man worked at the job I give him. They were a Jewish family who pretended that they weren't Jewish and, certainly, that their son was not Jewish, and what was insane about this, and I understood it was insane when I was a boy, is that while they went around telling everybody – insisting – that they were not Jewish, their grandfather lived with them and he dressed in a long black coat and he had the tassels, the twirly hair locks, and he wore a black hat and he had the shawl. And my mother said to me at the time, "If he isn't Jewish, nobody's Jewish." But the mother was insisting, to the point of changing her son's name, that they were not Jewish. They were from Vienna.

Now, I knew all this as a journalistic fact and could report it. I also knew that up the street there was another Jewish family who hated them because they were denying they were Jewish. And the old man in this other household used to stand up on his front porch stairs and spit at them when they went by. And I asked as a kid, why? And they said because they say they're not Jewish. That, journalistically, I could report on. I understood, at the age twelve, what was going on there.

Also on our thirteenth birthdays I discovered what prejudice was for the first time, except it was really weird, because I was told by my Jewish friends that I was a *goy* and they couldn't see me any more because they were now men. And I said to them, "What is a *goy*?" And they said, "You eat unclean food. You're unclean." And I came home telling my mother this, crying. So I could write about that journalistically, too. I also had a boxing match with the kid downstairs. One day, it all coalesced for me so that I wrote the story called "Our Thirteenth Summer" in which I described the people downstairs. I described the other Jewish family, and then I described what happens on the thirteenth birthday in which I find that they are no longer my friends, that I am this unclean person and they're not going to see me anymore. Then, on the birthday of the kid downstairs, when he's turning thirteen but they are pretending that he's not Jewish, the kid comes out and he's been forced by his father to learn how to box, and he's being forced to box me. I've already beaten this kid up once in my life. I couldn't fight him. This is true. I couldn't fight him. I knew he couldn't hurt me. In effect, I just kind of sat down, to his astonishment. And I remember as a child thinking, I'm glad my father isn't here watching this because if he was here I would have to beat him up. I'd have to do what adults expected me to do. Instead, I just sat down and he went inside and his father embraced him and there was a whole bonding and I sat on the curb taking the boxing gloves off that the kid had brought me. Now all of that is journalistically true, right? I shaped it and I understood the significance of the Jewish kid in the other family yelling at the old man as he went by, when his father said, "You're not Jewish." The kid said to the old man, "You might as well be from Mars." I've never forgotten that. I sat on the curb and I suddenly found that the only person standing beside me, this person who had accepted defeat, was the old Jewish guy, the grandfather, who was looking down at me. And here's where the fiction came in. He never said anything to me in real life. He just stood there looking at me and I knew that his sympathy was with me, but he didn't know what to say, or couldn't say it, or wouldn't say it, but nothing was said. So I made up the lines and this became the fiction. I made up the lines where the old man smiles and talks to me as I'm taking off the boxing gloves:

"It's not so easy to hurt you," he said.
"Nope," I said.
"You would make a good Jew," he said.
"How would you know," I said, real sharp, "you're not Jewish."
"No, that's right," he said, smiling a little more, and then he leaned down and whispered, "I'm the man from Mars."

Those lines are the only fictional thing in the whole experience, the rest is journalistic reporting;

but that little twist is what gives it the other level, or dimension of understanding, of how you're never quite sure who the victim may turn out to be, and who the light unto the world might turn out to be, and who is actually unclean, who is a *goy*. So the question is – and this relates to what I was saying about Genesis – when I made up those four lines, was I in fact lying on behalf of fiction? I don't believe it. I believe that that's what was in the heart of that old man as he stood looking at me. And I believe that's what he would say to me. It resonates as true through the whole story, because it is true to all the journalistic detail of the story.

WK: Your version of his truth.

BC: Absolutely. But the truth inherent in the detail because the truth that emerges out of my imagination doesn't violate the reported detail, therefore the ending does not seem forced. Short stories that seem forced in their endings – trick endings, or unnecessary endings – are not true to the reportage. After all, it was Tolstoy who said that all great storytelling starts with reporting. If it's not true to the reporting and the rest of the story, it's false. The reader knows it's false. No reader ever suggested to me that that's not what the old man would say.

WK: This constant rage for authenticity, for historical accuracy, and biographical truth is really bothersome nonsense. The truth is that the truth is not only better off, but more visible, more tellable and, really, more authentic as a lie. And I think your experience with the Hogg poems illuminates this brilliantly.

BC: It fascinates and amuses me in the best sense that Hogg, in the lives of some people, has become a real presence. There are friends of mine who don't call me by my name. They call me Hogg. John Montague, nine out of ten times will not call me Barry, he'll call me Hogg. This is kind of wonderful, amusing, even enchanting, but I remember when I started out, and I'm sure this is true for all kinds of writers, I was trying to learn how to write poems but I'd never really thought of myself as a poet. I'd fiddled, but I'd never really written what I would call a poem. And then, for reasons I don't know to this day, I started writing poems that reflected my experience in the Middle East and my relationship with a woman there. It wasn't until I had written about ten such poems that I realized these poems represented the voice of the egotistical "I" – you know, seen through my own lyric eye. Even at that stage I began to suspect the persuasiveness – not the authenticity of the experience, but the persuasiveness of the voice – if it was in that "I." And when you start suspecting yourself, you're in trouble. I do not remember how I actually came up with the name Hogg, but I remember the day that I stroked out all the "I"s, the personal pronouns, and wrote in *Hogg*. I felt this terrific release. Nothing in the poem had changed. It was a release of detachment and it wasn't that it allowed the reader to detach himself from me, as Eliot has argued about this matter, it allowed me a distance from myself, allowed me to be, ironically, in the voice of Hogg, more authoritative, more authentic, more honest about what I'd actually experienced personally. It was no longer my problem, it was Hogg's problem. So I went on writing the Hogg poems and they were published and achieved a certain notoriety.

Then the story of Hogg gets even more complicated because I went back to Jerusalem fifteen years later. I had no desire to see the woman with whom I had been involved. I went with Claire, who was having an exhibition of her work there. I had a desire to see Yehuda Amichai. I wanted to see Jerusalem again and I did and I came home, my imagination triggered. I started writing poems and I decided, since my mother had died, I'd make my mother the muse figure. So I published *Stone Blind Love* – poems set in Jerusalem around the death of a mother. I had no sooner published it than I thought, "This is a fake, all of this experience is Hogg's experience in Jerusalem. I've made a terrible mistake here. It's not that the poems aren't true, it's not that the lines aren't true, it's not that the experience isn't real and authentic, I've just named the wrong people." So I told this to my publisher and she said, "Well, do it right." So I did. I was blessed that my publisher would do this. That's why the second Hogg book came along. *Stone Blind Love* doesn't exist anymore, because I put it all back into the experience of Hogg, which is exactly what it was, because I am Hogg, that's all, and my mother had nothing to do with it, God bless her. I've written other things about my mother. She doesn't belong in the poem. And so the authenticity of the voice is still the same, the details are the same – you can check one against the other – the poems are the same, it's just that they are all attributed now to Hogg instead of me. Is this some kind of subterfuge?

WK: It certainly is, and you should be ashamed of yourself.

BC: Of course, I should be ashamed of myself, but then, if Yeats could do it, if Lowell could do it, if everybody else could do it, why can't I?

WK: There's no reason. And you are right that everybody does it. We hear over and over writers talking about the voice as the key to creating character. I've worked years on a novel and had it go nowhere until the voice clicks into place for me; but when I do finally hear it speak I'm liberated from the unknown. This suggests that the individual imagination is really

the final arbiter of what is true and not true in anybody's writing. It's not the reader, it's never the critic, it's the writer alone with all those possible voices;
and then one voice makes itself clear, and by happy
chance the game begins, and the truth gets told.
Sometimes.

BC: Happenstance, accident – something suddenly
seems to evolve naturally out of a situation, something not intended. What was never intended was
that your friend, the poet Jim Hart, Carly Simon's
husband, would suddenly show up unannounced at
your house. Remember that night. I nearly fell out of
my chair when I saw he was carrying a copy of the
Hogg poems and who could have guessed that he
intended to read, at supper, my poem "Sisyphus the
Crack King." I didn't know that he had been a crack
addict. Then he read it and what was interesting was
the way he read it – in a totally different speed and
rhythm than I have done, although as I told Jim afterwards, I have always felt when I read the poem that I
was not getting it quite right. I was reading it with
heavy syncopation in terms of stresses per line, and
he read it as someone frenetic would read it, rushing
across the beat. He told me afterwards that what
interested him about the poem and what made it so
authentic – I think he said it was the most authentic
voice of the crack addict that he knew of in poetry –
was the way the rhymes and the rhythms impelled the
reader to go forward at a faster and faster speed; and
of course speed is one of the effects of crack – I'm
told. What's really curious about his authenticating
the voice of Sisyphus is that I have never taken crack.
I've never even smoked hashish. I'm strictly what you
would call a boozehound. In terms of the authentic
voice, I said to Jim, "This makes me the Stephen
Crane of crack," because, just as Stephen Crane had

never been to war and wrote the greatest war novel in American history, I've never done crack and here I'm being told I have the authentic voice of the crack addict. There is something very mysterious here but it has happened many times over in literature – that the writer somehow projects himself into a world he has never known. I don't know how to explain it, because I agree with Tolstoy that the basis of all great writing is reporting, and reporting is the eye that sees with its own authority and trusts that authority. So when I wrote the poem I was trusting the authenticity of my own eye as I imagined myself inside the head of a crack addict. And the image I carried forward was of Sisyphus, who, in his addiction, rolled the stone, or rock – which is another word for crack – up the inside of his head in the way he rolled the stone up the hill, and then he watched it go back down, then he rolled it up and watched it go back down. So in a sense, I suppose, Sisyphus was the original crack addict.

In terms of everything I've said about authenticity of voice, this is a leap that is puzzling to me. I take the compliment as it is given because it's an authentic voice but then this is what has always bedeviled people who have tried to rationally explain where authenticity in the writer's eye and the writer's voice comes from. The imagination can break through boundaries into authenticity of experience simply by imagining. Certainly from Coleridge on, people have been trying to figure out how the imagination works and I can't explain it any better than Coleridge.

WK: That voice from the interior comes and goes, capriciously. It did for Coleridge with his opium dream, which was interrupted by a visitor, and most of it then lost to memory, except for the fragment we know as "Kubla Kahn." We are at the mercy of a capricious instrument, the imagination.

BC: An extension of this question is something I have played with all through my fiction. To imagine how a woman thinks and feels and speaks. The first story I tried this in was "Crow Jane's Blues." The second was a story called "A Terrible Discontent," and both are in *The Black Queen Stories*. Then finally I wrote a novel, *When Things Get Worst*, and what I was attempting to do in that was not only see a situation or a relationship from a woman's point of view, but actually inhabit a woman's voice. I certainly got away with it in "Crow Jane's Blues," but that's only seven pages. "A Terrible Discontent" is a little longer – people like that story very much, particularly women, which pleases me – but again, it's eleven pages. What I wanted to do was a short novel in the voice of a woman, in which she would talk, not only about the landscape, the relationships between men and women, family relationships, but all the way down to the most basic experiences – what it's like to be penetrated by a man, and not only penetrated but to feel a female orgasm. In other words, I tried to write a story which "only a woman could write." And I have had no one complain to me that the voice is false, or that it doesn't sound like a woman, or that it sounds like a man. Quite the reverse. All the readers who've written about it, and all the readers I respect, have simply accepted that this is the voice of a woman. Now, to make this more mysterious, at least to myself, I wrote that book at the racetrack in Toronto. I started writing it with a sense of being possessed. The races run every half hour and when I was not looking into the horses, this would leave fifteen minutes between races. I would hear this woman talking to me and so I would stand at the counter, alone with my notebook, and write in her voice, telling her story. I was in a state of extraordinary concentration.

This had a terrific effect on my concentration on the horses, too. I had one of the greatest summers betting the horses that I've ever had in my life.

I used to look up and I'd see that it was time and I'd put down my pen and go over to the woman in the wicket who looked after me, and I'd make my bet. I'd go back to my book, I'd watch the race, I'd win the race. I'd think "good," and I'd start writing in the voice of this woman again. I did this day after day after day. I could hardly wait to get to the racetrack because it was an exhilaration, and I felt that if I broke this rhythm the woman might leave me, her voice might stop; also the winning streak might stop. So I did a chapter, and then another, and then I stopped for a break. I came down to Albany, to visit with you and Joe Gagen, wondering when this woman would next speak to me. I marched – strolled, would be a better word – in the St. Patrick's Day parade with you and we stopped in at *Sweet Lorraine*'s tiny café. I sat down beside you, and we ordered drink. I looked around that little bar at the locals, at what I thought was serious in-breeding among the neighbours – which seemed to remind me of the country story that I was telling through the voice of this woman – and I said out loud to myself, "This is daughter-fondling country. I can't see anybody in this room who has more than two fingers of forehead." I heard a little Whoop inside my brain. I took this line back to Toronto and went to the racetrack about two days later. I was standing there with my book and I heard: "This is daughter-fondling country and nobody here's got more than two fingers of forehead." That woman was talking to me again and I never looked back. I kept on going and going and I finished the novel.

And so, now, suddenly everything between us has dovetailed – here we are at a racetrack, engaging the mysteries of writing, wondering at how the imagination projects itself into a voice that it shouldn't know, a knowing, an inner intimacy that is a mystery akin to knowing the inner voice of a crack king. There it is, all wrapped up nicely for us – authenticity of voice, imagination, and our time here at the racetrack.

As a matter of fact, with the waning of the afternoon, this is where we conclude our talk, the event punctuated by a trip to the betting window by Mr. Callaghan who, after sips of the Hennessey cognac that arrived at the table, places two wagers on the ninth race, a trifecta, and an exacta. "Americanbid" wins it, "Regal Pro" is second, "Run for Mom" third, and Callaghan smiles at the finish and hands the interviewer the winning exacta ticket, a gift horse of sorts, a betting man's way of buying a drink for the interviewer, who has been busy examining the results of his tape recording and could not have been expected to do any handicapping, which is, anyway, the lowest form of truth-seeking. Callaghan also flashes his own winning trifecta ticket, which pays four times what the exacta pays, but who's counting? The day at the track thus ends on a universally solvent note and we move toward the interviewer's home pool table for a few games of eight ball, the music of Champion Jack Dupree, and then to dinner before a plate of fifteen blessed lobsters. Fifteen. But who's counting?

APPENDIX A

Four Hogg Drawings

APPENDIX B

Translation in *Exile: The Literary Quarterly*

VOLUME 1, #1 (1972)

Samar Attar (Arabic, Syrian), "The Return of the Dead," poem trans. by author.

Yehuda Amichai (Hebrew, Israeli) three short poems, trans. Harold Schimmel.

Michel Deguy (French), a poem trans. Serge Fauchereau and John Montague.

Marie-Claire Blais (Quebecoise), second chapter from the novel *Le Loup*, trans. Louise Delisle.

VOLUME 1, #2 (1972)

Yehia Hakki (Arabic, Egyptian), short story "An Empty Bed," trans. Samar Attar.

Robert Marteau (French, living in Canada), six poems, trans. John Montague.

Claude Gauvreau (Quebecois), short play, poem, essay, trans. Ray Ellenwood '.

VOLUME 1, #3 (1974)

Roch Carrier (Quebecois), "Hunting les Anglais," trans. Sheila Fischman.

Jacques Ferron (Quebecois), *Papa Boss* (60-page novella), trans. Ray Ellenwood.

VOLUME 1, #4 (1974)

Françoise Xenakis (French), "She'd Tell him on the Island: A Play for Stereophonic Radio," trans. Margaret Pacsu.

Philippe Thoby-Marcelin (Haïtian/U.S), four poems, trans. Ray Ellenwood.

Marie-Claire Blais (Quebecoise), from *St. Lawrence Blues*, trans. Ralph Manheim.

VOLUME 2, #1 (1974)

Yehuda Amichai (Hebrew, Israeli), four poems from the war, trans. by the author.

Jacques Ferron (Quebecois), *Quince Jam*, complete novella, trans. Ray Ellenwood.

Yannis Ritsos (Greek), trans. Nikos and Gwendolyn (MacEwen) Tsingos.

Mercè Rodoreda (Catalonian), two stories, trans. David Rosenthal .

VOLUME 2, #3-4 (1975)

Joyce Mansour (French) *Jules César* (novella), trans. Ray Ellenwood. (Also trans. of short texts for Jean Benoît objects).

Yannis Ritsos (Greek), "Helen," long poem, trans. Nikos and Gwendolyn MacEwen.

VOLUME 3, #1 (1975)

Marie-Claire Blais (Quebecoise), "The Testament of Jean-Le-Maigre to his Brothers," draft of part of a novel never published, trans. Ray Ellenwood.

Yehuda Amichai (Hebrew, Israeli), *The Travels of a Latter-Day Benjamin of Tudela*, long poem, trans. Ruth Nevo.

Joyce Mansour (French), eight poems, trans. Ray Ellenwood.

André Frenaud (French), eight poems, trans. Evelyn Robson and John Montague.

Mercè Rodoreda (Catalonian), "A Letter," trans. David Rosenthal.

VOLUME 3, #2 (1976)

Jacques Ferron (Quebecois), three stories, trans. Betty Bednarski; and "Claude Gauvreau" trans. Ray Ellenwood.

Claude Gauvreau (Quebecois), "Ode to the Enemy" and "Three Dramatic Objects," trans. Ray Ellenwood.

Philippe Jaccottet (French) three poems, trans. John Montague.

Jaime Gil de Biedma (Spanish), four poems trans. Elaine Kerrigan.

VOLUME 3, #3-4 (1976)

Réjean Ducharme (Quebecois), "The Zone of Hardy Deciduous Forests" from *L'Hiver de force*, trans. Ray Chamberlain.

Yannis Ritsos (Greek), *Orestes*, trans. Nikos Tsingos and Gwendolyn MacEwen.

Pierre Jean Jouve (French), three poems, trans. John Montague.

VOLUME 4, #1 (1976)

Breyten Breytenbach (Afrikaans, South Africa), ten poems plus "Vulture Culture," poems and non-fiction piece trans. by André Brink.

France Théoret (Quebecoise), "The Sampler," trans. David Ellis.

Nicole Brossard (Quebecoise), "The Writer," trans. David Ellis.

Marie-Claire Blais (Quebecoise), "Marcelle," trans. David Ellis.

VOLUME 4, #2 (1977)

Yehuda Amichai (Hebrew, Israeli), "Seven Laments for the Fallen in the War," trans. by the author and Ted Hughes.

Jacques Ferron (Quebecois), from *The Cart*, trans. Ray Ellenwood.

André Frenaud (French), sixteen poems, trans. John Montague and Evelyn Robson.

Paul Celan (German), eighteen poems, trans. Michael Hamburger.

VOLUME 4, #3-4 (1977)

Marie-Claire Blais (Quebecoise), *The Ocean*, play trans. Ray Chamberlain.

Robert Marteau (French), from *Pentecost: A Novel*, trans. David Ellis.

VOLUME 5, #1-2 (1977)

Roch Carrier (Quebecois), Part 1 of *The Garden of Earthly Delights*, trans. Sheila Fischman.

Robert Marteau (French), from *Atlante*, trans. Barry Callaghan.

Jaime Gil de Biedma (Spanish), four poems, trans. Anthony Kerrigan.

VOLUME 5, #3-4 (1978)

Claude Estaban (French), "Transparent God", poems trans. John Montague and Evelyn Robson.

Jacques Ferron (Quebecois), "La Sorgne", trans. Ray Ellenwood.

Robert Marteau (French), from *Atlante*, trans. Barry Callaghan.

Marie-Claire Blais (Quebecoise), from *Nights in the Underground*, trans. Ray Ellenwood.

Guillevic (French), "Carmac," poem trans. John Montague.

Victor-Lévy Beaulieu (Quebecois), from *A Québécois Dream*, trans. Ray Chamberlain.

VOLUME 6, #1-2 (1979)

The first number with no translations.

VOLUME 6, #3-4 (1979)

Robert Marteau, from *Treatise on Tincture and White*, trans. Barry Callaghan.

VOLUME 7, #1-2 (1980)

Réjean Ducharme (Quebecois), from *Bittersea*, trans. David Homel.

Louis Goulet (Manitoba Métis), "She Wins," trans. Ray Ellenwood.

Archambault Theatre Collective (Quebecois), "Scenes of Maximum Security," from *It don't Mean Nothing*, trans. Ray Chamberlain and Ray Ellenwood.

VOLUME 7, #3-4 (1981)

Raymond Queneau (French), "Exercises in Style," trans. M.B. Thompson.

Jacques Ferron (Quebecois), from *The Cart*, trans. Ray Ellenwood.

Claude Gauvreau (Quebecois), four plays, trans. Ray Ellenwood.

Marie-Claire Blais (Quebecoise), from *Deaf to the City*, trans. Carol Dunlop.

VOLUME 8, #1-2 (1981)

Victor-Lévy Beaulieu (Quebecois), from *Jos Connaissant*, trans. Ray Chamberlain

Italo Calvino (Italian), from *If on a Winter's Night a Traveller*, trans. William Weaver (name not given in magazine).

Stéphane Mallarmé (French), "The Afternoon of a Fawn: Eclogue," trans. Marc Widershien.

Jaroslav Hasek (Czech), *The Red Commissar*, trans. Sir Cecil Parrott

Michel Beaulieu (Quebecois), from "Spells of Fury," poems trans. Arlette Francière.

VOLUME 8, #3-4 (1981)

Yehuda Amichai (Hebrew, Israeli), "Great Tranquility: Questions and Answers," poems trans. Tudor Parfit and Glenda Abramson.

Aharon Appelfeld (Hebrew, Israeli), from *The Age of Wonders*, novel trans. not listed

Miodrag Pavloviæ (Serbian), "Singing at the Whirlpool," poems trans. Barry Callaghan.

Boris Pasternak (Russian), "The Subline Malady," poem, trans. Mark Rudman.

Nicole Brossard (Quebecoise), "Aroused," poem sequence, trans. Alexandre L. Amprimoz.

Tomas Tranströmer (Swedish), four poems, trans. Göran Malmquist.

Yehuda Amichai (Hebrew, Israeli), "To Love in Jerusalem," play trans. Richard Farber.

Gérard Bessette (Quebecois), from *The Cycle*, novel trans. A.D. Martin-Sperry.

Imants Ziedonis (Latvian), from *Flowers of Ice*, prose pieces, trans. Barry Callaghan.

Nikola Petkovic, "The Hoppers," short story trans. Slobodon Drenovac.

Tristan Corbière (French), "The Wandering Mistrel and the Pardon of Saint Anne," poem, trans. Peter Dale.

Robert Marteau (French), "Three Sonnets," trans. Barry Callaghan.

Jaime Gil de Biedma (Spanish), three poems, trans. Elaine Kerrigan.

Arie van den Berg (Dutch), *Owls*, poems, trans. Scott Rollins and Peter Nijmeijen.

Roland Giguère (Quebecois), ten poems, from *Rose and Thorn: Selected Poems*, trans. Donald Winkler.

Gilles Hénault, from *Signals for Seers*, poems, trans. Ray Ellenwood.

Yves Theriault (Quebecois, Acadian of part Montagnais ancestry), "Missus Anna," short story trans. Ray Ellenwood.

Andrei Voznesensky (Russian), from *The Ditch: A Spiritual Proceeding*, poems/prose trans. Barry Callaghan and Natalia Mayer.

Aristophanes' *The Birds* (Ancient Greek comedy-drama) adapted by Gwendolyn MacEwen.

Attilio Bertolucci (Italian), eight poems, trans. Charles Tomlinson.

Michel Tremblay (Quebecois), from *The Guid-Sisters*, play trans. William Findley and Martin Bowman into modern Scots from the Quebecois joual, *Les belles soeurs.*

Mihály Kornis (Hungarian), "Petition," short story trans. Ivan Sanders.

Jean Joubert (French), four poems, trans. Hilary Davies.

Roland Giguère (Quebecois), from *Rose and Thorn,* prose poems, trans. Donald Winkler.

Iván Mándy (Hungarian), "Night of the Sweat-Soaked Shirt," short story, trans. Chris Outtram and Éva Rácz.

Rita Tornborg (Swedish), "Kajamec," short story trans. Patricia Campton.

Michel Beaulieu (Quebecois), "Among Other Cities," long poem, trans. Arlette Francière

Mimmo Morian (Italian), *Seven Solitudes for an Island*, poem sequence, trans. Mark O'Connor

Slavko Mihalic, poem from *Black Apples*, trans. Bernard Johnson.

Kazuko Shiraishi (Japanese), four poems, trans. Sally Ito.

Ivan Drach (Ukrainian), four poems, trans. Paul Nemser, Mark Rudman, Carol Muske, and Paula Schwarts.

Charles Baudelaire (French), "The Voyage," poem, trans. Peter Dale.

Nikola Šop (Croatian), "Cottages in Space," long poem trans. Branko Brusar and W.H. Auden.

Pierre Morency (Quebecois), two poems, trans. Alexandre Amprimoz.

Pier Paolo Pasolini (Italian), two poems, from "Ali Blue-Eyes," and "Teorema (an Aside)," trans. Antonino Mazza.

Gunter Kunert (German), "In the Closet," short story trans. Hans Werner.

Milivoj Slavicek (Croatian), four poems, trans. Branko Gorjup and Jeannette Lynes.

Heinz Piontek (German), "Other Catchwords," short prose trans. Ken Fontenot.

Gabriele Eckart (German), "Feldberg and Back," short story trans. Wayne Kvam.

VOLUME 14, #4 (1990)

Osman Lins (Portuguese, Brazil), "Pastroral," short story trans. Adria Frizzi.

Naguib Mahfouz (Arabic, Egyptian), "The Mosque in the Narrow Lane," short story trans. Nadia Faraq, revised by Josephine Wahba and Barry Callaghan.

VOLUME 15, #1 (1990)

Antun Šoljan (Croatian), "Stone Thrower," poem trans. Charles Simic.

Pierre Morency (Quebecois), "Personal Effects," poem trans. Alexandre Amprimoz.

Gunter Kunert (German), "Dreamchild," short story trans. Hans Werner.

Ihor Kalynets (Ukrainian), three poems, trans. Marco Carynnyk.

VOLUME 15, #2 (1991)

Vasyl Holoborodko (Ukrainian), "Katerina (fugue)," poem trans. Bohdan Boychuk.

Vasko Popa (Serbian), "Give Me Back My Rags," poem sequence trans. Charles Simic.

Jude Stéfan (French), six poems, trans. John Montague.

VOLUME 15, #3 (1991)

No translations.

VOLUME 15, #4 (1991)

Gaston Miron (Quebecois), six poems, trans. Paul Savoie.

Hans Joachin Schädich (German), *East/West Berlin*, prose trans. Hans Werner.

Hélène Dorion (Quebecoise), "Out of Focus," long poem trans. Andrea Moorhead.

Friedrich Christian Delius (German), from *The Pears of Ribbeck*, novel trans. Hans Werner.

VOLUME 16 #1-4 (1992)

These issues were replaced by *15 Years in Exile Vols 1 and II* (reprinted pieces in English and English translation taken from *Exile's* first fifteen years), and *Exile's Exiles: The Happy Few* (this volume plus the combined Exile 16.2 and 16.3 volume are photographs of Exile authors and reproductions of their actual handwriting).

VOLUME 17, #1 (1992)

Ivan Slamnig (Croatian), *Squares of Sorrow*, poems, trans. Milka Lukic.

Ivana Malenkova (Serbian), *Festivals of Babylon*, poems, trans. Milka Lukic.

Tomaz Salumun (Slovenian), three poems, trans. Michael Biggins.

Claire Dé (Quebecoise), "A Devouring Love," short story trans. Sam Leibman.

VOLUME 17, #2 (1993)

No translations.

VOLUME 17, #3 (1993)

Francic Ponge (French), three poems, Trans. John Montague.

VOLUME 17, #4 (1993)

Jacques Brault (Quebecois), from *On the Road No More*, poems trans. David Sobelman.

VOLUME 18, #1 (1994)

No translations.

VOLUME 18, #2 (1994)

Primo Levi (Italian), twelve poems, trans. M. L. Rosenthal.

VOLUME 18, #3 (1994)

Rakel Liehu (Finnish), *Cubisms*, poems trans. Seija Paddon.

Claire Dé (Quebecoise), "Slices of Mealtime," short story trans. Lazer Lederhendler.

Giuseppe Ungaretti (Italian), "Day by Day 1940-1946," poem sequence trans. Diego Bastianutti.

VOLUME 18, #4 (1994)

Tristan Bernard (French), "The Exile," play trans.

Armando Pajalich (Italian), "On the 18th Anniversary of P.P. Pasolini's Murder," poem, trans. by author.

Fluvio Tomizza (Italian), "A Better Life," short story, trans.

VOLUME 19, #1 (1995)

Sappho (Ancient Greek), eight poems, trans. by Anita George.

VOLUME 19, #2 (1995)

Andrea Zanzotto (Italian), eight poems, trans. Beverly Allen and Gino Rizzo.

VOLUME 19, #3 (1995)

A.B. Yehoshua (Hebrew, Israeli), "Night Babies," play trans.

VOLUME 19, #4 (1995)

Hans Sahl (German), four stories, trans. Hans Werner.

VOLUME 20, #1 (1996)

Gérald Tougas (Quebecois), "Fête du Canada Day," short story trans. Rachelle Renaud.

VOLUME 20, #2 (1996)

Claire Dé (Quebecoise), from *Soundless Loves*, novel trans. Lazer Lederhendler.

VOLUME 20, #3 (1996)

Vesna Parun (Croatian), five poems, trans. Branko Gorjup and Jeannette Lynes.

Slavenka Draculic (Croatian), from novel *The Taste of a Man*, no translator name listed.

VOLUME 20, #4 (1996)

Gottfried Benn (German), twelve poems, trans. James Lawson.

VOLUME 21, #1 (1997)

Katarina Frostenson (Swedish), two stories, trans. Joan Tate.

Wislawa Szymborska (Polish), twelve poems, trans. Marta Zaborska-Quinn

Ferida Durakovic, from *Heart of Darkness*, three poems, trans. Amela Simic.

VOLUME 21, #2 (1997)

Andrea Zanzotto (Italian), from *Going Sewing*, poems, trans. Beverly Allen and Gino Rizzo.

VOLUME 21, #3 (1997)

Andreï Makine (French, Russian), from *Once Upon the River Love*, novel trans. from the French by Geoffrey Strachan.

Miljenko Jergovic (Serbian), two stories, trans. Stela Tomaševic.

VOLUME 21, #4 (1998)

Mirkka Rekola (Finnish), from *Sky on Duty*, eleven poems, trans. Hebert Lomas

Pierre Nepveu (Quebecois), ten poems, trans. Donald Winkler.

VOLUME 22, #1 (1998)

Ismail Kadare (Albanian), from *The File on H*, novel trans. David Bellos.

Patrizia Cavalli (Italian), eight poems, trans. Judith Baumel, Francesca Valente, Kenneth Koch, and Robert McCracken.

Réjean Ducharme (Quebecois), from "The Daughters of Christopher Columbus," prose trans. Will Browning.

VOLUME 22, #2 (1998)

Claire Dé (Quebecoise), from *The Sparrow Has Cut the Day in Half*, novel in verse, trans. Lazer Lederhendler.

Michel Deguy (French), *A Poleoscope*, long poem, trans. Christopher Elson.

Aude (Quebecoise), "The Indiscernable Movement Called Life," and "The Ferryman," short stories, trans. Jill Cairns.

VOLUME 22, #3 (1998)

No translations.

VOLUME 22, #4 (1998)

Yehuda Amichai (Hebrew, Israeli), "Jerusalem is a Merry-Go-Round," poem trans. Aloma Halter.

Pierre Morency (Quebecois), *Glimmer on the Mountain*, long poem trans. Brenda Casey and Elizabeth Hahn.

VOLUME 23, #1 (1999)

Ludwig Zeller (Spanish, Mexico & Chile), four poems, trans. A.F. Moritz.

David Huerta (Spanish, Mexico), six poems, trans. Mark Schafer.

VOLUME 23, #2 (1999)

Mónica Lavin (Spanish, Mexico), "Home Again?" short story trans. Arturo V. Degade and Barry Callaghan.

Pia Pera (Italian), from *Lo's Diary*, novel trans. Ann Goldstein.

VOLUME 23, #3 (1999)

Ryszard Kapuscinski (Polish), eight poems, trans. Diana Kuprel and Marek Kusiba.

Jaime Sabines (Spanish, Mexico), from *Night Flight*, poems, trans. Colin Carberry.

Jean Barbe (Quebecois), from *How to Become a Monster*, novel trans. Patricia Wright.

VOLUME 30, #3 (2006)

Piera Mattei (Italian), "North," short story trans. by Adrian Cook.

VOLUME 30, #4 (2007) (SPECIAL 120TH ISSUE)

Marie-Claire Blais (Quebecoise), from *Augustino and The Choir of Destruction*, novel trans. Nigel Spencer.

Gonçalo M. Tavares (Portuguese), *Mr. Brecht*, prose poems, trans. Desirée Jung.

Book-length Publications of Translations by Exile Editions

Aristophanes. (Ancient Greek.) *The Birds, after the play of Aristophanes*, Gwendolyn MacEwen, 1993.

Amichai, Yehuda and Ritsos, Yannis. (Hebrew, Greek.) *Amichai and Ritsos: Two Long Poems, "Travels of a Latter-day Benjamin of Tudela" and "Helen,"* trans. Ruth Nevo (Amichai) and Nikos and Gwendolyn Tsingos (Ritsos), 1976. English and Hebrew, facing pages.

Amichai, Yehuda. (Hebrew, Israeli.) *Travels: a Bilingual Edition*, trans. Ruth Nevo, 1986. Hebrew and English, facing pages. (Republished 2001, Picas Series.)

Archambault Theatre Group. (Quebecois.) *No Big Deal!*, trans. David Homel, 1982.

Aristophanes. (Ancient Greek.) *The Birds*, trans. Gwendolyn McEwen, 1993.

Aude. (Quebecoise.) *Human*, trans. Nora Alleyn, 2006.

___. *The Indiscernible Movement*, trans. Jill Cairns, 1998.

___. *The Whole Man*, trans. Jill Cairns, 2000.

Beaulieu, Michel. (Quebecois.) *Countenances*, poems trans. Josée Michaud, 1986.

___. *Kaleidoscope: Perils of a Solelmn Body*, trans. Arlette Francière, 1998.

___. *Perils of a Solemn Body*, poems trans. Arlette Francière, 1988.

___. *Spells of Fury / Charmes de la Fureur*, trans. Arlette Francière, 1984. French and English, facing pages. (Republished 2003, Picas Series.)

Beaulieu, Victor-Lévy. (Quebecois.) *Jos Connaissant, A Novel*, trans. Ray Chamberlain, 1982.

___. *A Québécois Dream*, trans. Ray Chamberlain, 1978.

___. *Satan Belhumeur*, trans. Ray Chamberlain, 1983.

___. *Steven Le Hérault*, trans. Ray Chamberlain, 1987.

Bessette, Gérard. (Quebecois:) *The Cycle*, trans. A.D. Martin-Sperry, 1987.

___. *Incubation, a Novel*, trans. Glen Shortliffe. 1986.

___. *Not for Every Eye,* trans. Glen Shortlifffe, 1984. (Republished 1994, Picas Series.)

Blais, Marie-Claire. (Quebecoise.) *The Ocean*, a play trans. Ray Chamberlain, 1977.

___. *Deaf to the City*, trans. Carol Dunlop, introduction by Richard Teleky, 2006. Exile Classics Series.

___. *Nights in the Underground*, trans. Ray Ellenwood, drawings by Mary Meigs, introduction by Janice Kulyk Keefer, 2006. Exile Classics Series.

___, and Mary Meigs. *Illustrations for To Novels by Marie-Claire Blais*, illustrations by Mary Meigs, text by Marie-Claire Blais, French and English bilingual edition, 1977.

Borduas, Paul-Emile et al. (Quebecois.) *Refus global / Total Refusal*, manifesto trans. Ray Ellenwood, 1985. (Republished 1998.)

Böszörményi, Zoltán. (Hungarian.) *Far From Nothing*, novel trans. Paul Sohar, 2006.

Brault, Jacques. (Quebecois.) *Fragile Moments*, trans. Barry Callaghan, 1985. French and English, facing pages. (Republished 2000, Picas Series.)

___. *On the Road No More*, trans. David Sobelman, 1993. French and English, facing pages.

Cavalli, Patrizia. (Italian.) *My Poems Will not Change the World: selected poems 1974-1992*, trans. Judith Baumel, Dina Boni, Barry Callaghan, Patrizia Cavalli, Mario Fazzini, Paulo Fietta, Kenneth Koch, Robert McCracken, Francesca Valente, Christopher Whyte, 1998. Italian and English, facing pages.

Dé, Claire. (Quebecoise.) *Desire as Natural Disaster*, trans. Lazer Lederhendler, 1995.

____. *The Sparrow Has Cut the Day in Half*, trans. Lazer Lederhendler, 1998.

____. *Soundless Loves*, trans. Lazer Lederhendler, 1996.

Delius, Friedrich Christian. (German.) *The Pears of Ribbeck,* trans. Hans Werner, 1991.

Drach, Ivan. (Ukrainian). *The Madonna of Chernobyl and Other Poems*, trans. Mark Rudman, 1989.

____. *Orchard Lamps*, ed. Stanley Kunitz, various translators, with woodcuts by Jacques Hniz-
dovsky, 1989.

Ducharme, Réjean. (Quebecois.) *Ha! Ha!* trans. David Homel, 1986.

Euripides, and Yannis Ritsos. (Ancient Greek and Modern Greek.) *The Trojan Women, Helen, and
Orestes*, trans. Gwendolyn MacEwen and Nikos Tsingos, 1990.

Ferron, Jacques. (Quebecois.) *The Cart*, trans. Ray Ellenwood, 1980. (Republished 1988).

____. *Papa Boss/Quince Jam/Credit Due*, prose texts trans. Ray Ellenwood, 1992.

____. *The Penniless Redeemer*, trans. Ray Ellenwood, 1984.

Gauvreau, Claude. (Quebecois.) *The Charge of the Expormidable Moose*, play translated by Ray
Ellenwood, 1996.

____. *Entrails*, trans. Ray Ellenwood, 1991.

Giguère, Roland. (Quebecois.) *Rose and Thorn: Selected Poems*, trans. Donald Winkler, 1988.

Hénault, Gilles. (Quebecois.) *Signals for Seers*, poems trans. Ray Ellenwood, 1988. (Republished
2000, Picas Series.)

Holoborodko, Vasyl. (Ukrainian.) *Icarus with Butterfly Wings and Other Poems*, trans. Myrosia Stefaniuk, 1991.

Hungarian Short Stories, ed. Paul Varnai, various translators, 1983.

Incontro: Where Italy and Canada Meet: Photographs by John Reeves, introduction by Francesca
Valente, various translators of the Italian texts, 1996.

Italville: New Italian Writing, ed. Lorenzo Pavolini, various translators, 2005.

Kalynets, Ihor. (Ukrainian.) *Crowning the Scarecrow*, trans. Marco Carynnyk, 1990. Ukrainian and
English, facing pages.

Lapointe, Paul-Marie. (Quebecois.) *The 5th Season*, trans. D. G. Jones, 1985.

Lords of Winter and of Love: A Book of Canadian Love Poems in English and French, ed. Barry
Callaghan, various translators, 1983.

Marteau, Robert. (French.) *Atlante*, trans. Barry Callaghan, 1979. French and English, facing pages.

____. *Eidolon*, trans. Barry Callaghan, 1990. Reprints of *Treatise on White and Tincture* and *Atlante.*
English and French, facing pages.

____. *Interlude*, trans. Barry Callaghan, 1982.

____. *Mount Royal*, novel trans. David Homel, 1982.

____. *Pentecost*, novel trans. David Ellis, 1979.

____. *Pig-skinning*, novella trans. David Homel, 1984. (Republished 2006, Picas Series).

____. *River Without End: A Logbook of the Saint Lawrence*, trans. David Homel, 1987.

____. *Traité du blanc et des teintures\Treatise on White and Tincture*, trans. Barry Callaghan, 1979.
French and English, facing pages.

____. *Venise en miroir/Venice at her Mirror*, poetic text trans. Alexandre Amprimoz, 1991.

____. *Voyage to Vendée*, trans. David Homel, 1987.

Mihalic, Slavko. (Croatian.) *Black Apples: Selected Poems 1954-1987*, tans. Bernard Johnson, 1989.
Croatian and English, facing pages.

Morency, Pierre. (Quebecois.) *The Eye is an Eagle*, trans. Linda Gaboriau, 1992.

____. *A Season for Birds*, trans. Alexandre Amprimoz, 1990. French and English, facing pages.

Nepveu, Pierre. (Quebecois.) *Romans-fleuves*, trans. Donald Winkler, 1998.

Neruda, Pablo. (Spanish, Chilean.) *100 Love Sonnets*, trans. Gustavo Escobedo, Introduction by
Rosemary Sullivan, paintings by Gabriela Campos, 2004. Spanish and English, facing pages.
(Republished 2007, Exile Classics Series.)

Ouellette, Fernand. (Quebecois.) *Wells of light*, trans. Barry Callaghan and Ray Ellenwood, 1989.
(Republished 2003, Picas Series.)

Pasolini, Pier Paolo. (Italian.) *Poetry*, selected and translated by Antonino Mazza, 1991.

Pasternak, Boris. (Russian.) *My Sister-life*, poems trans. Mark Rudman with Bohdan Boychuk,
1989.

Pavlovic, Miodrag. (Serbian.) *Kaphke/Links,* trans. Bernard Johnson, 1989. Serbian and English, facing pages.

___. *Singing at the Whirlpool,* trans. Barry Callaghan, 1983. Serbian and English, facing pages.

___. *A Voice Locked in Stone,* trans. Barry Callaghan, 1985. Serbian and English, facing pages.

Pelchat, Jean. (Quebecois.) *The Afterlife of Vincent Van Gogh,* trans. Lazer Lederhendler, 2001.

Riel, Louis. (Quebecois.) *Selected Poetry of Louis Riel,* trans. Paul Savoie, 1993. French and English, facing pages. (Republished 2000, Picas Series.)

Sabines, Jaime. (Spanish, Mexican.) *Weekly Diary and Poems in Prose & Adam and Eve Poems,* trans. Colin Carberry, 2004. Spanish and English, facing pages.

Salivarová, Zdena. (Czech.) *Ashes, Ashes, All Fall Down,* trans. Jan Drábek, 2000. Picas Series.

Schäedlich, Hans Joachim. (German.) *Eastwestberlin,* trans. Hans Werner, 1992.

Simonsuuri, Kirsti. (Finnish.) *Boy Devil,* novel trans. by Seija Paddon, 1992.

Slavicek, Milivoj. (Croatian.) *Silent Doors,* trans. Branko Gorjup and Jeanette Lynes, 1988. Croatian and English, facing pages.

Šoljan, Antun. (Croatian.) *The Stone Thrower and Other Poems,* trans. Charles Simic, A.S. Tomson, A. Nizeteo, G. Marvin Tatum, A.R. Mortimer, Bernard Johnson, 1990. Croatian and English, facing pages.

Tremblay, Michel. (Quebecois.) *The Guid Sisters,* trans. William Findlay and Martin Bowman, 1988. Translation of the Quebecois joual play *Les Belles Soeurs* into modern Scots. (Republished 2000, Picas Series.)

Ungaretti, Giuseppe. (Italian.) *A Major Selection of the Poetry of Giuseppe Ungaretti,* trans. Diego Bastianutti, 1997. Italian and English, facing pages.

Vorobyov, Mykola. (Ukrainian.) *Wild Dog Rose Moon,* trans. Myrosia Stefaniuk, 1992. Ukranina and English, facing pages.

Werup, Jacques. (Swedish.) *The Time in Malmö on the Earth,* trans. Roger Greenwald, 1989.

Zeller, Ludwig. (Spanish, Mexican.) *Totem Women,* trans. Susanna Wald, sculpture by Claire Weissman Wilks, 1993. Spanish and English, facing pages.

Ziedonis, Imants. (Latvian.) *Flowers of Ice,* trans. Barry Callaghan, preface by John Montague, 1987.

Zigaina, Giuseppe. (Italian.) *Passolini Between Enigma and Prophecy,* trans. Jennifer Russell, 1990.

CONTRIBUTORS

BRUNELLA ANTOMARINI teaches Aesthetics and Contemporary philosophy at John Cabot University in Rome. She holds degrees in Foreign Languages and Literatures, Philosophy, and a PhD in philosophy at Gregoriana University, Rome. She has published many articles on the question of form in art, about poetry from an anthropological point of view, and on the relationship between art and cognition. She runs a yearly poetry festival "InVerse," devoted to Italian poets in English translation. She has published *La percezione della forma nell'estetica di Hans Urs von Balthasar* (Aesthetica edizioni, Palermo, 2004); *L'errore del maestro* (Derive Approdi, Roma 2006); *Pensare con l'errore* (Codice edizioni, Torino 2007, forthcoming in September).

ALEXANDRE AMPRIMOZ is a professor, a distinguished semiotician, a translator, linguist, and storyteller, and the author of some twenty-five books. He published a collection of short stories in English, *Too Many Popes*, in 1990.

MARGARET ATWOOD is the author of more than forty books of fiction, poetry, and critical essays. Her most recent book, *Moral Disorder*, is a collection of interconnected short stories and was published by Nan A. Talese/Doubleday. Her novel, *Oryx and Crake*, was short-listed for the Man Booker Prize and the Giller Prize in Canada. Her other books include the 2000 Booker Prize winning, *The Blind Assassin*, *Alias Grace*, which won the Giller Prize in Canada and the Premio Mondello in Italy, *The Robber Bride*, *Cat's Eye*, *The Handmaid's Tale* and *The Penelopiad*. Margaret Atwood lives in Toronto with writer Graeme Gibson.

SUSAN BECKMAN is a writer and journalist.

MICHAEL BELL was the founding Director of the Carleton University Art Gallery, Ottawa. He took on the position after a distinguished career in the visual arts, including stints at the National Gallery of Canada, the Ontario Arts Council, and the McMichael Canadian Collection. He retired from the Carleton University Art Gallery in 2004.

MARIE-CLAIRE BLAIS of Canada is the internationally known author of more than twenty-five books. She is a three-time winner of the Governor General's Award for Fiction, and has been awarded the Athanase-David Prize, the Médicis Prize, the Molson Prize, and Guggenheim Fellowships. She lives in Quebec and Florida. *Augustino and the Choir of Destruction* is the final volume of a trilogy, and it will be published in English by Anansi in May 2007.

JON BROOKS was recently named "Best Songwriter of 2006" by the international Green Man Review. He is part unrepentant idealist, part fallen mystic, part secular preacher, part Gen X Cohen, Cave and Cash. A troubadour wholly devoted to the song as a necessary means toward greater social justice, his inspiration is drawn from those living on the outskirts of approval. Brooks maintains, "only a stranger will save this world." His first CD (January 2006), 'No Mean City,' is a 13-song novel revealing the homelessness of Toronto's streets and soul. His new CD (May 2007), 'Ours And The Shepherds,' is a collection of Canadian war stories from WWI through to current missions in Afghanistan, and is named after the Dorothy Day quote, 'whose fault is it? Ours and the shepherds.' Jon Brooks lives in Toronto. For more information about his songs and purpose please visit www.jonbrooks.ca.

HAYDEN CARRUTH lives in the hills of upstate New York. He has published more than thirty books, chiefly poetry, but including four books of criticism, and two anthologies. He has received fellowships from the Bollingen Foundation, the Guggenheim Foundation, the National Endowment for the Arts, a Lannan Literary Fellowship, the Paterson Poetry Prize, the Carl Sandburg Award, the National Book Award and the National Book Critics Circle Award. His most recent books are *Scrambled Eggs and Whiskey, Collected Longer Poems, Collected Shorter Poems, Suicides and Jazzers* and *Reluctantly.*

BILL CASSELMAN has written ten books about Canadian words and one medical dictionary. He was a columnist for *Maclean's* magazine and *Canadian Geographic*, and a freelance producer at CBC Radio and CBC TV for twenty years. Bill was one of the founding producers of "This Country in the Morning," a seminal program that introduced Peter Gzowski to national radio audiences. His books include the bestselling *Canadian Sayings* in three volumes, *As The Canoe Tips: Comic Scenes from Canadian Life* and *Casselman's Canadian Words*. His humorous word studies continue on his website: www.billcasselman.com.

GEORGE ELLIOT CLARKE, born in Nova Scotia, is the author of the acclaimed works *Whylah Falls, Beatrice Chancy, Execution Poems, Blue,* and *Québécité*; a critical study, *Odysseys Home: Mapping African-Canadian Literature*; a novel, *George and Rue*; and in association with photographer, Ricardo Scipio, *Illuminated Verses*. His honours include the Governor General's Award for Poetry, the Martin Luther King Jr. Achievement Award, and the Pierre Elliott Trudeau Fellowship Prize.

LAUREN B. DAVIS is the author of The Radiant City, (HarperCollins Canada 2005), a finalist for the Rogers Writers Trust Fiction Prize; The Stubborn Season (Harper Collins Canada, 2002), chosen for the Robert Adams Lecture Series; as well as a collection of critically acclaimed short stories, Rat Medicine & Other Unlikely Curatives (Mosaic Press, 2000). Her short fiction has also been nominated for the CBC Literary Awards and she is the recipient of two Mid-Career Writer Sustaining grants from the Canadian Council for the Arts - 2000 and 2006. Born in Montreal, Davis now resides in Princeton, New Jersey. For more information, please visit her website at: http://www.laurenb-davis.com.

MICHEL DEGUY is among the most influential of France's poets. His many publications include: *Donnant Donnant, Jumelages, Made in USA, Tombeau de Du Bellay, Figurations, Actes,* and *Oui Dire.*

ANN DIAMOND is a journalist and the author of several books.

CHRISTOPHER DODA is a poet and critic living in Toronto. His first collection of poetry, *Among Ruins*, was released in 2001 by the Mansfield Press and his second, *Aesthetics Lesson*, will appear in 2007. He is a two-time winner of the Critic's Desk Award for short reviews from Arc magazine. Trained as an archivist, he currently works for the Information and Privacy Office at York University.

RAY ELLENWOOD is a retired professor of English, York University. He has published ten books of translation, French-to-English, mostly of Quebec literature, including the manifesto, *Refus global,* by the Montreal Automatist Movement. Besides a number of articles on the dancers, writers, and artists of that group, he has published *Egregore: A History of the Automatist Movement of Montreal* (Toronto: Exile Editions, 1992). He continues working on projects related to his previous research.

TIMOTHY FINDLEY, one of Canada's finest writers, published during his lifetime (1930- 2002) collections of stories and novels, including: *The Last of the Crazy People, The Wars, Famous Last Words, Dinner Along The Amazon, Not Wanted on the Voyage, Stones, Headhunter, The Piano Man's Daughter, You Went Away*, and *Inside Memory: Pages from a Writer's Notebook.*

ADELE FREEDMAN is a writer and critic.

VERA FRENKEL is a multi-disciplinary artist and her installations and new media projects have been shown at the Venice Biennale, documenta IX, MoMA, the Goeteborg Konstmuseum and the Freud Museum London, among other venues. Her touring project on the travails of a dysfunctional cultural organization, *The*

Institute™: *Or, What We Do for Love* (www.the-national-insti-tute,.org/tour) was installed most recently at the National Gallery of Canada, Ottawa, marking her 2006 Governor General's Award in Visual Arts and New Media. *Of Memory and Displacement*, a 4-disk DVD/CD-ROM collection of Frenkel's video-tapes, media works and writings, with commentary by others, is now available from Vtape Distribution, Toronto. In 2007, Frenkel was inducted into the Royal Society of Canada (Acade-mies of Arts, Sciences and Humanities). Recent publications include "A Place for Uncertainty: Towards a New Kind of Muse-um," in *Museums after Modernism: Strategies of Engagement* (Blackwell Publishing, U.K. 2007).

GALE ZOË GARNETT's debut novel, *Visible Amazement* (Canada, 1999) has since been published in the US, France and Germany. The French version was chosen as one of the best books of sum-mer, 2001. Her novel, *Transient Dancing* was published in 2003. Zoë's third book, the novella *Room Tone* (2007), was reviewed in *The Globe and Mail* as a "wonderfully realized beautiful book" by a "masterly writer," and compared to Kundera and Marquez. Her short story, "Your Children Are All Dead, Missus?" was cho-sen for CBC's Fall Festival of Fiction. "Broken Things" (short story), "If I Had a Lover, I Would Make My Own Pickles" (poem) and excerpts from her first two novels have appeared in *Exile*. Zoë also works as an actor in theatre, film, television, radio and animation. She is a member of Artists Against War, Writer in Residence with Literature for Life (a reading and writing centre for young single mothers) and produced and appeared in "Get-ting it Write!," a benefit for The Stephen Lewis Foundation. With the support of The Writers Union of Canada (TWUC) and SLF, she initiated the CanadaAfrica KidLit BookLift, bringing Canadi-an children's books to The Nyaka AIDS Orphans School in Nyakagyezi, Uganda.

BRANKO GORJUP is the chief editor of the Peter Paul Bilingual Series of Contemporary Canadian Poetry (English/Italian) in which the following authors have appeared: Irving Layton, Gwendolyn MacEwen, P.K. Page, Al Purdy, Margaret Atwood, Michael Ondaatje, Margaret Avison, Dennis Lee, and Dionne Brand. He assembled a special issue, *Oceano Canada*, for Mon-dadori's *Nuovi Argomenti*, introducing Canadian contemporary writing in English to an Italian readership. *White Gloves of the Doorman: The Works of Leon Rooke*, published in 2004, brings together essays, reviews, and interviews from an international rostrum of contributors, a new bibliography and a DVD-docu-mentary on the author. Gorjup taught Canadian literature in universities in Canada and Italy. Presently he resides in Los Angeles and Toronto.

JIM HART of the United States is a gentleman of letters, a publisher, the poet of *Milding: poems,* and husband to Carly Simon.

JANICE KULYK KEEFER has published numerous works of poetry, fiction and literary criticism. A graduate of the University of Toronto and the University of Sussex, she teaches English and Creative Writing at the University of Guelph. Her latest publications are *Midnight Stroll* (poetry) and the novel *The Ladies' Lending Library*.

MICHEAL KEEFER is Professor of English at the University of Guelph, a former president of the Association of Canadian College and University Teachers of English, and a winner of the Renaissance Society of America's Nelson Prize. He has published widely on Renaissance literature and philosophy, and on the contemporary North American "culture wars." His recent publications include two editions of Marlowe's *Doctor Faustus* (Broadview Press, 2007), as well as essays on Helen of Troy, textual-critical theory and practice, globalization and imperial geopolitics, the war in Iraq, false-flag terrorism, and electoral fraud in the United States and Haiti.

WILLIAM KENNEDY is an American novelist, author of "The Albany Trilogy" – *Legs, Billy Phelan's Greatest Game,* and *Ironweed* – as well as *Quinn's Book, Very Old Bones, The Flaming Corsage,* and *Roscoe.* His non-fiction has been collected in *Riding the Yellow Trolley Car.* Among his many awards, The Pulitzer Prize, the National Book Critics Circle Award, and a McArthur Foundation grant. He is a member of the American Academy of Arts and Letters.

DIANA KUPREL is the editor of *idea&s: the arts & science review,* published by the University of Toronto. She is also the English translator of Zofia Nalkowska's *Medallions,* a book of creative non-fiction on the Holocaust, as well as poetry and the early reportages of Ryszard Kapuscinski.

DAVID LAMPE, Professor Emeritus specializing in Middle English, Renaissance and Contemporary literature at the State University of New York at Buffalo, is the author of *The Trees Walked.*

PATRICK LANE lives near Victoria, British Columbia with his companion, the poet Lorna Crozier. His most recent publications are, *Go Leaving Strange,* poetry from Harbour Publications, *What the Stones Remember,* from Trumpeter Books in Boston, and *There Is a Season,* from McClelland & Stewart. His new poetry collection, *Last Water Song,* will be published in September, 2007, and his novel, *Red Dog Red Dog,* in spring 2008 from McClelland & Stewart.

DENNIS LEE is the author of more than twenty books, including *Civil Elegies*, which won the Governor General's Literary Award, and *Alligator Pie*, the children's classic. Among many other honours, he was Toronto's first poet laureate from 2001 to 2004. His newest book of poetry is *yesno*, a sequel to *un*.

ROBERT MARTEAU was born in 1925 and is the French author of some forty books of poetry, reflections on art, memoirs, critical history, and novels. He has – since 1990 – written a sonnet almost every day. Among his translations, *Les Livres de Hogg*. Callaghan has translated his *Atlante*, his *Traité du blanc et des teintures*, and is completing Marteau's latest work, *Laure*.

KATHLEEN MCCRACKEN is the author of six collections of poetry including *Blue Light, Bay and College* (Penumbra Press, 1991), which was shortlisted for the Governor General's Award for Poetry in 1992, *A Geography of Souls* (Thistledown Press, 2002) and *Mooncalves* (Exile Editions, 2007). Her poems have been published in *The Malahat Review, Poetry Canada Review, Exile, Poetry Ireland, New Orleans Review* and *Grain,* and she has given readings in Canada, Ireland, the United Kingdom and the United States. Kathleen is currently Lecturer in English Literature at the University of Ulster in Northern Ireland. She has published scholarly articles on the poetry of Derek Mahon, Paul Muldoon and Ciaran Carson, as well as on Irish cinema and First Nations Canadian writing. A critical monograph entitled *Radical Vision: Reading the Poetry of Paul Durcan* is forthcoming from Bloodaxe Books in 2008.

BRUCE MEYER is author of over twenty books including *The Golden Thread: A Reader's Journey Through the Great Books*, and six collections of poetry: *The Open Room, Radio Silence, The Presence, Anywhere, The Spirit Bride* and *Oceans*. His previous collection of short fiction, *Goodbye Mr. Spalding*, was acclaimed by TV Ontario's *Imprint* as one of the classics of contemporary baseball fiction. Broadcaster, critic and professor at St. Michael's College Continuing Education Program and Laurentian University in Barrie, Meyer lives in Toronto and appears frequently on *CBC Radio One* and TV Ontario.

ANNE MICHAELS is a poet and novelist. Her work has been translated into more than thirty languages and her internationally award-winning novel *Fugitive Pieces* has been made into a feature film.

JOHN MONTAGUE was born in New York (28 February 1929) and brought up in Garvaghey, County Tyrone. He has published a number of volumes of poetry, two collections of short stories and a memoir including: *Death of a Chieftain* (1964), *The Rough*

Field (1972), *The Faber Book of Irish Verse* (1974), *Selected Poems* (1982), *The Dead Kingdom* (1984), *The Figure in the Cave* (1989), *An Occasion of Sin* (1992), and *Smashing the Piano* (1993).

DOUG (DOUGIE) RICHARDSON, the stellar tenor saxophonist, was born in 1937 and raised in the Kensington Market/Spadina Avenue area of Toronto. He died in 2007. Having met Callaghan in 1954 or 1955, he was, at the time of his death Callaghan's oldest friend. Over the last ten or fifteen years, on more occasions than not when Callaghan was reading from his work in public, Dougie Richardson accompanied him. He also played at the *Exile* and Exile Editions reading evenings. During his career, Richardson played all across North America with Ornette Coleman, Ernest Dawkins, the Ramones, James Brown, Roland Kirk, The OJs, The Platters, Percy Sledge, Ben E. King, Bo Diddley, Chuck Berry, Etta James, and a dozen more. His CDs are *Doug Richardson*, *Winning Ticket*, as well as four CDs with the Toronto band Kollage, the last called *At This Time*.

PAUL WILLIAM ROBERTS lives in Toronto but has written from various outposts in the world. His two novels are *The Palace of Fears* and *Homeland*. His non-fiction: *A War against Truth*, *Smokescreen*, *The Demonic Comedy*, *Journey of the Magi*, *Empire of the Soul*, and *River in the Desert*. He was given the Canada PEN Paul Kidd Courage Award, honouring bravery in journalism.

RAY ROBERTSON is the author of the novels *Home Movies*, *Heroes*, *Moody Food*, *Gently Down the Stream* and *What Happened Later*, as well as a collection of non-fiction, *Mental Hygiene: Essays on Writers and Writing*. He lives in Toronto.

LEON ROOKE of Canada is the author of, among other books, *Oh!*, *Who Goes There*, *Fat Woman*, *Shakespeare's Dog*, *The Face of Gravity*, *A Good Baby*, *The Magician of Love*, *The Beautiful Wife*, and most recently, poems, *Hot Poppies*.

JOE ROSENBLATT was born in Toronto in 1933. He became interested in writing through his association with the worker poet Milton Acorn in the early sixties and the metaphysical poetry of Gwendolyn MacEwen. By 1966 he had his first book of poetry published and he also received a Canada Council grant which allowed him to leave his job as a freight handler of the old Canadian Pacific Railway and devote the next year to writing and travelling. Over the years, Rosenblatt has written more than twenty books of poetry, several autobiographical works and his poems have appeared in over thirty anthologies of Canadian poetry over his forty year career as a poet. His poetry books have received major awards, such as the Governor General's award for poetry in 1976 and the BC Book Prize in 1986. He has travelled widely giving readings of his poems in Europe, Canada and the United States. Several bilingual volumes of his poetry have been published in Italian with translations by Prof. Alfredo Rizzardi of the University of Bologna, and Ada Donati of Rome. His most recent poetry volume, *Parrot Fever* was published by Exile Editions, 2002. His poems have also been also translated into French, Dutch, Swedish and Spanish. For the past twenty years he has been living in a resort community of Qualicum Beach on Vancouver Island.

NORMAN SNIDER is considered one of the premier magazine journalists in Canada by author Peter C. Newman. Snider has been nominated for four National Magazine Awards, appearing in such publications as *Toronto Life, Saturday Night, Macleans,* and *Rolling Stone.* For seven years, he was a weekly columnist for Canada's National Newspaper, *The Globe and Mail.* As well as the bestselling true crime book, *Smokescreen* (Stoddart), Snider is also the author of a work of political journalism *The Changing of the Guard* (Lester & Orpen Dennys), a Book of the Month Club selection. Snider has also written extensively for movies and television such as the Juno award-winning, internationally-recognized psychological drama *Dead Ringers* (dir. David Cronenberg, starring Jeremy Irons), 20th-Fox 1989, the crime drama *Call Me: The Rise and Fall of Heidi Fleiss,* (USA Network, 2004) directed by Emmy-winner Charles McDougall, starring *The Sopranos'* Jamie Lynn Sigler, *Rated X,* Showtime Network, 2000 (dir. Emilio Estevez, starring Charlie Sheen), and the crime thriller *Valentine's Day,* 1998, HBO, starring Mario Van Peebles. He has also worked with renowned directors Bob Rafelson, Edward Zwick, Norman Jewison, and Atom Egoyan. Snider's collection of non-fiction, *The Roaring Eighties and Other Good Times,* will appear in 2007.

DAVID SOBELMAN of Toronto, Canada, is a poet, essayist, screenwriter, story editor, director, producer, translator and philosopher. Sobelman is the director of *The McLuhan Probes*; the writer-director of *Space Symphony* and *The Leonardo Project: Making the Invisible Visible;* he's the award winning co-writer and senior producer of *Runaways: 24 Hours on the Street;* and the writer who conceived and co-produced the highly acclaimed *McLuhan's Wake.* His first book of poems, *After the End,* was published by Guernica in 2006. He is currently writing *ElectriCity: a work in Progress,* a multi-platform project, consisting of a book, a feature-length documentary, a companion DVD, a website and bits of bite-sized mobile content. He's also working on *The Buried Life*, his second book of poems. "Fishing for Hogg in the Midnight Sun," and "My Old Friend, the Literary Journalist," are from *Belletters*, Sobelman's book of 26 letters, each describing a facet of the literary identity.

ALEF GRAF VAN STEIJN is a retired entrepreneur and philosopher and lover of literature. He lives on a lake, near Granada, in the Netherlands.

ROSEMARY SULLIVAN is the author of the #1 national bestseller *The Red Shoes: Margaret Atwood, Starting Out*. Her biography of poet Gwendolyn MacEwen, *Shadow Maker,* won the Governor General's Award for Non-fiction, the Canadian Authors Association Literary Award, the City of Toronto Book Award and the University of British Columbia Medal for Canadian Biography. *By Heart: Elizabeth Smart/A Life* was nominated for a Governor General's Award. Sullivan is the author of three collections of poetry and the editor of six anthologies of poetry and prose. Her latest books are: *Labyrinth of Desire: Women, Passion, and Romantic Obsession*, *Cuba: Grace Under Pressure*, and *Villa Air-Bel: World War II, Escape*. She is a professor of English at the University of Toronto.

JOAN THOMAS is a writer and journalist.

MICHAEL TRUSSLER teaches English at the University of Regina. He's published literary criticism, poetry and short fiction. *Encounters*, a collection of short stories, won the City of Regina and Book of the year Awards at the Saskatchewan Book Awards in 2006. Hagios Press will publish his first poetry collection, *Accidental Animals* in 2007.

PRISCILA UPPAL is a poet and fiction writer born in Ottawa and currently living in Toronto. Among her publications are five collections of poetry: *How to Draw Blood From a Stone* (1998), *Confessions of a Fertility Expert* (1999), *Pretending to Die* (2001), *Live Coverage* (2003), and *Ontological Necessities* (2006); all with Exile Editions; and the novel *The Divine Economy of Salvation* (2002), published to critical acclaim by Doubleday Canada and Algonquin Books of Chapel Hill and translated into Dutch and Greek. Her poetry has been translated into Korean, Croatian, Latvian, and Italian, and *Ontological Necessities* was recently short-listed for the prestigious Griffin Prize for Excellence in Poetry. She has a PhD in English Literature and is a professor of Humanities and English and member of the Faculty of Graduate Studies at York University and Coordinator of the Creative Writing Program. For more information visit priscilauppal.ca.

SEÁN VIRGO was born in Malta of Irish parents. He lived in South Africa, Malaya, Ireland and the UK, before becoming a Canadian. He has spent time on both the west and east coasts, in southern Ontario, and now lives in rural Saskatchewan. He has published a novel, *Selak,* and his most recent collection of stories is *Begging Questions* (Exile Editions, 2006).

DAVID WEVILL teaches literature and creative writing at the University of Texas, and is retiring this year. He is a dual citizen, Canadian-American, and has published ten books of poetry, five with Exile Editions, including his most recent, *Asterisks* (2007).

Printed in July 2007 at Gauvin Press, Gatineau, Québec